One World Anthropology and Beyond

This volume offers a multidisciplinary engagement with the work of Tim Ingold. Involved in a critical long-term exploration of the relationships between human beings, organisms, and their environment, Ingold has become one of the most influential, innovative, and prolific writers in anthropology in recent decades. His work transcends established academic and disciplinary boundaries and his thinking continues to have a significant impact on numerous areas of research and other intellectual and artistic spheres. The contributions to this book are drawn from several fields, including social anthropology, archaeology, rock art studies, philosophy, and science and technology studies. The chapters critically engage with Ingold's approaches and ideas in relation to a variety of case studies that include the exploration of Australian rock art, electricity in Pakistan, Spanish farmhouses and sensory dimensions of educational practices. Emphasising the importance of dialogue and debate, there is also a response to the contributions by Tim Ingold himself. The volume will appeal to a wide range of audiences and provide new avenues of theoretically informed anthropological exploration into the many realities and expressions of human life.

Martin Porr is Associate Professor of Archaeology at the University of Western Australia.

Niels Weidtmann, philosophy, is Director of the College of Fellows – Center for Interdisciplinary and Intercultural Studies at Eberhard-Karls Universität Tübingen, Germany.

Routledge Studies in Anthropology

Suckling
Kinship More Fluid
Fadwa El Guindi

Amerindian Socio-Cosmologies between the Andes, Amazonia and Mesoamerica
Toward an Anthropological Understanding of the Isthmo–Colombian Area
Edited by Ernst Halbmayer

Africa and Urban Anthropology
Theoretical and Methodological Contributions from Contemporary Fieldwork
Edited by Deborah Pellow and Suzanne Scheld

Human Trafficking, Structural Violence, and Resilience
Ethnographic Life Narratives from the Philippines
Amie L. Lennox

Knots
Ethnography of the Moral in Culture and Social Thought
Edited by David Lipset and Eric K. Silverman

Secular Narrations and Transdisciplinary Knowledge
Abdelmajid Hannoum

One World Anthropology and Beyond
A Multidisciplinary Engagement with the Work of Tim Ingold
Edited by Martin Porr and Niels Weidtmann

https://www.routledge.com/Routledge-Studies-in-Anthropology/book-series/SE0724

One World Anthropology and Beyond

A Multidisciplinary Engagement with the Work of Tim Ingold

Edited by Martin Porr and Niels Weidtmann

Routledge
Taylor & Francis Group
LONDON AND NEW YORK

First published 2024
by Routledge
4 Park Square, Milton Park, Abingdon, Oxon OX14 4RN

and by Routledge
605 Third Avenue, New York, NY 10158

Routledge is an imprint of the Taylor & Francis Group, an informa business

British Library Cataloguing-in-Publication Data
A catalogue record for this book is available from the British Library

ISBN: 9780367755133 (hbk)
ISBN: 9780367755201 (pbk)
ISBN: 9781003162773 (ebk)

DOI: 10.4324/9781003162773

Typeset in Sabon
by Newgen Publishing UK

Contents

Figures

Contributors

Benjamin Alberti is a professor at Framingham State University.

Balanggarra Aboriginal Corporation is a Registered Native Title Body Corporate and represents the interests of the Balanggarra People in the Northeast Kimberley, Western Australia.

Anna Bloom-Christen is an anthropologist with a philosophy background. She is currently teaching at the University of Heidelberg and the University of Basel, where she is also working on her second book project concerned with habits of attention.

Stephanie Bunn lectures in Social Anthropology at the University of St Andrews, Scotland, and conducts research into Central Asian felt textiles and basketry worldwide.

Dylan Gaffney is an anthropological archaeologist with an interest in human behavioural plasticity. He is currently a Research Fellow at St John's College, Oxford.

Ralf Gisinger is a DOC-Fellow of the Austrian Academy of Science (ÖAW) and research fellow at the University of Vienna (Department of Philosophy).

Melanie Greiner is a co-director of the Kocherwerk – Haus der Verbindungstechnik, a museum dealing with the historical development of the screw and fastening industry in Southern Germany. She holds an M.A. degree in anthropology, geography and economics from Ruprecht–Karls University Heidelberg.

Emily Grey is a PhD Candidate at the Centre for Rock Art Research + Management, University of Western Australia.

Laura Harris is a cultural sociologist with an interest in contemporary visual art, its spaces, circulation, and meanings. She is currently an Anniversary Fellow at the University of Southampton looking at experimental film-making and the cultural sociology of place. She completed her PhD in collaboration with Bluecoat, a contemporary arts centre in Liverpool, in 2020.

Maike Melles is a sociocultural anthropologist and currently a PhD candidate at Goethe University Frankfurt.

Ana Paula Motta has recently completed a PhD at the University of Western Australia, where she looked at social identity and human-animal relations in the rock art from the north-eastern Kimberley, Australia.

Antony Pattathu is a Habilitation Candidate at the Department of Social and Cultural Anthropology and a founding member of the Interdisciplinary Center for Global South Studies at the University of Tübingen.

Irina A. Ponomareva is a postdoctoral researcher at the University of Barcelona.

Martin Porr is Associate Professor of Archaeology and a member of the Centre for Rock Art Research + Management at the University of Western Australia.

Quirin Rieder is a PhD student and University Assistant at the Department of Cultural and Social Anthropology, University of Vienna.

Niels Weidtmann is Director of the College of Fellows – Center for Interdisciplinary and Intercultural Studies at the University of Tübingen.

Leor Zmigrod is a Research Fellow at the University of Cambridge.

Acknowledgements

This volume is both a book about Tim Ingold's work and a book with Tim Ingold. We hope that it will raise the awareness for and visibility of his many contributions and ideas. Although we are very happy with the final product, we also need to stress that it is not possible to capture the richness and depth of Tim Ingold's *oeuvre* in a few chapters. It is not our intention to provide a comprehensive overview of Tim Ingold's work and his many academic achievements. As we outline in the introductory chapter, however, we definitely believe that his work deserves wider recognition and productive and critical engagement. The relevance of his work is enormous, and it is rich across many different fields in the sciences, social sciences, and humanities.

The book has its origins in a workshop held at the *Forum Scientiarium* at the University of Tübingen (Germany) in September 2019. Like previous workshops at the Forum (now to be continued at the *College of Fellows*), it was specifically designed and accessible for PhD students and early career researchers only. It was clear that any publication should reflect this heritage and with this book, we wanted to give early career researchers the opportunity to engage with Tim Ingold's work in writing and as part of a major international publication. The current book is mostly due to the hard work of all of our authors, who sometimes worked through difficult professional and personal circumstances during a disruptive global pandemic.

The book would also not have been possible without the energy and commitment of Tim Ingold himself. He provided detailed and insightful suggestions for each chapter. Everyone's work has greatly profited from this engagement. Through his input, the process of writing the individual chapters and compiling them for this volume became very much a process of writing *with* Tim Ingold and not just about his work. Finally, we are, of course, also grateful that he contributed the response chapter to the volume.

As editors, we want to thank the following reviewers for their work on the book's manuscripts: Heribert Beckman, Mathew Chrulew, Eric Eggert, Jeanne Féaux de la Croix, Ursula Frederick, Nick Gestrich, Joakim Goldhahn, Chris Gosden, Zouhair Hammana, Christoph Hubatschke, Andrew M. Jones, Tristen Jones, Darren Jorgensen, Max Kramer, Johannes Kuber, Melissa

Marshall, Oscar Moro Abadía, Alessandro Rippa, Sasha Rossman, Guido Sprenger, Paul Taçon, Bruno Vindrola, Carsten Wergin, Darryl Wilkinson, and Thomas Wynn. We thank Udo Keller Foundation Forum Humanum for financial support of the workshop mentioned above and Katherine Ong for her patient and professional guidance of the volume at the publisher. Finally, we want to thank Marco Wallis for his crucial assistance with the compilation of the index.

Martin Porr wants to thank Christine and Erik for their ongoing support. Martin has been working on this volume for most of the time on Whadjuk Noongar Boodjar. He wants to thank the Whadjuk Noongar Traditional Owners for their past and present care for Country. Always was, always will be.

Part I

Introduction

Tim Ingold – biographical and research overview[1]

Martin Porr, Niels Weidtmann, and Tim Ingold

Tim Ingold is Professor Emeritus of Social Anthropology at the University of Aberdeen, Scotland. He had previously spent 25 years at the University of Manchester, where he was appointed Max Gluckman Professor of Social Anthropology in 1995. Ingold moved to Aberdeen in 1999, where he established the UK's newest Department of Anthropology and directed the University's strategic research theme on 'The North' (2011–2017). During his career, he has carried out ethnographic fieldwork among Saami and Finnish people in Lapland, and has written on comparative questions of environment, technology, and social organisation in the circumpolar North, as well as the role of animals in human society, on issues in human ecology, and evolutionary theory in anthropology, biology, and history.

A key aspect of Ingold's work continues to lie in his critical exploration of the links between environmental perception and skilled practice. In this he has aimed to replace traditional models of genetic and cultural transmission with a relational approach focusing on the growth of embodied skills of perception and action within social and environmental contexts of development. More recently, he has pursued three lines of inquiry that emerged from his earlier work, concerning the dynamics of pedestrian movement, the creativity of practice, and the linearity of writing. These all came together in a project funded by the UK Economic and Social Research Council (2005–2008), entitled 'Explorations in the comparative anthropology of the line'. Ingold has subsequently taught and written on a series of issues at the interface between anthropology, archaeology, art, and architecture. From 2013 to 2018, he directed the project 'Knowing from the Inside: Anthropology, Art, Architecture and Design' (2013–2018), with funding from the European Research Council. He officially retired from the University of Aberdeen in 2018 but continues to research and write as an independent scholar.

Ingold's research career can roughly be divided into four phases: the first from 1970 to 1988, the second from 1988 to 2002, the third from 2002 to 2018, and the fourth from 2018 and continuing.

The first phase began with his doctoral research among Skolt Sami people in the far northeast of Finland. Here, he studied the local-level ethnopolitics of a small and apparently endangered minority but soon became caught up in what, for the people themselves, were much more pressing questions

DOI: 10.4324/9781003162773-2

surrounding the management of their reindeer herds and the contingencies of making ends meet in an environment that otherwise offered meagre returns from fishing, berry-gathering, and casual labour on road-building sites. These issues became the subject of his doctoral dissertation and first book *The Skolt Lapps today* (Ingold 1976).

Arriving at the University of Manchester in 1974 as a lecturer in social anthropology, Ingold was responsible for teaching classes in ecological anthropology. He soon became immersed in the literature on human–environmental relations with a particular focus on relationships between humans and animals. Since the Sami were, at least nominally, pastoralists, he initially considered situating his research within the field of comparative studies of nomadic pastoralism. Most of these studies, however, were located in ethnographic regions – North and East Africa, the Mediterranean, Southwest and Central Asia – in which conditions were so very different from what he had encountered in Lapland that it was hard to find any grounds for systematic comparison. Much more promising comparative possibilities were offered by studies of other Indigenous peoples around the circumpolar North, many of whom lived by hunting, or by some combination of hunting and herding. Ingold's second book, *Hunters, pastoralists, and ranchers: Reindeer economies and their transformations* (1980), compared peoples from around the North for whom the reindeer or caribou was a mainstay of livelihood. In this work, human–animal relations – and especially the question of whether or in what sense these relations could be considered 'domestic' – took centre stage.

Together with his teaching in ecological anthropology, this research eventually drew Ingold into the field of hunter-gatherer studies. Work in this field addressed topics at the heart of the human condition in a way that studies of pastoralism, at least at that time, did not. Relevant questions included: What constitutes an environment for human beings and how can they be said to adapt to it or to transform it? What does it mean to make and use tools, and when does making and using amount to a 'technology'? How do people relate to, or exercise rights over, lands and waters, and what does it take for these relations to be understood as forms of property or tenure? If movement is a condition of human life, then how do the movements of people designated as 'nomadic' differ from those of people characterised as sedentary? What does it mean to store stuff for the future, and how does storage affect the quality of social relations? How do people reconcile their sense of autonomy with their dependence on others?

In addressing these and other topics, Ingold started from a premise that seemed unassailable at the time, namely that all human beings are necessarily caught up in two, ontologically distinct systems of relations: ecological relations with non-human components of the environment and social relations with one another. The issue, then, always boiled down to that of how these two relational systems intersect. The exploration of this issue set the agenda for his book *The appropriation of nature: Essays on human ecology and social relations* (1986).

While following these research interests, Ingold was also confronting a series of broader theoretical problems founded on the conviction that what we say about social life and culture must at least be consistent with what biological science teaches about human evolution. It soon became evident that in order to advance an integration of the two fields of social anthropology and evolutionary biology it would first be necessary to unravel the many different understandings of the paired concepts of history and evolution that had been proposed – sometimes as equivalents, sometimes in opposition – by advocates of radically different positions both on the nature of change and on the question of human uniqueness. The result was a systematic inquiry into how these concepts were reflected in the fields of biology, history, and anthropology, from the mid-nineteenth century to the present, leading to Ingold's fourth book, *Evolution and social life* (1986). While the book was intended to be a monument of theoretical integration, it turned out, in his own retrospective assessment, to be a failure. For in the very course of writing it, Ingold's own thinking was undergoing a profound shift, occasioned primarily by his encounter with the process philosophies of Henri Bergson (1911) and Alfred North Whitehead (1929). It was a shift that, in the book, remained incomplete and unresolved.

Only some years later, in 1988, would Ingold eventually recognise that the only way forward was to seek a rapprochement with a biology that was developmental rather than evolutionary in orientation. Previous attempts at integration, Ingold realised, had foundered on an absolute incompatibility between the kind of 'population thinking' which was axiomatic in mainstream evolutionary biology and the 'relational thinking' fundamental to contemporary social anthropology. The new synthesis, however, was supposed to be relational through and through, and this necessitated a search for alternative sources. In biology, Ingold turned to Susan Oyama's (1985) foundational work on what has since come to be known as 'developmental systems theory', or DST (Oyama, Griffiths, and Gray 2001). In philosophy, he turned to the phenomenological writings of Martin Heidegger (2010) and, above all, Maurice Merleau-Ponty (2008). It was also necessary to incorporate thinking from psychology, a discipline with which Ingold had hardly engaged until then. Here, he turned to the ecological approach to perception founded by James J. Gibson (1979). It was this engagement with ecological psychology that really distinguished the second phase of Ingold's research.

At that time, ecological anthropology had reached an impasse, centred on the question of how to position culture in human–environmental relations. Some saw culture as the human means of adaptation *par excellence*. Others saw it as an autonomous system of meaning, transcending the ecological nexus and setting the very conditions of adaptation. Gibson, by contrast, proposed a way of understanding how animals, whether human or non-human, can perceive their environment directly, in the very course of acting in it, in ways that answer to their current practice. This not only offered a way through the impasse; it also helped to break down the increasingly problematic bifurcations between human and non-human, and between culture and nature. In short, ecological psychology promised just the kind of relational perspective that Ingold was looking for at this time. This realisation was, however, complemented by a simultaneous reading of the work of Jakob von Uexküll (1957), retrospectively acknowledged as the founder of biosemiotics (Brentari 2015). Like Gibson, von Uexküll had placed the animal at the centre of its own perceptual world, but in other respects his approach differed radically from Gibson's. For Gibson, the animal *discovers* meanings in the environment, in the form of what he called its affordances; for von Uexküll, the animal *projects* meanings onto its environment, to form what he called its *Umwelt*. In a paper, published in 1992, 'Culture and the perception of the environment', Ingold presented the first attempt by any anthropologist to compare the approaches of Gibson and von Uexküll, and to examine the relevance of their ideas for anthropology.

Ingold pursued these themes through a series of essays composed in the 1990s, most of which were originally commissioned as special lectures or conference presentations. In many of these, he continued to develop his earlier interests in hunting-and-gathering and pastoral societies, looking again at issues of perception, human–animal relations, and domestication. Other essays took up the questions of what it means to perceive a world, to dwell in it, and to move around in it. Some focused on the meanings of environment and landscape; others on human–animal differences. He also explored the concept of skill, understood in terms of the coordination of perception and action, and its bearing on ideas of technology, of language and intelligence, and of the evolution of so-called 'modern humans'. These essays were eventually revised and assembled into a single volume entitled *The perception of the environment: Essays on livelihood, dwelling and skill*, published in 2000. One chapter, 'A circumpolar might's dream', a reanalysis of Hallowell's classic work on Ojibwa ontology, anticipated many of the ideas that have more recently been promulgated in anthropology under the twin rubrics of perspectivism and the 'ontological turn'. Another, 'Ancestry, generation, substance, memory, land', explored understandings of these five dimensions of indigeneity in terms of a contrast between genealogical and relational models. In 'Stop, look and listen! Vision, hearing and human movement', Ingold argued for a new approach to perception, derived from Gibson and Merleau-Ponty, through a critique of approaches being proposed at the time by advocates of the 'anthropology of the senses'. The essay that perhaps had the greatest bearing on his subsequent work, however, was entitled 'To journey along a way of life: Maps, wayfinding and navigation'. This text explicitly took up the contrast between Gibson's approach to wayfinding, understood as a movement along what he called a 'path of observation', and theories of cognitive mapping, which conceptualise navigation in terms of the location and integration of point-specific images within an overarching mental representation.

Despite their diverse themes, the thread running through all essays in *The perception of the environment* was the ambition to critique and move beyond the dominant paradigms of neo-Darwinian biology, cognitive science, and cultural anthropology, by bringing both 'developmental systems' thinking in biology and 'ecological' thinking in psychology into a dialogue with 'relational' thinking in anthropology. This underlying ambition, in turn, laid the foundation for the third phase of Ingold's research.

The starting point for this phase was the idea that life is not lived in locations but along paths or lines. Thus, the 'way of life' has to be understood quite literally, not as a received body of tradition handed down independently and in advance of its enactment in the world, but as a creative and improvisatory process of finding a way through a world of relations and processes that are forever unfolding. Here, the figure of the *line* took centre stage. Ingold pursued this theme in three directions: the dynamics of pedestrian movement, the creativity of practice, and the linearity of writing. The research on walking, carried out together with Jo Vergunst, resulted in the co-edited volume *Ways of walking: Ethnography and practice on foot* (Vergunst and Ingold 2008). Contributors to the volume discussed how walking along together, as opposed to the face-to-face encounter, is a primary form of human sociality, and how it resembles storytelling as a way not just of going from place to place, but also of making the places themselves. In his research on creative practice, Ingold returned to the writings of Whitehead and Bergson with the aim of decoupling the idea of creativity from that of innovation, linking it instead to a sense of improvisation, as a movement that is continually attentive to the comings and goings of human and non-human others. These themes were explored in a co-edited volume on *Creativity and cultural improvisation*, published in 2007 (Hallam and Ingold 2007), and based on contributions to the eponymous 2005 conference of the UK Association of Social Anthropologists. In the same year, Ingold published his book *Lines: A brief history*, which had evolved from his 2003 Rhind Lectures (Ingold 2007). While the lectures had focused on the linearity of writing and drawing, the book presented a much broader approach to understanding the relation between movement, knowledge, and description.

Key to this new research direction was the distinction between two kinds of line: the gestural trace and the point-to-point connector. Lines of the first kind, typically made by hand, or by walking, comprise what Ingold called the *meshwork*. Travellers, improvising their passages through the world along the paths of the meshwork, and attending and responding to surrounding conditions as they go along, are seen as *wayfarers*. In this sense, wayfaring is opposed to *transport*, the carrying across of persons or goods from point to point, even as the meshwork of wayfaring lines is opposed to the network of punctual interconnections. For Ingold, wayfaring is fundamental to living beings' habitation of the earth.

These ideas were further developed in a collection of essays published under the title *Being alive: Essays on movement, knowledge, and description* (Ingold 2011). In one essay, for example, Ingold explored how developments in footwear, street-paving and transport contributed to an assumed separation between locomotion and cognition that underpins much work in cognitive science. In another essay, he returned to his earlier comparison of the approaches of Gibson and von Uexküll, in seeking to understand how animals perceive the world around them, finding a possible resolution in the philosophy of Gilles Deleuze (Deleuze and Guattari 2013). A further theme of many of the essays in this volume is what Ingold calls the *logic of inversion*, characteristic of modernity, which turns the lines along which life is lived into boundaries within which it is contained, thus converting emplacement into enclosure, travelling into transport, and ways of knowing into transmitted culture. Throughout these essays, Ingold aims to shift the focus from ready-made objects to the processes of their generation or dissolution – a shift that requires us to *follow the materials* as they flow, mix, and mutate.

During this phase of his research, while Ingold continued to draw on the ecological psychology of James Gibson, he also became increasingly aware of its limitations. While it gives the perceiver an active and exploratory role, the world perceived seems static, as if it were already laid out. In *Being alive*, he sought to overcome this limitation, for example by diverting attention from features of terrestrial layout to the atmospheric dynamics of wind and weather, thereby situating the wayfarer at the heart of a world in continuous flux. Thus, the wayfarer's line not only leaves its trace on the ground but also threads through an atmosphere. In order to understand the relation between lines and atmosphere, Ingold realised, he would have to synthesise lineaology with meteorology. In his book *The Life of lines*, published in 2015, he set out to do just this. The book has three parts. The first, 'Knotting', focuses on the many ways in which lines are enmeshed in the formation of the ground, its features, and inhabitants. In the second, 'Weathering', the argument turns to the atmosphere, showing how light and sound, in particular, can be understood as atmospheric phenomena. In the third part, however, the argument is brought back to the perennial question of what it means to be human, or to lead a human life, in an ever-unfolding world of lines and atmosphere. His answer is that humans are not so much beings as *becomings*. In their doings and undergoings, they are 'humaning'. Or in a word, to human is a verb.

Once again, the inspiration for this move came in part from Gibson's ecological psychology. It was linked to the idea that perceiving is about attending to things, and that attention is a skill that can be honed through practice. Gibson called this 'the education of attention'. In a landmark article, 'From the transmission of representations to the education of attention', Ingold set out an ecological alternative to the dominant view that culture consists of systems of representation, transmitted by social learning from one generation to the next (Ingold 2001). Against this, he argued that the variations that we are inclined to call cultural are in fact variations of skill, and that skills are not transmitted ready-made but learned anew in each generation under the guidance of already accomplished practitioners. This theme continues to resonate in Ingold's work. He has repeatedly returned to the argument against transmission in critiquing neo-Darwinian models of genetic and cultural evolution, in an attempt to replace them with a relational approach. In this, the volume *Biosocial becomings: Integrating social and biological anthropology*, co-edited with Gisli Palsson, represents a milestone (Ingold and Palsson 2013). The book is perhaps the first to set out a coherent approach to human evolution founded upon a relational ontology, from the viewpoint of social anthropology,

In the third part of *The life of lines*, Ingold returned to the theme of the education of attention, comparing Gibson's approach with that of the educational philosopher Jan Masschelein (2010). This led him to further develop his arguments *against* transmission, and *for* attention, which he went on to elaborate in his book *Anthropology and/as education* (Ingold 2018a). The key thesis of the book is that anthropology, understood as a way of going along *with* and learning *from* others, is itself educational in practice and intent. The practice of going along with and answering to others is what Ingold calls 'correspondence'. This notion of correspondence lies at the heart of his ongoing attempts to reunite perception with imagination, understood not as a power of mental representation but rather as a way of entering creatively into the very becoming of things – of moving 'upstream' to the moment of their incipient formation. It is precisely in its failure to offer a convincing account of imagination that Ingold finds the Gibsonian approach to perception most wanting. The attempt to rectify this failure underlies most of the chapters in his latest essay collection, *Imagining for real: Essays on creation, attention, and correspondence* (Ingold 2022a).

Since 2002, most of Ingold's work has been situated at the interface between anthropology (broadly conceived to include social and biological anthropology as well as archaeology), art, and architecture. From 2003 to 2010, he taught a course at the University of Aberdeen entitled *The 4 As*. The As in question were anthropology, archaeology, art, and architecture, and the themes tackled ranged from design and making, materials, form and function, movement and gesture, the senses in perception, and craft and skill, to lines, drawing, and notation. This course formed the basis of his book *Making: Anthropology, archaeology, art, and architecture* (Ingold 2013), as well as a successful application to the European Research Council for an Advanced Grant. The project, entitled *Knowing from the Inside* (KFI), set out to forge a new synthesis at the confluence of anthropology, art, architecture, and design, based on the premise that in all four disciplines, knowledge grows from the crucible of our practical and observational engagement with the world around us – that is, from thinking *with*, *from*, and *through* beings and things, not just *about* them. The overall aim of KFI was to show how research underpinned by this premise could make a difference to the sustainability of environmental relations and to the well-being that depends on it.

Following the completion of the KFI project, Ingold formally retired in 2018. However, his research and writing have continued unabated. A short book, *Anthropology: Why it matters*, published in the same year, introduced his vision of the discipline and its future to a general readership (Ingold 2018b).

The first pandemic year of 2020 saw the publication of *Correspondences*, a collection of his personal reflections on a range of recent art–anthropology collaborations (Ingold 2021). In the following year, *The perception of the environment* and *Being alive* were published in new editions, to coincide with the publication of *Imagining for real*. Together, these three essay collections form a trilogy, wrapping up the past three decades of Ingold's work. In the same year, a special issue of the journal *Theory Culture and Society*, co-edited with Cristian Simonetti, came out under the title 'Solid fluids: New approaches to materials and meaning', based on a project funded by the British Academy between 2015 and 2019 (Ingold and Simonetti 2021). Even more recently, drawing on experience from the KFI project, Ingold has put together an edited volume on alternative pedagogies, entitled *Knowing from the inside: Transdisciplinary experiments with matters of pedagogy*. The volume was published in March 2022 (Ingold 2022b).

Beyond all that, Ingold's current long-term plan is to return to the field in Finnish Lapland, and to pick up from where he left off in 1980. Enough of theory! It's high time he became an ethnographer again.

Note

1 This text was adapted from www.timingold.com/research-statement, with kind permission.

References

Bergson, H. 1911. *Creative evolution*. London: Macmillan.
Brentari, C. 2015. *Jakob von Uexküll. The discovery of the Umwelt between biosemiotics and theoretical biology*. Dordrecht: Springer.
Deleuze, G. and F. Guattari 2013. *A thousand plateaus: Capitalism and schizophrenia*. London: Bloomsbury Academic.
Gibson, J. J. 1979. *The ecological approach to visual perception*. Boston: Houghton Mifflin.
Hallam, E. and T. Ingold, eds. 2007. *Creativity and cultural improvisation*. Oxford/New York: Berg.
Heidegger, M. 2010. *Being and time* (J. Stambaugh, trans.). Albany: State University of New York Press.
Ingold, T. 1976. *The Skolt Lapps today*. Cambridge: Cambridge University Press.
——— 1980. *Hunters, pastoralists, and ranchers: Reindeer economies and their transformations*. Cambridge: Cambridge University Press.
——— 1986. *The appropriation of nature. Essays on human ecology and social relations*. Manchester: Manchester University Press.
——— 1992. Culture and the perception of the environment. In *Bush base – forest farm: Culture, environment, and development*. E. Croll and D. Parkin, eds. Pp. 39–56. London: Routledge.
——— 2000. *The perception of the environment. Essays in livelihood, dwelling and skill*. London: Routledge.

——— 2001. From the transmission of representations to the education of attention. In *The debated mind: Evolutionary psychology versus ethnography*. H. Whitehouse, ed. Pp. 113–153. Oxford: Berg.
——— 2007. *Lines. A brief history*. New York: Routledge.
——— 2011. *Being alive. Essays on movement, knowledge and description*. London: Routledge.
——— 2013. *Making. Anthropology, archaeology, art and architecture*. London: Routledge.
——— 2015. *The life of lines*. London: Routledge.
——— 2016 [orig. 1986]. *Evolution and Social Life* (Second ed.). London: Routledge.
——— 2018a. *Anthropology and/as education*. Abington: Routledge.
——— 2018b. *Anthropology. Why it matters*. Cambridge: Polity.
——— 2021. *Correspondences*. Cambridge: Polity Press.
——— 2022a. *Imagining for real. Essay on creation, attention and correspondence*. London: Routledge.
Ingold, T., ed. 2022b. *Knowing from the inside. Cross-disciplinary experiments with matters of pedagogy*. Sydney: Bloomsbury Publishing.
Ingold, T. and G. Palsson, eds. 2013. *Biosocial becomings. Integrating social and biological anthropology*. Cambridge: Cambridge University Press.
Ingold, T. and C. Simonetti. 2021. Introducing solid fluids. *Theory, Culture & Society* 39(2):3–29.
Masschelein, J. 2010. The idea of critical E-ducational research – E-ducating the gaze and inviting to go walking. In *The possibility/impossibility of a new critical language of education*. I. Gur-Ze'ev, ed. Pp. 275–291. Rotterdam: Sense Publishers.
Merleau-Ponty, M. 2008. *Phenomenology of perception*. London: Routledge.
Oyama, S. 1985. *The ontogeny of information: Developmental systems and evolution*. Cambridge: Cambridge University Press.
Oyama, S., P. E. Griffiths and R. D. Gray, eds. 2001. *Cycles of contingency: Developmental systems and evolution*. Cambridge, MA: MIT Press.
Vergunst, J. L. and T. Ingold, eds. 2008. *Ways of walking. Ethnography and practice on foot*. London: Routledge.
von Uexküll, J. 1957. A stroll through the worlds of animals and men: A picture book of invisible worlds. In *Instinctive behaviour: The development of a modern concept*. C. Schiller, ed. Pp. 5–80. New York: International Universities Press.
Whitehead, A. N. 1929. *Process and reality: An essay in cosmology*. Cambridge: Cambridge University Press.

1 Being alive and educating attention

The persistent value of the work of Tim Ingold

Martin Porr and Niels Weidtmann

Introduction

Over the last decades, Tim Ingold has become one of the most influential, innovative, and prolific academic researchers and writers. His work has been transcending established academic and disciplinary boundaries, particularly between social and biological anthropology. He has been described as "one of the most original and radical thinkers alive" (T. H. Eriksen, in Ingold 2018a:148 [back cover]). He has significantly influenced the development of the academic field of anthropology for more than four decades. He has held significant positions within the field and has been the editor of many important volumes and journals. Of course, he has also published many single-authored books and journal papers. However, although this impression is only based on a minuscule sample, his books rarely feature prominently in bookstores. His work does not appear to have the same public recognition as other authors writing within a comparable space and in a similar spirit. Prominent examples would be Bruno Latour, David Graeber, Marshall Sahlins, or Philippe Descola. While we do not want to provide a quantitative analysis of these observations, it seems quite extraordinary that until now, there has not been a single edited book that is either dedicated to Tim Ingold or engages systematically with the wealth of his work over the last four decades. To our knowledge, there has so far been only one special issue in a journal (*Interdisciplinary Science Reviews* 43, 3–4, 2018) with such an aim and orientation. This book simultaneously is and is not an attempt to fill this gap. It wants to make the case for the value of a critical engagement with the work of Tim Ingold. However, in writing this book and putting the individual chapters together, we are also aware that it will not be possible to come even close to a comprehensive or adequate assessment. We hope to provide some inspiration for others to follow in our footsteps and continue the explorations outlined in this book. We also hope to convey the inspiration that we and the authors have found in engaging with Tim Ingold's many contributions. As will become clear in the individual chapters, this engagement is not always frictionless and straightforward. And that is how it should be. The chapters are reflections of the correspondence between different lives,

DOI: 10.4324/9781003162773-3

perspectives, and understandings. They are reflections of thinking with Tim Ingold.

This book is the product of a workshop held at the Forum Scientiarum at the University of Tübingen, in September 2019.[1] The workshop was jointly organised by Niels Weidtmann and Martin Porr. Tim Ingold was able to visit Tübingen for this occasion and over three days, participants were able to discuss their work at this forum together with Tim and among themselves. The workshop was specifically aimed at early career scholars and postgraduate research students, and in order to reflect the many different areas to which Tim Ingold has contributed, it avoided disciplinary restrictions. These two aspects are preserved in this volume. The authors include almost all of the workshop participants together with two further scholars (Alberti, Bunn), who have previously made significant contributions with reference to Ingold's work or have even had an institutional affiliation with him. While the original workshop contributions were focused on the participants' own work, for the chapters in this book contributors were asked to relate their research critically to some aspect of Ingold's work. The range of different disciplines is considerable, even in this relatively short book. The chapters are therefore arranged into four different sections, which reflect both the expertise of the volume's contributors and some of the most important areas of Tim Ingold's *oeuvre*. In this way, we hope to demonstrate the transdisciplinary character of both, as well as the interconnectedness of the chapters.

In this introduction, we provide some brief thoughts on the enduring value of Tim Ingold's work and his thinking. To fill the gap mentioned above, we want to draw attention to the relevance of his contributions to a range of current issues and challenges in academia and beyond. This aim is related to a discussion during the above-mentioned workshop about the political dimensions of Ingold's work, which can appear to be less obvious and more implicit compared to the work of other contemporary anthropologists. While this introduction will not outline Tim Ingold's career in chronological fashion (on this, the reader is directed to the biographical and research overview and the chapter below by Bunn), we will address some of its key topics, which have guided him through the last decades of his professional life.

Being and becoming human

Anthropology is the study of human beings. It is a field of inquiry concerned with understanding humans and their numerous behaviours and actions. Humans and their lives are complex and have many dimensions. They can be studied from a multitude of perspectives and different aspects can be selected for interrogation. While it is often said that anthropology is a relatively recent academic discipline that was only formalised in the late 19th century, the systematic study of human beings by other human beings has a long history. Anthropology does not have a real beginning and it continues to have very fuzzy boundaries. As an academic field, the discipline has undergone numerous phases of conceptual and institutional fusion and fission, which cannot be adequately addressed here. However, one specific aspect that has impacted the field throughout is the distinction and the relation between the biological and social or cultural aspects of human existence. The conceptualisation of this aspect reflects the ontological definition of human beings and their relationships with each other and their environment. It bears on the difference between relational and realist understandings of humanity, and on whether or in what ways culture may be distinguished from nature, or history from evolution. As such, it impacts on the acceptance and implementation of theories and methods, the research process itself, and the status of the knowledge produced. Most importantly, it has been at the core of Tim Ingold's work from the very beginning of his academic career.

One of the most striking features of the current institutional landscape of anthropological research is the widespread separation of social/cultural from biological anthropology. In many universities, these two fields rarely collaborate with each other and are often situated in different administrative entities with contrasting academic cultures and separated along a science/humanities distinction. This characterisation is of course a stark simplification. But there is little doubt that the separation has grown stronger over recent years (Kuper and Marks 2011). Since the establishment of anthropology as a university-based field of study, approaches towards the many dimensions of the study of human beings have been variously defined and institutionalised in different ways. Inspired by the holistic vision of German-born and educated Franz Boas, anthropology was founded in the United States as a four-field discipline that aimed to unite physical anthropology, cultural anthropology, linguistics, and archaeology. Until the mid-20th century, it was usual for researchers to move between these fields in integrating their respective insights. This unified approach had many advantages, but it also had its negative sides. It was common to draw causal connections across different sources and domains in order to account for social, cultural, psychological, and biological similarities. These arguments were made principally with reference to a biologically essentialist framework, which finds its expression in the implicitly and explicitly racist interpretations that dominated the field until the mid-20th century. After the Second World War, racism was discredited within and outside of academia, but biological and other forms of essentialism continued to guide research and political decision-making. In numerous contributions, Tim Ingold has engaged with this complex field and has shown how the institutional separation of social and biological anthropology rests on fundamentally different understandings of human beings and how they can and should be studied. He distinguishes between two ontologies, relational and populational (Ingold 2018a:104). The latter is related to essentialist thinking in assuming that human beings are constituted by entities that provide the blueprints of their physical bodies and the templates for their actions. This way of thinking is evident, for example, in evolutionary psychology and cognitive science. All Darwinian approaches towards human behaviour, while nominally eschewing essentialism in their embrace of population thinking, in fact reproduce a human essentialism in their commitment to a realist and positivist programme of science and research that places human ways of knowing over and above the world they profess to know. Many researchers have chosen to resolve the divide between social and biological anthropology by collapsing the former into the latter.

Tim Ingold has engaged with the distinction between social and biological anthropology for a long time. He has been one of the very few researchers within social anthropology who has never lost sight of the biological dimension of human existence. But this inclusion did not lead to a surrender to the forces of biological determinism, materialism, and essentialism. He, rather, continues to advocate for a dissolution of the distinction between the biological and the social (Ingold 1998, 2004). One of the key features of his thinking is the acknowledgement that the biological organism and the social person are one and the same. Human beings are not composed of different components or aspects with different causal mechanisms. This approach requires the acceptance of the fundamentally relational constitution of human beings. Such an understanding is anti-essentialist and dynamic. Human being is always human *becoming*. The consequences of such a framework are profound (Ingold and Palsson 2013). It shifts attention away from lines of descent, populations, or individual organisms to an understanding of human beings "as neither genetically nor culturally preconfigured but as ever-emergent outcomes of developmental or ontogenetic processes" (Ingold 2018a:104). Central to this is an aspect traditionally neglected or excluded from mainstream anthropological thinking, namely ontogenesis. Ingold places ontogenetic development at the centre, together with processes of growth and learning. In doing so, he questions the idea of cultural or biological inheritance and the idea that human beings are somehow constituted by elements that precede their existence (Ingold 2022b). The endeavour of anthropology is consequently not aimed at establishing the hidden causes that drive human existence (e.g., genes, memes, algorithms, etc.). Far from restricting or narrowing down the understanding of human life, anthropology seeks to reveal the continuous emergence of difference in activity. Anthropological research itself becomes a part of these ongoing patterns of corresponding lives and lines. It does not allow for a full or complete description of a human being, a social group, or a society, since these things are never complete but always work in progress. So too is research.

Racism and Black Lives Matter

A series of recent global crises has exposed many crucial fault lines within and between countries, their economies, and social fabric. In the United States, the killings of Breonna Taylor, Ahmaud Arbery, George Floyd, Tony McDade, Atatiana Jefferson, Aura Rosser, and many more Black Americans led to mass protests and demonstrations in 2020 (Flewellen et al. 2021).

The protests spread to other Western countries such as the United Kingdom, Australia, Canada, and France. The movement drew on the term *Black Lives Matter* to hold these various initiatives together, to draw attention to the injustices and systemic racism that persist in these countries, and to demand meaningful changes (Ray 2020; Szetela 2020). The Covid-19 pandemic rendered some of these disparities hyper-visible and made it obvious that African American people are exposed to significantly higher health risks in the United States. Accordingly, death rates due to Covid-19 were disproportionately higher among the African American population (Vasquez Reyes 2020; Marcantonio et al. 2021). Similar structural inequalities exist in other countries as well with similarly devastating consequences (Kirby 2020). However, the pandemic has not only exposed social and economic disparities along racial lines within countries. It also makes more obvious the deeply ingrained inequalities between countries across the globe and, particularly, between the Global North and the Global South (Kelley et al. 2020). These aspects are intertwined with ongoing issues surrounding unsustainable resource extraction economies, labour exploitation, and the degradation of ecosystems (Powers et al. 2021; Solomonian and Di Ruggiero 2021). More broadly, the current situation of our global society still reflects the racial logic that has fuelled the development of the global European-dominated colonial system of the movement and exploitation of people and resources over the last 500 years (Andrews 2021).

Anthropologists, archaeologists, and academics from related fields have actively engaged with these developments and challenges as commentators, participants, and researchers. Many Black and Indigenous academics have also been directly impacted by the events, emotionally, personally, and professionally. These events have also reignited discussions about the existing disparities and injustices within academia itself and how these can be addressed (e.g., Flewellen et al. 2021).[2] It has, of course, been recognised for a long time that the anthropological disciplines themselves are products of European colonialism and that they originated during the height of European colonial and imperial dominance during the 19th century. The legacies of this history are the subject of ongoing studies and critiques (Ashcroft, Griffiths, and Tiffin 1995; Liebmann and Rizvi 2008; Bhambra 2014; Porr and Matthews 2020). However, only relatively recently have academic anthropologists begun to engage with the hidden and deep influences of colonial thought on their ontologies and epistemologies (Mignolo and Walsh 2018; Bhambra and Holmwood 2021).

It is not surprising that within the anthropological disciplines, the fields of palaeoanthropology and biological anthropology have been experiencing the most profound challenges in relation to racist legacies and ideas. While most researchers today accept the racist history of these fields and the problematic practices of some of the most prominent founding figures, it is much more difficult to accept its ongoing influence on today's practices and frameworks (Marks 2008, 2012; Kuljian 2016; Mullings et al. 2021). These difficulties have surfaced, for example, in the fierce debates about the racist dimensions in the work of C. Darwin and E. O. Wilson (Fuentes 2021; McLemore 2021). In this context, the questions should not revolve around a historical assessment and an evaluation of possible historical continuities. Rather, the interrogation needs to focus on the question of whether anthropological research itself may be suffused with racist tendencies due to the biological essentialism on which it rests (Marks 2017).

During the course of his career, Tim Ingold has repeatedly but not extensively engaged with notions of race and racism. For him, this topic has not been a specific or separate area of inquiry. Nor, so far, has he explicitly engaged with postcolonial or decolonial literature. However, as outlined in the previous section, a fundamental critique of key aspects of the foundations of racist thought constitutes a central element of Ingold's thinking. It is a consequence of his understanding of the relational, dynamic, and ongoing constitution of human beings. In the book *Evolution and social life* (orig. 1986), for example, he critiques racist ideas in the context of a discussion of evolutionary thought (see also Ingold 2006), and analyses Franz Boas' not entirely coherent views on the relationship between race and culture (Ingold 2016:44–47, 314). Subsequently, in *The perception of the environment* (Ingold 2000), racism is critiqued as a reflection of the genealogical model, which assumes "that persons embody certain attributes of appearance, temperament and mentality by virtue of their ancestry, and that these are passed on in a form that is unaffected by the circumstances or achievements of their life in the world" (137). While this understanding itself has a long history and has been expressed in various forms, with the development of molecular sciences, its most recent formulations are couched in implicit or explicit forms of genetic determinism. Tim Ingold is, however, clear about the dangers of this, concluding that "so long as it is assumed that the biological constitution of human organisms is given as a genetic endowment, there can be no escape from racism" (Ingold 2000:389). In general, anthropology can only move forward if the demons of racism are exorcised. Such a movement will necessitate a much more fundamental revision of anthropological thinking, entailing a rejection of essentialist concepts of biological inheritance and cultural transmission, and their replacement by an understanding of human beings as the active and situated producers of their lives that repudiates any division of humanity into discrete races or cultures (Ingold 2018a:123–129). Thus, while race and racism have not been at the forefront of Tim Ingold's work, he has provided some of the most powerful and elaborate arguments for their rejection, as well as suggesting ways to take future research beyond them.

The crisis of education and the university

Turning to a very different side of Ingold's work, on the subject of education, in democratic societies, the most important task of schools and universities is to educate free and self-determined citizens to form a tolerant community oriented towards the wellbeing of all. Education must not foremost be a matter of providing students with the best possible prerequisites for life outside school and university; it is not a tool to master the challenges of 'real life'. Instead, the aim of education should be to enable students to participate in life and to interact with the world. Education must lead pupils and students out into the world and help them to find their own way to live their lives, instead of imparting knowledge that is supposed to help them brave the perils of life. Referring to the work of educational philosopher Masschelein, Ingold reminds us that the term 'education' comes from the Latin 'ex-ducere', literally meaning 'to lead out' (Masschelein 2010:48). Education is about leading life, not about managing life.

Following Dewey (1966), Ingold argues that education essentially helps to ensure the continuity of life (Ingold 2018a:3). In this context, education is not merely a means towards continuing life, but is itself a way of doing so. Generations overlap, old and young live together for a while, exchange ideas, and learn from each other. It would be a misunderstanding, however, to think that seniors would simply pass on their knowledge to juniors, who would then multiply it and pass it on to the next generation. If knowledge were merely transmitted and accumulated, it could only be *about* the world, requiring of its recipients that they keep their distance, rather than joining *with* the world and participating in its formative processes. The knowledge they acquire would not affect them personally. For Ingold, to the contrary, the task of education is first and foremost to enable people to participate. This has implications for how teaching and learning must be done. The learner can only participate in life and the world – rather than simply having knowledge presented to her – if she receives answers to questions that she asks herself. If a person has no questions, then the answers are none of her business. But even when a person has questions, she cannot simply take over the answers but must acquire them herself. Teachers can therefore only tell of ways in which they themselves have found answers. Learners must follow these paths themselves and search for answers in their turn. The answers they find may be much the same, but they have to be obtained for themselves. Learning is a matter of experience. We grow by experience. That is the meaning of education.

A good example of such a learning process is playing a musical instrument. The practitioner follows her teacher when she tries to play a piece as the teacher plays it for her. However, this is not a matter of simply copying the teacher's actions. Instead, the practitioner must enter the music in such a way that she 'inhabits' it (Ingold 2014:131) to make it sound. Here, Ingold draws attention to yet another aspect that is equally important and most often overlooked. For it is not the case that only the student learns; the teacher also learns in exchange with her student. Teaching and learning fundamentally make up a process in which both sides, teacher and learner, move forward and share experiences, and from which they both emerge transformed. Parents learn from their children, teachers, and professors from their students, the old from the young. That is what makes living together possible. Ingold therefore sees one of the greatest abuses of our education system in the fact that it separates the very young from the very old. "Both are excluded from making a collective future" (Ingold 2021). The young are prepared for 'real' life, the old are separated from it. 'Real' life apparently only consists of adult working life. Education, according to this conception, serves to cope with the challenges of working life.

In keeping with this critique, Ingold comes out strongly against the increasing corporatisation of universities. Many universities today serve as engines of the so-called global knowledge economy. However, only knowledge that can be detached from experience and objectified can be commodified. It must be based on facts, which should be subject to independent verification. Such facts come from 'hard' sciences – that is, sciences which are themselves impervious to the reality they investigate, and which position themselves, accordingly, in opposition to it. Life, however, is not built from facts; it is in constant motion and change and can therefore only be researched by going along with it, through participatory observation. This is 'soft science' which "bends and deforms when it encounters other things" (Ingold 2018a:69).

What is true for learning, then, is also true for research. It follows paths in search of truth but can never attain truth itself. The pathways do not lead to a destination, but to new life and creative reality. The knowledge that such research produces does not consist of facts but is 'knowing-in-being' (Ingold 2018b); it is not found 'out there' but disclosed 'from within' (Ingold 2018b:4). This understanding of research, however, has no place in a university that is run on the corporate model. Ingold had to learn this as well, and in 2016 he and a small group of like-minded colleagues and students at the University of Aberdeen wrote a manifesto entitled 'Reclaiming Our University' (Ingold 2016), which called for the fortunes of the university to be controlled once again by its members and for the university to take more seriously its civic task of educating responsible citizens.

So, what would the university of the future look like? It must be a place where people from all walks of life and from all over the world come together to study in a spirit of tolerance and justice. It should be a place of education where research means participatory observation and where scientists themselves are deeply involved and immersed in what they do. Anthropology, for Ingold, has a leading role to play in making this vision a reality.

The Anthropocene and the future of humanity

The term *Anthropocene* attests to the reality that human influence on nature has become so great as to become a leading force in shaping the history of the earth. Humans have become a geological force. Whether the Anthropocene began with the establishment of the Western colonial system in the 15th century, the development of modern science in the early 17th century, the expanding industrialisation in the 19th century or the atomic age in the 1950s, remains controversial (Lewis and Maslin 2015). For Tim Ingold, it is much more important that the devastating impacts on the environment must end quickly if the earth is to remain habitable. The forces at work in the Anthropocene are so destructive because nature is seemingly only shaped and exploited according to abstract human ideas. At the same time, nature's (and human) inherent vitality is denied and neglected. Only in the era of naturalism, modern technology, and capitalism – all peculiar to Western modernity – has nature been taken purely as a resource to be exploited and used. The consequent damage is not restricted to the exploitation of nature alone but affects how humans understand their relationship with nature. Ingold's analysis in this respect comes close to Heidegger's thinking about technology (Heidegger 1977:3–35). Like Heidegger, Tim Ingold is not concerned with demonising individual technical developments, but rather with pointing out how the technoscientific approach to nature obscures its inherent creativity. If nature is only approached as a resource, then it is deprived of its own creative power and appears to be fixed, static, and lifeless. It is reduced to mere material for human interventions in the world. Equally, human beings themselves are denied crucial aspects of their existence. They end up split between bodies in nature and minds without it: the former reduced to mechanisms; the latter elevated to a suite of capacities for directing their operations. Ingold therefore demands that we once again situate ourselves as humans in the midst of the living world. The destructive forces of the Anthropocene cannot be tamed merely by substituting the exploitation of nature with a sustainable use of resources. Sustainability thinking is still based on an understanding of nature as a mere resource for the human design of the world. This understanding of nature, which is deeply engrained in public consciousness, can only be broken by our learning to experience ourselves anew as beings deeply and irreducibly immersed in, and connected with, our environments. It is with precisely this dimension of experience that Tim Ingold is primarily concerned.

To illustrate the inseparability of humans from their surroundings, and to show that their actions are fundamentally carried out in interaction with the many forces of their environments, Ingold adduces such seemingly mundane examples as flying a kite, chopping wood, or simply walking (Ingold 2011). The fundamental creativity of all action is most obviously revealed in the work of art. From arts and artists, we learn that creativity is not exhausted in the event of thinking up something new and making it from available resources. An artist acts in a way that is truly creative only when she brings the material and environment of her work into play so that they themselves come to life. Creativity is less about producing something new than about bringing the material to life. Rather than being directed at final products, it is about initiating new beginnings. Ingold therefore insists upon a conceptual distinction between novelty and newness (Ingold 2022a:26). Novelty refers to something that appears for the very first time, whether in the life of an individual, or in the entirety of human history; thus, with respect to novelty, creation is bound to originality. By the notion of newness, on the contrary, Ingold, following Bergson (1922), means 'ceaseless upspringing' (cited in Ingold 2022a:26). With respect to newness, creativity does not come to an end with the creation of something new but rather means the process of living and acting along with the vitality and creativity of the environment. Creativity can therefore only emerge where humans engage with the materials in their environment, instead of subjecting them to abstract ideas. Recalling Wieman (1961), Ingold says that creation is not so much done by humans as undergone by them (Ingold 2014:126). The mere recombination of existing resources may be innovative, but action becomes creative only through the discovery of the creative potential that lies in the environment itself and by helping it to unfold.

The creative potential of the environment is not simply present, however, but must first be discovered or imagined. This is what Tim Ingold calls "imagining for real", a phrase he uses for the title of his latest book (Ingold 2022a). In imagining, nature is discovered in its creative vitality. And this discovery is itself a creative act. Creativity, thus, is always in the interplay of humans and their environment. Rombach has coined the term 'concreativity' to point out this interplay (Rombach 1987, 1994). The closeness of Ingold's thought to Rombach's structural-genetic approach is extensive in many other respects, even though Ingold appears to be unaware of his work, possibly because it remains largely unknown outside of German-speaking academia.

Like Rombach, Ingold also points out that both humans and environment are underpinned by their genesis. He speaks of the 'ontogenetic turn' (Ingold 2018:167). That human beings are alive means first and foremost that they exist in permanently striving beyond themselves. Life, therefore, is no inherent characteristic of human beings, but is the generative process of their becoming and longing (Ingold 2018:160). Human life itself is a creative process. Ingold recalls Whitehead (1926), who makes no distinction between creativity and creature: "There is only one entity which is the self-creating creature" (cited in Ingold 2022a:25). What is said here about human beings, however, truly applies to the whole of nature. Nature itself is alive and creative. The future of humanity depends essentially on opening up to this creativity anew instead of merely recombining existing and preformed resources. We need to provoke and promote it through our own creative actions that initiate, in the sense of Hannah Arendt (1958), a new beginning. "For only by restoring faith and hope in the perpetuity of beginning – or, in a word, in *creation* – can we open a real future to coming generations" (Ingold 2022a:28).

Conclusion

Tim Ingold has provided a body of work of immense scope and richness. He has influenced the fields of anthropology, human evolutionary studies, design, archaeology, philosophy, human geography, and many more. Some of these influences are reflected and discussed in the chapters assembled in this volume. Many more could be added and discussed. In this short introduction, we have tried to provide some further areas and themes with a focus on some of the most significant challenges for the world today. We believe that anybody can find valuable aspects in Ingold's work and can integrate them into their own journey and development. This engagement should not happen uncritically, and it should be conducted as a dialogue and as an ongoing correspondence. These elements are learning opportunities. Tim Ingold's vision of anthropology is holistic and does not accept established institutional and academic boundaries. Many aspects of his work have far-reaching relevance within academia and beyond because they have to do with understanding human existence and life itself, and this automatically encompasses every researcher and her or his actions. His understanding of research rests on the idea of involvement and engagement. It is opposed to detachment and abstraction. He has repeatedly stated that he understands anthropology as philosophy with the people in (e.g., Ingold 2018a:4). It is about understanding forms of existence in ongoing processes of dialogue and exchange. This is a mutual process that requires care, attention, and respect. It requires us to take the other seriously and accept the intertwined nature of learning and the creation of knowledge. The process can be bumpy and can take participants along unexpected pathways. One of the most enlightening aspects of Ingold's work lies in his own intellectual development and how its crucial junctures have shaped his thinking (e.g., Ingold 2018b). It is a testament to the freedom, openness, and curiosity that should guide every research endeavour and the philosophy that drives Ingold's inquiries. Unfortunately, within the current political climate, scarred by the ongoing influence of destructive neoliberal ideologies and the commodification of knowledge, such a vision is often seen as naïve and anachronistic. Yet, Tim Ingold's encompassing vision of research provides a powerful counternarrative. The key aspects outlined above – engagement, attention, care, respect – are not restricted to research with human beings; indeed, any such restriction would be incompatible with the anthropology he advocates. They are rather extended to the world of dynamic materials and non-human actors, all constituted in relation to each other. In this respect, Ingold's thinking shows some convergence with the logic and ethics of Indigenous ways of knowing (Porr and Bell 2012), as well as with the currently fashionable trope of the 'ontological turn' (e.g., Kohn 2015; Holbraad and Pedersen 2017). Ingold's perspective, however, has developed along its own trajectory. Although it seems difficult to assimilate Tim Ingold's work into existing intellectual currents, he provides a vision for some of the most pressing political, environmental, and social challenges of our time that takes us far beyond the age-old divisions between nature and culture, and between science and the humanities. Given the way the problems in the world right now are intertwined, this is exactly what we need.

Notes

1 We would like to thank the Udo Keller-Foundation for the generous support of the initial workshop.
2 There are many excellent online resources available to engage with racism in anthropology and archaeology and related fields. Because of lack of space, only two can be listed here, which include a wealth of further resources: www.americananthro.org/ParticipateAndAdvocate/Landing.aspx?ItemNumber=25744 (American Anthropological Association) and www.societyofblackarchaeologists.com/ (Society of Black Archaeologists).

References

Andrews, K. 2021. *The new age of empire. How racism and colonialism still rule the world*. Dublin: Allen Lane.

Arendt, H. 1958. *The human condition*. Chicago: Chicago University Press.

Ashcroft, B., G. Griffiths, and H. Tiffin, eds. 1995. *The postcolonial studies reader*. London: Routledge.

Bergson, H. 1922. *Creative evolution*. Translated by Arthur Mitchell. London: Macmillan.

Bhambra, G. K. 2014. Postcolonial and decolonial dialogues. *Postcolonial Studies* 17(2):115–121.

Bhambra, G. K. and J. Holmwood 2021. *Colonialism and modern social theory*. Cambridge: Polity.

Dewey, J. 1966. *Democracy and education: An introduction to the philosophy of education*. New York: Free Press.

Flewellen, A. O., J. P. Dunnavant, A. Odewale, A. Jones, T. Wolde-Michael, Z. Crossland, and M. Franklin. 2021. "The future of archaeology is anti-racist": Archaeology in the time of Black Lives Matter. *American Antiquity* 86(2):224–243.

Fuentes, A. 2021. "The Descent of Man", 150 years on. *Science* 372(6544):769.

Heidegger, M. 1977. *The question concerning technology and other essays*. Translated by William Lovitt, New York/London: Garland Publishing.

Holbraad, M. and M. A. Pedersen. 2017. *The ontological turn. An anthropological exposition*. New Departures in Anthropology. Cambridge: Cambridge University Press.

Ingold, T. 1998. From complementarity to obviation: On dissolving the boundaries between social and biological anthropology, archaeology and psychology. *Zeitschrift für Ethnologie* 123:21–52.

——— 2000. *The perception of the environment. Essays in livelihood, dwelling and skill*. London: Routledge.

——— 2004. Beyond biology and culture. The meaning of evolution in a relational world. *Social Anthropology* 12(2):209–221.

——— 2006. Against human nature. In *Evolutionary epistemology, language and culture. A non-adationist, systems theoretical approach*. N. Goutier, J. P. Bendegem, and D. Aerts, eds. Pp. 259–281. Dordrecht: Springer.

——— 2011. *Being alive. Essays on movement, knowledge, and description*. London/New York: Routledge.

——— 2014. The creativity of undergoing. *Pragmatics & Cognition* 22(1):124–139.
——— 2016a. *Evolution and social life*. 2nd Edition. London: Routledge.
——— 2016b. Reclaiming our university. The manifesto. https://reclaimingouruniversity.wordpress.com/ (accessed 03/06/2022).
——— 2018a. *Anthropology. Why it matters*. Cambridge: Polity.
——— 2018b. From science to art and back again: The pendulum of an anthropologist. *Interdisciplinary Science Reviews* 43(3–4):213–227.
——— 2018c. *Anthropology and/as education*. London: Routledge.
——— 2018d. Anthropology between art and science. An essay on the meaning of research. *FIELD. A Journal of Socially Engaged Art Criticism* 11. https://field-journal.com/issue-11/anthropology-between-art-and-science-an-essay-on-the-meaning-of-research (accessed 03/06/2022).
——— 2018e. One world anthropology. *HAU Journal of Ethnographic Theory* 8(1/2):158–171.
——— 2021. *Facing the Anthropocene*. Timothy Ingold in Conversation with Norman Wirzba. www.youtube.com/watch?v=dd9UUDdSaBA (accessed 03/06/2022).
——— 2022a. *Imagining for real. Essays on creation, attention and correspondence*. London: Routledge.
——— 2022b. Evolution without inheritance. Steps towards an ecology of learning. *Current Anthropology* 63/Supplement 25:S32–S55.
Ingold, T. and G. Palsson, eds. 2013. *Biosocial becomings. Integrating social and biological anthropology*. Cambridge: Cambridge University Press.
Kelley, M., R. Ferrand, K. Muraya, S. Chigudu, S. Molyneux, M. Pai, and E. Barasa. 2020. An appeal for practical social justice in the COVID-19 global response in low-income and middle-income countries. *The Lancet* 8(7):E888–E889.
Kirby, T. 2020. Evidence mounts on the disproportionate effect of COVID-19 on ethnic minorities. *The Lancet* 8(6):547–548.
Kohn, E. 2015. Anthropology of ontologies. *Annual Review of Anthropology* 44:311–327.
Kuljian, C. 2016. *Darwin's hunch. Science, race and the search for human origins*. Auckland Park: Jacana Media.
Kuper, A. and J. Marks 2011. Anthropologists unite! *Nature* 470:166–168.
Lewis, S. L. and M. A. Maslin 2015. Defining the Anthropocene. *Nature* 519:171–180.
Liebmann, M., and U. Z. Rizvi, eds. 2008. *Archaeology and the postcolonial critique*. Lanham, MD: AltaMira Press.
Marcantonio, R., D. Javeline, S. Field, and A. Fuentes. 2021. Global distribution and coincidence of pollution, climate impacts, and health risk in the Anthropocene. *PLoS ONE* 16(7):e0254060.
Marks, J. 2008. Race. Past, present, and future. In *Revisiting race in a genomic age*. B. A. Koenig, S. Soo-Jin Lee, and S. S. Richardson, eds. Pp. 21–38. New Brunswick: Rutgers University Press.
——— 2012. Why be against Darwin? Creationism, racism, and the roots of anthropology. *Yearbook of Physical Anthropology* 55:95–104.
——— 2017. *Is science racist?* Cambridge: Polity.
Masschelein, J. 2010. E-ducating the gaze: The idea of a poor pedagogy. *Ethics and Education* 5(1):43–53.
McLemore, M. R. 2021. The complicated legacy of E. O. Wilson. www.scientificamerican.com/article/the-complicated-legacy-of-e-o-wilson/ (accessed 03/06/2022).

Mignolo, W. D. and C. E. Walsh. 2018. *On coloniality. Concepts, analytics, praxis.* Durham: Duke University Press.

Mullings, L., J. Benn Torres, A. Fuentes, C. C. Gravlee, D. Roberts, and Z. Thayer. 2021. The biology of racism. *American Anthropologist* 123(3):671–680.

Porr, M. and H. R. Bell 2012. 'Rock-art', 'animism' and two-way thinking: Towards a complementary epistemology in the understanding of material culture and 'rock-art' of hunting and gathering people. *Journal of Archaeological Method and Theory* 19:161–205.

Porr, M. and J. M. Matthews, eds. 2020. *Interrogating human origins: Decolonisation and the deep human past.* Archaeological Orientations. London: Routledge.

Powers, M., P. Brown, G. Poudrier, J. Liss Ohayon, A. Cordner, C. Alder, and M. G. Atlas. 2021. COVID-19 as eco-pandemic injustice: Opportunities for collective and antiracist approaches to environmental health. *Journal of Health and Social Behavior* 62(2):222–229.

Ray, R. 2020. Setting the record straight on the movement for Black Lives. *Ethnic and Racial Studies* 43(8):1393–1401.

Rombach, H. 1987. *Strukturanthropologie. "Der menschliche Mensch".* Freiburg/München: Alber.

——— 1994. *Der Ursprung. Philosophie der Konkreativität von Mensch und Natur.* Freiburg: Rombach.

Solomonian, L. and E. Di Ruggiero 2021. The critical intersection of environmental and social justice: A commentary. *Globalization and Health* 17:30.

Szetela, A. 2020. Black Lives Matter at five: Limits and possibilities. *Ethnic and Racial Studies* 43(8):1358–1383.

Vasquez Reyes, M. 2020. The disproportional impact of COVID-19 on African Americans. *Health and Human Rights* 22(2):299–307.

Whitehead, A. N. 1926. *Religion in the making: Lowell Lectures 1926.* Cambridge: Cambridge University Press.

Wieman, H. N. 1961. *Intellectual foundations of faith.* London: Vision Press.

Part II

Knowing, perceiving, and attending

2 Introduction

Knowing, perceiving, and attending

Niels Weidtmann and Martin Porr

Children are born into very specific and dynamic social, material, and spatial environments. They therefore initially acquire their knowledge of the world through their engagement with these environments before the boundaries of their experiential world gradually shift. For example, young children are astonished when they first learn that other children also have mothers and fathers, since their knowledge of mothers and fathers is initially based exclusively on their experiences with their own parents. Even when they learn that all children have parents, however, this does not become merely abstract knowledge. What it means to have parents – or perhaps to no longer have them at some point – can only be understood based on personal experience. It is not a mere fact to have parents; instead, it reflects an experiential reality of security and protection, but possibly also pain, loss, and helplessness that goes far beyond the fact. Without these experiences, it would remain largely unclear what the difference is between parents and other persons. But not only is knowledge of the world acquired through experience, children themselves simultaneously mature in their own personalities in this process. An example of this is that babies explore their own bodies and put their hands and feet, and later also toys, in their mouths. In this way they appropriate their own body and learn to distinguish it from the wider environment. When Plessner argues that people not only *have* their bodies, but at the same time *are* these bodies ("Leib") (2003:238), it is because people perceive and explore the environment beyond their body with the help of this very body. We do not explore *either* our body *or* the environment beyond the body; rather, we explore the environment *through* our body. But this is only possible because we experience ourselves as corporeal beings. The appropriation of one's own body, which we can observe in the toddler, thus goes along with the formation of a corporeal ego. Just as much as knowledge of the world is based on experience, so too is knowledge of the human self.

What is said here about one's own body can be extended to things beyond the body. Gregory Bateson (1973) draws on the example of the blind man with his cane, already introduced by Merleau-Ponty (2013) (cited in Ingold 2000:18). The blind man feels his environment by his cane as if through an

DOI: 10.4324/9781003162773-5

extended arm. It is not that the blind man feels the walking stick, he does this only when he concentrates on it specifically or does not hold it in his hand but must search for it first; instead, he feels the external environment through the cane. The cane is integrated into his own body schema. Other aspects of the environment may not only be integrated into the body schema but become an integral part of one's own personality as well, for example, one's own children. Parents themselves are fundamentally transformed by having children; in fact, they grow up together with their children. This affects how they perceive the world, how they behave, what values they hold, and at the same time, it changes their self-image and self-conception.

These examples show that it is short-sighted to compare perception to the way a computer processes data. Perception does not mediate between the external world and the mind. Instead, it is a form of living participation in the continuously moving and changing world. Such participation has an ontological character, which Heidegger expresses by the formula "being-in-the-world" (Heidegger 2010). The human mind, too, has therefore to be understood not as opposed and alien to the world, but as in correspondence with the world. Ingold describes impressively how he was blown away by the insight that the biophysical organism and sociocultural person are one and the same (Ingold 2000:3).

The decisive influences for such an ecological understanding of human perceiving and knowing are drawn from the works of Gibson, Bateson, Merleau-Ponty, Heidegger, and others. From Gibson (1979), Ingold adopts the appreciation of attention; he elaborates this aspect further and finally uses it to replace – in the form of what he calls attentionality – the supposed intentionality of perception, as it has been elaborated above all by Husserl (1999, 2001). A simple example of the importance of attention is in walking (Ingold 2011). If the ground is uneven, the walker must pay attention to the ground conditions with each step and adapt her posture to the conditions as they unfold. What seems to be of little relevance in relation to walking, since the required attentionality only penetrates into consciousness in exceptional cases, in fact applies to every kind of action. Human action can only succeed if it is attentive to the things and circumstances which it has to deal with. Circumstances make demands of the agent, to which she must respond in her actions. Here, according to Ingold "the relation between intention and attention is reversed" (2017:19). Such attentionality, to be sure, means much more than simply responding to the demands that the environment places on the person. The agent must engage with the circumstances and correspond with them. The environment is not in opposition to action but becomes a co-agent. A simple example is the splitting of wood, which must be done along the grain (Ingold 2018:163). If the axe follows the structure of the log, then the wood goes along with the movement, as it were, indeed it virtually leads the axe in the right way. Ingold speaks of correspondence and of the fact that such action runs along the conditions of materials. Humans and environment act together; humans do not impose on nature a form that is alien to it.

Such knowledge, which is acquired in attention to and close interaction with the environment, is less an abstract knowledge than a skill. The concept of skill echoes Merleau-Ponty's proclamation, adopted from Husserl, that consciousness is originally less an "I think" than an "I can" (Merleau-Ponty 2013). It is skills that enable humans competently to navigate a constantly changing world and environment. The distinctive feature of skills is that they are not a knowledge *of* the world, but knowledge in dealing *with* the environment and living *in* the environment. Skills and environment correspond with each other. This means on the one hand that skills reflect the specific environment, but, on the other hand, that the environment is discovered and perceived in a way that corresponds to the skills. Ingold can therefore claim that "what we are accustomed to call cultural variation in fact consists of variations of skills" (Ingold 2000:5). An anthropology interested in such cultural variations should therefore be interested in people's skills.

References

Bateson, G. 1973. *Steps to an ecology of mind*. London: Fontana.

Gibson, J. 1979. *The ecological approach to visual perception*. Boston: Houghton Mifflin.

Heidegger, M. 2010. *Being and time*. Translated by Joan Stambaugh, revised by Dennis J. Schmidt, Albany/New York: SUNY Press.

Husserl, E. 1999. *The idea of phenomenology*. Collected Works 8. Dordrecht: Springer.

Husserl, E. 2001. *Logical investigations*. Vol. 1+2. London: Routledge.

Ingold, T. 2000. *The perception of the environment. Essays on livelihood, dwelling and skill*. London: Routledge.

Ingold, T. 2011. *Being alive. Essays on movement, knowledge and description*. London: Routledge.

Ingold, T. 2017. On human correspondence. *Journal of the Royal Anthropology Institute* 23(1):9–27.

Ingold, T. 2018. One world anthropology. *HAU Journal of Ethnographic Theory* 8(1/2):158–171.

Merleau-Ponty, M. 2013 [1945]. *Phenomenology of perception*. Translated by Donald A. Landes. London: Routledge.

Plessner, H. 2003. Lachen und Weinen. Eine Untersuchung der Grenzen menschlichen Verhaltens (1941). In H. Plessner, *Ausdruck und menschliche Natur*. Gesammelte Schriften Bd. VII. Pp. 201–387. Frankfurt/M.: Suhrkamp.

3 Anthropology with Tim Ingold and friends

Stephanie Bunn

Introduction

A while ago, I was asked to give a short series of lectures to anthropology students at the University of St Andrews about the work of Tim Ingold. When I mentioned it to Tim, he said, "Fine, just so long as you don't call it 'The anthropology *of* Tim Ingold …' " Hence this chapter is entitled 'Anthropology *with* Tim Ingold and friends' …

When I first met Tim, he was soon to become my academic supervisor at the University of Manchester from 1989 to the late 1990s, through both my masters and doctoral research, so it is quite challenging to write about him from this perspective. At the time, he was senior lecturer and director of postgraduate admissions, so it was almost a chance meeting, and I was not aware of my good fortune immediately. Tim was very generous with his time, ideas, and scholarship, frequently leaping up to stride at great speed down the department's corridor to make photocopies of articles that I simply 'had to read'. He'd lend me treasured books, such as Gregory Bateson's *Steps to an ecology of mind* (1972), which I studied so thoroughly that all the pages fell out. I felt that many of the new scholars whose ideas he introduced me to were indeed his 'thinking friends', a diverse group of anthropologists, philosophers, ecologists, artists, and others, whose many perspectives somehow converged into the writings of this new-thinking anthropologist.

At the time, Tim was becoming known for his innovative writing on human–environment relations. He was immensely busy, editing the *Journal of the Royal Anthropological Institute* and convening the famous Manchester GDAT Debates (Group for Debates in Anthropological Theory), which he had founded in 1988 and which discussed themes such as 'the concept of society' and whether aesthetics could be a cross-cultural category (Ingold 1996). Having done field research among Saami reindeer herders in Finland in the 1970s and 1980s, Tim had already established his reputation through his work on human–animal relations and had begun developing his unique and very philosophical approach to ecological and evolutionary anthropology,

DOI: 10.4324/9781003162773-6

declaring during our sessions that 'Anthropology is philosophy with the people in'. His concern with anthropology and creativity was still largely to come.

Two key underlying concerns in Tim's work, which were particularly inspiring and novel, were developing during the period I studied with him. Much of his subsequent work, I think, is set within the context of these critical early themes. On the one hand, he aimed to reconcile the contradictions between the biological and the social, asking how we could consider people both as organisms and as social beings at the same time – and exploring "the mutualism of person and the environment" (1992:40). On the other hand, he aimed to address problems inherent in scholarly attempts to analyse the world in a retrospective, post facto, kind of way, an approach very common in anthropology of the late 1980s and early 1990s. This latter approach reflected a tendency to project the analysis of events or artefacts 'backwards', based on the finished product, ascribing a kind of a priori plan to human action, whether the subject under discussion was cultural transmission, tradition, the environment, or craft.

In his introduction to *The perception of the environment*, Tim describes his realisation of the first concern as follows:

> I had argued that human beings must simultaneously be constituted both as organisms within systems of ecological relations and as persons within systems of social relations. The critical task for anthropology, it seemed, was to understand the reciprocal interplay between the two kinds of systems, social and ecological ...
>
> I continued to be troubled by the inherent dualism of this approach, with its implied dichotomies between person and organism, society and nature. I vividly remember one Saturday morning in April 1988 – an entirely ordinary one for Manchester at that time of year, with grey skies and a little rain – when, on my way to catch a bus, it suddenly dawned on me that the organism and the person could be one and the same ... Instead of trying to reconstruct the complete human being from two separate but complementary components, held together with a film of psychological cement, it struck me that we should be trying to find a way of talking about human life that eliminates the need to slice it up into these different layers.
>
> Why had this view, that the person *is* the organism, and not something added on top, eluded me for so long?
>
> (Ingold 2000:3)

This approach challenged the assumption that every person is a discrete entity, *prior* to their engagement with others. People, Tim argued, aren't born finite, complete, and discrete, with their characteristics bestowed upon them in advance. Nor are they like biological blank sheets, ready to be inscribed with culture. Anthropologists of that time, such as Clifford Geertz (1973), had declared, in contrast, that "humans inhabit discursive worlds of culturally constructed significance laid on to the substrate of an undifferentiated and continuous terrain" (Ingold 2000:172), and that these would vary from society to society.

One challenge for anthropologists of the 1980s was that juxtaposing cultural relativism with ecological ideas could yield very contradictory outcomes. On the one hand, an implication of the cultural relativist approach was that societies inscribed a grand script of culture, which was somehow different from nature, onto an environmental canvas, so that the natural environment became a kind of backdrop onto which different cultures inscribed different forms of culture: as Geertz (1973:5) put it, "man is an animal suspended in webs of significance he himself has spun". On the other hand, the models developed by ecologists at the time tended to ascribe a determining role to the environment that left little scope for human intentionality, save as an adaptive afterthought. Until that point, Tim had also argued that intentions were constituted in relations between persons, while as organisms, humans related to nonhumans and other components of the natural environment. The problem, he realised, was that this would mean human life is conducted simultaneously on two levels: the social domain of interpersonal relationships and the ecological domain of inter-organism relations. And it is contradictory, as he now argues, to have people living a split-level existence, half in nature and half in culture; half organisms, half persons. Tim's new way of thinking about humans as organisms within an environment proposed instead that humans are 'condensations' of all their life experiences and relationships, physically and socially. To understand this requires a kind of "relational thinking" (Ingold 2000:3).

Similarly, in regard to his critique of analysing cultural forms by working backwards from finished products, Tim's argument was that events or products are the result of practices, and as such are improvisatory, emergent, conducted as life is lived. This calls for an understanding of the difference between being and becoming. For Tim, it also challenged the perceived difference between innovation and tradition, since improvisation "characterizes creativity by way of its processes", while the way we think about innovation or tradition characterises creativity "by way of its products" (Ingold and Hallam 2007:2). Hence, Tim developed an affinity with thinkers such as Heidegger on the relationship between building and dwelling (1971). These concerns were to provide a strong lead into his future work on skill, and hence to creativity, as discussed in the second part of this chapter. As his ideas crystallised, he began to put them together into his major work, *The perception of the environment* (2000), which is probably (in this author's view) the most significant book he has written, so I'll begin by considering why I think the two key terms of the title of this book – 'perception' and 'environment' – are so important.

Perception

The ecological psychologist James Gibson, author of two seminal works – *The senses considered as perceptual systems* (1966) and *The ecological approach to visual perception* (1979) – critically influenced Tim's thinking on perception and, linked to this, affordances. Gibson could be considered one of his earlier 'thinking friends'. For Gibson, perception is the achievement not of a mind in a body, but of the organism as a whole as it moves around in its environment. He draws attention to two key aspects of sensing or perception. Firstly, Gibson shows how sensing isn't passive. The senses, he says, are active perceptual systems rather than consisting simply of receptors which pick up sensations (such as of heat, light, pressure, odours, and so on), sending them on their way to the brain for processing. Through this, secondly, Gibson shows that perception is not a linear, sequential process from world to mind; rather, it is a form of direct experience. "The pattern of the excited receptors is of no account: what counts is the external pattern that is temporarily occupied by the excited recipients as the eyes roam over the world, or as the skin moves over an object" (Gibson 1966:4). Finally, Tim followed Gibson in seeing affordances as properties of elements of an environment, "what it provides or furnishes, either for good or ill" (Ingold 1992:42). These are most certainly not features added on to a neutral object, although inhabitants may perceive their value differently.

From this perspective, we don't sense by default; sensing is both active *and* receptive, we both experience sensations and detect or actively perceive them. In other words, we don't just see, we also look; we don't just hear, we also listen; we both smell and sniff, and while we may physically feel sensations, the process of touch is also active. The point is that if sensing were purely passive, then seeing, for example, would take place in the brain. However, for both Gibson and Ingold, perception takes place in a process in which the whole body is in action, paying attention. Thus, sensing is not ultimately 'mental'; rather, it unites body and mind in direct engagement with the world. It takes place, and is experienced, in the direct involvement of people in their environments (see Ingold 2000, Chapter 14).

One point worth noting, in regard to touch, is that while vision and hearing enable us to position ourselves within and appreciate the environment at distance, through touch or the haptic system, using the hands and other parts of the body, we come into direct and immediate physical contact with the environment. Furthermore, we get information about the environment beyond the body. Through engaging with tools and other implements, whether a stick, a hammer, or an axe for chopping wood, or even using the body as an instrument itself, through dance, or climbing, or walking, we come to know what the wider environment feels like and what we feel like within it. Through touch and movement, the boundaries of the body are breached, and connections are made with people, animals, and materials.

The body is no longer entirely on its own; a connection has been made – a kind of engagement. Furthermore, because the hands can also act along with feeling, they can change the world while sensing it. Herein lies the connection with skill. Gregory Bateson, another of Tim's 'thinking friends', tells us that mind is active throughout the entire body. Further, it is 'not limited by the skin', but also immanent in 'pathways and messages beyond the body' when engaging with the environment, and is thus immanent in the ecosystem, even in the 'total evolutionary structure'. This 'circuit of mind' in the environment reflects how the skilled maker engages with materials. Thus, in active perception and creative action, mind is effectively connected with the body, the environment, and society (Bateson 1972:429–436).

Environment

In regard to environment, Tim has often emphasised that we cannot consider environment as '*space*' because, for him, space is empty. Here again he agrees with Gibson (1979). *Environment*, by contrast, is something of which humans are a part and with which they actively interact, and which interacts with them. The environment is certainly not a blank sheet upon which humans inscribe the forms of culture, nor is it a backdrop to human action (a notion frequently used in anthropological analysis until this point). It is rather a domain that persons, both human and non-human, *inhabit*.

Much of Tim's approach to humanity's place in the environment, and to 'animals as nonhuman persons', has arisen through his interest in circumpolar hunting and herding peoples. Among such peoples, whether the Saami, with whom he worked, or North American or Siberian hunting peoples, the environment is understood to be animate, a vital living place in which humans are just one element. Here, Tim complements Gibson's ecological approach by noting how hunting peoples, in particular, have tended to treat the natural environment as if it was sentient, and its inhabitants as social beings like themselves. Therefore, if a community says that an element of the environment such as a rock *did* something, or that thunder *said* something, this reflects their perspective on the environment. And in Tim's view, it is not up to anthropologists to reframe such perspectives, nor to treat them simply as metaphors. Key anthropological friends here include Irving Hallowell on the Ojibwa (1960), Richard K. Nelson on the Koyukon (1983), and Nurit Bird David on the Nayaka (1990). In *The perception of the environment*, Tim puts it thus:

> The Ojibwa, however, do not make this assumption. Persons, in the Ojibwa world, can take a great variety of forms, of which the human is just one. They can also appear in a variety of animal guises, as meteorological phenomena such as thunder or the winds, as heavenly bodies such as the sun, and even as tangible objects such as stones … (…) Moreover

> (...) persons can be encountered not only in waking life but also, and equally palpably, in dreams and in the telling of myths. And most importantly they can change their form.
>
> (Ingold 2000:91)

One of Tim's key examples comes from a celebrated account by Hallowell with reference to Chief William Berens:

> I once asked an old man: 'Are *all* the stones we see about us here alive?' He reflected along while and then replied, 'No but, *some* are'.
>
> (Hallowell 1960:24, cited in Ingold 2000:96)

Another example comes from Nelson's work on the Koyukon:

> The proper role of humankind is to serve a dominant nature. The natural universe is nearly omnipotent, and only through acts of respect and propitiation is the well-being of humans ensured ... in the Koyukon world, human existence depends on a morally based relationship with the overarching powers of nature. Humanity acts at the behest of the environment. The Koyukon must move *with* the forces of their surroundings, not attempting to control, master, or fundamentally alter them. They do not confront nature, they yield to it.
>
> (Nelson 1983:240, cited in Ingold 2000:68)

In his concern to understand the relations between humans and nonhumans, Ingold argues that whatever applies to organisms in their environment has to include humans as well. We see here the divergent influences of Gibson – who defined the environment as consisting "of the earth and the sky with objects on the earth and in the sky, of mountains and clouds, fires and sunsets, pebbles, and stars" (1979), (perhaps presaging Tim's (2010) concern with weather), and the subtly different perspective of Jacob von Uexküll who developed the notion *Umwelt* (1957).

For von Uexküll, an animal's life world – what it perceives and what it does in its immediate environment – is uniquely comprehensible and meaningful to that animal and equates to its *Umwelt*. "All animals, from the simplest to the most complex, are fitted into their unique worlds with equal completeness", he says (von Uexküll 1957:11). Gibson, von Uexküll, and Ingold might agree that the meaning in an animal's world emerges through a very close relationship between their perception and their actions on the world. But for von Uexküll, the *Umwelt* is different from how 'a neutral' human observer might perceive the environment that surrounds a creature, and he also argues that this reflects a uniquely human capacity to endow the environment with different potentials and meanings – representations. A simple world, according to von Uexküll, corresponds to a simple animal, a well-articulated world to a complex one.

Here, Tim contrasts the significance of Gibson's notion of affordances as *potentials* or *properties* intrinsic to an object or material, which were 'taken up' by human and nonhuman animals (Ingold 2011:79), with von Uexküll's *Umwelt*, where such potentials are more like 'qualities bestowed upon things' by a creature reflecting its specific use and need. In his earlier work (1989), Tim had indeed seen humans as uniquely capable of standing back and reflecting on the conditions of existence, so that making and using things was understood as a kind of 'cultural ordering of things' (Ingold 2000:178). But this, he acknowledges later, "is now a source of considerable embarrassment" (ibid.). It reflects a view of nature as a source of raw materials available for projects of cultural construction, and again, the retroflexive approach he came to reject, as discussed above.

Evidently, any model developed by ecological thinkers, including Gibson, about the relations between organisms and environments has to include humans. The implications of this are – and here the literature on hunter-gatherers complements that of Gibson (1979, Chapters 1–3) – that the environment has a vitality, and equally, aspects of it have personhood.

Building and dwelling

To explore this further, Tim considered how humans and nonhumans construct their own environments through inhabitation and making home, rather than simply as the result of a plan, as architecture is often assumed to be created. He compared the human house, the beaver's lodge, and the mollusc shell (e.g., Ingold 2000:172–188). While scholars tend to treat contemporary city architecture as a product of human intention and as the planned work of a lone creative individual, vernacular architecture is considered to be the product of culture, where the plan of what is to be made is found in tradition. But the houses of animals, whether a beaver's lodge or a bird's nest, are said to be the products of instinctive behaviour. The animal must work to implement what biologist Richard Dawkins (1999) has christened its 'extended phenotype'. But the mollusc needs to do no work to build its shell; it just grows, along with the rest of its body, apparently under genetic control.

This way of thinking posits several parallel yet discontinuous models of development, depending on the sources of the 'plan'. These sources range from genes to instinctive behaviour, to tradition, to the lone individual. Yet, none of these factors directly address the generative process of growth and becoming, nor the improvisatory aspect of creativity and making mentioned above. Instead, they treat animal constructions as assemblages of sensory practices with no intention of any kind, and vernacular dwellings as similarly lacking in intention, since the 'plan' is embedded in tradition. Yet, all of these makers engage with the environment, through acts of care, or through a need for shelter, growth, and inhabitation. Their processes of building and dwelling are improvisatory and responsive. The resulting structures emerge through an engagement between organism and environment that cross-cuts the emergent boundaries between them.

These contrasting ways of thinking about how humans and animals construct or build aspects of their environment, and inhabit it, are summed up in what Tim calls the 'building perspective' and the 'dwelling perspective'. Here, his 'anthropological friend' is the German philosopher Martin Heidegger who wrote about this relationship in his *Poetry, language, thought* (1971). In discussing the difference between building and dwelling, Tim considers what it takes for a house to be a home. He draws on Heidegger's discussion of the origins and meaning of the old German word *Bauen* and old English *buan*, both of which, Heidegger says, condense the building of the home and living in it into a single term, with meanings of both building and inhabiting. So, the building of a house or home includes the care, attention, and senses of inhabitation that we bring to dwelling in our environments. Ingold and Heidegger both argue that we don't dwell because we have built, that is, we don't live in preconstructed worlds. Rather, "we build and have built because we dwell", as Heidegger (1971:148) pronounces. So, while human homes, whether vernacular and embedded within 'traditional practices', or architecturally designed apartments, may seem planned in an ongoing way, their construction nevertheless incorporates the dwelling and the generative engagement with the environment by generations of past inhabitants.

Thus, humans and non-humans build in the process of being involved in many ways of inhabiting their world, their environment. This is not an inscription of precise design onto material. Builders may envision form in advance of construction, but even this envisioning is an activity in the real world. All forms, then, "arise as a kind of crystallization of human activity within an environment" (Ingold 2000:186).

The move to creativity

In 1999, Tim Ingold moved from Manchester to take up a newly established Chair of Anthropology at the University of Aberdeen. This move also marked a time of increased focus on anthropology and creativity, leading to his subsequent work on lines. Bringing with him the ideas he had begun to develop on skill, and working with new colleagues such as Elizabeth Hallam, refocussed Tim's direction to explore creativity as a process in action, in relation to what is usually called 'tradition'. He describes this most succinctly in the preamble to the 2005 conference of the Association of Social Anthropologists, held in Aberdeen, on *Creativity and Cultural Improvisation*, and in the introduction to the eponymous volume, co-edited with Hallam (Hallam and Ingold 2007).

> There is no ready-written script for social and cultural life. People have to work it out for themselves as they go along. Though the idea that folk in 'traditional' societies are destined to follow routines transmitted as a legacy from the past might find few anthropological adherents today, we

> have not entirely thrown off the yoke of a way of thinking that pits individual invention against cultural convention.
>
> (ASA theme 2005)

With the conference theme, Ingold and Hallam's aim was to challenge 'the polarity between *novelty* and *convention*', and, following Edward Bruner (one of Tim's more understated thinking friends), they drew upon improvisation as a way of exploring creativity which encompassed both these aspects of tradition. Bruner had proposed that people everywhere "construct culture as they go along and as they respond to life's contingencies" (1993:326). In effect, by associating creativity with improvisation rather than innovation, Ingold and Hallam were able to touch on a truth about the way people work and make things, while at the same time accepting that any continuity of tradition is more of a matter of 'carrying on' than 'cultural transmission' (Ingold and Hallam 2007). Tradition is creative and improvisatory because it is carried on in practice, in action, in life as it is lived, rather than through the precise execution of a preconceived plan. If there are rules to be followed, they are in the nature of 'non-specific' guidelines, sufficiently loosely formulated as to be adaptable to variable circumstances (Ingold and Hallam 2007:2). Moreover, as Tim also emphasises, continuity in tradition is due not to passive inertia, but to its active regeneration, through the generations, driven by a will to do rather than just passively to replicate.

Ingold and Hallam raise four key themes in their introduction to *Creativity and cultural improvisation* (the conference publication). These are that creativity and improvisation are generative, relational, temporal, and the way we work.

Creativity is generative precisely because it is not a retrospective act but *gives rise* to the cultural forms of people as they go about their lives in an improvisatory way. This view also references Tim's concern with building and dwelling, again challenging the idea that whether something is made or grown, the end product (if indeed there can ever be said to be a finishing point) is an outcome designed in advance. There is, in effect, a gap between the ideal and the outcome, and this is filled by makers and builders, both human and nonhuman, acting in the world. This approach also challenges the notions that creativity is purely individual, and that it results in innovation. That, he would argue, entails a backward reading of creativity.

In arguing that creativity is relational, Ingold and Hallam show how it is not so much a quality found in solitary individuals, but lies in their attunement to others, and comes into being through relationships and through time. This goes against the approach, founded in commodity capitalism, which sets the creativity of individuals in opposition to the constraining force of society, enacted in the breach of social norms. Rather, Ingold and Hallam argue, the activities which emerge through our social relationships enable us to participate in each other's coming-into-being throughout our lives, whose very entwinement amounts to social constraint. Of course, the non-conformist has to react against *something*, with actions that only make sense against the background of established norms. Nor need these actions be spectacular: as Bruner observes, "even little people in the routine and everyday" can change the world (Bruner 1993:321). But creativity is not just about change. As Ingold and Hallam show, there is creativity even in the maintenance of tradition, as practitioners have to improvise to get things right, to keep on track under varying conditions of performance. As a force of improvisation, tradition can be forward looking, keeping abreast of the times, taking account of new developments while carrying on from predecessors. Because it is relational it 'goes along', through entangled ways of life, and is progressively created within the community.

In emphasising that creativity is temporal, Tim also shows how the reproduction or regeneration of traditional practices is not about endless replication interspersed with novel and innovative events. This would be to value only the new, and to disregard it once it had become 'old'. It would take creativity outside of time, not to allow for change and the improvisatory nature of work in an ongoing way. Thus, the past is not finished business, set off against the present. Rather, the past is continuously active in the present, pressing towards the future. This concern with the temporal reflects Tim's interest in Bergson's notion of duration. Tim found great pleasure and inspiration in the work of this French philosopher, Henri Bergson, a 'philosophical friend' and author of *Creative evolution* (1911). Bergson argued that in living life we are inside of time, experienced as duration. That is, as living beings, we know what it is to work, to hurry, have patience, or to age, through our experience of being in time. One thing we are not is outside of the 'river of time', on the bank looking at it as it travels past us, although this is often how we may try to analyse and talk about it.

Crucial to Bergson was the idea that creation is movement, and in this movement, whether the movement of life, or of growth, lies the essence of time as duration. Life and work within duration, says Tim, is an ongoing generative movement set within "the circulation and fluxes of the materials that surround us and indeed of which we are made" (Ingold and Hallam 2007:11). The materials of our world are therefore life-giving and creative in themselves. Bergson's approach to time, as a kind of moving line of life which we live, has long been critical to Tim's thinking. Bergson further emphasises that while we may tend to treat living beings that move as externally bounded objects, or as containers for life, in reality, he argues, life is not contained inside things, it is movement itself – the living being, then, is "a progress, ... the very permanence of its form is only the outline of a movement" (Bergson 1911:135).

Finally, in proposing that creativity is the way we work, Tim shows that life, art, and tradition are not only unscripted but unscriptable. This is because life is a movement within a world of continuous flux. So, to keep going, we have to be open and responsive to variation. His 'thinking friend' here is the former designer and lecturer at the Royal College of Art, David

Pye. Writing of the 'workmanship of risk', Pye maintains that the good craft worker has to let go of the will to control, and in doing so, takes the risk that the work may be spoiled. The "quality of the result is continuously at risk during the process of making" (1968:20). The alternative – a pre-planned, controlled approach to work and life – is what Pye calls "the workmanship of certainty". It may have more predictable outcomes but lacks the creative and improvisatory flair of the workmanship of risk. Echoing this, fluency in work, as Bergson argues, lies not in a series of controlled steps, but emerges through a flow of practices, from past to future, every moment prefiguring future movements, and yet building upon the past.

Lines of creativity

Tim's concern with creativity was also inspired by a practice- and student-led study group which flourished during his later years at the University of Manchester. I recall the group of 20 or so students and staff making knots, baskets, having improvisational choirs, lessons in Alexander technique, and other activities. Tim expanded this in Aberdeen, creating a lecture series which he called the '4As' – anthropology, archaeology, art, and architecture, the connection being that these disciplines all entail ways of knowing through making. They also all employ quite similar methodologies, allowing for an emergent, quite intuitive approach, which features observation, description, and propositions, following the classical, Malinowskian approach to 'foreshadowed problems'. Some of the visual material linked to this research was first exhibited alongside the 2005 ASA conference, in the exhibition *Fieldnotes and Sketchbooks* at Aberdeen Art Gallery, curated by Wendy Gunn (2009).

Following on from the seminal ASA conference, Tim's work developed along more specific themes, on the one hand focussing on the narrative, temporal, and processual nature of lines, on which he based the book *Lines*, and on the other hand, focussing on a range of themes including materials, the weather, inscription, and meshworks, resulting in the volumes *Being alive* (2011) and *Making* (2013), and edited volumes such as *Redrawing anthropology* (2011) and *Making and growing* (co-edited with E. Hallam in 2014).

His focus on lines expanded through a whole series of parallel ideas linked to the possibility that, whether people are walking, talking, gesturing, sharing stories, arguing about genealogies, singing, weaving, sharing traditions, dancing, drawing, or writing – and in many other activities – the one thing they have in common is that they are proceeding along lines, albeit of different kinds. I have to confess that I was quite sceptical when Tim first started talking about lines. I've never been keen on linearity, and it seemed like an odd sort of subject for an anthropologist to be interested in. And he himself says that at first, colleagues looked at him with blank incredulity when he talked about this new research interest. "Did they mishear me: was I talking about lions?" (Ingold 2007:1).

Well, they didn't; he *was* talking about lines. And in both *Lines*, and following this, *The life of lines*, he has used lines of different kinds to talk about multiple social phenomena, all drawn together because they 'proceed' along lines. Here, the ideas of his 'thinking friend' Bergson, on time, have been further crystallised through the writings of philosopher Gilles Deleuze and psychoanalyst Félix Guattari, who had come up with the idea that as "individual or group ... we are composed of lines ... or rather, of bundles of lines" – lines of flight, lines of becoming (Deleuze and Guattari 1987:223). As for Bergson so for Deleuze and Guattari, these lines of flight or becoming are like the river of life, sweeping between the riverbanks, carrying on, unmeasurable, with no beginning or end. For Ingold, the point was that as anthropologists, we have been standing on, and concentrating on, the banks while losing sight of the river. So, rather than regarding social life as if we are on the riverbanks and cutting up life's activities into static sections for observation and analysis, we need to think about human life in movement. This, Tim says, requires a temporal approach to everything from materials to awareness. Everything is in process.

A further inspiring and significant 'thinking friend' of Ingold, with a parallel concern with lines, was the Swiss-German artist Paul Klee. Klee produced works of art often linked to musical forms, exploring how compositions, melodies, and harmonies might be resolved into colour, shape, and line, while still embodying a sense of movement and timing similar to that of musical performance. In his teaching at the Bauhaus School and in his writing about drawing, Klee, too, echoes Bergson, emphasising how the most authentic and active kind of line arises from movement and moves for movement's sake. This, Klee says, is the line that develops freely and in its own time, the line that 'goes for a walk' – that is "a walk for a walk's sake" (Klee 1961). In his paintings and drawings, Klee literally takes the viewer for a walk around the images on the paper.

Following Klee, Tim (2007:73) contrasts this moving, melodic line with the line in a hurry, going from point to point in a sequence, as quickly as possible, where each segment of the line is predetermined by the points it connects. "More like a series of appointments than a walk", says Klee (1961:109), in similar vein.

In *Lines*, Tim explores language, music, and inscription; textiles, from threads and traces to design; trails, tracks, and storylines; genealogical lines; and drawing, writing, and calligraphy. Having not understood the 'point' (of lines) 12 years ago, I now realise that this approach – to examining life in movement – was ahead of its time. It allows us to take new perspectives on multiple social phenomena through what could be seen as one form or feature in common, the line. In seeing how lines can be observed as static series of segments, or processes in flow, one can learn about walking from the point of view of drawing, for example. Or genealogies from the point of view of a river in flow.

Consider, for example, the relation between walking and drawing. Both, Tim proposes, are modes of *wayfaring*. For an Inuit hunter, travelling over ice and sea, as soon as a person moves, he becomes a line – hunting is looking to see where your line crosses another's; the whole area is replete with paths and journeys, lines of travel (Ingold 2007:76). Batek food gatherers in Malaysia similarly follow a trail or line, in their case of the growth of roots and tubers, while they gather food. For Foi food gatherers in Papua New Guinea, journeying is similarly "never a matter of getting from one point to another"; on the way is work, gathering fruit, rattan, edible insect larvae. In all these cases, "life happens while travelling" (Aporta 2004; Lye 2004; Weiner 1991; cited in Ingold 2007:76). This kind of wayfaring, according to Ingold, stands in contrast to what he calls *transport*. With transport, the emphasis is on the destination. Tourism, for example, focusses on arrival, while the journey is virtually expunged from memory.

> Transport, then, is distinguished not by the employment of mechanical means but by the dissolution of the intimate bond that, in wayfaring, couples locomotion and perception. The transported traveller becomes a passenger, who does not himself move but is rather *moved* from place to place.
>
> (Ingold 2007:78)

Wayfaring also contrasts with the colonial approach to mapping, where lines denote territorial boundaries and arterial routes rather than paths and journeying. The opposition, here, is between a kind of travel that is active and attentive, and one that is passive and possessive.

Likewise with drawing, a pencil, brush, or marker may be intentionally moved, or literally 'drawn', over a surface, marking it and leaving a trace. What interests Ingold about drawn lines is, again, their movement, and the relationship between drawing and gesture. Almost every hand-drawn line, he argues, is the trace of a gesture and gestural lines express the movement that generated them (e.g., Ingold 2007:26). The hand that draws is therefore also one that feels, one that expresses feeling, and one that tells a story. And what interests him is the human activity in the drawing and the way that drawing is a way of telling by hand.

The philosopher Maurice Merleau-Ponty sees it like this:

> There is a human body when, between the seeing and the seen, between the touching and the touched, between one eye and the other, between hand and hand, a blending of sorts takes place–when the spark is lit between sensing and sensible.
>
> (1964:163)

Drawing, he says, is the "way that humans and the world become enlaced such that inside and outside are not opposites" (1964:180). Similarly, architect Juhani Pallasmaa (2009:69) describes observational sketching as a haptic exercise: "As I sketch a contour of an object, human figure or landscape,

I actually touch and feel the surface". This could also be encompassed by Bateson's (1972) notion of a circuit of mind in the environment. It is what Paul Klee would call the 'mediating line', and in terms of the interiority of drawing, he describes how "a certain fire flares up, it is conducted through the hand, flows to the picture and there bursts into spark, closing a circle whence it came: back into the eye" (1961:78).

But drawing, of course, doesn't just consist of gestural lines. Consider certain geometric diagrammatic lines, where what is connected are abstract points rather than real materials and forces. Or return, for example, to map-making or cartography, where the only connections are 'lines of occupation' across what is perceived to be a 'blank surface', riding 'roughshod over the lines of inhabitation' (Ingold 2007:81). But, while these kinds of lines may connect 'nodal points of power', they also divide. Such 'ghostly lines', as both Ingold and Gibson describe the phenomenon, often have no physical counterpart, and may also be encountered as survey lines, or star maps, or as physical borders which have no local rationale. Again, there is a contrast between an action that pays attention and works within the moment, and a more passive, possessive line, between a descriptive line and a prescriptive one.

Knowing from the inside

In 2012, Tim Ingold was awarded a grant from the European Research Council (ERC) to devote his time to the study of this 'inside way' of working and thinking. The project, *Knowing from the Inside* (KFI), ran from 2013 to 2018, and involved PhD students, postdoctoral research fellows, colleagues, and many visiting scholars from around the world. The aim of the project was to dedicate time to exploring the approach outlined in this chapter through the kinds of research methods it calls forth. This meant trialling new and emergent methods of thinking with, from, and through persons and things, in practice. The practices involved ranged from dance and Scottish basketry, to walking, architecture, and making art in Japan. The focus was on learning and learning how we learn. The project was interdisciplinary, but at the same time it challenged the received idea of the academic discipline as a territorially demarcated field of study.

For everyone involved, the KFI project opened a space to develop these kinds of ideas in an open, encouraging, and intuitive way. It was an opportunity to try out anthropological ideas through unconventional methods and to explore the unknown. An edited volume with chapters by some participants in the project has just been published (see Ingold 2022). Other outcomes, from workshops and exhibitions, to publications and films will make themselves known for years to come. There are many ways of 'doing anthropology', and not everyone may agree with Tim's approach. What his work has done, however, is to influence not just anthropological thinking, but how those who respect and value his work or have worked with him will be doing anthropology from now on.

References

Aporta, C. 2004. Routes, trails and tracks: Trail breaking among the Inuit of Igloolik, *Études/Inuit/Studies* 28(2):9–28.

Bateson, G. 1972. *Steps to an ecology of mind*. London: Granada.

Bergson, H. 1911. *Creative evolution*. London: Macmillan.

Bird David, N. 1990. The giving environment: Another perspective on the economic system of gatherer-hunters, *Current Anthropology* 33:25–47.

Bruner, E. 1993. Creative persona and the problem of authenticity. In *Creativity/anthropology*. S. Lavie, K. Narayan, and R. Rosaldo, eds. Pp. 321–334. Ithaca: Cornell University Press.

Dawkins, R. 1999. *The extended phenotype. The long reach of the gene*. Revised edition. Oxford: Oxford University Press.

Deleuze, G. and Guattari, F. 1987. *A thousand plateaus: Capitalism and schizophrenia*. London: Athlone Press.

Geertz, C. 1973. *The interpretation of cultures*. New York: Basic Books.

Gibson, J. 1966. *The senses considered as perceptual systems*. London: George Allen and Unwin Ltd.

Gibson, J. 1979. *The ecological approach to visual perception*. Boston: Houghton-Mifflin.

Gunn, W., ed. 2009. *Fieldnotes and sketchbooks: Challenging the boundaries between description and processes of describing*. Frankfurt am Main: Peter Lang.

Hallam, E. and Ingold, T., eds. 2007. *Creativity and cultural improvisation*. Oxford: Berg.

——— 2014. *Making and growing: Anthropological studies of organisms and artefacts*. London: Ashgate.

Hallowell, A. I. 1960. Ojibwa ontology, behaviour and world view. In *Culture in history: Essays in honour of Paul Radin*. S. Diamond, ed. Pp. 19–52. New York: Columbia University Press.

Heidegger, M. 1971. *Poetry, language, thought*. New York: Harper and Row.

Ingold, T. 1989. The social and environmental relations of human beings and other animals. In *Comparative socioecology*. V. Standen and R. A. Foley, eds. Pp. 495–512. Oxford: Blackwell.

——— 1992. Culture and the perception of the environment. In *Bush base, forest farm: Culture, environment and development*. E. Croll and D. Parkin, eds. Pp. 39–56. London: Routledge.

——— 2000. *The perception of the environment: Essays in livelihood, dwelling and skill*. London: Routledge.

——— 2007. *Lines: A brief history*. London: Routledge.

——— 2010. Footprints through the weather-world: Walking, breathing, knowing. *Journal of the Royal Anthropological Institute* 16(S1):S121–S139 (Special Issue: Making Knowledge).

——— 2011. *Being alive. Essays on movement, knowledge and description*. London: Routledge.

——— 2013. *Making. Anthropology, archaeology, art and architecture*. London: Routledge.

Ingold, T., ed., 1996. *Key debates in anthropology*. London: Routledge.

——— 2011. *Redrawing anthropology: Materials, movements, lines*. London: Ashgate.

——— 2022. *Knowing from the inside. Cross-disciplinary experiments with matters of pedagogy*. Sydney: Bloomsbury Publishing.

Ingold, T. and Hallam, E. 2007. Creativity and cultural improvisation: An introduction. In *Creativity and cultural improvisation*. E. Hallam and T. Ingold, eds. Pp. 1–24. Oxford: Berg.
Klee, P. 1961. *Notebooks, V1: The thinking eye*. J. Spiller, ed. London: Lund Humphries.
Lye, T. P. 2004. *Changing pathways: Forest degradation and the Batek of Pahang, Malaysia*. Lanham, MD: Rowman and Littlefield.
Merleau-Ponty, M. 1964. Eye and mind. In *The primacy of perception*. Trans. Carleton Dallery. James E. Edie, ed., Pp. 159–190. Evanston, IL: Northwestern University Press.
Nelson, R. K. 1983. *Make prayers to the raven: A Koyukon view of the northern forest*. Chicago: University of Chicago Press.
Pallasmaa, J. 2009. *The thinking hand: Existential and embodied wisdom in architecture*. Chichester: John Wiley.
Pye, D. 1968. *The nature and the art of workmanship*. Cambridge: Cambridge University Press.
von Uexküll, J. 1957. A stroll through the worlds of animals and men: A picture book of invisible worlds. In *Instinctive behaviour: The development of a modern concept*. C. H. Schiller, ed., Pp. 5–80. New York: International Universities Press.

4 Artworks at a threshold

Thinking with Tim Ingold about art gallery technicians

Laura Harris

Art galleries are places where audiences are invited into the imaginative space of art, populated by artful things, practices, and histories. They often play host to artworks which evidence a skilful process of making, and the relationship between artwork and artist is conventionally understood as a hallmark of authenticity from which value and meaning arises. However, between the artist's studio and the gallery-going public comes a whole host of intermediaries who realise the artwork's transition from one context to the other. In this chapter I will focus on gallery technicians as one part of this intermediary process, use ideas drawn from Tim Ingold's work to illuminate their often "invisible" work (Crain, Poster, and Cherry 2016), and, in so doing, trouble the conventional location of skill and making in the art gallery. Seen in this way the art gallery emerges as a unique site of practice, steeped in its own set of skills and demands, and corresponding with (but not collapsing into) the artworks that are carefully placed within it.

After positioning the chapter in relation to Ingold's work, I will move on to give three empirical examples of the skill of gallery technicians drawn from a study of the installation process at a gallery of visual art. The first example is a wall-mounted series of basket-like objects that make up Dan Coopey's artwork *Dry* (2017); the second details the installation of *Genesis*, a several-tonne marble sculpture by Jacob Epstein (1929–1930); and the final is a sculptural work, *Sugar and Spice (Economic Model)* by contemporary artist Jo Stockham (1989–2017). My discussion of these artworks zooms out from the micro-level, intricate process of installing *Dry,* to the context of *Genesis* in the particular material environment of the gallery, to finally take a wider view of the social and cultural conventions feeding into the gallery technician's practice as they install *Sugar and Spice (Economic Model)*. In the conclusion, I will point to the implications that this approach to studying the gallery, and the skill invested in it, has on the conventional notions of distributing value in such spaces.

DOI: 10.4324/9781003162773-7

Threshold and skill

In order to get close to the skilled practice of gallery technicians, my study is located in the liminal time and space when an artwork is in transit. In the gallery context, this transition period is referred to as the "installation" or "install." This is when the gallery is closed to the public and populated by a host of intermittent workers like gallery technicians or electricians. As one exhibition is removed (or "deinstalled") the cultural and material conditions open up for a new exhibition to take over the same gallery space. Things that were previously understood as art might shed this meaning, and be reinterpreted as waste to be removed, while other things are gathered together so that they can adequately bear the artistic visions of artists and curators (both professions which are routinely understood to be the creators of meaning in the gallery space). To achieve this, gallery technicians undertake a skilful process of manoeuvring the artwork into its desired spot in the gallery, while remaining sensitive to the subtleties of meaning that hang in the balance.

Ingold offers a useful way to conceive of the install. In their jointly written introduction to the volume *Making and Growing*, Elizabeth Hallam and Ingold talk of a "threshold" that things cross when moving from creation to employment, a threshold that is usually called "finishing" (Hallam and Ingold 2014:2). "Makers of every profession," they write "appear to stand at the threshold, in amongst the stuff and tackle of their trade, easing the way for their ever-varying, protean material to pass from one form of life to another" (Hallam and Ingold 2014:2). In sociological writing on art, the often-ambiguous process of 'finishing' an artwork has been studied in relation to the artists and when (or indeed if) they decide that the artwork is complete (Becker, Faulkner, and Kirshenblatt-Gimblett 2006). The process of "finishing" an artwork typically refers to the passage from artist to audience or market, but this smooth process is complicated by, for example, the constant repetition, reinterpretation, and experimentation that is the hallmark of artistic genres like jazz. In fact, artworks cross many thresholds as they are moved through social, cultural, and material contexts. En route to a gallery-going public, an artwork such as those of interest to this chapter crosses a particular threshold from being in transit, through being installed, to being positioned towards a visiting public. It is gallery technicians who labour at this threshold, who ease the artwork's passage from "one form of life to another," and my interest here is in the skill they practise when they do so (Hallam and Ingold 2014:2).

Threshold is one pillar of my Ingoldian study of gallery technicians, and skill is the other. Ingold has returned to thinking and studying skill throughout his writing (Ingold 2000, 2017b). It is one of the central motifs in his approach to how human beings live, dwell, and create in the world. For the purposes of this chapter, I am borrowing Ingold's description of skill as a processual practice. He writes: "Practitioners, I contend, are wanderers, wayfarers, whose skill lies in their ability to find the grain of the world's becoming and to follow its course while bending it to their evolving purpose" (Ingold 2011:211). Skilled practice is therefore an iterative and emergent process of attunement between a body and the thing worked upon. Works of art and craft are often valued and spoken of in exactly this way, as artists experiment with and skilfully manipulate their media in the pursuit of new and engaging aesthetic forms. Gallery technicians, by the same token, engage with artworks in exploratory ways, albeit to different ends; their concern is with realising the artwork in the specific time and place of an exhibition. To rephrase Ingold, the gallery technicians' skills lie in their ability to find and follow the grain of an artwork to realise it in situ, and to do so while bending their practice to the purposes of artist and curator.

Taken together, skill and threshold offer useful ways to conceptualise the time–space of the gallery install. The install is characterised by being a process of becoming; the things gathered not yet stabilised in the horizons of meaning that the coming exhibition will establish. Once the exhibition opens to the public, the space will continue to generate ever new potential experiences and meanings. The aim of the install, therefore, is not to take the artworks out of life, but to set them on a particular life course in the particular time and space of the gallery. This is the threshold, from one context of production to one context of consumption, that gallery technicians skilfully ease artworks over.

I will now offer three examples of gallery technicians practising this skill. The examples I use come from a yearlong multimedia ethnographically informed study that I completed in 2017–2018 at Bluecoat, Liverpool's centre for the contemporary arts. My focus was an exhibition entitled *In the Peaceful Dome*. The exhibition brought together contemporary artists alongside historical works in a survey show that took the history of the arts centre itself as a subject. A broad range of artworks and art forms were on display, from sculptures, to paintings, to screen-based works and mixed-media installations. This required the workforce to respond, adapt, and learn afresh with each new artwork over the two week install period in October 2017 when, closed to the public, the galleries were passed over from one exhibition to the next.

Dry (Coopey 2017)

The installation of every art object demands skills of varying degrees. The first focus of this chapter is an artwork comprised of six woven basket-like objects from English artist Dan Coopey's 2017 series *Dry* (2017) which demanded a highly skilled install. A self-taught basket weaver, Coopey weaves with rattan to create slimline objects, like elongated amphora, ribbed latterly in a way suggestive of hands shaping clay on a potter's wheel. Each basket encloses an oddity (including chewing gum and terracotta) to which viewers have no access. Coopey's practice troubles the distinctions between art and craft, usefulness and display, while it consciously draws attention to its material properties, both present (rattan) and absent or obscured (clay). On encountering these objects in my fieldwork, I immediately classified them as ripe for Ingoldian attention, basketry being a topic in Ingold's writing on skill and material (Ingold 2000:339–448). As I followed the materials however, I felt myself pulled away from Coopey and the material and cerebral subtleties of his work, and towards *Dry* as it appeared and was worked with at the install.

Dry was delivered to Bluecoat disaggregated. The artist was not present at the install, supplying only photographs of previous installations, photographs which were devoid of people or action. The photographs showed artworks as they exist in the social imaginary: stable and intellectually coherent objects, out of touch. Each of the six woven objects is installed on two or three dowels which jut out, perpendicular to the gallery wall, and which slot into the ridges of the baskets to hold them upright. They sit in a neat and ordered line on the gallery wall, with the different arrangements of dowel and different forms of the baskets similar enough to form an assembly (Figure 4.1).

This lack of clear, explicit, or in Ingoldian terms "articulated" (Ingold 2017a:97) instruction presented, or so I assumed, a challenge for the two gallery technicians tasked with installing the series (one a paid gallery technician, the other a volunteer). Not only did they have to render the artwork

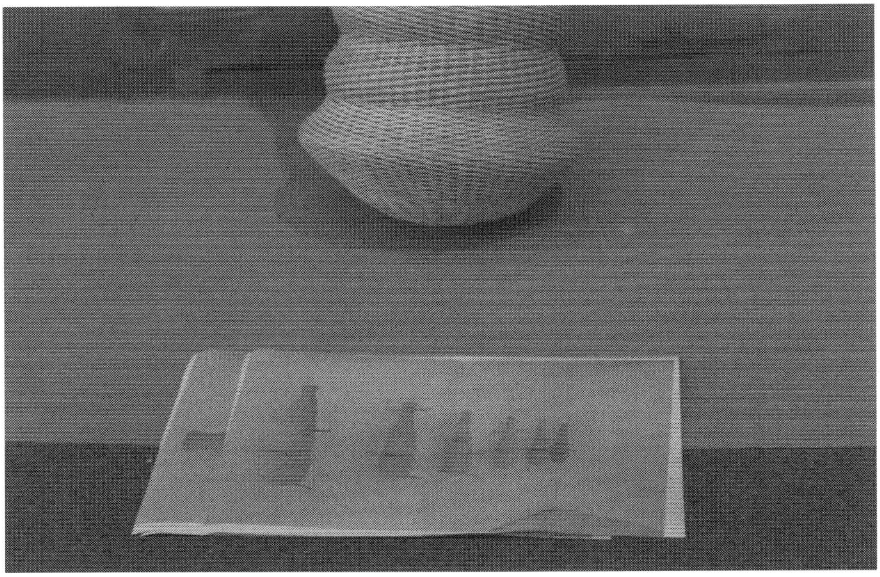

Figure 4.1 Artist Dan Coopey's series *Dry* (2017) awaits installation. The bottom of a basket-like item is resting on the floor. Beneath it is a photo of the artwork in situ, showing six of the baskets balanced on dowels along a white wall (photo by L. Harris).

in the form it was intended by the artist, but they also had to do so in a way that left no trace of their action (as is conventional in the gallery space). The difficulty lay in the successive nature of *Dry*'s installation. Unlike art works secured in place with one consolidating action, *Dry* demanded a series of delicate negotiations of balancing rattan basket on dowel. One slight misstep with one dowel would frustrate the successful hang of that basket, and the different shapes of each of the six baskets called for subtle variations in centres of gravity, weight, and snugness of dowel.

Skill, Ingold writes, is "an inherently uncertain business," which demands sensitive adjustment of movement in response to a "close perceptual monitoring of the task at hand," requiring a practitioner to feel their way forward through a "volatile and ever-changing environment" (Ingold 2017b:160–161). The installation of *Dry* took several hours of trial and error, teamwork, and conversation, throughout which the technicians felt their way towards completing the task. With each dowel, the basket was held in place, the hand rescinding only enough weight to see if the basket would hold. While the hand of one technician held the thing in place, the other's hand would reposition, adjust, and tweak the hang into shape. Often, one attempt to balance the basket would fail or send it skewwhiff, only for a slight twist to make everything fall into place. Only once the dowel could take over from the twisting, holding hand could it be considered to be in its rightful place (Figure 4.2).

Dowel, basket, and body: each element in the installation of *Dry* moved in concert with the others. In this way the skill of the body was indivisible from the process it was embroiled in. This skill *was* the actualisation of an art object in time and place; the ability of *Dry* to hang on the gallery walls was testament to the work of the hands it no longer needed to hold it up. As the gallery technicians felt their way forward through the installation, in the same gesture they were peeling their skilled hands and visible presence away from the object. The minimalism and simplicity of *Dry* as it is encountered by audiences does little to make present the skill of the gallery technicians, who worked between image, material, and social convention in order to push *Dry* over the threshold from installation to public appreciation.

Genesis (Epstein 1929–1930)

The second example I will draw on is *Genesis*, a sculpture by British sculptor Jacob Epstein made between 1929 and 1930. Made of white marble from Seravezza in Italy, the sculpture weighs several tonnes. It depicts a mask-wearing, nude and distorted body of a pregnant woman, and is marred by the male, colonial gaze endemic to modern art history. It was previously exhibited at Bluecoat in 1931 when 50,000 visitors were charged six pence to see the "controversial" sculpture—Bluecoat raised substantial and critical funds through the spectacle, and it has become a part of Bluecoat's institutional storytelling (Bluecoat 2021). This historic connection to Bluecoat

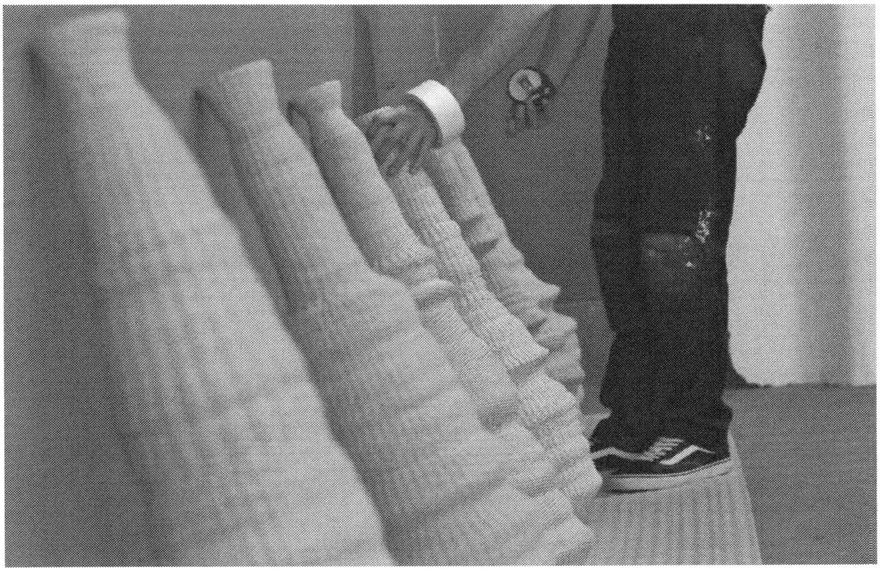

Figure 4.2 A gallery technician begins to install the series *Dry* (2017) by artist Dan Coopey. Six basket-like objects rest against a grey wall. A gallery technician with paint-splattered black trousers and masking-tape and measuring-tape in hand reaches out to one of them (photo by L. Harris).

justified its place as the centrepiece of *In the Peaceful Dome*. The sculpture has been owned by Manchester's The Whitworth gallery since 1992 and its nearly 60km journey to Bluecoat required a long and involved administrative process.

On the day of the move the skill sets of the gallery technicians were called upon, alongside a specially hired company of art movers and their equipment, to realise *Genesis* in situ at Bluecoat. Boxed in a large wooden crate emblazed with the word 'FRAGILE,' *Genesis* presented a substantial material challenge. Where *Dry* required delicacy and a certain lightness of touch, *Genesis* required brute force at the same time as a recognition of fragility (as well as the expense and risk involved in insuring such a sculpture).

Despite the wealth of resources invested in the move, the course of the process was critically endangered by a tiny, and previously unnoticed, material fact of Bluecoat's gallery. The following, from fieldnotes, describes *Genesis*' arrival at Bluecoat:

> It was very hard to get [the sculpture] into the gallery as there is a small step. There is also a slight ledge that is part of the door frame, which presented difficulty.

As *Genesis* was unloaded from its transportation lorry it was skilfully manoeuvred into position at the threshold of the gallery and the street. Countless artworks have passed this threshold without issue; however, the particular relationship between the boxed *Genesis* and the material fact of Bluecoat's gallery made this ledge of significance. The situation that emerged was a bottleneck of agency, relational to the weight of the sculpture and the height of the ledge. These facets corresponded with one another, exerting their combined influence by curtailing the smooth running of the intended series of events.

What followed was a collaboration between gallery technicians and art movers, utilising the resources at their disposal and displaying a degree of improvisation that is often the hallmark of refined skills-person-ship. The gallery's stores provided no tool perfect for the job, no obvious solution to the problem at hand. Instead, gallery technicians bricolaged together a device from available sheets of wood which acted as a makeshift ramp and wedge. Together with the combined strength of the technical team, this device was able to break the bottleneck that had arisen, and facilitate the delivery of *Genesis* to progress, safely, skilfully, and securely, as it should. The utilisation of this device showed a high degree of responsiveness, of adaptiveness, and of collaboration between people and their materials, in order to improvise and feel their way towards a shared goal. Where *Dry* evidenced a delicate image of skill, familiar to the imaginary of an artisan absorbed in their work, *Genesis*' installation showed skill in another light: physical and blunt, but nonetheless attuned.

In Ingold's work, skill is entangled with his broader set of ideas including the ways that things interrelate or correspond, and an understanding of agency as a property of an unfolding action (Ingold 2017b). The entanglement of these concepts is evidenced by this episode of *Genesis* and the ledge. In Ingold's terms, the resolution of the problem was achieved by the coming together of the wedge device and gallery technician's ingenuity and strength which realised an agency that diverted the course of the action in a profitable way. The example, therefore, shows that gallery technicians' skills are not only practised on the intimate level of the artwork, but equally on the wider context of the gallery as a material site. The ledge, in this instance, reminds us that the process of skill is not only a negotiation between technician and artwork but also between technician, artwork, and gallery (and many other potential correspondents). No matter how much specialist equipment and planning went into the install, in the heat of the moment the vital agential ingredient was the skilled practice of the gallery technicians, thinking on their feet and responding with their bodies.

Sugar and Spice (Economic Model) (Stockham 1989–2017)

The final example I will be employing in this chapter moves away from the more material focuses of the previous two, turning instead to the social and cultural elements of installing an artwork which are equally as central to the skill of gallery technicians. The example concerns *Sugar and Spice (Economic Model)* (1989–2017), a sculptural artwork by contemporary artist Jo Stockham. Stockham's artistic practice is informed by feminism, often taking aim at the male-dominated fields of art and politics with a wry sense of humour. Her artworks, while deeply political and often conceptual, are also intriguing not only for the skilled practice of her making but also the materials she selects to work with. *In the Peaceful Dome* showed several of her artworks, but the focus here is on a piece which featured the frame of a large globe, encrusted with white sugar. Hanging from the centre of the frame by a fine thread was a delicate girl's dress, cut from the pastel pages of the *Financial Times*, recalling a sewing pattern, and moving gently in the currents of the air. The piece spoke to many of Stockham's major themes—global trade, the brutal histories of commodities like sugar, and the impact of this on women and girls—and this cerebral, meaningful element of the work became a stake in its installation (Figure 4.3).

The install that I observed was a busy social, as well as material, site. The course of action depended not only on material facts, but on social relationships, orderings, and power structures at play in the gallery as a place of work. Unlike Coopey (detailed above), Stockham was able to make the journey from her base in London to Liverpool in order to contribute to, participate in, and supervise the installation of her artworks. By choice or circumstance, not every artist showcased in *In the Peaceful Dome* was

Figure 4.3 Artist Jo Stockham leans over the large, white globe frame of *Sugar and Spice (Economic Model)* (1989–2017). In the middle hangs a cut out of a girls' dress made from yellowed pages of the *Financial Times*. I am helping Stockham to hang the dress using invisible fishing wire. Behind us, outside a window, a pram is pushed along the city street (photo by L. Harris).

present at the install, vesting in Bluecoat the trust that their work will be installed appropriately and with due care. Stockham's presence, by contrast, introduced another variable for the gallery technicians to navigate as they worked towards installing the exhibition: the explicit appeals of the artist to ensure the installation matched her intentions for the artwork.

Sugar and Spice (Economic Model) is, of all the artworks introduced in this chapter, the easiest to install. It presents no particular challenge in terms of its construction nor its manoeuvrability. The globe frame was simply placed on a small plinth and the central dress strung up by the artist herself (with my helping hands). The process was complicated, however, by the spatial relationships that the artwork was placed into in the gallery. *Sugar and Spice (Economic Model)* was displayed in the same room as *Genesis* in a curatorial attempt to counterpose the male gaze of the marble sculpture with the feminist critique of Stockham's work. This room featured more of Stockham's artworks, including a series of two-dimensional (2D) works hung on the wall, as well as wall decals, two display cabinets of small curiosities, and a window giving out on to a busy Liverpool shopping street. The room ran a risk of being crowded, of clouding the curatorial vision of the space with a glut of artworks and information. As such, the spatial relationships between artworks had to be sufficiently able to suggest a conversation without either overpowering the other. This became the core challenge of installing *Sugar and Spice (Economic Model)*.

This was captured in one episode of the installation process. Two gallery technicians were on hand as the curator and Stockham discussed the placement of *Sugar and Spice (Economic Model)*. The following is an indicative excerpt from the ensuing discussions (which I was recording):

[Gallery technician #1 moves plinth]
Curator: It's a bit close to there [*Genesis*] now isn't it? But that can move …
Gallery technician #1: It can do, in a way …
Curator: And it's a bit close to there [other artwork] now isn't it …?
Artist: Yeah
Gallery technician #1: Oh yeah …
[Gallery technician #1 moves plinth back]
Gallery technician #2: Do you need something attached to the ceiling?
Artist: No.

The discussions continued as the group attempted to arrange the room such that the artworks were afforded, in the curator's words, "space to breathe." *Genesis* remained immovable throughout. As the artist and curator assessed the emerging spatial relationships in the gallery, the gallery technicians manoeuvred the artworks according to their direction, allowing them to experiment with and experience the different spatial possibilities of the assembly of artworks all the while feeding in information about the technical aspects of the process (e.g., attaching something to the ceiling). At the same time, they expressed and actioned their familiarity with art world parlance—responding to veiled directions like giving artworks "space to breathe"—as well as conventions in the hanging of visual art exhibitions (such as hanging things from the ceiling).

This episode shows the gallery technicians attuning their material practice to the general conventions and aesthetics of the visual art gallery as well as the lively, changeable, and experimental thought processes of artist and curator. Where *Genesis* allowed me to add the particular material facts of the gallery space into my description of gallery technician's skill, *Sugar and Spice (Economic Model)* allows me to expand this further, encompassing the social action surrounding artworks at the time of their installation as well as the cultural conventions informing the placement of artworks in gallery spaces. The complex and entangled interlocutors in the gallery technician's skilled practice speak to the relationality that is the centre of Ingold's writing as a whole, not least his understanding of skill.

One final aspect of the installation of *Sugar and Spice (Economic Model)* warrants attention in this discussion of the art gallery install as a site of skill from an Ingoldian perspective: the function of speech. Many discussions of skill (or tacit knowledge) take philosopher Michael Polanyi at his word when he writes that "we know more than we can tell" (Polanyi 1966:4). In a 2017 paper Ingold laments that this often leads to the cliched image of the silent craftsperson, unable to express adequately in words what they "know" with their body (Ingold 2017b:160). Ingold rejects this impulse to do away with language when discussing skill. He argues that "in our eagerness to reclaim skill, let us not give up too hastily on verbal expression" (Ingold 2017b:160).

While Ingold's argument hinges on the affective quality of the spoken word and the skilfulness of the verbal arts, it also makes clear that speech and language have a role to play in skilful practice more generally, and that skilled practice is often accompanied, or indeed facilitated by, speech. This was clearly evidenced by the installation of *Sugar and Spice (Economic Model)*, likewise of *Dry*, and, though to a lesser degree, of *Genesis*. To varying degrees, each install was accompanied by speech and by words, although not necessarily by logical, coherent propositions. Speech was broken, gestural, often monosyllabic, but nonetheless generative and conductive. Speech therefore acted as a connective tissue, allowing gallery technicians to enter into the flow of one another's work and to understand their intentions, and to collectively bend their practice towards the changeable desires of artist and curator. The work of gallery technicians epitomises Ingold's argument that skill and sound are inextricable, particularly, I would argue, in a context like the gallery install where the practice of skill is collective and social.

Conclusion

Like any skilled craftspeople, gallery technicians at work at an install offer an excellent case study for the application of Ingold's writing on skill. The installation context can be understood as an institutionalised threshold, a liminal time–space in which things are laboured upon in order to pass over from the time–space or the install to that of public appreciation. Ingold's work offers a way to shed light on the install as a context of skilled practice by engaging with the flows of activity which carry the space and the things within it over this threshold. To focus on the gallery install is therefore to complicate conventional understandings of making in the art gallery which routinely flatten out the full body of the labour of an exhibition of art in the service of establishing a direct relationship between artist and audience, via curator. In this concluding section, I will question how this broadened understanding of skill in the gallery relates to the conventional distribution of cultural value in the gallery.

Contemporary art galleries in the United Kingdom, like the one studied here, are associated with conventions guiding their aesthetic presentation. *In the Peaceful Dome* adhered to a convention which sees pale or neutral walls and strip lighting act as a supposedly neutral backdrop against which art is presented. However, as Henri Lefebvre reminds us, these conditions of apparent neutrality demonstrate that a space "has already been the focus of past processes whose traces are not always evident" (Lefebvre 1976:31). As this chapter has evidenced, the install is one context of such "past processes" which contribute to the exhibition as it comes to be. The erasure of the traces of work and skill practised by gallery technicians at the install is a necessary condition for the apparent neutrality of the gallery space to be maintained. In other words, a part of the skill required of gallery technicians is the ability to conduct their practice in such a way as to leave no clear and obvious trace of their work. For this reason, gallery technicians can be studied alongside other workers whose labour is made "invisible" in the same contexts that derive their value from their labour (Crain, Poster, and Cherry 2016).

One conventional function of the gallery space is to establish the authorship of artworks in such a way as to link the artwork with the ideas, skills, and histories of this artist's practice. This is achieved through labels, explanatory texts, marketing, gallery tours, informal conversations with gallery invigilators, and a host of other institutional practices which corroborate the artwork's value and meaning in relation to the artist. At the same time, the gallery technicians—whose work I have shown in this chapter to be deeply enmeshed in the process of bringing artworks to the public—are routinely uncredited. This is the material correlate of social and material conventions which venerate the artist over the vast network of labour that they are engaged in. Although gallery technicians may indeed have no claim on, or indeed interest in, authorship, this distribution of cultural value has knock-on effects on the evaluation of their labour in the gallery as a place of work. Both artists and gallery technicians often work in conditions of precarity, depending on intermittent work, short-term contracts, and all the burdens and barriers this brings with it. Gallery technicians, however, face the double bind of enduring this precarity alongside their 'invisibility' which can itself be a driver of further precarity (Crain, Poster, and Cherry 2016).

In this chapter I have not been motivated by an interest in establishing a hierarchy of skills in the art gallery, or by arguing that gallery technicians ought to be valued in the same ways as artists. Rather, the intention has been to use Ingold's work to look at the install as an understudied context of skilful practice in the world of art. In so doing, I have attempted to trouble conventional understandings of where skill and making sit in the gallery space. Ingold's work offers the tools to interrogate three empirical examples which I have drawn from a gallery install: *Dry*, *Genesis*, and *Sugar and Spice (Economic Model)*. This has allowed me to demonstrate the uniqueness of gallery technicians' skills which negotiate creatively between various pressures and interests in the service of an artwork and the social, cultural, and material contexts of its display. In this chapter I have aimed to show the vital plurality of skills required by an exhibition of art, beyond notions of creative practice typically associated with the space; to render visible the skills of gallery technicians in the study of art galleries.

References

Becker, H., R. Faulkner, and B. Kirshenblatt-Gimblett. 2006. *Art from start to finish: Jazz, painting, writing, and other improvisations*. Chicago: University of Chicago Press.

Bluecoat n.d. *Genesis: Return to bluecoat*. MyBluecoat. https://mybluecoat.org.uk/my-bluecoat-stories/genesis-return-to-bluecoat/ (accessed 03/06/2022).

Coopey, D. 2017. *Dry*. Rattan. www.dancoopey.com/dry.html (accessed 03/06/2022).

Crain, M., W. Poster, and M. Cherry 2016. *Invisible labor: Hidden work in the contemporary world*. Berkeley: University of California Press.

Epstein, J. 1929–1930. *Genesis*. Marble. Manchester: The Whitworth.

Hallam, E. and T. Ingold 2014. *Making and growing: Anthropological studies of organisms and artefacts*. Abingdon: Routledge.

Ingold, T. 2000. *The perception of the environment: Essays on livelihood, dwelling and skill*. Abingdon: Routledge.

Ingold, T. 2011. *Being alive: Essays on movement, knowledge and description*. Abingdon: Routledge.

Ingold, T. 2017a. *Correspondences: Knowing from the inside*. Aberdeen: University of Aberdeen.

Ingold, T. 2017b. Five questions of skill. *Cultural Geographies* 25(1):159–163.

Lefebvre, H. 1976. Reflections on the politics of space. *Antipode* 8(2):30–37.

Polanyi, M. 1966. *The tacit dimension*. Chicago: University of Chicago Press.

Stockham, J. 1989–2017. *Sugar and spice (economic model)*. Mixed Media.

5 In the slipstream of participation

Attention and intention in anthropological fieldwork

Anna Bloom-Christen

Introduction

For many people, the idea of anthropology may immediately and irresistibly conjure a certain image of the *anthropologist*. They may envisage a man, somewhat academic-looking and almost certainly Caucasian, weighed down with a camera and notebooks, sitting in the midst of a tribe of scantily clad, bush-dwelling 'natives'. They may picture his excitement as he frantically scribbles down or otherwise records the various activities—dancing, chanting, crafting—that make up the culture of that 'tribe'. Every now and then he will be asked to throw a spear or eat a snake, which he will do with the engaging conviction of an adventurer or the aloof reluctance of a gentleman.

This image is, of course, a stereotype. Like other stereotypes of its kind—the bearded philosopher who uncovers universal truths without ever leaving the familiar comfort of his study or the crazy-haired chemist mixing bottles of many-colored liquids to produce increasingly dramatic explosions—it simplifies or overlooks the diversity that nowadays exists amongst both researchers and their research interests. Yet, we can also find some insight contained within this image—insight that is reflected in how anthropologists themselves have understood what is central to their own discipline. Paul Atkinson and Martyn Hammersley take anthropological fieldwork to involve

> the ethnographer overtly and covertly, in people's daily lives for an extended period of time, watching what happens, listening to what is said, asking questions—in fact collecting whatever data are available to throw light on the issues that are the focus of the research.
>
> (2007:248)

Thomas Hylland Eriksen defines anthropology as "the comparative study of cultural and social life", whose "most important method is participant observation, which consists in lengthy fieldwork in a specific social setting" (2010:4). The common thread between the stereotype and these attempts at a scholarly definition is that the essence of anthropology as a discipline

DOI: 10.4324/9781003162773-8

resides not only in *what* anthropologists study (the subject-matter of anthropology), but also in *how* they study it (the methodology of anthropology). If the anthropologist's goal is, at its most general level, an understanding of the variety of forms that human cultures and practices take, then what distinguishes them from their colleagues in sociology or history departments (who many times share overlapping goals) is their conviction that the best route to achieve this goal is through a methodological procedure of active engagement with the cultures that are being studied.

This method of engaged observation is typically discussed under a range of headings, including 'fieldwork', 'ethnography', and 'participant observation'. Rather than getting into the complex debates on the methodological underpinnings of anthropology, I here want to examine a core characteristic of empirical, participatory knowledge gain crucial for all of the above labeled bundles of anthropological methods; that characteristic is *attention*.

Attention is crucial for participant observation in that it steers us towards what we deem to matter. Broadly defined, paying attention is an act of directing the mind. But how exactly do we get to pay attention? What is attention? In this contribution, I want to highlight avenues on how to frame, explore, and justify knowledge claims based on participation by means of looking into the phenomenon of attentionality. I will explore Tim Ingold's notion of attention and habit, link it with Elizabeth Anscombe's notion of intention, and set the newly paired concepts in relation to participation. My aim is to show how Ingold's impactful argument for the centrality of attention provides an important point of intersection to the groundbreaking philosophical work of Anscombe, whose treatise on intention has sustainably transformed philosophy of action, but so far rarely left its disciplinary boundaries.

This chapter is organized in five sections. Section 1 broaches the issue of participation in the history of anthropology, examining how participant observation was employed and conceptualized at its origins and engaging anthropology's own understanding of its defining methodology. Section 2 will spell out a set of interrelated core concepts for anthropological methodology. I will offer an Ingoldian take on the significance of attention and habit for anthropological fieldwork in relation to what I call non-propositional knowledge. Section 3 will consider intention as a way of framing attention in its potential form, and highlight problems with an overemphasis of a specific, narrow notion of intention. Section 4 will follow Ingold's suggestion to prioritize attention over intention with regard to its ability to implement the non-conscious, non-planning realm of habitual action. Finally, Section 5 will offer an alternative to the previously discussed, narrow notion of intention. I will suggest that when framed as an inner striving—a self-induced movement—intention represents the beginning, not the effect, of attention. Bringing into focus Elizabeth Anscombe's broader notion of what intentions are, I will conclude that attention, although habitual, is always intentional.

1 Participant observation: Emergence of an attentive method

> The empiricist [...] thinks he believes what he sees, but he is much better at believing than at seeing.
>
> Santayana (1923:201)

Observation is part of the history of Western scientific thinking, a crucial cornerstone of the 'scientific method'; it takes a leading role in any empirical research where data are consistently and unobtrusively collected. When Francis Bacon's proposal for a scientific method that relied on repeatable observations gained traction in the seventeenth century, the sciences as we understand them today began to act on the assumption that observation is essential for the extraction of scientific knowledge (Hallam 1854:514–517). This idea built the foundation of empiricism. Most prominently found in the works of the so-called British Empiricists, including Locke (1975 [1689]) and Hume (2014 [1738]), empiricism holds that all theories—including theories about social life—must be tested against observation of the natural world.

With this development, the seed for subsequent positivist thinking was planted and continued to infiltrate the methodology of anthropological research. The belief that only observational evidence that is rationalized with the tools of logic can be a source of scientific knowledge affected anthropology in the sense that it became standard practice to think of observation as a method in its own right.[1] The underlying presumption was that observation can be practiced objectively, and that the social world can be analyzed and dissected in the same way that experiments are conducted in the natural sciences.[2]

In adopting a methodology of *participant* observation, social anthropology is moved by the conviction that when researching the social life of others, mere observation is not enough. The ethnographer must participate in the social practices of others, using her body as a 'research tool' to access their lifeworlds. One of the figures who had a profound influence on the professional identity of modern anthropology in this respect is Bronisław Malinowski, to whom the original idea of systematic definition and use of participant observation as a method is often attributed.[3] In *Argonauts of the Western Pacific* (1961 [1922]), Malinowski propounded a methodological shift that would sustainably change the face of anthropology. His vision of how "to grasp the native's point of view, his relation to life, to realize *his* vision of *his* world" (1961 [1922]:25, original emphasis) was research in situ. Rather than conducting observatory studies from the vantage point of missionary verandas and colonial houses, Malinowski found it indispensable to share in the lives and activities of those being studied. Participant observation, as Malinowski would have it, demanded a research period of at least one seasonal cycle, learning and working in the native language, and becoming a member of the community that is being studied. He thereby challenged the hitherto dominant paradigm of research conducted from afar.

Overall, participant observation emerged as a principal approach to ethnographic research in the first half of the twentieth century. The veranda was abandoned for *the field*, and 'armchair anthropologist' became a pejorative term. In Geertz's interpretive anthropology of the early 1970s, the discipline found a first powerful response to its entrenched positivism (Geertz 2004 [1973]).[4]

It is worth pausing to consider why anthropologists should have been so dissatisfied with the prevailing methodology adopted by the sciences, as the reason for this discontent will offer us first clues as to how (not) to frame attention. The term 'observation' comes with heavy historical baggage. It was a technical term used by the police of absolutist France in the first half of the seventeenth and the second half of the eighteenth century, closely linked to the French *surveillance*. To observe was to spy on suspect individuals with the propounded objectivity of an absolute state.[5] These connotations are obviously unfortunate for those wishing to observe their research partners' activities openly and respectfully.

Another crucial omission from the traditional empiricist picture is any real attempt to reflect on what makes us observe certain things in the first place. What Tim Ingold has labeled *attentionality* (2018a) has been explored in detail under the heading of *awareness* (orig. *Aufmerksamkeit*, expressed in German as the tension between *Sehen* and *Beobachten*) in two closely related papers by Gerd Spittler (2001) and Till Förster (2001). According to this account, seeing and observing are different in that only the latter practice necessarily requires awareness. Spittler and Förster argue that much of the everyday life of others is *not* accessible through observation, which they describe as a conscious and intentional act, preceded by a preexisting awareness of what one wants to observe (Förster 2001:6–7). Being able to observe certain visible parts of our everyday world emerges from awareness, which in turn has to grow gradually and contextually, through participation. In line with this, Ingold's idea of attentionality encompasses awareness "not *of*, but *with*" its object—or rather, its subject—thus "turn[ing] othering into togethering" (2018a:26).

Despite the many advantages of a method in which observation occurs in combination with active participation, participant observation has repeatedly been subject to challenges and subsequent alterations (Stoller 1989; Marcus 1998; Jackson 2005; Kesselring 2017). One clue to the conceptual challenges inherent in participant observation is contained in its name. Participation and observation are ostensibly two quite distinct types of action; as such, participant observation can seem to involve an uneasy combination of two bodily activities that at first might appear mutually exclusive.

This conceptual tension has led to a heated debate. Some scholars think of participant observation as an oxymoron (Behar 1996; DeWalt and DeWalt 2002; Okely 2012), arguing that observation inherently generates the kind of distance that participation is intended to overcome. According to this view, the lumping together of the two terms obliterates a vital distinction between a (seemingly) passive, objective endeavor and its active, subjective counterpart. The dichotomy between these concepts is, to critics of participant observation, a problem glossed over by the unreflected grouping of the two terms. Okely suggests that we should not understand participation and observation as a continuum, but find distinctive places for each (2012:79–80). For Förster (2011:5–12), the conceptual combination occludes the scientific history of observation, as evoked above.

Responding to these criticisms, Ingold has argued that there is no contradiction between participation and observation; on the contrary, the one is impossible without the other (2018a:23–27). According to Ingold, observation is one sensory way of paying attention. Moreover, to pay attention entails that the movements of the observer are already coupled, in perception and action, to those of the things that hold her interest. This stance has a Heiddeggerian flavor, as it was Heidegger (1953) who proposed, in exploring the notions of understanding and interpretation, that "any simple pre-predicative seeing of what is at hand is in itself already understanding and interpretative" (149, my translation). Thus, the participatory coupling of perception and interpretation is a precondition for observation. Retracing the etymological origins of observation, and reaching further back in time—beyond its above-mentioned French connotation of surveillance connected to the traditional empiricist picture—Ingold's understanding of what it means to observe is closer to its Latin meaning found in the Oxford English Dictionary (2020), according to which observing a practice means to act in accordance with it. In effect, according to this view, one cannot observe what another is doing without already participating with them in at least this minimal sense. Observation, too, is participatory in nature.

This apparent disagreement can be resolved by noting that the two views point to different aspects of participant observation that in many ways complement each other. Conceptually, it makes sense to distinguish participation from observation, as the first camp suggests, for it helps us remember what conceptual heritage and baggage *observation* has shouldered when empiricism began to flourish. In practice, though, our being oscillates between observation and participation—or rather, in Ingold's view, it *is* participatory insofar as it is observing—and it seems awkward to cling to the distinction *as* we walk, dance, or craft something together. Rather, the flow of everyday life allows us to immerse ourselves in observations, participations, and everything in-between.

But how do we get to direct our senses towards what matters in a specific social setting in the first place? Ingold offers a strategy on how to frame observation in a way that sets it apart from the above-described, traditional notion of disengaged surveillance 'from above'.

2 Attention, habits and non-propositional knowledge

One of the primary motivations behind the method of participant observation is to harness non-propositional knowledge—knowledge that pertains to doing things—through the creation of intimate social spaces that only become intelligible when one participates in them over a longer period of time. The continuance of participation ensures coherence with the broader social context, thus yielding justification. Indeed, continuous participation may be the only way to gain knowledge of the subtle webs of sociality, notably those exhibited through habitualized activity.

But what are habits? Are they a result of, or do they make us who we are? Ingold follows John Dewey, who, elaborating on the subject of agency, found that "every experience enacted and undergone modifies the one who acts and undergoes, while this modification affects, whether we wish it or not, the quality of subsequent experiences. For it is a somewhat different person who enters into them" (Dewey 2015:35, quoted in Ingold 2018a:22). On the one hand, habits seem to 'make us' do things, and thus shape our acting. On the other hand, we may choose to do certain things repeatedly, thus producing and shaping habits actively. The sharp distinction between active agency and passive suffering is dissolved into a continuous circle of undergoing and enactment. We are what we repeatedly do. Elaborating on habits of attention, Ingold suggests that the part of habits that shape our identities must be seen as a manner of becoming, not of being: "The 'I' of habit [...] falls in the slipstream of action" (Ingold 2018a:24). Habits, then, are the manifestations of a continuous carving out of who we are about to become. I will return to this point in more detail shortly. For now, it is sufficient to say that much of our everyday life is habitual, and the challenge of participant observation is to find a balance between immersion and paying attention.[6]

Kristin Surak, exploring the tension between routine and rupture, reminds us that we "take much for granted in the flow of a situation. Moving into a new social world, however, disrupts many of the assumed and automatic ways of being to which we are accustomed" (2017:324). Supposedly, this rupture is what makes us pay attention to what otherwise would "go largely under the experiential radar" (2017:313). The epistemological position of the anthropologist at the beginning of her empirical research period is, in this respect, advantageous: She will notice what might have slipped into the habitual, non-propositional realm of local actors. The link between habits and non-propositional knowledge should be clear: The more habitual our interactions become, the less we consciously think and talk about them in propositional form. Why should we? One function of routine is precisely to enable us to think about and tend to other things than sitting, walking, or driving.[7] We might be well able to report on request what it is we are doing, but we are likely to encounter difficulties when asked to describe how we move—for instance our fingers to tie shoelaces or our upper bodies to dance the polka. Not because it is an impossible task to explain in propositional form, but because we lack practice in doing so. Parents might (re-)learn how to explain the tying of shoelaces, but more likely, they will kneel down, and let their children watch, who gradually, through observation and practice, will learn how to do it themselves.

Now, let me return to Ingold's evocative picture of the 'I' falling into the slipstream of action. Understood in the sense that we are what we repeatedly do, human habits appear as a crucial aspect to incorporate in anthropological fieldwork, yet at the same time beyond recognition once acquired. To complicate matters even more let me mention a psychological phenomenon, which, in honor of the following poem, has been called the *centipede effect.*

> A centipede was happy—quite!
> *Until a toad in fun*
> *Said, 'Pray, which leg comes after which?'*
> *Which threw her mind in such a pitch,*
> *She laid bewildered in the ditch*
> *Considering how to run.*[8]

Habits automatize tasks to reduce attentive efforts, but come at the cost of the centipede effect, where attention impairs the ability to perform that task—much like the centipede tripping on its own legs. As Ingold reassures himself while he prepares for a hike, "walking is just a habit; it is sedimented in my body and I can do it more or less without thinking" (2018a:23). But what if our task is to think about, and put into words, what it is for a specific group or individual to walk? The anthropological challenge of conveying non-propositional knowledge explained through the role of habit, then, can be framed as the need for attentiveness to what has its natural place in the unheeded realm of intentions.

Ingold himself opposes the idea that intentions are more fundamental to understand human action than attention, claiming that "attentionality takes ontological priority as the fundamental way of being in the world, whereas intentions are but milestones thrown up along the way" (2018a:25). Before assessing this claim, let us look at what an anthropology of intentions would have to offer.

3 Anthropology of intentions

Alessandro Duranti begins his book *The anthropology of intentions* (2015) by declaring that both anthropology and philosophy have overstated their case concerning the place and relevance of intentions for human agency. While a whole generation of philosophers of action, according to Duranti, claims intentions to be fundamental for understanding human agency, anthropologists time and again point out that intentions are a specifically Western ingredient in (the conception of) agency and do not matter for some societies, where people have been said to exclusively focus on the outcome of their actions. Duranti seeks to demonstrate that intentions do not *necessarily* play as central a role in a thorough explanation of shared human agency as some philosophers want to have it. At the same time, however, intentions *possibly* matter even in societies "where people have been said to avoid reading the minds of others" (Duranti 2015:1). Evaluating long-term fieldwork data from Samoa and the United States, and borrowing from Husserl, Duranti proposes an "intentional continuum" (2015:233), which, in a nutshell, encompasses the idea that there are variations in degrees of intentional awareness across both solitary and collective intentional action. Duranti then moves to critique John Searle's influential notion of 'collective intentionality'. Searle, himself arguably in favor of a clear-cut argument rather than getting into the messiness of fieldwork scenarios, fostered "a preference of simplification over complexification" and a "professed dislike of ambiguity" (Duranti 2015:4). Supported by long-term research on jazz improvisation in the United States, Duranti convincingly problematizes Searle's overemphasis of a causal planning structure of intentional action (2015:212–228). His alternative proposal is to draw from Husserl's conception of the aforementioned 'intentional continuum' and of intersubjectivity, thus giving preference to a phenomenological view of the role of mental states like intentions.

Duranti's preference of a phenomenological approach over a Searlian analytic action theory has been critically discussed by Eve Danzinger. As she points out, Duranti's suggestion to "take Husserl's ideas as the platform for all understanding of human interaction everywhere is not subjected by Duranti to the same empirical scrutiny with which he treats Searle" (2017:452). For one thing, following Danziger, cross-cultural variability in attitudes to others' mental states is not more clearly elaborated upon in Husserl's use of intentionality. Also, there is a set of preconditions one must subscribe to in order to follow this alternative path: According to Husserl, intersubjective knowledge is both temporally and logically *prior* to self-knowledge. One knows oneself *in virtue of* knowing "the Other". Danziger rightfully asks: "[T]o what extent and in which of many possible senses does intersubjective knowledge empirically 'precede' other kinds of knowledge?" (2017:452). Duranti's comprehensive book does not explicitly argue this point, but takes Husserl's insistence on the temporal priority of the social as given.[9]

Seeing the whole extent of this challenge a phenomenological anthropology of intentions faces, we can summarize a set of problems and a problematic solution. Duranti's book delivers an example of the fruitful employment of phenomenological theory, but without justification of its epistemological grounding. The problematic solution takes the form of an overemphasis on a phenomenological understanding of intentionality. The underlying set of problems persists: Despite the promise participation offers in providing access to non-propositionally encoded forms of cultural knowledge, it remains unclear how the empirical data gathered through participant observation—that is the part of it that represents non-propositional knowledge—can be put into words. The issue is twofold. We cannot simply ask and note down our research partners' explanations. At the same time, we have to be careful not to get so immersed as to submerge the precious knowledge that is the fabric of our ethnographies by giving into the force of habit ourselves. The challenge of participant observation is to access this kind of, at times, habitual, and often non-propositional knowledge embodied in practices or customs, and to find an intelligible way to communicate it, all while remaining in the slipstream of participation. One way to avoid these problems is to refrain from couching participation in terms of intentions altogether.

4 Ingoldian attention

What, then, is it that makes us engage, notice, and potentially understand the lifeworld we are embedded in? Ingold's answer is attention. Exploring the question of what it means to lead a life, and what the difference is between leading and merely living it, Ingold follows the philosopher Jan Masschelein, who proposes that "attention makes experience possible" (2010:282, quoted in Ingold 2018a:30). Drawing on the notion of human life as constant, yet uncertain changing and becoming, Ingold rejects the standard conception of agency that heavily relies on the idea of being in command. Assuming that agency is not to be assumed in advance of action, "as cause to effect, but is [...] transforming from within the action itself" (2018a:24), Ingold proposes to turn the contested noun into a gerund, and to replace 'agency' with 'becoming agent' or 'agencing', which leads him to the French *agencement*. Rather than framing agency in terms of volition, and thus of intentionality, Ingold proposes a conceptual triad of *agencement*, attentionality, and habit.

To follow the principle of habit is to acknowledge that "one is never fully the master of one's own acts; [...] to lead life is not necessarily to be in command" (Ingold 2018a:24). In this sense, Ingold asserts, the conception of intention is a misfit for conceptualizing action by life-leaders, since it suggests the intended path to be taken no matter what. For the example of going for a walk, preference should be given to attention over intention, for it takes, as Ingold notes, attention to stay en route: one has to *respond* to the specific, at times unpredictable ways the weather changes, paths bend, and blisters grow.

Expanding this example to a participatory act, we can easily see how walking *together* fosters a shared horizon. Perhaps the most obvious aspect of this shared experience is that when we walk alongside someone, we share the same view ahead. The possibility of re-habitualizing one's attention—or, as Masschelein (2010) puts it, of e-ducating the gaze—in the case of walking together, is at least partially enabled by the possibility of shared immersion in a perceptual field. Our research partner can point to something, and we can respond with acknowledgment. And while we might differ in our respective interpretations of what we see, we can learn, by following our research partner's ostensive gesture and gaze, where to look, and eventually also what to look *for*.

Here, participation becomes the teacher of observation, as walking together teaches us to see things 'with the eyes' of our guiding research partners. This communion can thus become a habituated form of practice, both in its participant and its observant dimension—a habitus, which communicates from body to body, non-propositionally. As such, it provides the very foundation of sociality upon which communication can then proceed and meanings can be shared. In this sense, attentionality is not only bound up with agencement and habit, but it is the beginning of participation.

Assessing this account, we can see that the alleged planning structure of intention plays a crucial role in Ingold's critique. Ingold suggests that in walking, "we must become responsive beings. Thus, even as I walk, I must adjust my footing to the terrain, follow the path, submit to elements. There is, in every step, an element of uncertainty" (2018a:23).

While it is certainly true that we cannot predict if our planned walk will turn out exactly as expected, this proclamation of uncertainty might strike us as surprising. After all, we have just learnt how habit can take away the burden of continuous, conscious paying attention to something. Within reasonable limits given by context and experience, we take our daily steps in tacit certainty.[10]

I take uncertainty to be a state of mind, not a state of the world. While we do say that 'these are uncertain times' or that 'the future is uncertain', what we mean is that *we* don't know how things stand or how they will develop. It might be that we encounter a hole in the very path we have walked many times. But the possibility of it being so is not a state of mind we constantly keep in the forefront unless we enter, so to speak, 'uncertain terrain', meaning that we have reason to *believe* that conditions might alter or that we do not know them. Again, it is not the terrain that is uncertain—indeed, if we took objects to have the capacity to produce mental states, the terrain, I dare claim, would be pretty confident of its state of being. Rather, it is us not knowing how it changes, shifts, and develops.

Yet, Ingold's argument seems to rely on a world-oriented notion of uncertainty, as it is the ever-changing world that is put into focus. This also gives him a springboard for his critique of a somewhat strict planning structure of intentions. Ingold illustrates how he gets ready for his walk by planning, and how this planning has the structure of intending to tease out the problem: to get fresh air, have time for contemplation, and see the countryside. A shift happens once he embarks on his walk. "Walking ceases to be something that I set my body to do, as a self-imposed routine. Rather, it seems that I *become* my walking, and that my walking walks me" (Ingold 2018a:23). Ingold thus suggests that life-leading agency is not to be understood as a given in advance of action, but rather "ever forming and transforming from within the action itself" (2018a:24). With reference to a passage in his book *The life of lines* (2015:141), he proposes that he is, as it were, tending to the action in thinking and doing, which are both not modes of being, but of becoming. Rather than putting the acting 'I' before the actual action as an overlooking, planning agent, he seeks "to put the 'I' who acts in the midst of the experience undergone" (Ingold 2018a:24).

Summing up, Ingold conceptualizes intention as a planning capacity. Confirming this reading, in 'The creativity of undergoing', Ingold proposes "that in undergoing, the relation of temporal priority between mastery and submission is the reverse of that which is assumed in the cognitive or intentionalist account of doing" (2014:137), implying that intentionalist accounts are cognitive at heart. Intentions thus reside in the conscious, cognitive realm and hinder a responsive *leading* of life in the becoming of every moment. Intentionalist accounts simply ignore the uncertainty and surprising nature of the present.

But are intentions always part of the cognitive realm? As I would like to suggest, intentions can also be defined more broadly, including embodied movements of life-leading beings. This broader way of framing intention shall be discussed in the following and final section.

5 Anscombian intention

Within philosophical approaches, the project of understanding participation is typically regarded as a specific iteration of what is perhaps the most general and fundamental question with which philosophers of action are concerned: What are intentional actions? In her 1957 book *Intention*, which by now has acquired the status of a modern philosophical classic, Anscombe sets up three conditions for intentional action, given for an *individual*. An action is intentional only if: (a) she who is doing something knows that she is doing it; (b) she knows that she is doing it *not* by observation; and (c) her doing it and knowing so is an act of practical reasoning.[11]

For Anscombe, intention is the peculiar teleological character that a certain kind of movement—namely intentional action—exhibits. The purposiveness of these movements is, as it were, constitutive of their being the movements they are. There would not be that sort of movement without it. This purposive ordering, then, exists only in virtue of being known by the agent. The agent's self-knowledge, what Anscombe takes to be practical knowledge, makes intentional action what it is. It does so in two ways: Both the intentional character and the existence of intentional actions derive from this special sort of self-knowledge that agents have. As Anscombe puts it, following Aquinas, "practical knowledge is 'the cause of what it understands', unlike 'speculative' knowledge, which is 'derived from the objects known' " (1957:87).[12]

As I would like to propose such an account is possible for *shared* intentional action as well. Anscombe does not identify a further factor that binds individual movements together, thereby turning them into an intentional action that is shared. Rather, she describes the inner constitution of what is one movement from the start. A shared intention is, according to this account, not a complex of individual cognitive attitudes that are separate from the movements they cause and guide. Rather, it is the teleological structure of this single movement. It is the manner in which the different bits that each of the participants do over time hang together, how all of them contribute to the realization of the shared intention. In other words, a shared intention is the special way a certain sort of movement, a shared intentional action, is real, is being performed, rather than some intention or complex of intentions distinct from the movement. In this way, an intention is not a causal planning structure, but rather the beginning of an action—for instance, of paying attention. The very feature of intention Ingold criticizes is thus eliminated in Anscombian intention, which neither entails nor suggests a planning theory of acting.

I take Anscombe to vindicate the Aristotelian view that action itself is the conclusion of practical thought. In Aristotle's *De Anima*, intentions (as *orexis*) are things that move their creator, the agent. They are a sort of desire, or appetite. In this sense, intending is not just a form of passive perception or readiness to perceive, nor does it have a mere planning structure. Rather, it is the beginning of attention—and thus a form of movement. Accordingly, any practical thought begins with intention. By taking intention to be not just the cause of what it understands (in the sense that intention comes first and only then movement kicks in), but in the sense that they are (in) the beginning of the movement, intentions become initial part of the action rather than its preceding cause. Harking back to Ingold's distinction between living a life and leading it, intending would entail the latter. In this way, intentionality can be framed as the human capacity—the readiness, the tension—to be an attentive agent in the lifeworld she co-inhabits.

Conclusion

The starting point of this chapter was the assumption that anthropologists are in the business of understanding their surroundings through a process of participation. From there, I explored the role of attention and intention for participant observation.

Participant observation, I would like to conclude, interlocks two distinct types of research. Observation, on the one hand, is guided by attention as framed by Ingold. What we pay attention to—that is, *how* we see things as well as *what* we notice—depends on our dispositions and habits. These tacitly guide our attention to what we normally intend to observe, or to the unusual: Attention emerges in situations where we have (been) trained to be observant, or where habits are disrupted by the *extra*ordinary. Either way, what we observe is affected by our habits about where to look, and what to look *for*.

Participation, on the other hand, *generates* attention, and therewith overlapping perspectives. Each time we join into a specific practice with others, we adjust our senses to what matters in the lifeworlds of those who allow us to participate. We are taught, by and by, where to look. In this way, observation is not opposed to participation, but bound up with it.

These two modes of perception are channeled by anthropologists as complementary methods to adapt their habits and dispositions to local processes of perceiving and doing things. Their aim is perceptual immersion, as I would like to call this gradual adjustment of the senses mediated by participation.

Perceptual immersion can be understood as a realistic goal or an unattainable ideal. Either way, I have tried to argue that the motivation that guides our attentive perception has itself an intentional structure. I have offered an augmented interpretation of how to conceptualize what it is to participate or, in Ingold's words, to "turn othering into togethering" (2018a:26). My proposal embraced an Anscombian, at heart Aristotelian, notion of intention that encompasses attention as its actualized mode. Building on Anscombe's philosophical contributions to philosophy of action, this notion of intention can greatly benefit from Ingold's conception of attention as a 'stretching towards'—*ad-tendere*—one's environment, while incorporating a teleological structure of human agency as a kind of 'movement before movement', a mode of being *in tension*.

I might be mistaken in thinking that making this conceptual distinction between attention and intention matters. 'Call it intention, then', you might think. Perhaps there is a point to be made about giving up certain words because they foster convolution of what should be unfolded, and replacing them with words that display what matters more clearly. Intentions and intentionality could then be replaced by attention and attentionality. But I hope, here, to have performed more than just a conceptual maneuver. Taking seriously Ingold's significant worry about a purely cognitive, causal account of human agency, I have portrayed an alternative. By taking intention to be more than a planning cause of action, but as the moving beginning of it, I have aimed to show that only an understanding of intention *as* movement is useful in understanding the dynamics of shared action. Incorporating this notion into Ingold's conception of attention reveals that attention is a variety and a specification of intention. Attention, then, is intention in situ.

Notes

1 Before the establishment of the experiment as the prevalent method of empirical research, observation had been regarded as a merely passive way to understand the natural world, whereas later it became part an active way to 'rip off nature's curtains'. For a historically minded discussion of the development of observation as a research method, see Kwaschik (2018).

2 For a compelling analysis of different modes of observation, see Gallagher's *Seeing without an I* (2015). Gallagher treats the difference between object-perception and person-perception and argues for fundamental differences in what he calls gaze, depending on whether one is interacting with others or gazing alone. According to Gallagher, one's observation practice changes fundamentally when practiced with others.

3 Before Malinowski, Rivers (1912) had already laid a first foundation for the method. It was Malinowski's writing, however, which gave participant observation its distinct shape.

4 For a comprehensive overview of the origins and evolution of social anthropology, see Clifford and Marcus (1986). For a critical extrapolation of these thoughts, see Hardin and Clarke (2012).

5 Bourdieu has dwelled on this connotation of observation in his *Outline of a Theory of Practice* (1977).
6 This is not to say that habits always weaken or inhibit our ability to articulate what we do. They can also lead to a refined articulation, as for instance in martial arts, where a master learns and teaches awareness of certain motion sequences. Also, craftsmanship, as Richard Sennett (2008) makes explicit, can foster refined articulation of trained, habitual movement.
7 However, as examples from the realm of art production and craftsmanship illustrate, we do not necessarily act unthinkingly when we act out of habit. Crafting techniques require both concentration *and* habitualized movement. For an insightful account on rhythm and focus, see Michele Feder-Nadoff's illuminating writing on herself becoming a coppersmith in Mexico (2019).
8 The poem was supposedly first published by Katherine Craster in 1871. Its earliest widely known mention, however, is in Lankester (1889:80).
9 To make matters more complicated, it should be added that phenomenology is concerned with the first-person point of view in the sense that 'the Other' helps the 'I' to re-cognise itself. The presupposition Duranti's account rests on thus only represents an argumentative steppingstone to get to a conceptual constitution of the 'I'. How exactly we get from this to a 'We' remains notoriously murky and is still hotly debated in contemporary phenomenology and social philosophy more broadly.
10 As mentioned, we can also think of practices that demand both habitual practice *and* concentration. One of Ingold's own examples is his experience of playing the cello (2018b), and we can think of any other practice in the realm of crafting or artmaking to see the importance of understanding habit not in the service, but also in opposition to automatization. My point here, however, is not about the level, quality or place of consciousness when executing a habitual task, but rather about the place of uncertainty when acting in an ever-changing world.
11 Compare §6 for (a), §§ 28–30 for (b) and §§42, 45 and 48 for (c).
12 Inner brackets refer to Thomas Aquinas, *Summa Theologica*, Ia IIae, Q3, art. 5, obj. 1.

References

Anscombe, G. E. M. 1957. *Intention*. Cambridge: Harvard University Press.

Atkinson, P. and M. Hammersley 2007. *Ethnography: Principle in practice*. London: Routledge.

Bacon, F. 1960 [1620]. *The New Organon and related writings*. Fulton Henry Anderson, ed. Indianapolis: Bobbs-Merrill.

Behar, R. 1996. *The vulnerable observer*. Boston: Beacon Press.

Bourdieu, P. 1977. *Outline of a theory of practice*. New York: Cambridge University Press.

Clifford, J. and G. Marcus, eds. 1986. *Writing culture: The poetics and politics of ethnography*. Berkeley and Los Angeles: University of California Press.

Danziger, E. 2017. Toward an anthropology of intersubjectivity. *HAU: Journal of Ethnographic Theory* 7(2):451–455.

DeWalt, K. M. and B. R. DeWalt. 2002. *Participant observation*. Plymouth: AltaMira Press.

Dewey, J. 2015 [1938]. *Experience and education.* New York: Free Press.
Duranti, A. 2015. *The anthropology of intentions: Language in a world of others.* Cambridge: Cambridge University Press.
Eriksen, T. H. 2010. *Small places, large issues: An introduction to social and cultural anthropology.* 3rd edition. London and New York: Pluto Press.
Feder-Nadoff, M. 2019. Bodies of knowledge: Towards an anthropology of making. *Entanglements* 2(1):59–75.
Förster, T. 2001. Sehen und Beobachten. *Sozialer Sinn* 2(3):459–484.
——— 2011. *Emic evaluation approach—Some remarks on its epistemological background.* In *The emic evaluation approach—Epistemologies, experience, and ethnographic practice.* T. Förster, B. Heer, M. Engeler, A. A. Kaufmann, K. Bauer, and K. Heitz, eds. Pp. 3–12. Basel Papers on Political Transformations. Basel: Institute of Social Anthropology, University of Basel.
Geertz, C. 2004 [1973]. Thick description: Toward an interpretive theory of culture. In *The interpretation of cultures: Selected essays.* C. Geertz, ed. Pp. 3–30. New York: Basic Books.
Hallam, H. 1854. *Introduction to the literature of Europe in the fifteenth, sixteenth, and seventeenth centuries: Volume 2.* Boston: Little, Brown & Company.
Hardin, R. and K. M. Clarke, eds. 2012. *Transforming ethnographic knowledge.* Madison: University of Wisconsin Press.
Heidegger, M. 1953. *Sein und Zeit.* Tübingen: Max Niemeyer.
Hume, D. 2014 [1738]. *A treatise of human nature.* Oxford: Clarendon Press.
Ingold, T. 2014. The creativity of undergoing. *Pragmatics & Cognition* 22:124–139.
——— 2015. *The life of lines.* Abingdon: Routledge.
——— 2018a. *Anthropology and/as education.* London: Routledge.
——— 2018b. From the north with my cello, or, five propositions on beauty. In *Anthropology and beauty: From aesthetics to creativity.* S. Bunn, ed. Pp. 449–464. Abingdon: Routledge.
Jackson, M. 2005. *Existential anthropology.* New York: Berghahn.
Kesselring, R. 2017. *Bodies of truth: Law, memory, and emancipation in post-apartheid South Africa.* Stanford: Stanford University Press.
Kwaschik, A. 2018. *Der Griff nach dem Weltwissen: Zur Genealogie von Area Studies im 19. Und 20. Jahrhundert.* Kritische Studien für Geschichtswissenschaft 229. Göttingen: Vandenhoeck & Ruprecht.
Lankester, E. R. 1889. The Muybridge photographs. *Nature* 40(1021):78–80.
Locke, J. 1975 [1689]. *An essay on human understanding.* Peter H. Nidditch, ed. Oxford: Oxford University Press.
Malinowski, B. 1961 [1922]. *Argonauts of the Western Pacific.* London: Routledge and Keagan Paul.
Marcus, G. 1998. *Ethnography through thick and thin.* Princeton: Princeton University Press.
Masschelein, J. 2010. E-ducating the gaze: The idea of a poor pedagogy. *Ethics and Education* 5(2):43–53.
Okely, J. 2012. *Anthropological practice: Fieldwork and the ethnographic practice.* London: Bloomsbury.
Oxford English Dictionary. 2020. www.oed.com/view/Entry/129883 (accessed 28/02/2021).
Rivers, W. H. R. 1912. A general account of method. *Notes and Queries on Anthropology* 4:108–127.

Schütz, A. and T. Luckmann. 1973. *Structures of the life-world: Vol. 1*. Translated by R. M. Zaner and J. T. Engelhardt, Jr. Evanston: Northwestern University Press.
Sennett, R. 2008. *The craftsman*. New Haven: Yale University Press.
Spittler, G. 2001. Teilnehmende Beobachtung als dichte Teilnahme. *Zeitschrift für Ethnologie* 126:1–25.
Stoller, P. 1989. *The taste of ethnographic things: The senses in anthropology*. Philadelphia: University of Pennsylvania Press.
Surak, K. 2017. Rupture and rhythm: A phenomenology of national experiences. *Sociological Theory* 35(4):312–333.
Waldenfels, B. 2004. *Phänomenologie der Aufmerksamkeit*. Frankfurt am Main: Suhrkamp.

6 Historicising creativity

An interdisciplinary perspective between the social and natural sciences

Dylan Gaffney and Leor Zmigrod

Introduction

In recent decades, anthropology has moved beyond the opposition between structure and agency and now tries to grapple with the improvisational ways by which we make our world (Leach 2012). This puts creativity at the heart of what it means to be human. But in what ways is human life creative? Tim Ingold has expressly addressed this topic in several influential works (Ingold 1986:173–221, 2007, 2010a, 2010b, 2011:210–219, 2013:7, 2014; Ingold and Hallam 2007). For Ingold, creativity is a process whereby humans submit to the flows of social life and materials and give form to themselves, each other, and the world around them. This kind of creativity is relational and historical, emerging over time from the correspondences between people and other organisms, and between people and things.

Although social scientists have dealt extensively with different constituents of relational creativity, including material culture and the human organism as a whole, there have been few attempts to incorporate an understanding of the brain into this framework. The first aim of this chapter is therefore to ask: how does the brain operate in these creative processes? The recent theoretical focus on the dialectic between people and other things has been driven by a justifiable shift away from cognitivist assumptions that exclusively situate creativity inside the physical brain. But is it possible to remove the 'ghost in the machine' (see Gosden 2010; Malafouris 2013:10) from human creative activities – that is, to remove creativity as an inherent essence from inside the brain – while still taking neural processes seriously? Doing so would allow us to involve the brain in creative action and to understand it as a vital material constituting, and constituted by, relational correspondences.

The second aim of the chapter is then to ask: how does a relational creativity that involves brain processes operate at different temporal scales? Creativity has been a focus of synchronic experimentation by psychologists and participatory observation by anthropologists, but we want to explore how creative thoughts and actions, and the capacities that underlie these activities, emerge temporally. To address these aims, we explain how creativity plays out at three timescales: in the everyday, across the lifetime, and

DOI: 10.4324/9781003162773-9

over the *longue durée* – during days, decades, and millennia. Because much of Tim Ingold's writing is an attempt to understand both the 'social' and the 'natural' within the context of generative history (e.g., Ingold 1998, 2004), we consequently provide an account that integrates the social and natural sciences.

Ingold on creativity

Ingold's work helps us to move past some of the conceptual limitations of the standard view of creativity in the social and natural sciences. Like other cultures, post-Enlightenment communities around the North Atlantic have developed their own unique epistemology to understand creativity (Lubart et al. 2019). Conventionally, this interpretation of creativity prioritises the inventiveness of individuals and the generation of novel end products including ideas, objects, and art. Since the mid-twentieth century, scientists have usually described creativity as something both novel and appropriate within a given social context (Mayer 1999). This definition pervades both the natural and social sciences, which essentially understand creativity as a gloss for **innovation** (e.g., Wilson 2017). In an attempt to investigate innovation empirically, psychologists of the late twentieth century hypothesised that it is the product of schematics generated in the brain (e.g., Boden 1998). These are what psychologists call 'representational' accounts and Ingold (2012) calls the 'hylomorphic model', whereby form is inscribed on the world by individual, rational agents.

To historicise innovation, scholars like Boden (1990, 2018) propose that ideas can either be individually creative, meaning they were entirely new for the person involved, or historically creative, meaning the new idea was produced for the first time in human history. In some instances, the evolution of innovation has been exclusively tracked by identifying a sequence of genius minds that generate historically creative outputs (e.g., Simonton 1999). As Ingold (2014:125) notes, this way of historicising creativity is actually static because it constructs a temporal sequence entirely from seemingly 'authentic' novel behaviours which are later replicated. "[W]hat is missing from the equation of creativity with innovation, then, is growth, becoming, the actual forming or making of things, or in a word, ontogenesis" (Ingold 2014:128).

Ingold and Hallam (2007) suggest **improvisation** helps to explain how creative ontogenesis occurs. Although humans are excellent imitators, we are very poor replicators; we continually reproduce the behaviours of other humans, but we tend to introduce variation, whether in mundane activities or in more extended task-specific practices (Gaffney 2019:200; Schillinger et al. 2015). Ingold and Hallam (2007) ascribe four characteristics to improvisational creativity: (1) it is generative, giving form to the world; (2) it is relational, responsive to the actions of others; (3) it is temporal, embodying duration; and (4) it is the 'way we work' in our everyday lives.

Elsewhere, Ingold (2010a) suggests that improvisation occurs without agency. This is primarily a reaction to anthropologists like Gell (1988) who suggested that the agency of the maker is revealed in creative outputs. Gell stipulated that we should look for agency in the object itself and trace it back to the mind of the person who made it, or, in fact, trace it outwards from certain end products that can affect the observer (Gell 1992). Ingold sees this as a backwards reading of the creative process and that we need to understand that life is not animated by humans inscribing their agency on the world, or bestowing secondary forms of agency into objects, but rather by living things, both human and non-human, going about their activities and submitting to the flows of materials.

Finally, in the context of improvisation without agency, Ingold (2014) seeks to prioritise the life '**undergoing**' in which people create themselves and one another. This is the creativity of becoming that energises much of Ingold's writing. Attending to social relations and all that entails – building friendships, recounting stories, telling lies, nurturing loved ones, generating obligation – is itself perhaps the most human of activities, but is rarely considered creative. Yet, by definition, undergoing transforms the net of relationships that make up our worlds, and, in so doing, brings forth elements of difference. We seek to provide detail about the organic and material processes that stimulate creative improvisation and undergoing. To do this, we now examine how the brain, as an organic material interlinked with a wider sensory system, contributes to vitalising human modes of creation.

Human brains: vital organic materials

"Psychologists have a peculiar idea of creativity", observes Ingold (2014:124). "They tend to think of it as … located somewhere in the mind-brain". Conversely, anthropologists have often implicitly decoupled the brain from the mind, thinking of the brain as the physical cortices and lobes within the skull, and the mind as something that does creative mental processing. If the brain and mind are separate, whether the mind is internal to the brain or distributed outside of the brain, it presents a conceptual problem (see Northoff 2018). This is because both frameworks locate physical properties on a separate plane to mental properties. We argue that the brain and mind are the same thing – constituted by neural processes that are both material (physical) and organic (living), inseparable from a wider sensory system that extends out into the world and constituted by its correspondences with this ecology.

Modern psychology and neuroscience have repeatedly shown that the brain is not neatly modular or insular from its surroundings. The idea of an embodied, situated brain goes back to the fundamental principles of ecological psychology, pioneered by J. J. Gibson and E. J. Gibson. These authors were highly influential to Ingold's work on *The perception of the environment* (2000:2–3) because they challenged the dichotomies between perception and action, and between organism and environment. All human perception is reactive, and all action is produced at the intersection of this ecologically sensitive perception and the environment. "We don't simply see, we look" noted E. J. Gibson (1988:5), "the visual system is a motor system as well as a sensory one". Sensation and movement are tightly interlocked: humans are attuned both to sensory stimuli and to ecological contingencies and so have evolved behaviours that allow environmental details to be revealed and deeply processed. In the words of Lobo, Heras-Escribano, and Travieso (2018:5), "perceptual systems orient the perceptual organs and make adjustments in the exploration to resonate when ecological information is picked up. [This] picking up is the reason why organism and environment are entangled in action-perception dynamics". The brain, nerves, and sensory organs consequently provide a system through which environmental stimuli can be perceived and remodelled in action.

Therefore, what *forms* brain matter does not necessarily and locationally begin in brain cells, but at the correspondence between the brain, the body, and the wider ecology. Indeed, Ingold (2010a), expanding on the work of Gregory Bateson (1972:429) and Andy Clark (1997:53), has often spoken of the brain, and even the organism, as a 'leaky' thing. It tends to form connections outside of the skull and body, and, in so doing, becomes deeply intertwined with its surroundings (Jasanoff 2018). We can therefore situate much of the potential for human creativity in our embodied neural and sensory systems that extend out into the world.

We now ask how creative activities 'grow' brains by stimulating neural connections, and in turn how these neural processes vitalise human activities. As Henri Bergson (2005 [1907]) noted, for creative ontogenesis and morphogenesis to occur, they need to unfold durationally: the past, in both its personal and collective forms, shapes perception, memory, and future imagination, and so creativity is fundamentally a temporal process of becoming. We explore this process on three different temporal scales – the everyday, the lifecycle, and the long-term.

The everyday

Having positioned the dynamic loops between perception and action within the extended and embodied neural system, we can now begin to historicise improvisational creativity on the everyday scale. How does creativity emerge in the context of the everyday from the correspondence between humans and their social and material environment? The specific mechanics of this everyday creativity can be understood in the neurobiology of learning: environmental stimuli are sensed and processed by bodily nerve endings that transmit an array of complex signals to sensory cortical networks, which materialise conscious percepts and actions. These processes simultaneously involve 'top-down' cognitive control and regulation of motor-sensory movement as well as 'bottom-up' stimuli-led reaction and generation.

It is possible to see the interaction between 'top-down' mental regulation and 'bottom-up' environmental influences across a range of everyday improvisational creativities and the emergence of creative undergoing (as shown by brain imaging in Figure 6.1). For example, during musical improvisation, areas of the brain linked to both cognitive control and spontaneous mind wandering are activated (Beaty 2015). In this way, the neuroscience of real-time musical creativity illustrates that improvisation is not purely a product of mental simulations or solely a response to external cues; there is continual generative and reactive coordination that buttress innovative and aesthetically rewarding creativity (Loui 2018).

Research on brain-to-brain coupling during verbal communication illustrates that when relaying a story, the speaker and listener's brains will exhibit similar neural dynamics (Hasson and Frith 2016), and the strength of their neural mirroring can predict the listener's comprehension of the speaker's story (Silbert et al. 2014; Stephens et al. 2010). One person's narrative production is therefore neurally interlocked with a listener's narrative comprehension, especially in successful social interactions and collective coordination (Fusaroli and Tylen 2015). This is not restricted to verbal exchanges; experiments that invite participants to tap their fingers in synchrony find that interpersonal coordination emerges from capacities to predict one's partner's upcoming action, but also by behavioural adaptability on a moment-by-moment basis, evidenced on the timescale of milliseconds (Konvalinka et al. 2010). Similarly, when children are asked to play a cooperative game with their parent, and, separately, with a stranger, there is brain-to-brain synchrony in child–parent games but not in child–stranger games (Reindl et al. 2018). The extent to which parents' and children's brains are synchronised during the cooperative game also predicts how successful their performance is. Correspondences can be, in part, revealed by the minds of participants and their existing emotional connections. Creative undergoing and improvisation are thereby mediated through the individual's control (involving the brain's internal processing) which is continually receptive to the actions of others, external cues, and the opportunities presented by the world.

The human experience of this everyday creativity as durational stems from the interaction between the brain's spontaneous activity and resting states, the sensory system, and the pace of the external world. Most people's brain frequencies, bodily rhythm, and daily practice synchronise over time with their wider ecology (Northoff et al. 2020). This wider ecology moves at different rates and scales due to variability in the temporalities of different materials and different organisms (Robb 2020). Alongside this, cognitive capacities like active attention (Zmigrod et al. 2019), imagination (Finke 1996), memory (Madore et al. 2015) and working memory (Takeuchi et al. 2011), and emotion (Bledow et al. 2003) are generative and build up by immersion with these different materials and organisms. These psychological capacities lead, and are led by, the kind of creative activities that people routinely

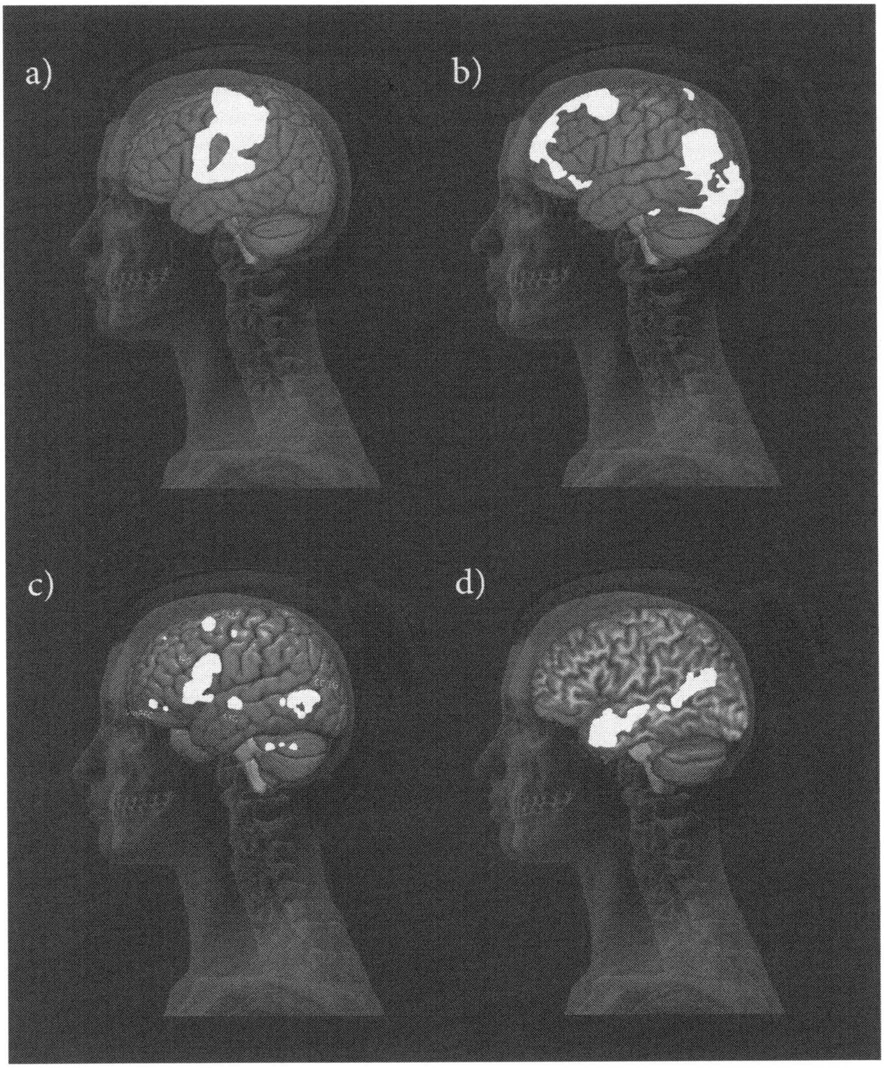

Figure 6.1 The brain, as part of the human organism, actively responds to creative action in the environment: (a and b) dorsolateral prefrontal cortex connectivity during musical improvisation; in (a) functional connectivity is associated with using different sets of piano keys and in (b) functional connectivity is associated with the goal of expressing different emotions (adapted from Beaty et al. 2016); (c) brain activity associated with original association tasks (adapted from Benedek et al. 2020); (d) brain activity associated with literal and metaphorical speech in narrative contexts (adapted from Hartung et al. 2020). Base image: Stocktrek Images.

practise, whether in the domain of music, storytelling, movement, dance, or existential becoming. But how do human capacities to lead, and to be led by, creative activities transform over a lifetime? To historicise creativity across this temporal scale, we must trace creativity – in its improvisational, innovative, and mutually-constructive forms – to birth.

The life cycle

Ingold (2014:127) encourages us to see creativity even in the conception of the individual: "I can think of no more creative process than that by which a baby … is 'knit together' in its mother's womb". Gestation is therefore the initial creative process which sets in motion the human lifecycle, including the development of neural and sensory systems. Ingold acknowledges that this is fundamentally a biosocial pathway, occurring both within, and in relation to, the parental body. When the newborn enters the world, it is already an environment with which it is acquainted, at least in terms of its creative, generative, and co-dependent capacities, because the womb too has these properties. The infant's motions and noises are consistently greeted by reactions from its caregivers; perception and action are thereby woven together into the fabric of the individual's existence from the very beginning. Early behaviours include eye contact, smiles, and positive vocalisations (Akhtar and Jaswal 2020), and these interactions come alongside a host of biochemical stimulants in both parent and child, such as neuropeptides flooding the body's endocrine system and encouraging social bonding (Atzil et al. 2017; Carter et al. 2008). These biochemical processes begin even during gestation; for instance, testosterone levels in amniotic fluids have an influence on early eye contact and bonding (Lutchmaya et al. 2002). In fact, the development of many core features that we understand to facilitate creative undergoing such as language use, the interpretation of facial expressions and gestures, and the understanding of emotion all rely on this early social bonding (Sherwood and Gómez-Robles 2017:400).

As the infant learns and engages with its surroundings, the brain and extended sensory system are constantly growing. The infant absorbs and reacts to the textures of relationships, materials, and perceptual stimuli, in which it becomes increasingly enmeshed. The child identifies patterns and anomalies – how things can come together, break apart, and be altered (see Brandt and Eagleman 2017) – continually building up these experiences as memory (Schneider and Ornstein 2015). Developmental psychology has illustrated that the infant's brain is malleable and receptive (Lindenberger and Lövdén 2019:202), and recent neuroimaging has shown that this plasticity is there from birth, moulded during early infancy when the individual is immersed into a world of sensory stimuli (Yin et al. 2020). In the domain of language, infants can distinguish between more variations in sound than older children or adults (Cutler 2012; Eilers et al. 1977). In the realm of social perception, newborns appear to identify emotions and infer intention from visual shapes (Chronaki et al. 2015). They test new sounds on their tongues, observe facial reactions with fascination, and demonstrate surprise when their expectations fail to materialise (Cheng et al. 2012). The capacity to predict initially underpins pretend play. Play allows toddlers and older children to build up sensory ways of knowing by following the tugs and pulls of desire that different materials animate (MacRae 2020). Imagination also generates a range of 'what if's' (Gotlieb et al. 2019) that shape future improvisation and innovation that the individual will engender over the lifespan.

Childhood creativity is afforded by the support directly provided by the wider community. As Vygotsky (1978) originally noted, learning in groups allows humans to perform a range of tasks that could not be achieved solely by individuals. For instance, social play allows for the development of perspective-taking, internal reflection, empathy, and exchange (Gotlieb et al. 2019), and mediating behaviours encourage children to rapidly navigate social interaction and to, on the fly, look for new directions and new paths to go down; the life undergoing, being mutually constitutive and improvisatory, begins from a young age.

Although growth is exploratory, children increasingly develop motor and cognitive control (Somerville and Casey 2010), which allows focussed attention to be given towards the task at hand. As such, both improvisatory and highly innovative action with extended technical sequences can begin to flourish. Such capacities underlie later processes of technical enskilment that go hand in hand with the development of adult social skills (Gowlland 2019). Learning these skills is conspicuous at first, but these motor-neural routines become habitualised as a person increasingly reproduces the same activities (Minar and Crown 2001), thus reducing the cognitive load of such tasks (Wood et al. 2002). Habitualisation, be it as everyday activities like walking, talking, and moving, or technical activities like craft production, in time shape a person's bodily dispositions (Mauss 1934). As Ingold (2000:186) has noted, in inhabiting their local environment, children "come literally to carry the forms of their dwelling in their bodies – in specific skills, sensibilities, and dispositions". Experts in these practices even enter 'flow states' which lead to an extended cascade of insights when executing challenging tasks allowing the person to self-scaffold into enhanced states of control and awareness (Csikszentmihalhyi 1990; Vervaeke et al. 2018). Flow states emerge, in particular, when an individual has become fluent in the materials and rhythms of their activity, which meld together to produce a seamless experience. In this way, highly skilled creativity is flexible and dynamic, responding to an 'open complex system', which promotes the exploration of possibilities *in action*. These states do not only arise as individual improvisatory experiences but can be synchronised amongst groups practising the same activities; undergoing that fosters enhanced states of togetherness (Noy et al. 2015).

These experiences, whether pretend play, social learning, or craft production leave their marks on the body, brain, and sensory system, forming neural pathways and lasting traces in the neocortical and hippocampal circuits (Lindenberger and Lövén 2019:212). The brain, in particular, continues to be reworked even after the individual is said to reach adulthood (Lebel and Beaulieu 2011). Although brain plasticity gradually declines throughout the lifecycle, the flexibility or the cognitive control to optimise these behaviours generally increases and then possibly declines in late adulthood (Figure 6.2). At the same time, wisdom involving genuine insight derived from cumulative experience and memory is thought to build up throughout life. The interplay between these capacities over the life course, and the interaction between individuals at different stages in their lives, assembles the means for the dynamic expressions of creativity that we think of as human-like. These interactions within the community represent emergent fields of creative potential during the lifecycle (see also Glăveanu 2020). On a deeper temporal scale, humankind represents the same field of emergent potential. This potential, especially as it relates to transformations to brain processes and sense making, has a long evolutionary history. We now turn to how these relational fields are reproduced and reconstituted across generations, and therefore how creativity has emerged within our genus over the *longue durée*.

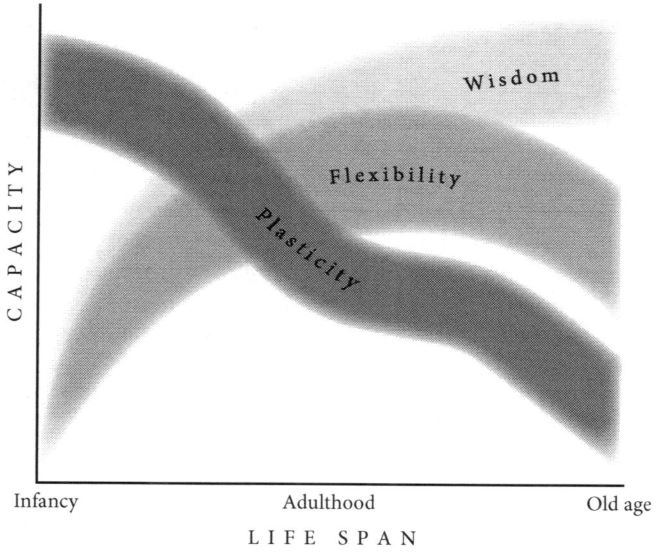

Figure 6.2 Changes to capacities for cognitive plasticity, flexibility, and wisdom across the lifespan (adapted from Kühn and Lindenberger 2016: 108 and Romer et al. 2017: 28).

The *longue durée*

Most attempts to understand the evolution of human creativity have favoured Neo-Darwinian models, which emphasise that genetic mutation under natural selection drove cognitive reorganisation, technological innovation, and the rapid onset of symbolic behaviour (Kozbelt 2019). Boden (2018) even sees this selection process itself as 'creative', but of a very different kind to human creativity. Essentially, what most of these studies do is identify the origins of novel organic or technological forms (historically creative evolution), which are then replicated or independently innovated by other individuals in the population (individually creative evolution).

Ingold (2002) has similarly sought to unite biological evolution and cultural change under one explanatory paradigm, but in a different way. Using a 'developmental systems approach', he accounts for not only selective pressures and differentiation at the population level, but also the developmental contexts that bring organisms and non-living things into being. This essentially shifts the focus of long-term change from replication to ontogenesis. Using this kind of relational model for change, the next step is to rethink how our capacities to live socially, and to improvise with different materials, emerged. This would allow us to better understand how particularly human styles of creativity evolved, while acknowledging an overarching creative advance of nature (following Whitehead 1919, 1929).

Human creativity has coevolved with the tools that our genus has produced, the activities we have undertaken, and the communities we have formed. Some technical activities that may have nurtured our species' capacities to improvise include the hunting of small and hard-to-catch animals (Ben-Dor and Barkai 2021), stone tool production and recycling (Davidson 2010), mark making (Malafouris 2021), the control of fire (Wrangham 2017), and long-distance mobility (Kuhn et al. 2016). Each of these practices that characterised forager livelihoods for many tens of millennia encouraged humans to respond, on the fly, to an open and complex system of possibilities, mediated by other organisms and materials. Similarly, social activities like gestural imitation (Nielsen 2012), music making (van der Schyff and Schiavio 2017), exchange (Oka and Fuentes 2010), and communal foraging (Churchill 1993) allowed humans to seamlessly coordinate and even shape the behaviours of others (Zawidski 2018).

As such, although the potential of human creativity is open-ended, the deep histories of tool making, problem solving, and communal life have in part tethered human behaviour along specific trajectories. These trajectories that we propel ourselves along are not fixed on a set course, but deeply rooted by past modes of becoming. We posit that these trajectories are activated and shaped by intergenerational correspondences: participation between generations, between masters and apprentices, adepts and neophytes, and parents and children (Gaut 2010). These correspondences do not result in the transmission of knowledge fully formed, but the mutual sharing of ideas, and the generation of new understanding between the young and old. It is what Ingold (2001), borrowing from Gibson (1979:254), has called the education of attention. This may take place in an institutional setting, like when children are closely monitored as they learn their parent's trade. Such correspondences are often reified as 'tradition' and lead to socialisation, enskilment, and technical mastery. Conversely, these correspondences may be serendipitous, like when children play with the offcuts of an adult's activities, or when adults learn to become parents by tending to their children. Human groups cannot produce long-term elements of difference without intergenerational correspondences; they are in fact complementary with, rather than in opposition to, the emergence of novel social forms (Dewsbury 2011; Glăveanu 2012).

The foundation for these kinds of intergenerational correspondences initially evolved amongst hominins in deep time. The practice of children and elders creating institutions, specifically kinship groups which denote ongoing obligation and reciprocity, arose sometime during the Plio-Pleistocene. Generating obligation encouraged humans to tend to familial relationships and may have gradually fostered metacognition and social awareness (Packer and Cole 2019). The ontogeny of play, including exploration that develops spatial cognition, pretend play that shapes the capacity to understand other people (Kavanaugh 2010), and divergent and convergent thinking with different materials (Gabora 2018) likely has a similar or even greater antiquity, and evolved both horizontally between children as they responded to what they perceived in their environment, and also vertically and obliquely as younger individuals observed their elders, and as elders provided guidance and instruction. So, improvisation and undergoing stimulated the growth of specific kinds of brains and sensory systems during individual life cycles, and the developmental systems that encouraged this growth were reproduced in deep time.

Not only do we reproduce our own behavioural trajectories, but these trajectories continually transform the material world around us, which presents us with an ever-changing developmental system in which to grow (see Malafouris 2014, 2015). As our improvisatory capacities have been nurtured, the human sensory system has increasingly become distributed out into a world that is human made, both in terms of the materials that we engage with, and the social fields that we learn within. Humans grow up in environments made by previous generations. To illustrate this, Ingold (2000:384) uses the example of a child growing up in an old house, not only surrounded by a nuclear family but supported by the work of those predecessors that built the house and furnished the materials for life within that home. In the same way, humankind has self-scaffolded its own affordances by the environments that we ourselves have carved out and crafted over the millennia.

Over time, our creative capacities have even become deeply rooted in our physiology and biochemistry. Although humans are born with remarkable neural plasticity, we are not born as blank slates. Our sulci – markers of brain organisation with important implications for improvisatory, innovative, and social behaviours – have been reconfigured as our species has stimulated specific neural centres. For instance, Beaudet (2017) shows how brain reorganisation over several million years emerged alongside language comprehension, while Wynn and Coolidge (2014) note that transformations to the cortical and subcortical neural substrates may underlie changes to working memory and therefore capacities for both improvisation and undergoing. These creative behaviours engineered developmental systems in which increasingly plastic brains and sensory systems, associated with specific alleles, were selected for (Barbot and Eff 2019). In turn, the genome's deeply rooted molecular and cellular mechanisms contributed to morphogenesis and therefore how these neural and sensory systems were continually brought into being (Fagiolini et al. 2009). This is to say that our creativity has shaped the selective pressures acting upon our creative capacities. As Laland and colleagues (2010) note, humans have become co-directors in our own evolution, altering the trajectory of our genome, material worlds, and social environments.

Conclusion

Throughout this chapter our aim has been to provide a temporal understanding of creativity, resolved across three different timescales: the everyday, the lifecycle, and deep time. We drew from a range of Ingold's writings that explicitly deal with creativity, as well as those that more generally develop a way of understanding life as a process of becoming. In doing so, we have also pushed Ingold's ideas towards an interface between empirical inquiry that characterises the natural sciences, and system thinking that characterises the social sciences.

Our argument began from the premise that human creativity not only gives form to the net of relationships that constitute the ecology, which continually reconfigures the conditions for creative expression, but also gives form to people themselves, including the human brain, the body, and the sensory system. Creating and becoming, then, are not merely states of activity in the world, but they are also fundamentally organic and material processes. We highlighted how everyday creative action promotes neurobiological and physiological transformations by forging new neuronal connections, activating brain networks in new configurations, and aligning bodily and culturally specific dispositions within the wider ecology. These biological changes to the organism, in turn, shape capacities for future improvisation and innovation.

Second, we showed that creativity is about growth throughout the life cycle. During infancy and childhood, humans begin to actively explore their world, and this results in novel encounters with a multitude of materials and other organisms. We described how these interactions encourage the development of complex neuromotor capacities such as walking, talking, language comprehension, and tool use, along with social skills like play and restraint. In doing so, the child partially sets its own conditions for future growth but is also scaffolded into new realms of possibility by the learning environment and wider social group.

Third, we noted that lives are lived not just between peers in a social group, but also as intergenerational correspondences between the young and old. Parents and children, masters and novices, learn and share knowledge together, generating novel albeit temporary social forms while, at the same time, reinvigorating or unravelling tradition. Through this process, improvisatory behaviours are nurtured, neural capacities are extended, and learning environments are transformed, which in turn sculpt the brain. We suggest that our species has altered our own behavioural trajectories over tens of thousands of generations by changing our learning environments, by changing the materials with which we engage the world, and by changing our neurobiological abilities. Creativity is then cultivated and shaped by people's daily activities and correspondences, but the ways that creativity unfolds developmentally and evolutionarily have become deeply rooted in our neural architecture and behavioural trajectories. As a species our creativity plays out durationally at different scales; on all timescales, we continually bring our own potential within reach and build connections between the known and the possible.

Acknowledgements

We thank Martin Porr and Niels Weidtmann for their organisation of the original workshop in Tübingen from which this piece of writing sprouted, and for their careful editorial comments. We also thank Tim Ingold for his thought-provoking discussion both at the workshop and in reply to this chapter. We lastly acknowledge two independent reviewers for their constructive and challenging input, which pushed our ideas in new directions.

References

Akhtar, N. and V. K. Jaswal. 2020. Stretching the social: Broadening the behavioral indicators of sociality. *Child Development Perspectives* 14(1):28–33.

Atzil, S., A. Touroutoglou, T. Rudy, S. Salcedo, R. Feldman, J. M. Hooker, B. C. Dickerson, C. Catana, and L. F. Barrett. 2017. Dopamine in the medial amygdala network mediates human bonding. *Proceedings of the National Academy of Sciences* 114(9):2361–2366.

Barbot, B. and H. Eff. 2019. The genetic basis of creativity. In *The Cambridge handbook of creativity*. J. Kaufman and R. J. Sternberg, eds. Pp. 132–147. Cambridge: Cambridge University Press.

Bateson, G. 1972. *Steps to an ecology of mind: Collected essays in anthropology, psychiatry, evolution and epistemology*. Chicago: University of Chicago Press.

Beaty, R. E. 2015. The neuroscience of musical improvisation. *Neuroscience and Biobehavioral Reviews* 51:108–117.

Beaty, R. E., M. Benedek, P. J. Silvia, and D. L. Schacter. 2016. Creative cognition and brain network dynamics. *Trends in Cognitive Sciences* 20(2):87–95.

Beaudet, A. 2017. The emergence of language in the hominin lineage: Perspectives from fossil endocasts. *Frontiers in Human Neuroscience* 11:427.

Ben-Dor, M. and R. Barkai. 2021. Prey size decline as a unifying ecological selecting agent in Pleistocene human evolution. *Quaternary* 4(1):7.

Benedek, M., J. Jurisch, K. Koschutnig, A. Fink, and R. E. Beaty. 2020. Elements of creative thought: Investigating the cognitive and neural correlates of association and bi-association processes. *NeuroImage* 210:116586.

Bergson, H. 2005 [1907]. *Creative evolution*. Arthur Mitchell, trans. New York: Cosimo Classics.

Bledow, R., K. Rosing, and M. Frese. 2013. A dynamic perspective on affect and creativity. *Academy of Management Journal* 56(2):432–450.

Boden, M. 1990. *The creative mind: Myths and mechanisms*. London: Weidenfeld and Nicolson.

Boden, M. A. 1998. What is creativity? In *Creativity in human evolution and prehistory*. S. Mithen, ed. Pp. 15–43. London: Routledge.

Boden, M. A. 2018. Creativity and biology. In *Creativity and philosophy*. B. Gaut and M. Kieran, eds. Pp. 173–192. London: Routledge.

Brandt, A. and D. Eagleman. 2017. *The runaway species: How human creativity remakes the world*. Edinburgh: Canongate.

Carter, C. S., A. J. Grippo, H. Pournajafi-Nazarloo, M. G. Ruscio, and S. W. Porges. 2008. Oxytocin, vasopressin and sociality. *Progress in Brain Research* 170:331–336.

Cheng, Y., S.-Y. Lee, H.-Y. Chen, P.-Y. Wang, and J. Decety. 2012. Voice and emotion processing in the human neonatal brain. *Journal of Cognitive Neuroscience* 24(6):1411–1419.

Chronaki, G., J. A. Hadwin, M. Garner, P. Maurage, and E. J. Sonuga-Barke. 2015. The development of emotion recognition from facial expressions and non-linguistic vocalizations during childhood. *British Journal of Developmental Psychology* 33(2):218–236.

Churchill, S. E. 1993. Weapon technology, prey size selection, and hunting methods in modern hunter-gatherers: Implications for hunting in the Palaeolithic and Mesolithic. *Archaeological Papers of the American Anthropological Association* 4(1):11–24.

Clark, A. 1997. *Being there*. Cambridge, MA: MIT Press.

Csikszentmihalyi, M. 1990. *Flow: The psychology of optimal experience*. New York: Harper and Row.

Cutler, A. 2012. *Native listening: Language experience and the recognition of spoken words*. Cambridge, MA: MIT Press.

Davidson, I. 2010. Stone tools and the evolution of hominin and human cognition. In *Stone tools and the evolution of human cognition*. A. Nowell and I. Davidson, eds. Pp.185–205. Boulder: University Press of Colorado.

Dewsbury, J. D. 2011. The Deleuze-Guattarian assemblage: Plastic habits. *Area* 43(2):148–153.

Eilers, R. E., W. R. Wilson, and J. M. Moore. 1977. Developmental changes in speech discrimination in infants. *Journal of Speech and Hearing Research* 20(4):766–780.

Fagiolini, M., C. L. Jensen, and F. A. Champagne. 2009. Epigenetic influences on brain development and plasticity. *Current Opinion in Neurobiology* 19(2):207–212.

Finke, R. A. 1996. Imagery, creativity, and emergent structure. *Consciousness and Cognition* 5(3):381–393.
Fusaroli, R. and K. Tylén. 2016. Investigating conversational dynamics: Interactive alignment, interpersonal synergy, and collective task performance. *Cognitive Science* 40(1):145–171.
Gabora, L. 2018. The neural basis and evolution of divergent and convergent thought. In *The Cambridge handbook of the neuroscience of creativity*. R.E. Jung and O. Vartanian, eds. Pp. 58–70. Cambridge: Cambridge University Press.
Gaffney, D. 2019. Technological process in pre-colonial Melanesia. In *Archaeologies of Island Melanesia: Current approaches to landscapes, exchange and practice*. M. Leclerc and J. Flexner, eds. Pp. 191–209. Canberra: Australian University Press.
Gaut, B. 2010. The philosophy of creativity. *Philosophy Compass* 5(12):1034–1046.
Gell, A. 1992. The technology of enchantment and the enchantment of technology. In *Anthropology, art and aesthetics*. J. Coote and A. Shelton, eds. Pp. 40–63. Oxford: Clarendon Press.
Gell, A. 1998. *Art and agency: An anthropological theory*. Oxford: Clarendon Press.
Gibson, E. J. 1988. Exploratory behavior in the development of perceiving, acting, and the acquiring of knowledge. *Annual Review of Psychology* 39(1):1–42.
Gibson, J. J. 1979. *The ecological approach to visual perception*. Mahwah, NJ: Lawrence Erlbaum Associates.
Glăveanu, V. P. 2012. Habitual creativity: Revising habit, reconceptualizing creativity. *Review of General Psychology* 16(1):78–92.
Glăveanu, V. P. 2020. *The possible: A sociocultural theory*. Oxford: Oxford University Press.
Gosden, C. 2010. The death of the mind. In *The cognitive life of things: Recasting the boundaries of the mind*. L. Malafouris and C. Renfrew, eds. Pp. 39–46. Cambridge: McDonald Institute for Archaeological Research.
Gotlieb, R. J., E. Hyde, M. H. Immordino-Yang, and S. B. Kaufman. 2019. Imagination is the seed of creativity. In *The Cambridge handbook of creativity*. J. Kaufman and R. J. Sternberg, eds. Pp. 709–731. Cambridge: Cambridge University Press.
Gowlland, G. 2019. The sociality of enskilment. *Ethnos* 84(3):508–524.
Hartung, F., Y. N. Kenett, E. R. Cardillo, S. Humphries, N. Klooster, and A. Chatterjee. 2020. Context matters: Novel metaphors in supportive and non-supportive contexts. *NeuroImage* 212:116645.
Hasson, U. and C. D. Frith. 2016. Mirroring and beyond: Coupled dynamics as a generalized framework for modelling social interactions. *Philosophical Transactions of the Royal Society B: Biological Sciences* 371(1693):20150366.
Ingold, T. 1986. *Evolution and social life*. Cambridge: Cambridge University Press.
Ingold, T. 1998. From complementarity to obviation: On dissolving the boundaries between social and biological anthropology, archaeology and psychology. *Zeitschrift für Ethnologie* 123(1):21–52.
Ingold, T. 2000. *The perception of the environment: Essays on livelihood, dwelling and skill*. London: Routledge.
Ingold, T. 2001. From the transmission of representations to the education of attention. In *The debated mind: Evolutionary psychology versus ethnography*. H. Whitehouse, ed. Pp. 113–153. London: Routledge.
Ingold, T. 2002. On the distinction between evolution and history. *Social Evolution and History* 1(1):5–24.
Ingold, T. 2004. Beyond biology and culture. The meaning of evolution in a relational world. *Social Anthropology* 12(2):209–221.

Ingold, T. 2007. Introduction. In *Creativity and cultural improvisation*. E. Hallam and T. Ingold, eds. Pp. 45–54. Oxford: Berg.

Ingold, T. 2010a. Bringing things back to life: Creative entanglements in a world of materials. *Realities Working Papers* 15:1–15.

Ingold, T. 2010b. The textility of making. *Cambridge Journal of Economics* 34(1):91–102.

Ingold, T. 2011. *Being alive: Essays on movement, knowledge and description*. London: Routledge.

Ingold, T. 2012. Toward an ecology of materials. *Annual Review of Anthropology* 41:427–442.

Ingold, T. 2013. *Making: Anthropology, archaeology, art and architecture*. London: Routledge.

Ingold, T. 2014. The creativity of undergoing. *Pragmatics and Cognition* 22(1):124–139.

Ingold, T. and E. Hallam. 2007. Creativity and cultural improvisation: An introduction. In *Creativity and cultural improvisation*. E. Hallam and T. Ingold, eds. Pp. 1–24. Oxford: Berg.

Jasanoff, A. 2018. *The biological mind: How brain, body, and environment collaborate to make us who we are*. New York, NY: Basic Books.

Kavanaugh, R. D. 2010. Origins and consequences of social pretend play. In *The Oxford handbook of the development of play*. P. Nathan and A. D. Pellegrini, eds. Pp. 296–307. Oxford: Oxford University Press.

Konvalinka, I., P. Vuust, A. Roepstorff, and C. D. Frith. 2010. Follow you, follow me: Continuous mutual prediction and adaptation in joint tapping. *Quarterly Journal of Experimental Psychology* 63(11):2220–2230.

Kozbelt, A. 2019. Evolutionary approaches to creativity. In *The Cambridge handbook of creativity*. J. Kaufman and R. J. Sternberg, eds. Pp. 109–131. Cambridge: Cambridge University Press.

Kühn, S. and U. Lindenberger. 2016. Research on human plasticity in adulthood: A lifespan agenda. In *Handbook of the psychology of aging*. K.W. Schaie and S. Wallis, eds. Pp. 105–123. Cambridge, MA: Academic Press.

Kuhn, S. L., D. A. Raichlen, and A. E. Clark. 2016. What moves us? How mobility and movement are at the center of human evolution. *Evolutionary Anthropology* 25(3):86–97.

Laland, K. N., J. Odling-Smee, and S. Myles. 2010. How culture shaped the human genome: Bringing genetics and the human sciences together. *Nature Reviews Genetics* 11(2):137–148.

Leach, J. 2012. Creativity as a social relation. In *Remediating the social, electronic literature as a model for creativity and innovation in practice*. S. Biggs, ed. Pp. 28–31. Edinburgh: ELMCIP.

Lebel, C. and C. Beaulieu. 2011. Longitudinal development of human brain wiring continues from childhood into adulthood. *Journal of Neuroscience* 31(30):10937–10947.

Lindenberger, U. and M. Lövdén. 2019. Brain plasticity in human lifespan development: The exploration–selection–refinement model. *Annual Review of Developmental Psychology* 1:197–222.

Lobo, L., M. Heras-Escribano, and D. Travieso. 2018. The history and philosophy of ecological psychology. *Frontiers in Psychology* 9:2228.

Loui, P. 2018. Rapid and flexible creativity in musical improvisation: Review and a model. *Annals of the New York Academy of Sciences* 1423(1):138–145.

Lubart, T., V. P. Glăveanu, H. de Vries, A. Camargo, and M. Storme. 2019. Cultural perspectives on creativity. In *The Cambridge handbook of creativity*. J. Kaufman and R. J. Sternberg, eds. Pp. 421–447. Cambridge: Cambridge University Press.

Lutchmaya, S., S. Baron-Cohen, and P. Raggatt. 2002. Foetal testosterone and eye contact in 12-month-old human infants. *Infant Behavior and Development* 25(3):327–335.

MacRae, C. 2020. Tactful hands and vibrant mattering in the sand tray. *Journal of Early Childhood Literacy* 20(1):90–110.

Madore, K. P., D. R. Addis, and D. L. Schacter. 2015. Creativity and memory: Effects of an episodic-specificity induction on divergent thinking. *Psychological Science* 26(9):1461–1468.

Malafouris, L. 2013. *How things shape the mind*. Cambridge, MA: MIT Press.

Malafouris, L. 2014. Creative thinging: The feeling of and for clay. *Pragmatics and Cognition* 22(1):140–158.

Malafouris, L. 2015. Metaplasticity and the primacy of material engagement. *Time and Mind* 8(4):351–371.

Malafouris, L. 2021. Mark making and human becoming. *Journal of Archaeological Method and Theory* 28(1):95–119.

Mauss, M. 1934. Les techniques du corps. *Journal de Psychologie* 32(3–4):271–293.

Mayer, R. E. 1999. Fifty years of creativity research. In *Handbook of creativity*. R. J. Sternberg, ed. Pp. 449–460. Cambridge: Cambridge University Press.

Minar, C. J. and P. L. Crown. 2001. Learning and craft production: an introduction. *Journal of Anthropological Research* 57(4):369–380.

Nielsen, M. 2012. Imitation, pretend play, and childhood: Essential elements in the evolution of human culture? *Journal of Comparative Psychology* 126(2):170–181.

Northoff, G. 2018. *The spontaneous brain: From the mind-body to the world-brain problem*. Cambridge, MA: MIT Press.

Northoff, G., S. Wainio-Theberge, and K. Evers. 2020. Is temporo-spatial dynamics the "common currency" of brain and mind? In quest of "Spatiotemporal Neuroscience". *Physics of Life Reviews* 33:34–54.

Noy, L., N. Levit-Binun, and Y. Golland. 2015. Being in the zone: Physiological markers of togetherness in joint improvisation. *Frontiers in Human Neuroscience* 9:187.

Oka, R. and A. Fuentes. 2010. From reciprocity to trade: How cooperative infrastructures form the basis of human socioeconomic evolution. In *Cooperation in economy and society*. R. C. Marshall, ed. Pp. 3–28. Walnut Creek, CA: Altamira Press.

Packer, M. J. and M. Cole. 2019. Evolution and ontogenesis: The deontic niche of human development. *Human Development* 62(4):175–211.

Reindl, V., C. Gerloff, W. Scharke, and K. Konrad. 2018. Brain-to-brain synchrony in parent-child dyads and the relationship with emotion regulation revealed by fNIRS-based hyperscanning. *NeuroImage* 178:493–502.

Robb, J. 2020. Material time. In *The Oxford handbook of history and material culture*. I. Gaskell and S. A. Carter, eds. Pp. 123–139. Oxford: Oxford University Press.

Romer, D., V. F. Reyna, and T. D. Satterthwaite. 2017. Beyond stereotypes of adolescent risk taking: Placing the adolescent brain in developmental context. *Developmental Cognitive Neuroscience* 27:19–34.

Schillinger, K., A. Mesoudi, and S. J. Lycett. 2015. The impact of imitative versus emulative learning mechanisms on artifactual variation: Implications for the evolution of material culture. *Evolution and Human Behavior* 36(6):446–455.

Schneider, W. and P. A. Ornstein. 2015. The development of children's memory. *Child Development Perspectives* 9(3):190–195.

Sherwood, C. C. and A. Gómez-Robles. 2017. Brain plasticity and human evolution. *Annual Review of Anthropology* 46:399–419.

Silbert, L. J., C. J. Honey, E. Simony, D. Poeppel, and U. Hasson. 2014. Coupled neural systems underlie the production and comprehension of naturalistic narrative speech. *Proceedings of the National Academy of Sciences* 111(43):E4687–E4696.

Simonton, D. K. 1999. *Origins of genius: Darwinian perspectives on creativity*. Oxford: Oxford University Press.

Somerville, L. H. and B. J. Casey. 2010. Developmental neurobiology of cognitive control and motivational systems. *Current Opinion in Neurobiology* 20(2):236–241.

Stephens, G. J., L. J. Silbert, and U. Hasson. 2010. Speaker–listener neural coupling underlies successful communication. *Proceedings of the National Academy of Sciences* 107(32):14425–14430.

Takeuchi, H., Y. Taki, H. Hashizume, Y. Sassa, T. Nagase, R. Nouchi, and R. Kawashima. 2011. Failing to deactivate: The association between brain activity during a working memory task and creativity. *NeuroImage* 55(2):681–687.

van der Schyff, D. and A. Schiavio. 2017. Evolutionary musicology meets embodied cognition: Biocultural coevolution and the enactive origins of human musicality. *Frontiers in Neuroscience* 11:519.

Vervaeke, J., L. Ferraro, and A. Herrera-Bennett. 2018. Flow as spontaneous thought: Insight and implicit learning. In *The Oxford handbook of spontaneous thought: Mind-wandering, creativity, and dreaming*. K. Christoff and K. C. R. Fox, eds. Pp. 309–326. Oxford: Oxford University Press.

Vygotsky, L. S. 1978. *Mind in society: The development of higher psychological processes*. Cambridge, MA: Harvard University Press.

Whitehead, A. N. 1919. *The principles of natural knowledge*. Cambridge: Cambridge University Press.

Whitehead, A. N. 1929. *Process and reality*. New York, NY: Macmillan.

Wilson, E. O. 2017. *The origins of creativity*. New York, NY: W.W. Norton and Company.

Wood, W., J. M Quinn, and D. A. Kashy. 2002. Habits in everyday life: Thought, emotion, and action. *Journal of Personality and Social Psychology* 83(6):1281.

Wrangham, R. 2017. Control of fire in the Paleolithic: Evaluating the cooking hypothesis. *Current Anthropology* 58(S16):S303–S313.

Wynn, T. and F. L. Coolidge. 2014. Technical cognition, working memory and creativity. *Pragmatics and Cognition* 22(1):45–63.

Yin, W., T. Li, S. C. Hung, H. Zhang, L. Wang, D. Shen, H. Zhu, P. J. Mucha, J. R. Cohen, and W. Lin. 2020. The emergence of a functionally flexible brain during early infancy. *Proceedings of the National Academy of Sciences* 117(38):23904–23913.

Zawidzki, T. W. 2013. Mindshaping. In *The Oxford handbook of 4E cognition*. A. Newen, L. de Bruin, and S. Gallagher, eds. Pp. 735–754. Oxford: Oxford University Press.

Zmigrod, S., L. Zmigrod, and B. Hommel. 2019. The relevance of the irrelevant: Attentional distractor-response binding predicts performance in the remote associates task. *Psychology of Aesthetics, Creativity, and the Arts* 13(1):15–23.

Part III

Anthropology and/as attention

7 Introduction

Anthropology and/as education

Niels Weidtmann and Martin Porr

In various contexts, Tim Ingold has argued that anthropology must abandon the standpoint of a pure and detached observer and must, instead, seek to participate in people's lives. Anthropological or ethnographic research has, of course, made much of the notion of 'participant observation'. However, Tim Ingold has been quite critical of this concept because the researcher invariably goes on subsequently to objectify her observations and insights. As a result, participation and observation are once again torn apart. While participation is based on experience and concerns the participant herself by way of her deep involvement, the scientific account of observation is designed to exclude all 'merely' subjective aspects. Ingold refers to Jackson's statement that "one can observe and participate successively but not simultaneously" (Jackson 1989:51, cited in Ingold 2000:60). It is precisely this understanding that he questions. Indeed, the attempt to objectify the experiences of participant observation is tantamount to a betrayal by the observer of the observed. This betrayal even affects the anthropologist herself since she distances herself from her own experiences by objectifying them. Ingold attributes the dilemma faced by the anthropologist to the deeply rooted assumption in science that only objective knowledge is valid and 'true'. According to this understanding, since objectivity is understood as the absence of subjective aspects, participation cannot lead to true knowledge.

The idea of objectified knowledge, however, fundamentally contradicts the concerns of anthropology. After all, anthropology is interested in people and not in data from which people have been removed, or in which people themselves have been transformed into data. Ingold therefore introduces the idea of participatory knowledge, in which observation and participation belong together. Thus, the apprentice learns from the master precisely by watching her and giving her a hand, i.e., by working together with her. She acquires the knowledge herself and, in this way, acquires skill. This form of knowledge is more fundamental than the objectifying knowledge of the sciences. After all, humans must first learn to find their way in the environment and to come to terms with their life. Knowledge, thus, is experiential first of all. Objectified knowledge, on the other hand, requires an abstraction from this

DOI: 10.4324/9781003162773-11

experiential knowledge. The latter, therefore, always is implicated in the former. In arguing along these lines, Ingold comes very close to the phenomenological tradition pioneered by Husserl, who drew attention to the process of abstraction in the mathematized sciences (Husserl 1970). For Ingold, however, Gibson has been more important than Husserl. From Gibson, he adopts the notion of an "education of attention" (Gibson 1979:254; cited in Ingold 2000:22). Without attention, the intention to learn remains without content.

Ingold's anthropological understanding of participatory learning and knowledge is also reflected in his characterization of the scientist. In the manifesto which Ingold and some of his colleagues authored in 2016 to reclaim the university from its increasingly business-focused orientation and move towards a more community-oriented and a civic purpose, they argued for an understanding of academics as professionals who have the trust of society and who should not be controlled by so-called professional managers (Ingold 2016). In contrast to professional managers, Ingold's academic professionals are like amateurs in that they are motivated, in Edward Said's words, "not by profit or reward but by love for and unquenchable interest in the larger picture" (Said 1994:76; cited in Ingold 2021:155). According to such a reading, the amateur is an involved scientist who does not distance herself from her object of investigation.

Today, there is an increased interest in the lifeways and ways of thinking of so-called Indigenous peoples. Especially their relationship with the natural world seems to present a range of exciting alternatives to the approaches and structures of 'Western' thought. With reference to Tim Ingold's work, however, we should resist the temptation to find alternatives or replacements to scientific thinking. Science can only be participatory if it resists the supposedly neutral standpoint from which different scientific approaches could be compared or even applied in a complementary way. Such an orientation is related to the Western distinction between nature and culture; it treats various sciences like different cultures that relate to nature in diverse ways. Ingold, on the other hand, understands participatory science as a way of continuing life (Ingold 2018a). This idea of science strives not for a timeless understanding but to correspond with lived experience. Ingold speaks in this vein of a "poetics of dwelling" (Ingold 2000:26). Different peoples and their relationship with nature, as well as their thinking and their convictions, must not be essentialized or 'frozen'. Instead, they must be seen in their own vitality; comprehension, therefore, depends on participation. The differences between peoples reflect the different experiences they have had and continue to have with ever-varying environments (Weidtmann 2016). These experiences do not divide but invite re-enactment and co-enactment. Ingold (e.g., 2018b) therefore speaks of people as undergoing differentiation within a common world, instead of existing irreconcilably side by side. From Escobar, he adopts the term 'pluriverse' (traced back to William James), which characterizes a world that leaves room for different worlds of experience (Escobar 2011:139, cited in Ingold 2018b:169; Escobar 2018).

References

Escobar, A. 2011. Sustainability: Design for the pluriverse. *Development* 54(2):137–140.

Escobar, A. 2018. *Designs for the pluriverse. Radical interdependence, autonomy, and the making of worlds*. Durham: Duke University Press.

Gibson, J. 1979. *The ecological approach to visual perception*. Boston: Houghton Mifflin.

Husserl, E. 1970. *The crisis of European sciences and transcendental phenomenology. An introduction to phenomenological philosophy*. Evanston: Northwestern University Press.

Ingold, T. 2000. *The perception of the environment. Essays on livelihood, dwelling and skill*. London: Routledge.

Ingold, T. 2016. Reclaiming our university. The Manifesto. https://reclaimingouruniversity.wordpress.com/ (accessed 03/06/2022).

Ingold, T. 2018a. *Anthropology and/as education*. London: Routledge.

Ingold, T. 2018b. One world anthropology. *HAU Journal of Ethnographic Theory* 8(1/2):158–171.

Ingold, T. 2021. In praise of amateurs. *Ethnos* 86(1):153–172.

Jackson, M. 1989. *Paths toward a clearing: Radical empiricism and ethnographic inquiry*. Bloomington: Indiana UP.

Said, E. 1994. *Representations of the intellectual*. London: Vintage.

Weidtmann, N. 2016. *Interkulturelle Philosophie. Aufgaben, Dimensionen, Wege*. Tübingen: Narr/UTB.

8 Experiences from within

Contributions of outdoor education to anthropology

Melanie Greiner

The ontological turn and the work of anthropology

Studying anthropology could arguably be described as one of the most challenging endeavours to undertake in the academic world. There are few disciplines that so persistently, self-critically, and passionately shake the foundations on which they are built. As Tim Ingold states in his book *Anthropology: Why it matters*, for anthropology students, even after years of study, it is possible to know less than when they started (Ingold 2018a:107). As an undergraduate student, I learned that anthropology is about humans and their various ways of living. From evolutionists to functionalists, structuralists, cultural relativists, cultural ecologists, and so on, these variations have been differently explained and evaluated. Humans, however, it is assumed, differ from non-humans because they have Culture. What humans do, what they believe in, how they speak, and how their society and institutions are structured vary around the world, and these differences are mostly seen as the results of diverse cultures. Thus, as a common statement goes: There is one nature and many cultures.

While the nature:culture debate has formerly appeared in anthropology in the guise of a conflict between realism and constructivism, more recent approaches question this dualism itself. Many anthropological case studies demonstrate that the nature:culture dichotomy is not a universal world order across all 'cultures' or 'societies'. Terms like 'nature', 'culture', and with it, numerous presuppositions connected to 'humanity', are contentious (e.g., Descola 2013; Descola and Pálsson 1996; Ingold 2000; Kohn 2013; Viveiros de Castro 1998). As a result, both the concept of Culture as a special characteristic of human beings and cultures as the common research area of anthropology have run into trouble. Across various disciplines, the nature:culture dualism has been replaced by new approaches of socio-natures, nature-cultures, multispecies communities, co-productive lifeworlds, assemblages, collectives, the network, the meshwork, the pluriverse, and more. The foci of research have shifted from humans to trans-species life-forms or socio-natural formations, performances, and practices of worlding, generating, and co-creating the world or even a multiplicity of worlds (e.g., Escobar 2018;

DOI: 10.4324/9781003162773-12

Haraway 1991, 2008, 2016; Henare, Holbraad and Wastell 2007; Ingold 2000, 2011; Kirksey and Helmreich 2010; Kohn 2007, 2013; Latour 1993, 2005, 2013; Law and Lien 2013; Mol 2002; Tsing 2015).

In his after-dinner speech held at *Anthropology and Science, the 5th Decennial Conference of the Association of Social Anthropologists of Great Britain and Commonwealth* (2003), Eduardo Viveiros de Castro argued that the ontological turn "[...] acts as countermeasure to a derealizing trick frequently played against the native's thinking, [...], by reducing it to the dimensions of a form of knowledge or representation, that is, to an 'epistemology' or a 'worldview'" (Viveiros de Castro 2003:13). However, with the ontological turn, problems that had already arisen with the Writing Culture debate (Clifford 1988; Clifford and Marcus 1986; Fabian 1983) are re-emerging. It can be argued that today's anthropologists still struggle with asymmetric circumstances of research and presentations – not of other cultures, but ontologies, or whatever anthropologists decide to call 'it'. Even if the ontological turn is treated strictly as a collection of methodological, analytical proposals, doesn't it foster a priori imperative pre-suggestions about the world? Does it really lead to taking others more seriously than before? The paradigmatic shift from cultural to ontological anthropology is still subject to critical debates (Bessire and Bond 2014; Carrithers et al. 2010; Graeber 2015; Heywood 2017; Holbraad and Pedersen 2017).

Despite the critique, the ontological turn has yet again shaken the foundations of the discipline of anthropology. Participant observation, data collection, comparative analysis, description – anthropological work always seems to be connected to an objectification through which researchers turn away from their research field, their subjects, and their own world of experience. Anthropology itself, therefore, is not free from fundamental problems of scientific inquiry, "for in order to turn the world into an *object* of concern, it has to place itself above and beyond the very world it claims to understand" (Ingold 2011:75; emphasis in the original). Thus, in many ways, anthropological work involuntarily maintains the very dichotomies some anthropologists would like to banish. In this regard, there is also one important aspect that is often overlooked: A large part of an anthropologist's work is educational. Naturally, the discussion about the ontological turn and its rejection of dualisms stretches forward into the study halls of anthropology as a subject, but rarely does it seem to change the practice of its education itself. Field and classroom seem to be worlds apart when it comes to the question of how insights from the ontological turn have changed the discipline, even though, as Ingold (2018b) argues, anthropology and education are basically congruent. Elaborating on basic arguments in Ingold's works (esp. Ingold 2018b, 2011, 2000), this chapter draws attention to the need of reassessing educational practice in anthropology in the light of the ontological debate.

Building-dwelling

Over the last decades, deliberately or not, Tim Ingold has become one of the key figures of the ontological turn. Influenced by his research with and comparative studies of northern circumpolar peoples and hunter-gatherer societies, as well as phenomenological approaches related to philosophy, psychology, cognitive anthropology, and biology, Ingold developed the 'dwelling perspective' and the 'building perspective'. I would like to introduce them briefly to show how the dissolution of the nature:culture dichotomy is related to the topic of education.

According to Ingold's 'building perspective' humans 'build' their world, both materially and ideally, on an external nature, arranging and interpreting it in multicultural ways. Every human perceives him- or herself as a "self-contained individual confronting a world 'out-there'" (Ingold 2000:173), whereas the world and the things within it become the objects of mental constructions and material transformative interventions. Inside and outside world are correlated through the body, which receives stimuli through the senses. The final processing of information takes place almost independently of the outside world in the human mind. While nature is defined as universal physical raw material, the different perspectives of the world are the result of diverging culture-specific cognitive and representational schemes, which are passed from one generation to the next (Ingold 2000:14–15, 40–41, 89–90, 103–105, 178–185).

The 'dwelling perspective', on the other hand, rests on the idea that 'building' is a priori only possible through 'dwelling'. This means that "the forms people build, whether in the imagination or on the ground, arise within the current of their involved activity" (Ingold 2000:186). Hence, thinking, meaning making, making plans, etc., do not take place 'in the head' of an individual vis-à-vis an external world, but world and human evolve together in everyday life activity as an 'indivisible totality' (Ingold 2000:19, 176, 186). Consequently, the idea of humans living as discrete entities in a social world outside of nature does make no sense. In the dwelling perspective, everything is entangled, and former domains, such as ideal and material, are inseparably enmeshed in the process of becoming. In this regard, neither is Culture a special characteristic of humans that sets them apart from other beings, nor are cultures, understood as cognitive and representational schemes, the reason for multiple world views layered upon a universal nature. At most, cultural variations are expressions of particularised ways of being involved within the coming-into-being of the world (Ingold 2000:5, 87, 96–97, 162, 168, 171, 185–188, 200).

Knowing-being

On the basis of his elaborations on the building and dwelling perspectives, Ingold develops two different models of (re-)generating knowledge. According to the 'genealogical model' (Ingold 2011:142, 157–158; Ingold 2000:134–139), biological reproduction is based on the transmission of genes and cultural reproduction is based on the transmission of cognitive representational schemes. In this case, transmission is understood as a transfer from point A to point B, whereby a corpus of information is passed on from one generation to the next, transferred from one person to the other as ready-made packages, or toolkits of instructions, norms, values, responsibilities, explanations, interpretations, or representations. This transfer seemingly happens independently from the actual lifeworld and in advance of its application. Through this 'logic of inversion', "beings originally open to the world are closed in upon themselves, sealed by an outer boundary or shell that protects their inner constitution from the traffic of interactions with their surroundings" (Ingold 2011:68). Knowing about the world and being involved in it seem to be separated in this understanding.

In contrast, in congruence with the dwelling perspective, the 'relational model' (Ingold 2000:97, 140–150, 177–188, 200) is based on the principle that everything unfolds in a continuously developing web of relations. In order to escape the logic of inversion, Ingold follows philosopher Gilles Deleuze and psychoanalyst Felix Guattari's (1987; Ingold 2011:13–14, 83–84) definitions of life as movement, and the organism as lines or bundle of lines. The fabric of the world, then, is "a field not of interconnected points but of interwoven lines; not a network but a *meshwork*" (Ingold 2011:70; emphasis in the original). Beings of all kinds, animate or not, continuously contribute to each other's lines, and by this, to the ever-evolving world. Hence, there are no discrete entities, no pre-existent cognitive and representational schemes, and no self-contained facts. There are only becomings or stories. Following these arguments, 'building' does not mean translating a mental image into material reality, but rather attending to the movements and properties of materials (Ingold 2013). Knowledge, according to this model, is obtained through 'wayfaring' – "a *movement along a way of life*" (Ingold 2000:146; emphasis in original). Instead of understanding education as a transmission from A to B; it is a correspondence of line A with B. Since organisms are the lines of their movements, knowing and being cannot be separated from one another.

Call for a change in (anthropological) education

"By general consent, the organisations of production, distribution, governance and knowledge that have dominated the modern era have brought the world to the brink of catastrophe" (Ingold 2018b:58). With this statement Ingold is in agreement with other scientists associated with the ontological turn who call for a change in the ways of understanding and leading life. Arguing that ontological schemes are (re-)emerging by their way of mediation, this shift needs a re-direction of education. In his book *Anthropology and/as education* (2018b) Ingold fosters a particular understanding of education as well as anthropology which run counter to the mainstream view of educational practice as the inter-generational transmission of authorised knowledge, or an anthropology making studies and theories of other people's lives by using epistemological methods similar to those used in the natural sciences. As already indicated in the previous section on the building perspective and the genealogical model, in both cases the logic of inversion separates the (re-)generation of knowledge from being within the actual lifeworld. It is through this separation that knowledge becomes objective, scientific, and hence, authoritative (Ingold 2011:75, 111, 113–114, 155; Ingold 2000:154, 212–215). To avert the catastrophe mentioned above, Ingold believes it is imperative that both mainstream education and the discipline of anthropology change their course. For him anthropology and education are basically congruent as they enable to enquire and expand the scope of dialogue about the potentials of human life from within. That is to say, both education and anthropology are ways of learning, studying, knowing, and conversing with others – not about vis-à-vis or from a point of view above or beyond the other. This undertaking demands care, responsibility, and humility in face of the knowledge that life and its continuity depends on leading it together (Ingold 2018b:iix–x, 58–63, 70–73).

Ingold sees another major problem in the rising marketisation of science. Constrained by the rules of a neoliberal market, it seems as if academic institutions have lost their educational commitment. Subordinated to a process of commodification, educational institutions increasingly serve as service providers, offering authority-approved content in predetermined ways to their customers, who value it particularly in terms of enhancing their employability. In anthropology too, knowledge production and transmission are more and more driven by the competition for innovation, excellence, and commercial value. No matter if related to research, tuition, or learning, in return for their money, governments, corporations, and other financing bodies expect quantifiable outcomes gained through clearly prescribed procedures. For Ingold these developments thwart the original purpose he intends for education and anthropology (Ingold 2018b:54–55, 70–74, 78).

In accordance with his elaborations on the dwelling perspective and relational model, Ingold promotes a more 'wayfaring-oriented' education which he defines as transformative shared experience of correspondence, a process of 'commoning' – attuning attention along a common line, but without submitting to pre-determined objectives (Ingold 2018b:4, 12–13, 17, 32). However, as Ingold states, nowadays the formal educational and academic system leaves only little room for such an approach. Ruled by the principles of transmission, "students are tied to an institutionalised regime of behavioural and disciplinary constraint, and teachers to the precisely scheduled delivery of a pre-scribed curriculum" (Ingold 2018b:46). In this regard, the discipline of anthropology too seems to be stuck within an institutionalised regime which prevents itself from examining and reassessing its (educational) practice. Not least due to this reason, in the following section, I will make an excursion into the field of outdoor education. Self-reflectively engaging with outdoor education approaches based in Australia and Germany, their diverging teaching aims, methods, and ways of dealing with the nature:culture dichotomy, I explore alternative directions where anthropology might go next.

Outdoor education I: *Experience the Australian Landscape*

Experience the Australian Landscape is the name of an outdoor education programme developed by Brian Wattchow, Mike Brown, and Philip Payne (2008, 2009, 2011) in which I took part as a student when I was on exchange at Monash University in Melbourne. Their approach is based on what they call a 'pedagogy of place' or 'slow pedagogy'. It is the result of their dissatisfaction with conventional outdoor education programmes. Mostly focusing on adventurous, challenging, fun outdoor activities, these basically use outdoor places as backdrop for the enhancement of individual, social, or technical skills. Furthermore, mainstream outdoor education activities aim at achieving fast, quantifiable results, such that learning objectives are already given. This leaves little room for participants to reflect on their experiences, e.g., to examine in-depth how 'the outdoors' is conceptualised, even less so, to develop a deeper environmental, location-related awareness. Concerning the formal education system in general, Wattchow and his colleagues criticise the preference for intellectual knowledge over sensual experience, thereby fostering a disembodiment, displacement, and de-contextualisation of knowledge. Instead, Payne and Wattchow (2009:30) suggest a place-responsive pedagogy, which "works to displace numerous dualisms and disconnections that still abound in environmental education: The body and mind; I, we, and world; self and other; ontology and epistemology". A pedagogy of place, they argue, positions humans within, not upon, the world and fosters an experience of deep immersion. Wattchow, Brown, and Payne developed their own curriculum to adjust to the challenges of a changing world which for them goes hand in hand with growing environmental issues. But instead of taking 'nature' as a given moral high ground, they almost completely let go of any concept of nature, since they are convinced that conventional outdoor education approaches, which, for instance emphasise nature conservation, do not acknowledge how people actually live and experience the world (Wattchow and Brown 2011:88). They argue that, with increasing age, physical experiences come to be subordinated to particular historical-cultural ideas and interpretations which not only seem to precede experience but put a limitation on one's perception. For them, this becomes particularly evident in the resort to an abstract and often controversial notion of nature (Wattchow and Brown 2011:62). The authors prefer instead to concentrate on the concept of place, as it "keeps bringing our attention back to the local, to the specific meanings and experiences that are attached to our embodied experience" (Wattchow and Brown 2011:85). As Wattchow and

Brown explain, students know a lot about global issues, climate change, loss of biodiversity, and social, economic, or political inequalities, but do not know what is happening in front of their own doors. Just as Ingold pointed out with regard to the genealogical model, a gap is inserted between knowing about something and being involved in it. With regard to the ethical question of human responsibility, Wattchow and Brown conclude that a focus on the local is necessary since "significant environmental and social challenges will always be felt and responded to, first and foremost, locally" (Wattchow and Brown 2011:197, 34, 48–49, 71–75, 91; Payne and Wattchow 2009:17, 25–27; Payne and Wattchow 2008:16–17, 27).

The unit *Experience the Australian Landscape*, which I took part in at Monash University combined classroom-based seminars with multi-day hiking trips. As Payne and Wattchow (2008:31) suggest, these components ideally form a slow re-cycling conversation. Before going on excursion, we were asked to reflect on previous environmental encounters, especially earlier childhood experiences, in order to analyse what each participant already knew, assumed, or presupposed in advance of terms like 'nature', 'wilderness', 'landscape', 'place', 'space', and, in general, 'being-in-the-environment'. This process served to expose how experiences had changed over the course of time and what expectations we were carrying into future experiences. Regarding the excursions it was important to the instructors to start at the campus, not – as usual for outdoor education – at a faraway spot, to show how everyday life was connected to other places. In terms of preparation, particular attention was paid to the purchase of local food and a minimum of technical instructions and equipment since risk and physical challenge were rather low and manageable. Last but not least, we were asked to leave nothing but footprints and to document our experiences in a field journal in the form of descriptions, poems, drawings, photos, songs, or film. Throughout the semester we were asked to hand in assignments based on aspects of our learning journeys, possibly, but not necessarily, in the usual academically standardised form of a written assignment.

For excursions, our class was divided into smaller groups, each accompanied by one of our lecturers or their student assistants. Also, during the field trips we had a lot of time to stroll around and follow our own interests. On our first multi-day excursion to Phillip Island, an inhabited island located about 130 km away from Melbourne and popular destination for short-term vacation, different tasks were set up to learn about historical, geological, biological, cultural, and economic aspects in relation to places our teachers pointed out along the journey. The first excursion was characterised by changing weather conditions and a lot of activities such as hiking, surfing, fantasy, and role-playing games. Visiting the local town to get involved with the local community was also part of the curriculum.

Back at the campus, the time between the first and the second field trip was used to reflect about and present our experiences as well as to prepare the next excursion, which this time was largely organised by us. We were

Figure 8.1 Camping on the coast. Photograph by M. Greiner.

instructed to design short teaching units which should then be carried out with the others. The second excursion to Snake Island, an uninhabited, remote island in southern Victoria, was also meant to highlight differences between seasons, weather conditions, and geographical features. For many students, including myself, the second excursion was much more intense and exhausting. Not only because it took place in cool, mostly rainy weather, but also as we walked several days, carrying our heavy backpacks filled with food, water, and camping equipment through wood-, scrub-, and heathland; swampy areas; and mudflats, following more or less existing pathways or the directions given by our instructors. On Snake Island, we did not pass human settlements but entered the heartland of mosquitos, something we experienced on every inch of exposed skin.

Having elaborated on the motivation, structure, and places of this particular kind of outdoor education approach I will now take a closer look at the course's aim, by reconsidering and reflecting on one of the key moments, which became part of one of my assignments.

On a rainy day we went to a coastal bay in order to learn surfing. After our teacher had given us equipment and minimum instruction, I entered the water. The rough surge made me feel human – made of earthly material, but different, because of my body temperature and ability to feel – I felt the

Figure 8.2 Walking together. Photograph by M. Greiner.

immense power of cold waves, tasted the salt in my throat, and the sharp stones under my naked feet. I needed protective equipment, a swimsuit, and shoes, to keep me warm and unharmed. This second skin enabled me to become part of the sea and to enjoy it, until at one point I lost control: A huge wave pushed me under water, twisted me around, and forced me to go with the flow. After this incident, sitting on the beach and taking a rest, I relished the rain falling down on me. What especially attracted my attention were the egg-size stones which were moving back and forth with every wave that was clashing on the beach – *Woosh-Clickclackclickclack-Woosh-Clickclackclickclack* – and I asked myself, how I differ from them. I guessed that the stones were passive, cold objects, from which I differ because I am able to feel, and to think and act in a self-determined manner. I thought that, in comparison to stones, I have a choice. Also, I had the impression that it was me giving the waves, the stones, and the environment its meaning. However, rethinking my field notes in an 'Ingoldian' manner, I might say as well, the place revealed itself to me. The stones moved with the waves, driven by the turbulent sea, and so I perceived them. Although from my experience stones have no consciousness and not the same intentionality of action as I have, they nevertheless interacted with me and influenced my thinking, doing, and writing. I witnessed how they were alive in their own way. In that moment at the beach, I felt completely at ease and immersed within the movement of the world.

Over the years, Brian Wattchow has collected and analysed many field notes from his students. Especially he wanted to know in which situations the relation to a certain place has been felt strongest. He made two significant observations (Wattchow and Brown 2011:112–122): Firstly, students, in the case of a strong place-responsiveness, struggled to put their experiences into words, because there were no words to describe them; and secondly, they felt particularly connected to a place when the perceived boundary between them and their environment dissolved, epitomised in "an experience of the limits of the body becoming porous and a feeling that the place entered the participant" (Wattchow and Brown 2011:117). Wattchow concludes that in order to achieve this kind of familiarity, it is necessary to accept a certain vulnerability by which one willingly opens up to a place. In this way teaching is not restricted to people, land itself is a teacher too (c.f. Raffan 1993). Therefore place-responsiveness cannot be taught by sitting in the classroom alone – by filling students' heads with knowledge – while embodied ways of knowing are completely neglected. To Wattchow and Brown, knowledge is not delivered but emerges within the manifold relations in which people, environment, and places are entangled. For them as educators, it follows, they

Figure 8.3 Rainy day on a coastal bay. Photograph by M. Greiner.

can only shape the opportunity for students to acquire knowledge for themselves by guiding them along the journey of their own experiences. Of course, this means that the outcomes are somewhat unpredictable (Wattchow and Brown 2011:74, 196). This closely resembles Ingold's argument that knowledge is not ready-made, but people "*grow into it*, through a process of what might best be called 'guided rediscovery'" (Ingold 2011:162; emphasis in original). The pedagogy of place developed by Wattchow, Brown, and Payne corresponds with Ingold's approach of a more *wayfaring*-oriented education, according to which the task of the teacher is to lead students out and become attentive. For Ingold becoming attentive carries an ethical dimension, since correspondence trains the ability to be responsive and being responsive, for him, means to care (Ingold 2018b:27–28, 70–71, 73–74). It is this kind of responsibility, care, and belonging that my education teachers also aimed for in their approach (Wattchow and Brown 2011:196).

Outdoor education II: *Natürlich Heidelberg*

In many ways, the above example of outdoor education is easy to reconcile with Ingold's approach because it tries to let go of all kinds of dualisms, a proposition which also hits the nerve of the ontological turn. But how to align it with research in a field in which the dichotomy of nature:culture strongly prevails? In the following section, I want to elaborate and reflect on a second outdoor education programme, which I encountered by doing research on the mediation of 'nature' through activities offered by the environmental education platform called *Natürlich Heidelberg*.

Based on the perception of increasingly serious environmental problems, numerous environmental educational programmes have emerged in Germany since the 1970s. At the core of this development lay the assumption that progress towards a modern industrial nation had been reached at the expense of nature. One of the goals of the first environmental programme passed in 1971 by the federal government was to raise the population's environmental awareness by anchoring topics from environmental planning and nature conservation in the curricula at all educational levels (Becker 2001; Beyersdorf 1998; Deutscher Bundestag 1971:9, 20).

In a sense this was a critique of the existing educational system since it had been unable to provide the necessary knowledge and skills that would have prevented the environmental crisis in the first place. As Yvonne Kehren writes in her study of the education for sustainable development (ESD), the 'ecological crisis' has triggered an 'educational crisis' (Kehren 2016:90–91). Today, environmental education in Germany is broadly understood as part of an ESD. Hence, it is not enough to educate people about environmental issues. New approaches integrate ecological, economic, and social issues equally and foster a holistic, lifelong, transformative education. The focus has shifted towards the interrelations of one's own actions with the lives of other people, future generations, and the planet as a whole, and the development of skills that enable people to take part in shaping a sustainable future. With the resolution of the United Nations on sustainable development as a general principle for humanity in the 21st century, ESD has gained much political relevance (Kehren 2016:93–94, 209–219; United Nations 1992: Agenda 21: Programme of Action for Sustainable Development; United Nations 2015: Transforming Our World, The 2030 Agenda For Sustainable Development).

The environmental education platform *Natürlich Heidelberg* (hereafter abbreviated as NH) was developed in 2007 by Friedrich Kilian and colleagues in the forestry department of the city of Heidelberg. Combining all three dimensions of sustainable development – economy, ecology, society – since its foundation, NH has been recognised several times as an exemplary ESD project by the Commission of the United Nations Educational, Scientific and Cultural Organization (UNESCO). In cooperation with municipal departments, local and regional associations, educational institutions, recreational facilities, farms as well as private individuals, NH offers a wide range of activities from survival, mushroom- and herb-identification courses, introductions to forestry, flora, fauna, geology, cultural history, to extreme sports, life coaching, creative work camps, green action days, theme weeks, and more. Another aspect of the NH programme is to train teachers from school to kindergarten in the fields of forest pedagogy, environmental education, and ESD, as well as to develop, maintain, and expand hiking routes, nature trails, learning landscapes, forest adventure locations, and forest kindergartens (Stadt Heidelberg 2021: *Umweltbildung Natürlich Heidelberg*).

All outdoor education events I participated in for my research, both within the framework of the NH leisure programme and in the course on *Forest Pedagogy for Early Childhood and Elementary Education* offered at the Heidelberg University for Education in cooperation with NH, took place during summertime. Not least for this reason I found most of the activities not only educational, but also recreational, which also aligned with the intentions of the people organising them. Events lasted from one hour to a day and group size was never more than a dozen people. Since I was interested in how 'nature' was mediated through the diverse range of activities offered by NH, it was important to me to get an insight into their programme that was as broad as possible. Usually, events took place at venues outside of the inhabited urban area, e.g., municipal forests, pastures, meadows, orchards, horticultural lands, and vineyards. In this regard, the frequent use of public transportation to get to designated meeting points for NH activities particularly attracted my attention.

On one occasion, the summer heat accumulated on the asphalt and made waiting at the bus stop quite exhausting. When I finally got on the bus, a wave of conditioned air hit me like a slap in my face. While the bus pushed through the busy afternoon traffic, I thought about the question of how 'nature' emerges through its way of mediation. The name of NH plays with the word *natürlich*, meaning 'natural' as opposed to 'artificial', but also

Figure 8.4 Atlas or a human carrying rubbish. Sculpture on the forest adventure trail in the municipal forest of Heidelberg. Photograph by the city of Heidelberg.

meaning ‘naturally’ – though for an anthropologist almost nothing comes ‘naturally’, especially not ‘nature’. The overall aim of the programme, as Kilian states, is “to perceive our wonderful natural space in an enjoyable and educational way and thereby to promote the responsibility of people to act sustainably” (Stadt Heidelberg 2014. NH Programm: 7; transl. M.G.). As emphasised in a personal conversation with the initiator, the programme aims at people’s longings in order to motivate them to go out into the outdoors, to get them involved and (re-)awaken their interest in nature, respectively the natural environment or cultural landscape. Passing traffic light after traffic light, the bus finally meandered its way up the hill into the forest to its final destination. Given this experience, I thought, it was not surprising that so many people I spoke to in my research defined nature as an alternative to everyday work and urban living space, an area to visit in leisure time for recreation and relaxation: 'green', 'quiet', 'undeveloped', 'technology-free', and full of opportunities for activities. However, I thought, does this imply a separation between everyday life and outdoor education experience? Regarding my question, the bus ride I experienced was part of the mediation of 'nature' too: driving out of the built-up city into the forest.

Depending on the activity offered, me and fellow participants walked along forest and meadow paths and occasionally off the beaten track. We stopped here and there whilst our guides told us about rock formations, agriculture, livestock farming, flora, fauna, forestry methods and certification systems, imported tree species, prominent personalities, Roman and Celtic settlements, ancient monasteries and trading paths, National Socialism, power conflicts, memorials of war and colonial times, romanticists, wild boars, and climate change. On the way our guides pointed to related landscape characteristics, sights, ruins, traces, markers, stones, plants, animals, and more. We learned about the meaning of cultural landscapes as hubs of biodiversity, to differentiate between apple varieties according to shape, colour, smell, and taste and prowled through the brushwood searching for mushrooms. We also learned to perceive nature as a teacher and a source of strength as we sat on the forest floor, meditating, listening to the sounds of the forest, and elaborating on the state of trance, the animation of nature, the importance of community, and the balance of life; we held a purification ceremony, burned salvia, hugged trees, and felt their energy and flow of time. We practised walking at a slow pace, expanding our field of vision, behaving bird-like or snail-like, perceiving the forest from the perspective of animals. Overall, we played lots of games enhancing skills such as orientation, mobility, coordination, endurance, strength, speed, creativity, and teamwork. We learned how to plan, implement, reflect, and evaluate child-friendly projects in forest pedagogy and to appreciate the forest as a place of learning. Along the way we perceived our environment in more and more detail and revived what I would call a child-like, open attitude towards experiences.

Through this 'guided (re-)discovery' not only the city of Heidelberg changed its face. I felt, heard, smelled, saw, and tasted what arose from the events, experienced emotional ups – meeting other people, physical exercise, being in the forest, playing games, relaxation – and downs – suffering from bad weather, losing orientation, lacking physical strength, fear of wild boars, collecting scratches and ticks. After years of living here it was only then I realised how much of the city area had slipped my notice, as if I had never really 'got out'. By this I mean that I had never really opened up to it this way, never got involved with, and reflected on the webs of its composition on

Figure 8.5 I'm a snail. Photograph by M. Greiner.

such a scale, about how humans for centuries have been entangled in more-than-human processes of ongoing formation, shaping together not least what I, in this particular case and time, experienced as 'nature'.

With regard to the ontological debate the two outdoor education approaches I presented in this chapter are very different. *Experience the Australian Landscape* has been developed by Brian Wattchow, Mike Brown, and Phillip Payne to approach the challenges of a changing world by directing students' attention to the manifold relations in which humans, non-humans, and particular places are entangled. In order to facilitate an experience of strong place-responsiveness and feelings of belonging, care, and responsibility, they are trying to overcome the dualisms inherent in the ontology of naturalism. In contrast, the environmental education platform NH acts as a service provider of educational, recreational outdoor education activities. Throughout the programme, the notion of 'nature', and with it the nature:culture dichotomy, was not only upheld but continuously (re-)generated in manifold, often inconsistent ways. Other participants; students; instructors; the environmental education platform NH; local, national, and international political institutions; literature on environmental pedagogy or forest education; etc., they all frequently referred to 'nature'. In the search for a more precise definition, I ended up lost in a jungle of terms, meanings, explanations, and references. As much as variable and situational the nature:culture dichotomy was constituted, its core remained untouched. Last but not least, this can be traced back to the historically grown, educational policy within which certain experiences and (re-) productions of 'nature' are conveyed. Following nowadays political agendas, the proclaimed goal is to transform society through a critical reflection and redirection of the relationship between nature and culture – but without dissolving the dualism as such. However, I argue, the educational approach of NH nonetheless corresponds with Ingold's idea of an open-ended, transformational education: It motivates people to go out of themselves; reawakens the senses, curiosity, and perceptiveness; draws attention to more-than-human subjects at hand; and enables participants to reflect on their own role in bringing about more sustainable ways of living.

Coming back to the overall aim of this chapter, in Germany environmental education has taken an interesting turn insofar as it has been recognised that it is not enough to change educational content if you want to bring about change in how humans live. The way in which it is conveyed must be revised too. In recent decades, new holistic, lifelong, experiential learning approaches have been developed that complement and take an influence on educational institutions such as kindergarten, school, or university.

Where anthropology might go from here

Starting from the question of what anthropology is about, I pointed out recent shifts within the discipline caused by the ontological turn. Elaborating on key aspects of Tim Ingold's works, I explored the implications of overcoming dualisms regarding the subject of education as it directly relates to the understanding of being in the world. Nowadays, a lecture called 'Introduction to Anthropology' would look different from the one I attended over a decade ago. But why has this change only affected the content and not the ways of mediation? In this respect, I argue, the consequences of the ontological turn have not yet been considered to their full extent, since education as one of the central aspects of anthropological work has been neglected.

As I wrote earlier, field and classroom seem to be worlds apart. There are many examples from the field that dismantle the universal validity of dualisms like nature:culture, human:non-human, ideal:material, subject:object, theory:practice, mind:body, history:evolution, self:other, and so on that stretch forward into the classroom as a subject of debates, but hardly foster any reflection on the practice of education. How is this possible? As Ingold argues in his book *Anthropology and/as education* a reassessment of mainstream educational practice is urgently needed. This starts with the understanding of education as the transmission of information from one head to another, premised on the model of the self-contained individual learning about a world, cultures, or 'it' 'out there', and continues through the formal processes that create scientific objectivity by abstracting knowing about the world from living within it. However, instead of seeing education as an integral part of anthropological work – meaning that anthropologists should pay the same careful attention to implicit assumptions as is done in relation to fieldwork – it is still often perceived as an inevitable supplement to the anthropologist's actual work (Ingold 2018b:72).

In this regard, Ingold's definition of education offers the possibility to turn away from the logic of inversion, which is keeping the field and the classroom apart, by letting the principles of education and anthropology converge upon a transformative process, in which older and younger generations, teacher and student, anthropologist and the people they work with, are together immersed in striving for correspondence. Moreover, through the process of 'commoning' – by attuning one's attention along a common line – humans not only join with other humans, but also with non-humans, plants, materials, etc. to ensure each other's continuity (Ingold 2018b:iix–ix, 3–4, 11, 38, 72–73). Given this redefinition of education, 'field' and 'classroom', or, in terms of this essay, 'outdoor' and 'indoor', become relative terms. Why, then, have I still turned to 'outdoor' education in search for a new perspective within anthropology?

Just like many scientists associated with the ontological turn, my outdoor education teachers in Australia, and my guides at NH, Ingold as well is trying to find better ways to deal with our fast-changing world. By reassessing the purpose of anthropological work, Ingold develops an ethic of care and responsibility which he wishes educational institutions to adapt. Anthropology, defined as "generous, open-ended, comparative, and yet critical inquiry into the conditions and potentials of human life" (Ingold 2018b:58), suggests a radical openness, an exposure of established positions in order to become attentive to what humans owe to other humans, non-humans, and, in short, everything, which enables the continuity of life (Ingold 2018b:27–28, 70–71, 73–74). In this regard, the excursion into outdoor education has been of particular interest since it allows for an education outside the doors that scholars have become used to keep closed in order to be recognised as proper academics.

References

Becker, G. 2001. *Urbane Umweltbildung im Kontext einer nachhaltigen Entwicklung: theoretische Grundlagen und schulische Perspektiven*. Bd. 7. Schriftenreihe Ökologie und Erziehungswissenschaft der Kommission Umweltbildung der Deutschen Gesellschaft für Erziehungswissenschaft. Opladen: Leske + Budrich.

Bessire, L. and D. Bond. 2014. Ontological anthropology and the deferral of critique. *American Ethnologist* 41(3): 440–456.

Beyersdorf, M., ed. 1998. *Umweltbildung. Theoretische Konzepte – empirische Erkenntnisse – praktische Erfahrungen*. Neuwied: Luchterhand.

Carrithers, M., M. Candea, K. Sykes, M. Holbraad, and S. Venkatesan. 2010. Ontology is just another word for culture: Motion tabled at the 2008 Meeting of the Group for Debates in Anthropological Theory, University of Manchester. *Critique of Anthropology* 30(2):152–200.

Clifford, J. 1988. *The predicament of culture: Twentieth-century ethnography, literature, and art*. Cambridge: Harvard University Press.
Clifford, J. and M. George, eds. 1986. *Writing culture: The poetics and politics of ethnography*. Berkeley: University of California Press.
Deleuze, G. and F. Guattari. 1987. *A thousand plateaus. Capitalism and schizophrenia*. Minneapolis: University of Minnesota Press.
Descola, P. 2013. *Jenseits von Natur und Kultur*. Berlin: Suhrkamp.
Descola, P. and G. Pálsson, eds. 1996. *Nature and society: Anthropological perspectives*. London: Routledge.
Deutscher Bundestag. 1971. *Umweltprogramm der Bundesregierung*. Drucksache VI/2710. Bonn: Bonner Universitäts-Druckerei. https://dipbt.bundestag.de/doc/btd/06/027/0602710.pdf (accessed 07/02/2021).
Escobar, A. 2018. *Designs for the pluriverse: Radical interdependence, autonomy, and the making of worlds. New ecologies for the twenty-first century*. London: Duke University Press.
Fabian, J. 1983. *Time and the other: How anthropology makes its object*. New York: Columbia University Press.
Graeber, D. 2015. Radical alterity is just another way of saying 'reality': A reply to Eduardo Viveiros de Castro. *HAU: Journal of Ethnographic Theory* 5(2):1–41.
Haraway, D. 1991. *Simians, cyborgs, and women: The reinvention of nature*. London: Routledge.
——— 2008. *When species meet*. Minneapolis: University of Minnesota Press.
——— 2016. *Staying with the trouble: Making kin in the Chthulucene*. Durham: Duke University Press.
Henare, A., M. Holbraad, and S. Wastell, eds. 2007. *Thinking through things: Theorising artefacts ethnographically*. London: Routledge.
Heywood, P. 2017. The ontological turn. In *The Cambridge encyclopedia of anthropology*. F. Stein, ed. www.anthroencyclopedia.com/printpdf/132 (accessed 31/01/2021).
Holbraad, M. and M. Pedersen. 2017. *The ontological turn: An anthropological exposition*. Cambridge: Cambridge University Press.
Ingold, T. 2000. *The perception of the environment. Essays in livelihood, dwelling, and skill*. London: Routledge.
——— 2011. *Being alive. Essays on movement, knowledge and description*. London: Routledge.
——— 2013. *Making. Anthropology, archaeology, art and architecture*. London: Routledge.
——— 2018a. *Anthropology: Why it matters*. Cambridge: Polity.
——— 2018b. *Anthropology and/as education*. New York: Routledge.
Kehren, Y. 2016. *Bildung für nachhaltige Entwicklung: Zur Kritik eines pädagogischen Programms*. Baltmannsweiler: Schneider Verlag Hohengehren GmbH.
Kirksey, E. and S. Helmreich. 2010. The emergence of multispecies ethnography. *Cultural Anthropology* 25(4):545–576.
Kohn, E. 2007. How dogs dream: Amazonian natures and the politics of transspecies engagement. *American Ethnologist* 34(1):3–24.
——— 2013. *How forests think: Toward an anthropology beyond the human*. Berkeley: University of California Press.
Latour, B. 1993. *We have never been modern*. Cambridge, MA: Harvard University Press.

——— 2005. *Reassembling the social: An introduction to actor-network-theory.* New York: Oxford University Press.

——— 2013. *An inquiry into modes of existence: An anthropology of the moderns.* Cambridge, MA: Harvard University Press.

Law, J. and M. Lien. 2013. Slippery: Field notes in empirical ontology. *Social Studies of Science* 43(3):363–378.

Mol, A. 2002. *The body multiple: Ontology in medical practice.* Science and Cultural Theory. Durham: Duke University Press.

Payne, P. and B. Wattchow. 2008. Slow pedagogy and placing education in the post-traditional outdoor education. *Australian Journal of Outdoor Education* 12(1):25–38.

——— 2009. Phenomenological deconstruction, slow pedagogy, and the corporeal turn in wild environmental/outdoor education. *Canadian Journal of Environmental Education* 14:15–32.

Raffan, J. 1993. The experience of place: Exploring land as teacher. *Journal of Experiential Education* 16(1):39–45.

Stadt Heidelberg. 2014. *NH Programm 2014.* Leimen: ColorDruckLeimen GmbH.

——— 2021. *Umweltbildung Natürlich Heidelberg.* www.heidelberg.de/hd,Lde/HD/Erleben/Natuerlich+Heidelberg.html (accessed 08/05/2021).

Tsing, A. 2015. *The mushroom at the end of the world: On the possibility of life in capitalist ruins.* Princeton, NJ: Princeton University Press.

United Nations. 1992. *Agenda 21: Programme of action for sustainable development.* New York: United Nations Department of Public Information. https://sustainabledevelopment.un.org/content/documents/Agenda21.pdf (accessed 07/02/2021).

——— 2015. *Transforming our world: The 2030 agenda for sustainable development.* New York: United Nations Department of Public Information. https://sustainabledevelopment.un.org/content/documents/21252030%20Agenda%20for%20Sustainable%20Development%20web.pdf (accessed 07/02/2021).

Viveiros de Castro, E. 1998. Cosmological deixis and Amerindian perspectivism. *The Journal of the Royal Anthropological Institute* 4(3):469–488.

——— 2003. *AND. After-dinner speech at 'Anthropology and Science', the 5th Decennial Conference of the Association of Social Anthropologists of the UK and Commonwealth 2003.* Manchester Papers in Social Anthropology 7. Manchester: University of Manchester.

Wattchow, B. and M. Brown. 2011. *A pedagogy of place. Outdoor education for a changing world.* Clayton: Monash University Publishing.

9 Decolonizing anthropology and/as education?

Antony Pattathu

Introduction

In March 2015, the *Rhodes Must Fall Campaign* at the University of Cape Town in South Africa led to a spark in decolonizing movements around the globe. The activists' demand was to remove the statute of the British imperial mining magnate and colonizer Cecil Rhodes. Within a month, the University of Cape Town decided to remove the statue, but the protest swept over to other universities in South Africa and most prominently also to Oxford, where the protests were centred on the statue of Cecil Rhodes at Oriel College. The demands were not limited to the statue itself but conceived of it as a symptom of the empire in order to address the colonization and exploitation of black people, the dynamics of which still shape the racial inequalities at the university and the colleges of Oxford today (Gebrial 2018:31). Both movements address institutional racism and white supremacy that the protesters have seen and experienced at their universities. In the wake of the protests, countless initiatives to decolonize curricula emerged and campaigns to rename streets and sites dedicated to colonialists gained more ground.[1] The student movements and the academic staff that have taken up the demands of the decolonizing movements have brought the topic of decolonizing anthropology into widespread prominence. Numerous publications preceding the movement, but many more texts published in its wake, address decolonization, speaking about the 'decolonial turn' (Grosfugel 2007; Maldonado-Torres 2007, 2017). In the context of anthropology, Jobsen and Allen referred to the scholarly networks from Africa and the African Diaspora in the 1980s, leading to Harrison's volume *Decolonizing anthropology*, as the 'decolonizing generation', emphasizing the disavowal of formative works (Allen and Jobsen 2016).

It is in this context that Tim Ingold (2018) has published his book *Anthropology and/as education*.[2] The book is an important intervention that departs from classical understandings of anthropology and education as fixed disciplines with top-down methodologies and theories of knowledge, learning and studying. It calls for a change in the way anthropology is

DOI: 10.4324/9781003162773-13

understood by making a case for the discipline's educational potentials that lie in its participatory nature of leading life with others, at the same time showing that education shares the same guiding principles as anthropology, and that characterize the educative process. Paying tribute to the philosopher, educator, and psychologist John Dewey, Ingold reassesses the principles of both disciplines on the basis of Dewey's thinking.

This chapter seeks to learn both from Ingold's (2018) approach and from the decolonizing efforts in anthropology. This might appear at first sight like a hopeless endeavour since the decolonizing project is scarcely mentioned in Ingold's works. Yet, I argue that these approaches can benefit from each other, both in the struggle to enhance the transformative potential of anthropology and in tackling the long-term effects of colonialism that are rooted in the canons of the discipline, in the institution of the university and in the way we teach anthropology. I understand this endeavour as an open process in which both sides will contribute to unearth the critical educative potential of anthropology. This chapter is, then, a form of 'commoning' which I take, according to Ingold, to be a form of sharing, which is both intergenerational and based on the experiences that the commoning parties can bring to their going along and becoming together. In this joining of experiences everyone involved needs to make an effort to find common ground. This common ground cannot be achieved if experiences are neglected or silenced. Commoning arises in relation to variation, which can be understood as the way the characteristics of each commoning party are shaped by time and the environment. Through variation, which gives every party its place, commoning can take place in acts of giving (Ingold 2018:4–6).

This concept of commoning, philosophically described as a way of leading life together, touches on the very predicaments and sensibilities that are necessary for a decolonial and critical education. It evolves out of Dewey's and Ingold's thinking, rooted in education and anthropology, but fails to consider the colonial legacies and complicities that each of these disciplines carries with it, and which can hinder the realization of the very potentials that the concept of commoning can give us.

Guiding principles of anthropology and/as education: Education over pedagogy and participant observation over ethnography

In Ingold's understanding anthropology is "a generous, open-ended, comparative, and yet critical inquiry into the conditions and potentials of human life in the one world we all inhabit" (2018:58). He distinguishes between anthropology and ethnography and makes the case to regard anthropology as education:

> On the side of anthropology, my approach runs counter to the commonplace identification of anthropology with ethnography – to the assumption that what anthropologists do is study other peoples and their worlds.

> What makes anthropology educational rather than ethnographic, I contend, is that we don't so much study others as study with them.
>
> (Ingold 2018:xi)

Ingold identifies here a major commonality between both disciplines, namely the principle of studying *with* people rather than studying *other* people: for anthropology this works through participant observation; for education this is embedded in a participatory practice that works against the idea of a unilateral transmission of knowledge. According to Ingold, it is from this foundational understanding of principles that guide both anthropology and education that the transformative educative potential of both disciplines emerges.

These common principles are reflected in his understanding of the distinction between the field and the classroom in anthropology: "we must repudiate, once and for all, the belief that what goes on in the classroom, under the rubric of teaching and learning, is but auxiliary to an anthropological project whose primary objective is ethnographic" (Ingold 2018:ix). Rather, learning and studying with one another should become the key educational exercise, which bears the same importance in the classroom as it does in the field (Ingold 2018:35).

In a similar vein, Ingold distinguishes education from the idea of pedagogy that, according to him, is based on a one-sided transmission or inheritance of authorized knowledge. He draws on Rancière's notion of the 'myth of pedagogy' to explain how the process of knowing is divided from knowledge, by pedagogues who use their power to ignore other ways of knowing not akin to theirs (Ingold 2018:34). Pedagogy is thereby turned into 'the other' of education, the latter characterized through a participatory process, a mutual attending[3] to ways of knowing and communication. Ingold proposes to conceive of education as exemplary of commoning in the aforementioned sense (Ingold 2018:1–6). He also argues for an appreciation of different ways of knowing that are part of the biographies of people. This makes it pertinent to raise the question of their respective histories and the histories of their environments. If people's biographies and voices are silenced in the dominant forms of history of countries or disciplines (Trouillot 2015), the question arises of how education through commoning can be attentive to these? Part of the answer is to be historically conscious of the colonial relations of power and roots of racism and its exclusionary mechanisms in the discipline and beyond, a historical consciousness and commitment that is expressed by decolonial movements and scholars alike.

Ingold's understanding of education and anthropology through participatory practice, commoning, and attention is based on principles similar to those underlying approaches to decolonizing anthropology. The latter propose a critical education, especially in regard to rethinking the observer-observed divide and the relationships between students and teachers as well as researchers and 'the researched'. Ingold's approach resonates with the core problematics related to such hierarchies of power in the field and the classroom, but he rarely addresses them directly. If anthropology for Ingold is 'philosophy with the people in' (Ingold 2014), then the decolonizing approach can help in merging anthropology and/as education with fostering a decolonial and historical awareness for the people. Ingold takes the route from the inside in his philosophical and phenomenological approach and based on his own experience. He merely implicates outside circumstances through the emphasis on environment and variation. By contrast, decolonizing approaches take as their point of departure questions of power dynamics tied to colonialism, to identities as well as experiences of exclusion, linked to the process of negotiating a certain historical narrative in a specific locality or discipline (Velásquez 2016:x). Even though the aspect of power relations is only addressed implicitly in Ingold's approach, the similarities between both approaches become most visible in the guiding principles and approaches to decolonize anthropology.

Guiding principles of decolonizing anthropology

The project of decolonizing anthropology is not confined to the disciplinary boundaries of anthropology but was and is heavily influenced by the work of decolonial thinkers outside of the discipline. The foundations for decolonizing anthropology were set by Faye Harrison, who was inspired by black feminist and decolonial thinkers. Her ground-breaking edited volume *Decolonizing anthropology* (2010) was, for example, inspired by Thiongo's (1986) *Decolonization of mind* and foregrounds perspectives and scholarship from the global south to address power relations and privilege in the discipline. She and the other authors in the volume also stress the responsibilities of the anthropologist in the field to engage and reflect along with the people they work with about their struggles. As in Ingold's description of the participatory aspects that give education and anthropology their transformative potential, Harrison emphasizes that one of the reasons for the transformative potential in decolonizing anthropology lies in its 'participatory ethic' (Harrison et al. 2017), an ethic that demands accountability for relationships and acknowledgement of the power dynamics that make them possible. More generally, decolonizing approaches aim to unveil the continuing presence of colonial pasts in contemporary universities, as the *Rhodes Must Fall* movement and other initiatives have shown in their collaborative work (Rhodes Must Fall Movement 2018).

Initiatives and scholars in the field have argued, and demonstrated, that decolonizing has the potential to transform both anthropology and the academy more widely. It is an ongoing process and calls for different arguments to be considered (Barnett-Naghshineh and Pattathu 2021; River and Fire Collective et al. 2021). Generally decolonizing aims at wider collaborations between civil society, academia, and politics, with no privileged point of departure (Mignolo 2018:108). As Fanon argued, it is a process that affects both colonizer and colonized. Both sides have therefore to decolonize and take responsibility for this process (Fanon 1963:35–36). This calls for critical analysis of the relations and ways of thinking that are formed, whether locally or on a global scale, by colonialism, empire, and the connected racisms in capitalist societies, which are perpetuated in different forms till today (Bhambra, Gebrial and Nişancıoğlu 2018:2). Decolonizing cannot be understood on a level of universal abstraction (Mignolo 2009:1), or as a blueprint to decolonize x, y, z; it has rather to be thought and taught through its localities. In the academy a critical focus on the processes of translation of forms of knowledge into academic language and hence knowledge production is necessary. Hence, these processes of translation can easily perpetuate a colonial divide, through language barriers and representation: The continuing hegemony of colonial power is most evident in the ways the languages of the powerful are given precedence over the languages of the colonized (Thiong'o 1986; Gutiérrez-Rodríguez 2010; Todd 2016). But it is also visible in the ways specific academic schools, anthropological traditions, or philosophies need to be cited, if work is to be published in certain journals. Here academic knowledge becomes a currency in the publishing and hiring industry, creating social inequality in the global neoliberal academic system. Kawa et al. (2019) have shown how this operates in the context of academic anthropology in the United States.

Since I am myself working on this topic, I am running up against what Sarah Ahmed has called 'brick walls' in the context of diversity work and academic institutions, a phenomenon that has to do with the hardening of histories that, in effect, nurture the institutional settings we move in. Ahmed understands these brick walls in both metaphorical and non-metaphorical senses; in so far as they pose an obstacle for some but not for others (Ahmed 2017:135f.). Decolonizing processes are not about diversity; they are about the histories and structures that have enabled the institution of the university and anthropology to be a predominantly white space[4] (Harrison 2010:1; Brodkin, Morgen and Hutchinson 2011). In the neoliberal university, and in anthropology, diversity has both an enabling and a restricting function, the terminology can bring the question of diversification of student and faculty bodies to the fore, but at the same time it can be void of meaning and rather a shield for the university or discipline to fence off accusations in regard to underlying structural problems, colonial histories, and racism (Ahmed 2012:3). This ambiguous effect of diversity work is also visible for decolonizing anthropology (Jobsen 2020:266–267). Let me elaborate on this.

Since I am engaging in the decolonizing project at my university, I have heard senior colleagues telling me: "Oh decolonizing? Again? Haven't we already done this, isn't that what the writing culture debate has already achieved, can we get anything new from this?" I have colleagues who tell me right out, that to engage in a discussion of decolonizing is a political endeavour – it is not an academic approach but playing at identity politics. By politicizing me in particular, and decolonizing approaches generally, as their *other*, they create the myth that their academic work carries no implicit or explicit political meanings. A resentment sets in even before a real form of commoning can take place. The sheer fact of engaging in the project of decolonizing, and of identifying with these ways of thinking and knowing, creates a 'wall' that stops any form of communication and learning with others. If the university would embrace a decolonial mission statement, I am pretty confident that these forms of politicizing would become less, and an increasing number of scholars would start using the terminology. This is already the case at some universities, where it can lead to turning decolonizing anthropology into a 'fix' that is characterized by gestures towards inclusion, a tick-the-box exercise that does not lead to structural changes in the discipline (Jobsen 2020:267).

The potential I see in decolonizing anthropology and/as education is exactly to pull down this wall between academic positionalities, localities, and responsibilities at institutional and educational levels. Connected to this, questions of colonialism, epistemology, diversity, and racism have to be tackled not only in our publications but also in our academic practices and classrooms, reforming the institutions we plan to be, or are or were, part of. This critical encounter with the colonial past, its power relations, and the question of race in anthropology has not yet translated into extensive changes within the racial and institutional structures of the discipline, also concerning which ways of knowing are allowed and which are dismissed in the classroom and the canon (Lewis 2019; Mogstad and Tse 2019; Sanchez 2019).

Decolonizing anthropology and/as education: Classroom, canon, and curriculum

Classroom, canon, and curriculum are crucial to defining and understanding what anthropology is, how it has been established over the centuries, and how the discipline is formed. Decolonizing anthropology and/as education should not be prescribed but should evolve out of a commoning, as an organic process based on the experience of students and staff. This has happened at many universities, where changes to canons and curricula have been made, in an effort to counter hegemonic Eurocentric narratives by rethinking their respective canons and reshaping them with scholarly works which have been marginalized or ignored due to institutional exclusionary mechanisms. For the canon of anthropology this means re-evaluating classics through decolonial perspectives and thinkers, to create a new narrative of anthropology that engages with its colonial continuities (Allen and Jobson 2016:131).

Decolonizing in the classroom also has to do with unlearning privilege, along with the idea of anthropology as the 'custodian of culture', as Girish Daswani pointed out in an interview (O'Sullivan 2019). When I used the interview to open a class on this subject, it served as a red thread for me and my students to talk about positionality and identity in terms of 'othering'. It also allowed us to scrutinize critically where we go when we do anthropology, and what an ethical relation between an undergraduate student of anthropology and local communities could look like. In my course I recognized that it is important to create a commoning with the students to unlearn the subject-object, researcher-researched divide, by considering our own intellectual genealogies in relation to the canon and the curriculum of anthropology. In this way, students can learn to be people who are humble about their privileges, who can go to another country and share life with local people with an awareness of the fundamental power imbalances and the colonial divides that inform the relationships they create and the questions they might want to ask (West 2016).

These learnings and approaches centring emotions as a core aspect connected to privilege and experiences of exclusion need to be integrated into the curriculum from the very start and over time. In particular, for the classroom, Ingold's referencing of Moten and Harney's concept of hapticality, from their book *The undercommons: Fugitive planning and black study* (2013), is very helpful in this regard: "a way of feeling through others, a feel for feeling others feeling you" (2013:98). It is a form of emotionality, of love, or empathy as Ingold describes it (2018:58). Yet Ingold is silent about the broader context of this concept. Moten and Harney show how hapticality is connected to the transatlantic slave trade from which logistics connected to capital and commodification evolved. For those affected by it, whom they call 'the shipped', denial was part of the need for hapticality: "Though forced to touch and be touched, to sense and be sensed in that space of no space, though refused sentiment, history, and home, we feel (for) each other" (Moten and Harney 2013:98).

What this reading of hapticality shows is the need to recognize denials as part of the experience. This example is emblematic of Ingold's way of addressing power relations. The contexts that explain structural forms of oppression and privilege are set aside to make way for an educative vision of anthropology that is a pure form of becoming from the inside without the "essentialist regression to primordial identity" (Ingold 2018:6).

Yet, people sometimes have to assume identities and claim their histories to gain a voice. Decolonial education in anthropology requires an emphasis on the complicities of anthropology in perpetuating the problems that we want to address or structurally change. We need hapticality and commoning to be a part of the classroom, but we cannot realize them without addressing the history of our discipline. This also means addressing the structural embeddedness of exclusionary moments within the classroom, curriculum, and the canon. The more we discuss the aspects of the colonial legacies of our discipline in the present, the more our students will become attentive to their own positionalities, their privileges, and their role as anthropologists in the world today. It is part of their process of learning and being with others to transfer the lived experience to words, images, and in the end to a published thesis, a book or even a movie. These practices involve power hierarchies which are hard to dismantle, hence thinking about forms of complicity becomes an important part of the educative process.

Moreover, decolonizing approaches ask to what extent the relation to the people that enable the anthropologist's experience can be an ethically responsible one, if they do *not* have the chance to enter the university system, and if their epistemologies and traditions never made their way into the canon of anthropology. These circumstances are well reflected in what Ramon Grosfugel (2016) has written about the 'westernized university', stating that the most privileged people in the canons of social science and humanities are 'western' male thinkers. This creates a knowledge gap and points to a deficit in westernized universities that is symptomatic of horizons that are narrow and provincial even as they pretend, at the same time, to be universal (Grosfugel 2016:29). Although anthropology is full of the most diverse ethnographies and works of scholars from the global south, some of these remain on the sidelines as 'tracking' material that is only cited for their ethnographic content and not for the theoretical advancements they have achieved for the discipline (Harrison 2010:7).

As Boaventura de Sousa Santos (2018) argues, when looking at the way knowledge systems and disciplines have been developed within the university as an institution, it becomes evident that hierarchies of knowledge are strongly influenced by the former colonial ties of researchers and their universities, which have led to countless 'epistemicides' (deaths of knowledge): "Unequal exchanges among cultures have always implied the death of the knowledge of the subordinated culture, hence the death of the social groups that possessed it" (De Sousa Santos 2014:92). Often the anthropologist seeks to translate or capture that knowledge with best of intentions, but at the same time an erasure takes place. Linda Tuhiwai Smith (1999) describes this as the 'ideology of research' that is blind to the fact that the very roots of research stem from colonial and imperial ties which are still active. She contrasts the ideological understanding that research is something done for the greater good with an indigenous perspective: "The word itself, 'research', is probably one of the dirtiest words in the indigenous world's vocabulary" (1999:1).

Like Ingold, Smith and Boaventura De Sousa advocate a shift in the ways of doing research, from knowledge about people to knowing-with people, a knowledge that is 'coknowledge'. De Sousa Santos, who coined the term, cautions that this is only possible if we are willing to participate in the social struggles of the people with whom we plan to create coknowledge, an aspect which is not addressed by Ingold (De Sousa Santos 2018:117, 147).

Whose works we read in our seminars, and the limited number of co-authorships between interlocutors and anthropologists that have been established since the 'writing culture' debate, are only some of the points that need to be addressed from the very start in teaching the coming generations of anthropologists. The quest for a decolonial anthropology and/as education that does not start in the field but in classrooms, canons, and curricula, has to begin with a process of correspondence.

An exploration in correspondence

Ingold's concept of correspondence is one of the foundations of his approach to *Anthropology and/as education*:

> It is the process by which beings or things quite literally co-respond or answer to one another over time, as for example in the exchange of letters or of words in conversation. It is comprised, [...] of the co-dependency of commoning and variation, of the way in which every being finds its singular voice in the sharing of experience with others.
>
> (Ingold 2018:26)

Correspondence is then based on the process of commoning and variation. While the first is close to what Dewey described as communication and connected to the experiences of the commoning people, as described in the introduction, the latter is characterized, in Dewey's words, as the environment changing and developing through time along with the conditions of the educative process (Ingold 2018:5–6).

Ingold stresses that it is not similarities that create an educational community, but differences. In his understanding, differences are prior to modes of identity since they make it possible for students to grow and learn from each other within this educational community. Through correspondence it is possible to create a change in an educational community from within (Ingold 2018:15, 22). It is connected to the biographies of the people who embark on this journey of education. To develop this idea, I would like to turn now to a little exercise in drawing narratives of life together, in the 'educational community' that is created through this volume.

In a recent article (2016), Tim Ingold reveals parts of his own biography from the days of his childhood with his father who was a renowned mycologist, his studies in natural science in Cambridge and his disappointment with the lectures, to the commencement of his studies in anthropology that he describes as a journey home (Ingold 2016:5–6). He draws on his intellectual genealogy describing his thoughts about the organism, connected to ideas of the mycelium leading him to his thoughts about the organism-person and its boundlessness. Debates in the discipline about the relations between biology and anthropology, the 'nature' versus 'nurture' debate, and Marxian critiques of vulgar materialism were important hooks in his thinking, bringing him to reflect on the commodification of science and how he remained true to a childlike enthusiasm for a science that is carried on through engagement with the things in the world. For him, these things are not objects; rather, he is leading up to an ontogenetic analysis that evolves from the inside. In the inside/outside dichotomy that he wants to transcend through this kind of thinking and being in the world (and in the academy), I find a point of correspondence in reflecting on my own biography.

I want to use this reflection on my own positionality as a basis for correspondence, and in order to take another step towards decolonizing anthropology and/as education. A lot of the things that Ingold writes about resonate with my own experience with anthropology, as what my university would regard as an 'early-career researcher'. One difference in our reflections is that Ingold wrote his article when he was about to reach retirement, looking back on four decades of teaching, while I am doing my post-doc looking back at roughly one decade of employment at the university. I see this part as an exercise for a critical decolonial education to reflect and put into practice forms of commoning and correspondence. At the same time, it is an attempt to cast my experiences in a way that might enable a coming together of the two approaches that are discussed here.

My own journey to become an anthropologist also starts in childhood. I was educated at school, by my relatives, and also by growing up in a small town near the French border in Southern Germany. My mother migrated from Kerala in India to support the German health-care sector as there was a huge need for health-care staff in the 1960s and 1970s, but already this worked through a certain narrative of power relations between formerly colonized and colonizers. Germany framed the training of young women as nurses as 'developmental aid' to India, although in practice, it essentially provided cheap labour for the German health-care market. When I was growing up, I had the privilege to have a very loving extended family with three mothers, my biological mother and two social mothers whose families became my extended family. In this way, there was a lot of commoning, correspondence, care, and attention. In the meeting of my parents and my social mothers, strangers joined to lead a life together. I grew up in the midst of all this, interested in the two cultures, the German and the Indian, which are both part of my becoming who I am.

Anthropology was for me the logical consequence of my way of being and becoming since I had effectively been doing, all my life, what it is the main task of the anthropologist to do: navigating, being nurtured, and being excluded, in between primarily two but actually more cultures. Most of my adolescent years were profoundly inspired by black culture and thinking since, in the forms of racism that I experienced, people rarely distinguished between Indian and Afro-Caribbean heritages. I was usually racialized as black in the German context and learned about the particularities of anti-black racism when I went to study anthropology in the United States. In Germany I was often told that race doesn't play an important role anymore in the discipline and that it is much more relevant to analyse class.[5] I focused on ritual and postcolonial studies, medical anthropology, and religion, but I kept thinking about race and colonialism.

Later I learned in the United Kingdom about the importance and contestation, from the 1970s until today, of 'political blackness' for finding voice and recognition (Alexander 2018),[6] and race and equality charters specifically addressing Black Asian and Minority Ethnic (BAME) students adopted by most universities. Yet, such charters do not even exist in the German university landscape. While diversity work in Germany is becoming increasingly relevant, the problems of translating this relevance into lived experience for students and staff at German universities remain ill-defined.

While I have laid out parts of my intellectual genealogy throughout this article, the biographical experiences I describe here, as in Ingold's biography, led to my realizing the need for decolonial thinking and approaches in the university and in anthropology. The relation of colonialism and the established sciences have fostered a deep-seated complicity running through the veins of academic disciplines. This colonial legacy creates a rift between those who are nurtured and privileged by the established body of a discipline and those who are also nurtured by this body, while simultaneously being excluded and racialized by it on the basis of their epistemologies, knowledge, identity, and experiences. Bridging this rift is part of the quest for decolonizing anthropology and/as education and hopefully the beginning of a longer correspondence.

Concluding reflection

The ideas of anthropology and/as education and the concepts of commoning and correspondence are closely connected to my own biography as an anthropologist, and that is why I am inspired to bring them to the classroom. But how can people who are continuously racialized engage in the forms of correspondence and commoning that Ingold describes, when their biographies are characterized by the fact that these very forms of correspondence and communing are denied to them?

To address experiences of denial and exclusion, which are built into the canons, classrooms, and curricula of anthropology, it is not enough to rely on the educative process from within. We need an anthropology and/as education that acknowledges the decolonial challenges we all face and that I have described throughout this chapter. For a critical decolonial anthropology and/as education, this means that it is necessary to become attentive, to recognize the identities, biographies, and histories of people who are marginalized and othered, for example as BAME or Black Indigenous People of Color (BIPOC), in different contexts of predominantly white societies. These categorizations are based on the shared and particular experiences of racism and exclusion along intersectional lines, despite of the abstract character, they remain necessary if people are to gain a political voice. In many ways it is up to these groups to reveal the conditions under which correspondence and communing is denied to them; this is also mirrored in the decolonizing practices and approaches in which BIPOC people are most active and tokenized for their labour (Doharty, Madriaga and Joseph-Salisbury 2020).

The institution of the university that is the ground for our academic projects enables and restricts correspondence in this regard, but it is also complicit, in its neoliberal form, in commodifying academic achievements, student learning, and knowledge production. These arguments and processes need to be part of decolonizing anthropology and/as education, as people still become objectified within and outside of the university. As Paulo Freire, another important educator and philosopher, said about the oppressed: "They cannot enter the struggle as objects in order later to become human beings" (Freire 2000:68).

We need forms of correspondence and commoning within anthropology that integrate these experiences and reflections, by making conscious efforts to transform our canons, curricula, and classrooms in this direction. While our colonial legacies are the brick walls of our discipline, which we have painted with new colours, we might need to leave that old house and find a new, more inclusive, and intersectional home. For that we might have to rethink our commitments and ethics with regard to the decolonial challenge, visible in 'racialized divisions of intellectual labour' (Shilliam 2018) that mirror the colonial legacies in our classrooms, canons, and curricula. Thinking and corresponding about decolonizing anthropology and/as education can bring us one step closer to this new home.

Acknowledgements

I would like to thank Eva Ambos, Annika Bohn, Zouhair Hammana, Max Kramer, and Tim Ingold for their helpful comments and reviews as well as the ongoing discussions on this chapter and the debate on decolonizing.

Notes

1 In the German context there have been broad initiatives of postcolonial and decolonial associations which demand and engage in decolonizing cities, museums, and remembrance culture. One prominent example is the initiative Decolonize Berlin, which brings together many local initiatives working in this field for the last decades in Berlin, in cooperation with the city administration (https://decolonize-berlin.de). Many other cities in Germany have similar initiatives.

2 In this chapter, I focus primarily on the concepts of 'commoning' and 'correspondence' as major points of convergence for both approaches.

3 Attention and being attentive are also central to Ingold's concept of education, and carry a range of meanings connected to care in the sense of stretching towards something, reflecting the etymological derivation of 'attend' from the Latin *ad-tendere* (2018:20).

4 Definitions and conceptualizations of whiteness are manifold. For a basic understanding it suffices to state in this context that whiteness works as a set of power relations, with its identifying noun 'white' as relational identity marker that creates exclusionary forces in its relation to other identities due to its hegemonial characteristics (Hartigan 1997:496; Ahmed 2007, 2017:54, 128; Moten and Harney 2013:55–56).

5 Doharty, Madriaga, and Joseph-Salisbury (2020) describe similar experiences and discussion of this argument in the context of whiteness, institutional racism, and microaggression on an academic staff level.

6 According to the website blackfemaleprofessorsforum.org the terminology refers to women of African, Caribbean, Asian, and Arabic descent to create empowerment, visibility, and solidarity within the group and to improve the situation on all levels for black female academics in the United Kingdom. At the present time, less than 2% of the roughly 18,000 professors in British higher education are black and female. The project is an example of the use of political blackness in academia in the United Kingdom.

References

Ahmed, S. 2007. A phenomenology of whiteness. *Feminist Theory* 8(2):149–168.

———. 2012. *On being included: Racism and diversity in institutional life*. Durham: Duke University Press.

———. 2017. *Living a feminist life*. Durham: Duke University Press.

Alexander, C. 2018. Breaking black: The death of ethnic and racial studies in Britain. *Ethnic and Racial Studies* 41(6): 1034–1054.

Allen, J. S. and R. C. Jobson 2016. The decolonizing generation: (Race and) theory in anthropology since the eighties. *Current Anthropology* 57(2):129–148.

Barnett-Naghshineh, O. and A. Pattathu. 2021. Introduction to the special issue: Decolonizing anthropology: Race, emotions and pedagogy in the European classroom. *Teaching Anthropology Journal* 10(4):1–16.

Bhambra, G. K., D. Gebrial, and K. Nişancıoğlu. 2018. Introduction: Decolonising the university? In *Decolonizing the university*. Bhambra, G. K., D. Gebrial, and K. Nişancıoğlu, eds. Pp. 1–18. London: Pluto Press.

Brodkin, K., S. Morgen, and J. Hutchinson. 2011. Anthropology as white public space? *American Anthropologist* 113(4):545–556.

Clifford, J. and G. E. Marcus. 2011. *Writing culture: The poetics and politics of ethnography*. Berkeley: University of California Press.

De Sousa Santos, B. 2014. *Epistemologies of the south. Justice against epistemicide*. London: Routledge.

———. 2017. *Decolonizing the university: The challenge of deep cognitive justice*. Newcastle: Cambridge Scholar Publishing.

———. 2018. *The end of the cognitive empire. The coming of age of epistemologies of the south*. London: Duke University Press.

Doharty, N., M. Madriaga, and R. Joseph-Salisbury. 2020. The university went to 'decolonise' and all they brought back was lousy diversity double-speak! Critical race counter-stories from faculty of colour in 'decolonial' times. *Educational Philosophy and Theory* 53(3):233–244.

Fanon, F. 1963. *The wretched of the earth*. New York: Grove Press.

Freire, P. 2000. *Pedagogy of the oppressed*. New York: Bloomsbury Academic.

Gebrial, D. 2018. Rhodes must fall: Oxford and movements for change. In *Decolonizing the university*. Bhambra, G. K., D. Gebrial, and K. Nişancıoğlu, eds. Pp. 19–36. London: Pluto Press.

Grosfoguel, R. 2016. The dilemmas of ethnic studies in the United States: Between liberal multiculturalism, identity politics, disciplinary colonization, and decolonial epistemologies. In *Decolonizing the westernized university. Interventions in philosophy of education from within and without*. Grosfoguel, R., R. Hernández, and E. R. Velásquez, eds. Pp. 27–38. Lanham: Lexington Books.

Grosfoguel, R., R. Hernández, and E. R. Velásquez, eds. 2016. *Decolonizing the westernized university. Interventions in philosophy of education from within and without.* Lanham: Lexington Books.

Gutiérrez Rodríguez, E. 2010. *Migration, domestic work, and affect: A decolonial approach on value and the feminization of labor*. London: Routledge.

Harney, S. and F. Moten. 2013. *The undercommons: Fugitive planning & black study*. Wivenhoe: Minor Compositions.

Harrison, F., ed. 2010 [1991]. *Decolonizing anthropology: Moving further toward an anthropology for liberation.* Arlington, VA: Association of Black Anthropologists, American Anthropological Association.

Harrison, F. V., C. McGranahan, K. Roland, and B. Williams. 2017. Decolonizing Anthropology: A Conversation with Faye V. Harrison, Parts I and II. Savage Minds. Uploaded on May 2 & 3, 2016. www.researchgate.net/publication/317804154_Decolonizing_Anthropology_A_Conversation_with_Faye_V_Harrison_Parts_I_and_II_Savage_Minds_Uploaded_on_May_2_3_2016 (accessed 29/08/2021).

Hartigan, J. 1997. Establishing the fact of whiteness. *American Anthropologist* 99(3):495–505.

Ingold, T. 1997. Eight themes in the anthropology of technology. *The International Journal of Social and Cultural Practice* 41(1):106–138.

———. 2000. *The perception of the environment: Essays in livelihood, dwelling and skill.* London: Routledge.

———. 2014. Anthropology and philosophy or the problem of ontological Symmetry. *La Clé des Langues.* http://cle.ens-lyon.fr/anglais/litterature/entretiens-et-textes-inedits/anthropology-and-philosophy-or-the-problem-of-ontological-symmetry (accessed 29/08/2021).

———. 2015. *The life of lines*. London: Routledge.

———. 2016. From science to art and back again: The pendulum of an anthropologist. *ANUAC* 5(1): 5–23.

———. 2017. On human correspondence. *Journal of the Royal Anthropological Institute* (N.S.) 23(1):9–27.

———. 2018. *Anthropology and/as education*. London: Routledge

Jobsen, R. C. 2020. The case for letting anthropology burn: Sociocultural anthropology in 2019. *American Anthropologist* 122(2):259–271.

Lewis, J. S. 2018. Releasing a tradition. *The Cambridge Journal of Anthropology* 36(2):21–33.

Marcus, G. E. 1995. Ethnography in/of the world system: The emergence of multi sited ethnography. *Annual Review of Anthropology* 24:95–117.

Mignolo, W. D. 2018. What does it mean to decolonize? In *On decoloniality. Concepts, analytics, praxis*. Mignolo, W. D. and C. E. Walsh, eds. Pp. 105–134. Durham: Duke University Press.

Mignolo, W. D. and A. Escobar. 2009. *Globalization and the decolonial option.* London: Routledge.

Mogstad, H. and L.-S. Tse. 2018. Decolonizing anthropology. *The Cambridge Journal of Anthropology* 36(2):53–72.

O'Sullivan, S. 2019. Decolonizing the classroom: A conversation with Girish Daswani. *Society for Cultural Anthropology*. https://culanth.org/fieldsights/decolonizing-the-classroom-a-conversation-with-girish-daswani (accessed 30/07/2021).

Rhodes Must Fall Movement, Oxford, Brian Kwoba, Roseanne Chantiluke, and Athi Nangamso Nkopo. 2018. *Rhodes must fall: The struggle for justice at the heart of empire*. London: Zed Books.

River and Fire Collective, A. Pattathu, O. Barnett-Naghshineh, A. Camufingo, et al. 2021. The fires within us and the rivers ahead. *Teaching Anthropology Journal* 10(4):92–109.

Sanchez, A. 2018. Canon fire. *The Cambridge Journal of Anthropology* 36(2):1–6.

Shilliam, R. 2018. *Race and the undeserving poor. From abolition to Brexit*. Newcastle upon Tyne: Agenda Publishing.

Smith, L. T. 1999. *Decolonizing methodologies: Research and Indigenous peoples*. Dunedin: University of Otago Press.

Thiong'o, N. W. 1986. *Decolonising the mind: The politics of language in African literature*. London: James Currey.

Todd, Z. 2016. An Indigenous feminist's take on the ontological turn: 'Ontology' is just another word for colonialism. *The Journal of Historical Sociology* 29(1):4–22.

Trouillot, M.-R. 2015. *Silencing the past: Power and the production of history*. Boston: Beacon Press.

Velásquez, E. R. 2016. Introduction. In *Decolonizing the westernized university. Interventions in philosophy of education from within and without*. Grosfoguel, R., R. Hernández, and E. R. Velásquez, eds. Pp. 4–16, Lanham: Lexington Books.

West, P. 2016. Teaching decolonizing methodologies. https://savageminds.org/2016/07/25/teaching-decolonizing-methodologies/ (accessed 29/08/2021).

Part IV

The life of lines, dwelling and growing

10 Introduction

The life of lines, dwelling and growing

Martin Porr and Niels Weidtmann

The chapters in this section present anthropological and philosophical perspectives on Tim Ingold's understanding of life as constantly immersed and involved in dynamic movement, engagement, and exploration. The world is saturated with dynamic potentials, and organisms live their lives through the creation of lines and pathways. In doing so, they are in continual correspondence with other lines of growth and development. In this understanding, an organism is fundamentally both product and producer of these relationships, and its existence does not precede its engagement with the real world. As outlined elsewhere in this volume (see e.g., Gaffney and Zmigrod), this understanding has crucial consequences for the relationship between biological and social anthropology and for Darwinian or populational approaches towards human evolution (see also e.g., Ingold 2007, 2004; Ingold and Palsson 2013). Here, however, the chapters refer to Tim Ingold's emphasis on a dwelling perspective and the related focus on temporal rhythms that create living spaces, buildings, and landscapes, i.e., the dynamic involvement of human beings in the world, and with the materials and forces that constitute it.

One of the defining aspects of Ingold's work is his rejection of the separation of the social and the biological in the conceptualisation of human beings and other organisms. This distinction is, of course, one of the defining characteristics of the structure of academia and its institutions, which are most often split between the natural sciences and the arts and humanities. It is not possible here to delve deeper into the dichotomising ways in which these fields are often perceived and presented, pitting quantitative modelling and prediction on the one side against interpretation and understanding on the other. Early in his life, Ingold intended to be a natural scientist and, perhaps, to follow in the footsteps of his father, who was a prominent mycologist. He has vividly described his early struggles with academic culture in the sciences and how science teaching at university erased all the fascination and wonder from scientific inquiry itself (Ingold 2016a:7). Anthropology seemed a more appropriate and a more holistic choice. However, during the early stages of his career as a lecturer, he was faced with the dichotomy again.

DOI: 10.4324/9781003162773-15

When he was asked to teach a course on *Environment and Technology* from 1974 onwards, and subsequently on *Environment and Economy*, the relationship between ecological and social aspects of human practices needed to be reinterrogated.

During this time, anthropology was successively dominated by the theoretical frameworks of neofunctionalism, cultural ecology, and neo-Marxism, which all conceptualised the relationship between ecological and social relationships in different ways. Ingold's major contribution in this context is the book *The appropriation of nature* (Ingold 1986), which – according to its subtitle – makes a fundamental distinction between 'human ecology' and 'social relations'. Shortly after the publication of this book, Ingold realised that such a perspective is untenable and "that the model of the human being as one-part organism and one-part person was not even an approximation to the truth" (Ingold 2016a:14–15). To progress beyond this would require a fundamentally different approach, which prioritises fields of relations over populations of individuals. It necessitated a move away from essentialist towards relational thinking. The early 1990s consequently marked a significant turning point in Ingold's work. From this time onwards, he increasingly explored approaches inspired by developmental biology, ecological psychology, and phenomenology, and authors such as M. Heidegger, H. Bergson, G. Bateson, and J. J. Gibson (see esp. Ingold 2000). In his most recent work, he has moved towards an even stronger relational ontological understanding, partly in correspondence with the writings of G. Deleuze and F. Guattari, and K. Barad (Ingold 2011, 2015, 2021).

It is not possible to cover all aspects of Ingold's later work here, and we will restrict ourselves to one core element only. Fundamentally, to move beyond the distinction between the social and the ecological meant that a range of anthropological and philosophical concepts had to be rejected or redefined. Ingold (2016b) invites us to think every living being as "a line or, better, as a bundle of lines" (10). It is part of an open-ended meshwork that consists of myriads of lines without beginnings and endings. Organisms are knots in this meshwork of interwoven lines (Ingold 2011:70) in which beings and materials contribute to each other and can, therefore, not be viewed as bounded or self-contained entities. There are only storied becomings (Ingold and Palsson 2013). To understand human actions in the world, Ingold proposes a focus on the confluence of forces and materials in which actors intervene, and from which artefacts emerge. In such an understanding, objects cease to exist as independent and static entities, tending rather to dissolve into dynamic flows of materials. This is a world of perpetual becoming and co-responsiveness. It requires a recalibration of the idea of ecology as well as the study of the interrelationships of things and actors in the world. Ingold's understanding of ecology is intentionally broad and encompasses the ecology of life, of materials, of learning, and so on (e.g., Ingold 2012, 2016b). Humans and other actors only exist through processes of involvement as they create their pathways through the world. Ingold (esp. 2000) has termed such an orientation the 'dwelling perspective'. It views the human being as constantly becoming with the environment. In this, processes of making and growing become indistinguishable.

These considerations, however, should not only be applied to the subjects and objects of anthropology, archaeology, or other academic disciplines. These practices are a part of the world and its continuously evolving meshwork. Consequently, research itself must be understood as an act of dwelling. It entails involvement and engagement. The archaeologist follows the assemblage and flow of things and materials in the landscape and in the soil. The interest of the archaeologist is directed at understanding the stories that have created and continue to create the landscape. It is about understanding how past populations have formed and shaped it. These are not acts of scientific detachment and analytical separation but "of engaging perceptually with an environment that is itself pregnant with the past" (Ingold 2000:189). Accordingly, anthropology becomes an inquiry that moves along with those that are studied. It participates in their lives and their activities in a mutually responsive fashion. In this way, research is no longer detached from its contexts and its subjects but becomes deeply involved and invested (Ingold 2016b:11). In consequence, it needs to be conducted with deep care and responsibility.

References

Ingold, T. 1986. *The appropriation of nature. Essays on human ecology and social relations*. Manchester: Manchester University Press.

——— 2000. *The perception of the environment. Essays in livelihood, dwelling and skill*. London: Routledge.

——— 2004. Between biology and culture: The meaning of evolution in a relational world. *Social Anthropology* 12(2):209–221.

——— 2007. The trouble with 'evolutionary biology'. *Anthropology Today* 23(2):13–17.

——— 2011. *Being alive. Essays on movement, knowledge and description*. London: Routledge.

——— 2012. Toward an ecology of materials. *Annual Review of Anthropology* 41:427–442.

——— 2015. *The life of lines*. London: Routledge.

——— 2016a. From science to art and back again: The pendulum of an anthropologist. *Anuac. Rivista dell'Associazione Nazionale Universitaria Antropologi Culturali* 5(1):5–23.

——— 2016b. On human correspondence. *Journal of the Royal Anthropological Institute (N.S.)* 23(1):9–27.

——— 2021. *Correspondences*. Cambridge: Polity Press.

Ingold, T. and G. Palsson, eds. 2013. *Biosocial becomings. Integrating social and biological anthropology*. Cambridge: Cambridge University Press.

11 Making (of) ecology

Philosophical perspectives on Tim Ingold

Ralf Gisinger

> In the analysis of concepts, it is always better to begin with extremely simple, concrete situations, not with philosophical antecedents, not even with problems as such (the one and the multiple, etc.). [...] I have only one thing to tell you: stick to the concrete, and always return to it.
>
> (Deleuze 2006:362–363)

In a letter to Jean-Clet Martin in 1990, French philosopher Gilles Deleuze (1925–1995) writes about his methodology, specifically from where to start philosophical investigations, which in his opinion should always centre around creating concepts (Deleuze and Guattari 1994:5). Although philosophy has to conceptualise through abstraction (maybe even its unique distinct feature), this illustrates one of the most common traps when doing philosophy. Speaking with Deleuze, philosophers develop 'pure concepts', but these are "inseparable from the passage from one concept to another" (Deleuze 2006:363). Thus, when examining a (philosophical) concept like multiplicity, Deleuze recommends starting with concrete questions (what is a pack (not a lone animal), what is an ossuary, what is a relic?) or examine the relationship between humans and animals, when talking about mimesis (Deleuze 2006:363). As I will show in the following text, Deleuze's demand can for sure be traced in the work of the anthropologist Tim Ingold, who is able to maintain a productive dialectic tension between the concrete and the abstract that should inspire philosophical texts as well as he did in his original field of anthropology.

Ingold's oeuvre and innovative approach, especially his theses on lines, making, dwelling, skill, or ecology serve as an integrating factor for disciplines like anthropology, archaeology, art, or architecture, where he has been widely received in the last few decades. Although Ingold derives many of his concepts explicitly from philosophical texts (e.g., Heidegger, Deleuze/Guattari, Merleau-Ponty, Bergson, Whitehead, Simondon) and also critically engages in contemporary philosophical discourses (Latour, Harman, Barad, Bennett, just to name a few),[1] he has not yet been a focal point of philosophical analysis. When Deleuze, as cited above, advises his philosophical

DOI: 10.4324/9781003162773-16

peer Martin to always start with the concrete, this seems like a paradigmatic instruction as to what a synthesis of anthropology and philosophy could look like and, as I will show, in this sense Ingold's work serves as a perfect example for such an interdisciplinary entanglement. Hence, I want to outline some examples where Ingold takes and creates philosophical concepts (consequently is *doing* philosophy),[2] further I will argue that Ingold's research should be vital for philosophy, in particular for philosophies of ecology, relational ontologies or materialist approaches. In a last step, I highlight some of the political implications of Ingold's research and plead for a so far neglected focus on the political through and with Ingold's ecologies.

I explicitly don't want to situate Ingold's texts in the field of anthropology or critically engage with his work from the standpoint of anthropology. But I take some of the philosophical themes, concepts, and references to achieve an interdisciplinary resonance of concepts that can be found in the work of Tim Ingold: A space of reciprocal resonance, where we are following the lines and traces of notions and ideas that transgress disciplinary boundaries. Methodologically, what Ingold calls resonance (Ingold 2000:199ff.) – and what we already can find in Simondon (1995:31) or Deleuze/Guattari (1994:23) – is much more than an academic text or a translating process between different fields. It is an attitude towards the world, an embodied *praxis* of correspondence/entanglement with the environment, with human (but also non-human) actors and things.

In what follows, I begin by outlining some reflections about "doing philosophy" as the creation or making of concepts (after Deleuze/Guattari). Although it is evident that Ingold at least in this sense is doing philosophy, I will focus on some innovative shifts that Tim Ingold's work provides, concerning his view on ecology and some of the concomitant philosophical premises and consequences: Ingold's focus on becoming, his rejection of the hylomorphic model, his ecology of materials and things as well as the in-between of relationality and ecology – *making* ecology along the lines of a life.

Making concepts: A philosophical operation

My aim with philosophical perspectives on Ingold's work is to create prospects for philosophy after Ingold by following his eclectic and prolific account of the material world and culture that deconstructs common Western dichotomies like subject–object or nature–culture/artifice. Ingold not only takes concepts from philosophy and enriches them with examples from an anthropological point of view, he himself makes philosophical contributions in the sense in which Deleuze/Guattari define in their last book *What is philosophy?* as the basic and most important philosophical operation: creating concepts. In their view, concepts do not simply reveal themselves to a philosopher (or anthropologist) as given; rather, their genuine task is to create (in a Nietzschean sense) concepts or, as Deleuze/Guattari also put it, to *make* concepts (Deleuze and Guattari 1994:5). This *creation* or *making* of concepts should in no way be mistaken for a voluntary act of a subject or a singular human being (author, philosopher, scientist, artist …).[3] A concept consists necessarily of components (more than one), combines them and therefore functions as a multiplicity (Deleuze and Guattari 1994:15). In the work of Ingold, one precisely encounters this (from the standpoint of philosophy) literally *creative* method.

In the following sections, I will briefly present these *concepts in the making* mainly with the example of 'ecology': Why ecology? Ingold can be a reference point for innovative ideas centred around 'neo-ecological thought' (Hörl 2017:6) and its transgression, because he himself uses ecological concepts to illustrate relationality and becoming (e.g., ecology of life, ecology of materials, or ecology of correspondence). *Ecology* was originally coined by German biologist Ernst Haeckel in 1866: "By ecology, we mean the whole science of the relations of the organism to the environment including […] all the 'conditions of existence'. These are partly organic, partly inorganic" (Haeckel 1866:286. trans. Robert C. Stauffer 1957). With the proliferation of ecology, especially in the last decades, we must reflect different meanings and uses of the concept. Firstly, ecology as a subdiscipline of biology focuses on these 'conditions of existence' as well as environments of organisms (but also extends to whole ecosystems); secondly, ecology has been adopted and appropriated in many other fields of study, both literally in its original sense (conditions of existence, environments, relations) and as a metaphor for complexity, connectedness, or interdependence (Bühler 2016:1–26). This proliferation of ecology – generalisation of ecology (Hörl 2017) – is a prime example of a concept that expands and extends its own boundaries by its significance, as it sprawls rhizomatically through all scientific disciplines, political discourses, or arts. Hence, ecology either disseminates in its meaning and relevance, or such an appropriation in different fields opens new possibilities and indicates an insistence of the concept. As Deleuze/Guattari would say: "[The concept] is not formed but posits itself in itself – it is a self-positing" (Deleuze and Guattari 1994:11) combined with creating and *making*.

But Ingold thinks of making much more along the lines of concrete, life-world practices. As Hörl puts it, Ingold has pushed paradigmatic turns in anthropology ('material culture', 'symmetrical anthropology') further and beyond himself by radicalising the question of 'making' (Hörl 2016:46). 'Making' for Ingold has to be understood as a process of growth (Ingold 2013:21) to take into account movements and the becoming of materials, and he positions himself against the hylomorphic model as well as preconceived concepts like subject, object, matter, or form – Ingold locates the problem in the static unification of becoming, processes, movements. "To read *making* longitudinally, as a confluence of forces and materials, rather than laterally, as a transposition from image to object, is to regard it as such a form-generating – or *morphogenetic* – process" (Ingold 2013:22). Ingold thinks *with* or *from* (the materials, the body), not *about* – he tries to follow the materials or what he calls the "matter-flow" (Ingold 2012:437).

Occurrences: Ingold's theory of becoming

Prioritising becoming, processes, motion before being, fixed substances, essences, or stasis is traditionally undervalued in Western thought, even though it could build on a long intellectual tradition of Heraclitus, Lucretius, Nietzsche, Heidegger, Bergson, Whitehead, Merleau-Ponty, or Deleuze. Ingold, too, proposes an ontology of becoming (instead of being), which has not being of being (Heidegger's 'Sein des Seins') at its core, but the becoming of being: becoming *is*. Such an ontology of becoming that also operates under names like event ontology or process ontology is mainly present in continental philosophy – Ingold's main references.[4]

In his critique of Graham Harman's OOO (object-oriented ontology; Harman 2017), Ingold notes that things do not just exist, they *occur*, they carry on along their lines (Ingold 2015:16). This means to grasp nature and matter as interactions (and repetitions) of events and processes (of material and forces), not as fixed form/matter in the hylomorphic model.[5] He develops an ontology of lines, but as a *life* of lines (instead of blobs), taking into account their flow. Ingold proposes an entangled world of knots or a world without objects (WWO against OOO) – a world of things (Ingold 2015:16). A life of lines follows Simondon's ontology that is ontogenesis (Simondon 1995:21ff.) and thus constitutes a theory of becoming around concepts like the line, the crease, the fold. Philosophically, this seems to align with a Deleuzian understanding of immanence (against transcendence), which he connects in his last text *Immanence: A Life* with vitalist principles (Deleuze 2001a). Subsequently, Ingold presents a form of vitalism that is *a* life in contrast to *the* life (Ingold 2015:143f.). The 'a' points to a virtual, impersonal, immanent field – Deleuze's 'transcendental empiricism' – where determination and identification have not taken place yet (Deleuze 2001a:26).

It is important to distinguish Ingold's focus on occurring instead of existing (Ingold 2008:1808) from a theory of the event, which plays a very important role in Heidegger's philosophy as well as in many post-Heideggerian philosophies and in French poststructuralism (e.g., Heidegger, Whitehead, Badiou, Deleuze). This is not a distinction *in kind*, but Ingold starts from a different point, where we can understand an occurrence much more casual than how an event often is characterised in a post-Heideggerian philosophical tradition (but also for example of Badiou or Deleuze). Unlike their theories of the event, Ingold's occurrence emerges not as an unpredictable, singular, and perturbating rupture or caesura, but instead starts from concrete practices in daily life. However, Ingold also ends up with ontologies (or ontogenesis) of the line (Ingold 2015:16), of immanence (Ingold 2000:422), of becoming, of movement. Deleuze illustrates those connections of becoming, line, and immanence with the example of music (as Ingold quite often likes to do) to show the fundamental difference between becoming (immanence) and development (transcendence):

> Is it by chance that music only knows lines and not points? It is not possible to produce a point in music.[6] It's nothing but becomings without future or past. Music is an anti-memory. It is full of becomings: animal-becoming, child-becoming, molecular-becoming. [...] Immanence. It is exactly the opposite of development, where the transcendent principle which determines and structures it never appears directly on its own account, in perceptible relation with a process, with a becoming.
>
> (Deleuze and Parnet 2007:33)

From hylomorphism to an ecology of materials and things

Ingold strongly opposes the Aristotelian hylomorphic model that emanates from the fundamental distinction between form (μορφή/morphḗ) and matter (ὕλη/hylē), thus he proposes another constitutive world-making relation: "the essential relation in a world in formation [...] is not between form and matter but between forces and materials" (Ingold 2013:45). The prioritisation of finished artefacts over properties of materials (Ingold 2012:427) is a problematic aspect of traditional Western thought with far reaching consequences regarding the *objects* of analysis not only in anthropology or archaeology, but also in philosophy. Instead of the materiality of things, Ingold is concerned with the properties of materials, which leads to what he calls an 'ecology of materials' (Ingold 2016). Ingold takes primarily from French Philosopher Gilbert Simondon (1924–1989) that the actual form-taking activity lies in the materials (Simondon 1995:37ff.). The examples of brickmaking (Simondon) and metallurgy (Deleuze/Guattari) show that the distinction between made artefacts and natural, grown organisms is blurred: *making* is to follow the (matter-)flow of materials (Ingold 2013:25). The shift from a hylomorphic model to materials/forces (with a focus on their genesis and mutations) offers a perspective beyond a static comprehension of the world and its human or non-human inhabitants that breaks with the subject–object distinction in favour of environmental and relational thinking.

As I elaborated before, ecology is traditionally understood as the science of the relationship of organisms to their environment, namely their organic and inorganic conditions of existence (Haeckel 1866). In Ingold's texts, ecology is transformed not only because of the necessary relational character of beings (relational ontology) or the dissolution of the subject–object dichotomy, but also because everything becomes a *thing*, whereat *things* are understood as "gatherings of materials in movement" (Ingold 2012:439). Even though there are some parallels and similarities between Ingold's position and some strands of 'new' materialism or so-called realist ontologies (e.g., opposition to subject–object dualism or the insistence of materials), where everything is conceived as objects, for example Harman's object-oriented ontology

(Harman 2017) or Timothy Morton's 'hyperobjects' (Morton 2013), one of the fundamental differences lies in Ingold's distinction between object and thing, which leads to his strong opposition to Harman's OOO.

Ingold's theory of the thing is obviously highly influenced by later texts of Martin Heidegger (1889–1976), mainly 'The Thing' and 'Building Dwelling Thinking', where Heidegger stresses the function of gathering or assembling for *the thing* (Heidegger 2001a:151) and also questions how things are *made*: "When and in what way do things appear as things? They do not appear *by means of* human making" (Heidegger 2001b:179). Furthermore, we and the world we live in are thing-ed [be-dingt], which means also conditioned and contingent (Heidegger 2001b:178). Ingold centres around this gathering aspect of the thing in a Heideggerian sense but cleared from some of Heidegger's mythical overtones (e.g., the fourfold): "Every thing, for Heidegger, is a gathering of materials in movement – a particular knotting together of the matter-flow – and to witness a thing is to join with the processes of its ongoing formation" (Ingold 2012:436).

For example, the body does not only interact with things but is a thing itself. Bodies correspond with their environment, they take materials in, process and discharge them – they 'leak', which indicates their necessary openness towards their surroundings. Therefore, Ingold's "shift of perspective from stopped-up objects to leaky things distinguishes the ecology of materials" (Ingold 2012:438). This shift implies that the world we *live* in cannot be totalised as an aggregation of things, but things exist (or occur) along the lines and flows of life. If we understand the thing in a Heideggerian sense as a focal point for assembling, then the Deleuzian/Guattarian concept of 'assemblage' [agencement] could be also useful, as I will show later with the example of nature.[7] Understanding the world as assembling assemblages – a multiplicity of assemblages – in any case goes beyond an aggregation of things and takes into account relationality.

Ecology of life

To engage with ecology (and its philosophical as well as political implications) means thus to look at the material conditions of existence (technical, economic, social, political) of humans and their 'milieus' (Deleuze and Guattari 1994:100) and to question their central positioning (anthropocentrism) through their embeddedness and entanglement in their environmental and material relationships. By dissolving the human in non-human structures (in the Hegelian sense: *Aufhebung*), a new image of thought emerges that proceeds in a non-subject-centred manner and undermines the seemingly self-evident division into subject and object (Deleuze and Guattari 1994:85; Harman 2017)[8] or what Ingold calls the "initial ontological dualism between the intentional worlds of human subjects and the object world of material things" (Ingold 2000:44). Through the lens of ecology and relationality, the subject is decentred through its material relations to environment (non-human, non-living), which must also include an ecology of thought, desire, and affects – in Deleuze's interpretation of Spinoza an 'ethology' (Deleuze 1988:122ff.), i.e., relations and capabilities of bodies or materials (to affect and to be affected) (Spinoza 1994): "*Affects are precisely these nonhuman becomings of man, just* as percepts [...] are *nonhuman landscapes of nature.*" (Deleuze and Guattari 1994:169; emphasis in original). Philosophy, according to Deleuze/Guattari, also means not to understand thinking as a (human) outside, from which 'nature' is contemplated or reflected upon, but rather creating assemblages of enunciation and affecting thought – thinking itself must become nature. This relation of mind and thought to nature is precisely what Ingold tries to describe with reference to Gregory Bateson's 'ecology of mind' (Bateson 1972) as 'ecology of life'. Bateson suggests, the "mind should be seen as immanent in the whole system of organism-environment relations in which we humans are necessarily enmeshed, rather than confined within our individual bodies *as against* a world of nature 'out there'" (Ingold 2000:16). But Ingold wants to go a step further, because Bateson still perpetuates what Ingold calls the "most fundamental opposition of all, between form and substance" (Ingold 2000:16): the hylomorphic model. Therefore, Ingold's ecology of life tries to treat the "organism plus environment" not as "a compound of two things, but one indivisible totality" (Ingold 2000:19). The question is, how to think this ecological totality without dissolving its inner differences and heterogeneity, for what I propose the notion of assemblage/*agencement*.

Which philosophy of ecology? Different concepts of nature

As stated before, with the proliferation of ecology there comes a certain ambiguity of the concept itself concerning mostly the respective underlying framing of nature. So which ecology are we talking about? A common understanding of the concept follows for instance the groundwork of 'deep ecology', coined by Norwegian philosopher Arne Næss (1912–2009), who carves out a possible relationship between philosophy and ecology. In the following, I will briefly present Næss' deep ecological approach as an example of a philosophy of ecology that builds on relationality, explain what concept of nature it is based on and why I would argue against such approaches. The terminology of Næss' 'deep ecology' (1989) distinguishes 'ecophilosophy' as the descriptive characterisation of the common problems of ecology and philosophy from ecology, which could be characterised according to the maxim "everything is connected with everything" (Næss 1989:35). This definition of ecology as fundamental connectivity, which may seem somewhat simplistic, can nevertheless be found in many ecologically inspired philosophies, ontologies, or epistemologies, and illustrates in a concise manner both the problems and the potential of the concept of ecology for philosophy. Although relation and relationships have to be a cornerstone of a philosophy of ecology (and its corresponding ontological, epistemological, or materialist premises), it makes more sense to focus on what Anna Tsing calls 'disturbance-based ecologies' (Tsing 2015:5) as opposed to romanticising concepts of nature of the kind that Næss indulges. Thus, my aim is, first, to emphasise with Nancy and Neyrat that connectedness always includes or even presupposes a form of separation, division, or spreading (Nancy 2015, as well as Neyrat's 'ecology of separation' (Neyrat 2017)) and second, to oppose a 'return to nature', a preservation of 'nature', or harmonious concepts of nature (Nancy 2008; Massumi 2009) and at the same time avoid imaginations of totality and completeness.

In this sense, Ingold may serve as a building block for such a philosophical position regarding ecology.

> I think it would be fair to say that in the scientific mainstream, ecology is still premised on a fundamental (and unaddressed) division between universal humanity and natural biodiversity, as if we humans were looking at (or intervening in) nature from without.
>
> (Ingold 2016:91)

This quote reveals two problems in the concept of nature that are intertwined but still conflicted: first, that nature is opposed to humanity, culture, society, or technology; second, that it is an abstract totality, detached from concrete processes, materials, practices. Human beings, of course, do not exist outside of nature, but this is not the only resignification regarding the notion of ecology that Ingold undertakes. For Ingold, ecology is not the study of organisms and their environments, but he aims for a broader understanding of concepts like nature, organisms, things, objects, humans, non-humans, society, and their relations (in-between): "both ecology and sociology merge in the study of the life of lines" (Ingold 2015:12). To reconcile these two aspects of nature, I build on Deleuze's/Guattari's concepts of assemblage [*agencement*] and multiplicity [*multiplicité*], as mentioned before, as a paradigmatic expression of an eco-philosophical concept of nature. Assemblages/*agencements* allow us to think in terms of the combination of nevertheless heterogeneous elements – but always on the same plane of immanence and becoming, which are supposed to enable relationality without totalisation.[9] In a very recent essay Ingold fittingly takes up the Deleuzian/Guattarian concept of *agencement* precisely to show a difference between assembling (additive relation) and gathering (conjunctive relation) which constitute two sides of *agencement* (Ingold 2020a:22).

On the basis of *agencement*, it is possible to develop an understanding of ecology that opposes the totalisation of nature, the earth, the planetary by understanding it as an ensemble of relationships, but neither regressing to an embellishment or idealisation of tribalism and nativism, nor evoking a natural state of 'planetary environmental sovereigns' (Luisetti 2018:4):

> Nature must be thought of as the principle of the diverse and its production. But a principle of the production of the diverse makes sense only if it does *not* assemble its own elements into a whole. […] Nature as the production of the diverse can only be an infinite sum, that is, a sum which does not totalize its own elements. There is no combination capable of encompassing all the elements of Nature at once, there is no unique world or total universe. *Physis* is not a determination of the One, of Being, or of the Whole. Nature is not collective, but rather distributive, to the extent that the laws of Nature […] distribute parts which cannot be totalized. Nature is not attributive, but rather conjunctive: it expresses itself through 'and', and not through 'is'
>
> (Deleuze 1990a:266–267)

With and beyond Spinoza's concept of nature, Deleuze thus shows the necessity of assembling (AND[10] – with Ingold – gathering) without totalising and outlines a relational ontology that has to be(come) ontogenesis.

Making ecology along the lines of a life

Ingold develops his thinking along the lines of concrete practices ('making')[11] that can help us understand the world in a holistic way against abstract and totalising categories. His use of concepts like meshwork, weaving, knots, etc. point to an understanding of the world that proposes ontogenesis instead of ontology. "We are not in the world, we become with the world; […] We become universes. Becoming animal, plant, molecular, becoming zero" (Deleuze and Guattari 1994:169). With Ingold, becoming takes a specific form of 'world-making' that is always making and remaking (Hörl 2016:45). Not to *be* (ecological or environmental), but always a *becoming* in the form of an imperative: Making ecology!

Whereas Latour's ANT (actor–network–theory) and also his political ecology are too static for Ingold's neo-vitalism/animism (he instead proposes, a little tongue-in-cheek, SPIDER – 'Skilled Practice Involves Developmentally Embodied Responsiveness'),[12] approaches like Jane Bennett's *Vibrant matter. A political ecology of things* (2010), for Ingold, operate with a problematic concept of agency (Ingold 2011:89ff.; Ingold 2013:96). Neither humans nor things (one should ask, if actually human beings are not things?) possess agency, they are possessed by action (Ingold 2016). When we talk about 'making', ordinarily we would presuppose an (human) actor who makes, thus possesses agency. What Ingold calls 'making' implies not a precedent subject or an actor who (intentionally) makes, but subject and object are always 'made' as well as embedded in a woven web of becoming, growth, lines… of life. Following Jean-Luc Nancy, Ingold proposes a kind of "action without agency, a doing-in-undergoing, an auto-fabrication, an anthropogenesis" (Ingold 2015:145).[13]

In-between relationality and ecology

Is there an intrinsic connection between ecology, environmentalism, and relational ontologies? Relationality has been shown to be a main component of many neo-ecological approaches: "ecological rationality is characterized by its radical revaluation of relationality" (Hörl 2017:6). Along these lines, Ingold proposes a synthesis of " 'relational' thinking in anthropology, 'ecological' thinking in psychology and 'developmental systems' thinking in biology" (Ingold 2000:4). As mentioned before, following Ingold we should speak of ontogenesis instead of ontology (Simondon 1995:21ff.) to focus on processes and relations instead of substances; becoming instead of being.

The problem with relationality is to not think or understand the relation itself: what a relation is, how it functions, is it internal or external? The difficulty lies in thinking the primacy of the relation over its terms as well as integrating different relations without an abstract or superordinate totality. How can we pose the relation *as such* without understanding it as substance or essence, therefore constructing a field of relationality? And how can we oppose "an ontology of the particulate that imagines a world of individual entities and events, each of which is linked through an external contact" (Ingold 2011:236)?

Ingold succeeds in dissolving the traditional dichotomies of Western thought between "person and organism, society and nature" (Ingold 2000:3) and consequently between subject and object or nature and culture, technology, or human beings. His ecology of life means to think the whole-organism-in-its-environment as an indivisible totality (in process) and not as a distinct entity with an equally distinct surrounding (Ingold 2000:19). Ingold develops an ecological anthropology that has to start in a field of manifold relations (from the in-between), where social relations of human beings are a subset of ecological relations (Ingold 2000:60). But maybe we should understand social relations not as a subset but *as* ecological relations?

This brings us to the question how relational ontologies (Bains 2017) are related to (political–philosophical) ecologies or can be made fruitful for them. The aim is to understand relation *as such*, that means as ontologically distinct from its terms (relata) (Massumi 2002:70; Barad 2007:139; 429). Thus, Karen Barad speaks of intra-action rather than interaction, so as not to presuppose the prior existence of independent, self-sufficient entities (Barad 2007:132ff.). On the grounds of relational ontologies this also results (regarding the political) in the impossibility of thinking the individual and society separately at all (Gisinger 2020). They belong to a common realm of relationality (Massumi 2002:71), which is based on the fundamental exteriority of relation (Deleuze and Parnet 2007:62; Deleuze 2001b) and simultaneously resists the subject–object dichotomy. But relationality in a Deleuzian sense (especially when accounting for the political implications) is never "flat" or an aggregation of harmonious connections, but assembles relations of power, desire, and forces,[14] what can be rudimentary also said for Ingold's concept of correspondence that is "longing for things rather than siding with them" (Ingold 2015:153).

Ecological politics?

When talking about relationality in an ontological, anthropological, or epistemological way and thinking an ecology that deals with environments in a field of growth, movements, lines (not of already constituted and fixed organisms, living or human beings), we must not forget the inherently political implications of the ecological question. Ecology should not be reduced to natural environment, but rather understood, as Ingold does, in a broad sense as 'conditions of existence' (Haeckel) which has to include economic, political, and technological conditions that are not outside of 'nature'. For example, Jean-Luc Nancy argues that technology is never external to nature, if nature has an outside at all: it is always within it, or technology is a specific unfolding of nature (Nancy 2015:46). Nancy criticises a confrontation between nature and technology that is based on an ecological 'protection' of nature from technological access or that subordinates technology to the purposes of a mythical nature: "An ecology properly understood can be nothing other than a technology" (Nancy 2008:42). Even if this statement seems a bit hyperbolic, it shows the necessary entanglement of technology and ecology and points out that these terms cannot be thought of mutually exclusive.

What is at stake for Ingold, regarding ecology, can be illustrated in his criticism of the way Bruno Latour writes about nonhumans. The nonhumans Latour evokes in his *Politics of nature* (Latour 2004), Ingold thinks, might just as well be inanimate, since their vitality contributes nothing to their networked convocation: "What draws them together are not trails of movement or growth, or of perception and response, but mutual, interactive effects in a network of effects that comprises the overall field of action. This is why Latour's political ecology fails *as ecology*" (Ingold 2016:436). Ingold proposes his concept of meshwork instead of network because in Latour's theory the primary function is cause and effect in a field, instead of taking the movements/lines of becoming into account. Ingold's meshwork tries to unify or entangle the 'flesh' of phenomenology (Merleau-Ponty) with the 'web of life' of ecology (Ingold 2012:437). The meshwork seems also much closer to the concept of *agencement*, as presented before. According to our relational premises, bodies are (in) movement and therefore in correspondence "with the things around them. This is to think of the body not as a sink into which practices settle like sediment in a ditch, but rather as a dynamic centre of unfolding activity" (Ingold 2012:437).

I would agree with Ingold's critique that Latour's political ecology fails as ecology, but there has to be a question of the political in an ecological context where Ingold seems quite tentative.[15] Ecologies, such as of the kind advanced by Næss, can incline towards a romanticism or nativism that idealises a traditional way of life against technology or modernity (back to "nature"). This is especially apparent in the work of Heidegger and his followers. Thus, it is necessary to think of an ecology which does not presuppose nature as an intact entity, which is exploited by technology, humans, etc. and which therefore does not interpret the history of humanity, technical progress, and the development of productive forces as a mere history of decay. But at the same time, we must ask how and whether ecological crises are necessarily related to the economic–political foundations of the capitalist system. Here, I would at least add this dimension to Ingold's account, when he describes the roots of ecological crisis in "disengagement, in the separation of human agency and social responsibility from the sphere of our direct involvement with the non-human environment [...]." (Ingold 2000:76) As Jason W. Moore (but also Timothy Morton or Donna Haraway) have noted in their critique of the concept of the Anthropocene, ecological crises cannot simply be understood as crises of humanity, the earth, the planet, or ecosystems. Rather, the irreducible connection with the capitalist mode of production, spheres of circulation, and consumption must be considered, what Moore therefore calls 'Capitalocene' (Moore 2017). Capitalocene is a complementary concept to the widespread and well-known notion of the Anthropocene as a new geological era, coined by the emergence, augmentation, and pervasiveness of mankind and its impact on the ecosystem. But to speak of the Anthropocene seems to presuppose a universalised or generalised abstraction of 'humanity' [anthropos], disregarding for example inequality, class, or imperialism. Hence, the notion of the *anthropos* unifies the irreducible differences of man in responsibility, causation, vulnerability, or power for the Anthropocene and its ecological implications. Moore argues (such as this chapter) to situate humanity in the web of life (without renouncing its distinctiveness), therefore, not to reproduce a human/nature dichotomy (in this sense according with Ingold) and at the same time investigate the political and economic causes of the devastating "capitalogenic" geological force (Moore 2017:597).

In this regard, ecological philosophy must also assert itself as a political–economic philosophy (stemming from the same word *oikos*), so as not to stabilise or reproduce the existing power relations in their economic and ecological form in either the appeal to the 'big picture' (Luisetti 2018) or individualistic, escapist solutions that identify ecology just with living more 'connected', i.e., more attentive, correspondent, or in harmony to and with 'our' environment.

Notes

1 For example, Ingold provides substantiated critiques of Bruno Latour's (2005) actor-network-theory (ANT) (Ingold 2011:89ff.) or Graham Harman's object-oriented ontology (OOO) (Ingold 2015:16).

2 'Doing' usually presupposes an intentional, self-conscious actor. Ingold asks, if there exists also 'doing', that is not done by us, a kind of 'action without

agency': "And as we owe our very existence to what has gone before, and as what comes after owes its existence, at least in part, to us, so our deeds belong to no-one: not to ourselves, not to others, but to history – or, better, to life" (Ingold 2015:145).

3

> Philosophers have not been sufficiently concerned with the nature of the concept as philosophical reality. They have preferred to think of it as a given knowledge or representation that can be explained by the faculties able to form it (abstraction or generalization) or employ it (judgment). But the concept is not given, it is created; it is to be created. It is not formed but posits itself in itself – it is a self-positing. Creation and self-positing mutually imply each other because what is truly created, from the living being to the work of art, thereby enjoys a self-positing of itself, or an autopoetic characteristic by which it is recognized. The concept posits itself to the same extent that it is created.
>
> (Deleuze and Guattari 1994:11)

4 But also, analytic philosophers like Donald Davidson could qualify as a representative of event ontology (Davidson 2001).

5 Karen Barad even goes a step further, speaking of intra-action instead of interaction between already preformed entities (Barad 2007:132ff.). Along these lines, Ingold pleads for the prefix *mid-* instead of *inter-*, but overall prefers his concept of 'correspondence' to do justice to the 'in-between' (Ingold 2015:152).

6 Following Kandinsky's argument in his essay 'Point and line to plane', where he describes the vital potential of the point in musical notation as a 'living thing', Ingold claims that points indeed can be produced in music (Ingold 2020b:211). Thus, the quote of Deleuze and Parnet seems a bit misleading but has not to be contradicting at all when we understand the point in music as part of an immanent becoming.

7 Ingold himself notes that the translation assemblage of the French *agencement* is not quite exact in a literal sense (because there would also exist the word *assemblage* in French), but a fortiori remains interesting in the context of the gathering quality of *things* that Ingold invokes (Ingold 2020a:20). In this paper I use both terms, because on the one hand the translation *assemblage* is common in the English scholarly discourse about Deleuze/Guattari, on the other hand I agree with Ingold that *agencement* means something different.

8

> Subject and object give a poor approximation of thought. Thinking is neither a line drawn between subject and object nor a revolving of one around the other. Rather, thinking takes place in the relationship of territory and the earth.
>
> (Deleuze and Guattari 1994:85)

9

> Thus, each individual is an infinite multiplicity, and the whole of Nature is a multiplicity of perfectly individuated multiplicities. The plane of consistency of Nature is like an immense Abstract Machine, abstract yet real and individual; its pieces are the various assemblages and individuals, each of which

groups together an infinity of particles entering into an infinity of more or less interconnected relations. There is therefore a unity to the plane of nature, which applies equally to the inanimate and the animate, the artificial and the natural. (Deleuze and Guattari 2004:254)

10 Deleuze uses capital letters for the AND when referring to the primacy of the relation to *being* itself. In French, ET (AND) instead of EST (IS) also functions as a homophone. "AND isn't even a specific conjunction or relation, it brings in all relations, there are as many relations as ANDS, AND doesn't just upset all relations, it upsets being, the verb ... and so on. AND, 'and ... and ... and ...' is precisely a creative stammering, a foreign use of language, as opposed to a conformist and dominant use based on the verb 'to be' " (Deleuze 1990b:44).

11 "Only if we are capable of weaving, only then we can make" (Ingold 2000:348). Here we can see that Ingold indeed starts with the concrete.

12 A very similar critique of Latour is made by Karen Barad on an ontological level when she disagrees with Latour on his prioritization of stability (Barad 2007:41).

13 This neither means that there are no subjects at all nor that we have no responsibility or accountability over actions but alludes to the ever-ongoing process of subjectivation (Foucault) and individuation (Simondon, Deleuze).

14 Andrew Culp's *Dark Deleuze* argues convincingly against interpretations of Deleuze that focus on connectivity and holistic relationality (Culp 2016).

15 Nonetheless there are a few indications in Ingold's research that point to such interpretations, especially in a text about dwelling as a potential foundation for a political ecology: "[T]he concept of nature, like that of society, is inherently and intensely political" (Ingold 2005:503).

References

Bains, P. 2017. *The primacy of semiosis: An ontology of relations*. Toronto: University of Toronto Press.

Barad, K. 2007. *Meeting the universe halfway. Quantum physics and the entanglement of matter and meaning*. Durham/London: Duke University Press.

Bateson, G. 1972. *Steps to an ecology of mind. Collected essays in anthropology, psychiatry, evolution, and epistemology*. Northvale/London: Jason Aronson.

Bennett, J. 2010. *Vibrant matter. A political ecology of things*. Durham/London: Duke University Press.

Bühler, B. 2016. *Ecocriticism. Grundlagen – Theorien – Interpretationen*. Stuttgart: J.B. Metzler.

Culp, A. 2016. *Dark Deleuze*. Minneapolis: University of Minnesota Press.

Davidson, D. 2001 [1980]. *Essays on actions and events*. Oxford: Oxford University Press.

Deleuze, G. 1988. *Spinoza. Practical philosophy*. Robert Hurley, trans. San Francisco: City Light Books.

——— 1990a. *The logic of sense*. Constantin V. Boundas, ed. Mark Lester and Charles Stivale, trans. New York: Columbia University Press.

——— 1990b. *Negotiations*. Martin Joughin, trans. New York: Columbia University Press.

——— 2001a. Immanence. A life. In G. Deleuze, *Pure immanence. Essays on a life*. Anne Boyman, trans. Pp. 25–34. New York: Urzone.
——— 2001b. Hume. In G. Deleuze, *Pure immanence. Essays on a life*. Anne Boyman, trans. Pp. 35–52. New York: Urzone.
——— 2006. *Two regimes of madness. Texts and interviews 1957–1995*. David Lapoujade, ed. Ames Hodges and Mike Taormina, trans. New York: Semiotext(e).
Deleuze, G. and F. Guattari. 1994. *What is philosophy?* Hugh Tomlinson and Graham Burchell, trans. New York: Columbia University Press.
——— 2004. *A thousand plateaus: Capitalism and schizophrenia*. Brian Massumi, trans. London: Continuum.
Deleuze, G. and C. Parnet. 2007 [1987]. *Dialogues*. Hugh Tomlinson and Barbara Habberjam, trans. New York: Columbia University Press.
Gisinger, R. 2020. *Philosophien der Pluralisierung. Begegnungen des Politischen zwischen Gilles Deleuze und Jean-Luc Nancy*. Paderborn: Wilhelm Fink Verlag.
Haeckel, E. 1866. *Generelle Morphologie der Organismen*. Berlin: Verlag von Georg Reimer.
Haraway, D. J. 2016. *Staying with the trouble. Making Kin in the Chthulucene*. Durham/London: Duke University Press.
Harman, G. 2017. *Object-oriented-ontology: A new theory of everything*. London: Penguin Random House.
Heidegger, M. 2001a [1971]. The thing. In M. Heidegger, *Poetry, language, thought*. A. Hofstadter, trans. Pp. 161–184. New York: Harper and Row.
——— 2001b [1971]. Building dwelling thinking. In M. Heidegger, *Poetry, language, thought*. A. Hofstadter, trans. Pp. 185–208. New York: Harper and Row.
Hörl, E. 2016. Ecologies of making. On Tim Ingold's general-ecological critique of worldmaking. In *+ultra knowledge & gestaltung*. N. Doll, H. Bredekamp, and Wolfgang Schäffner, eds. Pp. 45–54. Leipzig: E.A. Seemann.
——— 2017. Introduction to general ecology. Ecologization of thinking. In *General ecology. The new ecological paradigm*. E. Hörl and J. Burton, eds. Nils F. Schott, trans. Pp. 1–75. London/New York: Bloomsbury.
Ingold, T. 2000. *The perception of the environment. Essays on livelihood, dwelling and skill*. London/New York: Routledge.
——— 2005. Epilogue: Towards a politics of dwelling. *Conservation and Society* 3(2):501–508.
——— 2007. *Lines. A brief history*. London/New York: Routledge.
——— 2008. Bindings against boundaries: Entanglements of life in an open world. *Environment and Planning A* 40:1796–1810.
——— 2011. *Being alive. Essay on movement, knowledge and description*. London/New York: Routledge.
——— 2012. Toward an ecology of materials. *Annual Review of Anthropology* 41:427–442.
——— 2013. *Making. Anthropology, archaeology, art and architecture*. London/New York: Routledge.
——— 2015. *The life of lines*. London/New York: Routledge.
——— 2016. Eine Ökologie der Materialien. *Zeitschrift für Medienwissenschaft* 14(1):87–94.
——— 2020a. In the gathering shadows of material things. In *Exploring materiality and connectivity in anthropology and beyond*. P. Schorch, M. Saxer, and Marlen Elders, eds. Pp. 17–35. London: UCL Press.

——— 2020b. Thinking through the cello. In *Thinking in the world: A reader*. J. Bennett and M. Zournazi, eds. Pp. 202–222. London: Bloomsbury.
Latour, B. 2004. *Politics of nature: How to bring the sciences into democracy*. Catherine Porter, trans. Cambridge: Harvard University Press.
——— 2005. *Reassembling the social. An introduction to actor-network-theory*. Oxford: Oxford University Press.
Luisetti, F. 2018. Geopower: On the states of nature of late capitalism. *European Journal of Social Theory* 22(3):342–363.
Massumi, B. 2002. *Parables for the virtual. Movement, affect, sensation*. Durham/London: Duke University Press.
——— 2009. National enterprise emergency. Steps toward an ecology of powers. *Theory, Culture & Society* 26(6):153–185.
Moore, J. W. 2017. The capitalocene, part I: On the nature and origins of our ecological crisis. *The Journal of Peasant Studies* 44(3):594–630.
Morton, T. 2013. *Hyperobjects. Philosophy and ecology after the end of the world*. Minneapolis: University of Minnesota Press.
Næss, A. 1989. *Ecology, community, and lifestyle. Outline of an ecosophy*. David Rothenberg, trans. Cambridge: Cambridge University Press.
Nancy, J.-L. 2008. *The sense of the world*. Jeffrey S. Librett, trans. Minneapolis: University of Minnesota Press.
——— 2015. Of struction. In *What's these worlds coming to?* Travis Holloway and Flor Méchain, trans. Pp. 42–58. New York: Fordham University Press.
Neyrat, F. 2017. Elements for an ecology of separation: Beyond ecological constructivism. In *General ecology. The new ecological paradigm*. Erich Hörl and James Burton, eds. James Burton, trans. Pp. 101–128. London/New York: Bloomsbury.
Simondon, G. 1995 [1964]. *L'individu et sa genèse physico-biologique*. Grenoble: Édition Jérôme Millon.
de Spinoza, B. 1994. *A Spinoza reader. The ethics and other works*. Edwin Curley, trans., ed. Princeton: Princeton University Press.
Tsing, A. L. 2015. *The mushroom at the end of the world. On the possibilities of life in capitalist ruins*. Princeton/Oxford: Princeton University Press.

12 Making and growing

The lives and deaths of a tree and a house in the Spanish dehesa[1]

Maike Melles

Introduction

"Imagine that the dehesa used to be full of *chozos*." Rafael,[2] an elderly villager who worked as a shepherd in his younger years, raises his right hand and moves it from the left to the right on a horizontal line as if he was actually watching the landscape from its edge. Sitting with him at a table in front of a wooden hut, I try to picture the dehesa of southwestern Spain as an inhabited landscape, bustling with human activity. In today's dehesa, I find it very difficult to imagine the presence of the numerous small shepherd's huts, the *chozos* mentioned by Rafael, which over time gradually disappeared from the landscape.[3] This unique landscape, usually located at a few kilometres' distance from villages and small towns, appears like a heavily hollowed out forest where the numerous holm and cork oaks grow several metres apart as in a savannah (Figure 12.1). Between the trees, herds of cattle, pigs, or sheep graze on spacious pastures. While until the middle of the 20th century, shepherds like Rafael used to roam the vast dehesa with their flocks and the swineherds went after the acorns in the autumn with a group of fattening pigs, today the landscape is divided into plots and enclosed. The livestock stays inside the fences day and night and is moved to another plot from time to time. When no grazing grass is left in the pasture, the farmers usually come by once a day to pour out animal feed from bags into troughs. "There are no shepherds anymore, there are only *ganaderos*," Rafael comments this modern simplification of sheep farming with a slightly contemptuous smile on his face: while in his days, shepherding used to be hard manual labour, Rafael uses the term *ganadero* to denote today's sheep farmers who enjoy many more technical conveniences, such as the cars which they drive to visit their flocks.[4] These means were unavailable to their ancestors, and Rafael proudly describes the skills it once took to be a good shepherd.

Nowadays, animals and plants may be said to be the principal dwellers in the dehesa. Long gone are the times when agriculture in southern Spain was a shared activity and hard physical labour performed by whole working families on farms in the possession of the wealthy. Traces of human habitation have over time withered and weathered away; only some scattered stone

DOI: 10.4324/9781003162773-17

Figure 12.1 Almost like a savannah: dehesa of holm oaks in Andalusia.

ruins of the more solid huts give vague testimony to the lived realities before agriculture was mechanised and livestock farming entered into competition with industrial animal production, prompting farmers to increase the animal load in their pastures which frequently suffer from overgrazing. Apart from the wide range of skills that were necessary to cope with the challenges of everyday life, Rafael also recounts social injustices and the times of scarcity and rampant poverty for those who made the most precarious living, like his own family who one day did not know where to gather food for the next. Our conversation took a yet more disquieting turn, however, when we were joined by Emilio, a close friend of Rafael's age. Continuing at first with our talk about the past hardships of a village life full of exhausting tasks, at some point I asked them about the relations between the employees and foremen or landowners. Emilio's face immediately darkened with what seemed to be deep-seated embarrassment: "The relations were not good." I could tell that this was not usually a topic readily discussed, as our lively and joking exchange suddenly turned into a restrained report delivered in single sentences and with a faltering voice. To put Emilio's and Rafael's account (and that of further interlocutors of mine) briefly, exploitation, abuse, and sexual assaults on the part of the superiors were no exception on the farms in rural Spain until the middle of the 20th century.[5]

Hence, my conversation with Rafael and Emilio switched from proudly presented accounts on the skilfulness in the management of everyday tasks in the dehesa via social inequalities and poverty to a visible uneasiness when asked about the relations between different status groups at that time. The instance led me to reflect more closely about the passage of time and the consequences of processes which lead to the deterioration of the material environment, organic and inorganic. Material leftovers may give rise to stories on the pleasant sides of past lives – such as skilfully mastering life together with loved ones – or, by contrast, act as unwelcome reminders of cruel realities (Filippucci 2017, 2020), in which case their decay may be very convenient for those who wish to forget (Fewster 2007). The dynamics emanating from the axiomatic continuance of life on the one hand and human practices of relating to nonhuman lifeways on the other are reflective of an interplay between the multiple temporalities inherent in landscapes of which the human lifespan is but one (Ingold 1993). In the following, I will draw on and critically examine Tim Ingold's concepts of dwelling, growing and making in their capacity to shed light on the nature of this complex interplay between the manifold human and nonhuman temporalities: while the dwelling perspective allows us to situate the human being in an engaging relation to their environment (Ingold 2000), growing is synonymous with an ongoing and all-encompassing process of 'becoming with' which to Ingold is, briefly put, the essence of life which all of its participants equally undergo (Ingold 2015). Making, the human engagement with the nonhuman world for the sake of production, is here subsumed as another way of growing, expressed in the phrase making-in-growing.

In the remainder of this chapter, I will first introduce the main features and vantage point making-*in*-growing provides on the passage of time, or the 'flow of life.' I will discuss the implication of Ingold's perspective for the distinction between organism and artefact at the example of the lives and deaths of a tree and a house in the Spanish dehesa. While in Ingold's perspective, the difference between organism and artefact is marginal at most, in my view they come to stand for two distinct modes of world formation and meaning making. I will then discuss the implications of an absorbent growing perspective as opposed to a perspective with a broader understanding of making, with particular regard to the human processes of remembrance and forgetting. I will argue that the environmentally situated approach Ingold proposes is not apt to deal with the complexities of remembering, especially in the case of absences and silences. I will conclude that while making-in-growing captures well the relentlessness of life's moving on, making should be embraced as a distinctively human endeavour to give meaning to life.

Making-*in*-growing: Ingold's interweaving perspective

One of Ingold's central concerns has been to undo frequently invoked oppositions of which that between human and nonhuman, or between culture or society on the one hand and nature on the other, is the most encompassing (Ingold 1993, 2000, 2005; Ingold and Palsson 2013; Hallam and Ingold 2014). Instead of rendering the nonhuman or 'natural' world ready-made and passive, awaiting interpretation by an observer whose mind is somewhat detached from the world, the dwelling perspective, famously introduced and gradually specified by Ingold (1993, 2000, 2005, 2011), seeks to re-embed the human being as an inhabitant of the world in their active engagement with the environment. This multi-relational immersion is achieved by prioritising process over product as the supposedly final form, e.g., in the making of artefacts. Regarding things not as finalities but as temporary forms of an active flow of materials is Ingold's approach to giving due credit to the fact that what we call life is a process with many participants: instead of thinking of things as accumulations of dead matter, the activity of the materials themselves is foregrounded, since they are as much part of the form-producing process as the human maker (Ingold 2013:21).

Ingold's thinking with materials seeks to overcome all too clear-cut divisions between a natural realm where organisms grow, and a cultural realm in which artefacts are made. According to Ingold, the transition from growing to making is widely perceived to occur as soon as the materials, e.g., grasses and wood, are taken away from their spheres of growth (the pastures and the tree) and turned into passive matter waiting to be artificially modified by a human agent, to be made into hay or a wooden figurine, for example (Hallam and Ingold 2014:3–4). However, Ingold opposes, human intention rarely translates one-to-one into an artefact, as the hylomorphic model suggests.[6] The way there is, to him, a passage with many participants, both human and nonhuman such as materials (Ingold 2000:87). "Far from being the inanimate stuff typically envisioned by modern thought, materials in this original sense are the active constituents of a world-in-formation. Wherever life is going on, they are relentlessly on the move – flowing, scraping, mixing and mutating" (Ingold 2011:28).[7]

The ongoing movement of materials is an instance of Ingold's 'new ecology,' according to which life is a "process wherein form is generated and held in place" (Ingold 2000:173). This process is best pictured as a continuous movement along (Ingold 2011:11–12), or a life-flow in which every participant is in constant becoming and along which new forms arise (Ingold 2011:24):

> There are human becomings, animal becomings, plant becomings, and so on. As they move together through time and encounter one another, these paths interweave to form an immense and continually evolving tapestry. Anthropology, then, is the study of human becomings as they unfold within the weave of the world.
>
> (Ingold 2011:9)

As the interplay between human and material becomings, making "draw[s] out or bring[s] forth [...] potentials immanent in a world of becoming" (Ingold 2013:31). Thinking with materials rather than objects allows us to think of a house not as short-lived and static but as the manifestation of a perduring (in its material components) and ever-changing (in its form) phenomenon (Ingold 2013:31). This constant becoming, in which Ingold closely follows Deleuze and Guattari (1988), is quite akin to the notion of growth "or concrescence as the fundamental condition of beings and things in a world that is always surpassing itself" (Hallam and Ingold 2014:3). Making is just another form of growth not by human imposition but by giving new form (Ingold 2000:88, 2011:215).

Given this clear conceptual stance and the often polemical demarcation from other lines of anthropological thought in Ingold's writings the question of a political dimension of dwelling, and making-in-growing, arises. Ingold himself explicitly addresses it as a matter of "clos[ing] the gap between human and nonhuman worlds" (2005:504), thus joining a range of authors who foreground ecological issues by pointing to more-than-human entanglements (e.g., Tsing 2013) and interspecies companionship (Haraway 2008). Thinking with human and nonhuman becomings has also paved the way for Ingold's theory of lines, which come to stand for the dweller's movement or 'wayfaring' along a life-path: "Along such paths, lives are lived, skills developed, observations made, and understandings grown" (Ingold 2011:12). What is bracketed in approaches foregrounding relationships of human becomings in 'correspondence' with nonhuman becomings (Ingold 2015:154–158), however, are relations *between* humans, in particular those of a difficult kind arising from malice. This shortcoming is due to the always singular and unmarked (in terms of social dimensions such as gender) perspective of an otherwise – i.e., in their tangible environment – highly situated human dweller. The conception of an individual 'itinerant wayfarer' (Ingold 2011:216) following a life-path that is ready to be enmeshed with those of others accounts for the movement side by side, but not for halting and confrontation.

Making *and* growing: distinct modes of world-formation

A grown house and a tree made

Ingold's making-in-growing sheds new light on what are usually considered two very different things: houses and trees. In this section, I want to lay out the consequences of Ingold's perspective for the understanding of difference or similarity between an organism and an artefact, in this case, a holm oak and a *chozo*. While the *chozos* whose presence, or rather absence, animated my conversation with Rafael and Emilio, quickly began to deteriorate once they were left for good, many of the dehesa's numerous holm oaks continued to grow, seemingly unaffected by the changing social dynamics of the mid-20th century (Figure 12.2). The life span of these trees may comprise between 200 and 500 years.[8] Shifting away from the standpoint of the human life span, which may be preceded and outlasted by those of houses and trees, and taking on a perspective that foregrounds the continuous flow of materials – continuous growth – we still see that both trees and houses may come into existence and pass out of it at some points in time. To Ingold, though materials may be shaped into a building block, their continued existence remains unaffected by the decomposition and eventual disappearance of the building. But does it follow that the deaths – the 'passing out of their form' – of an oak tree and an old shepherd's hut in the Spanish dehesa are just the same?

Usually, we would assume that organisms like the dehesa's oak trees are grown and that artefacts like the shepherd's huts were made. Making-in-growing, however, postulates that houses are grown, too, and that trees may also be considered made (Ingold 2013:22). A first look at the Spanish *chozos* makes clear that both straw and stone huts were once part of the environment "conventionally described as 'built'" (Ingold 2000:172). By shifting analysis from the house-as-artefact to the house-as-material (Bunn 2014:168), the house ceases to be perceived as an enclosed object, and instead the activity of its materials such as stone and clay come to the fore – and so does the

Figure 12.2 Centuries of growth: a holm oak full of acorns in Extremadura.

growth of all participants in the house-forming process (Figure 12.3). The building is a form which emerges in the moment that the human builders give a new form to the clay by, first, firing it into bricks, and second, using it for construction. Whenever humans build a house, according to Ingold, they follow the flow of active materials (2011:213–215). Skill refers to the makers' attending to the materials by corresponding their practice to the flow, which means that they are always able to improvise their movement in response (Ingold 2013:48). This improvisation is, to Ingold, the essence of human creativity (2011:216).

Making-in-growing renders making a variety of growing: while the material flow continues, the house as the 'final form' is but a moment in the life-path of stone (Ingold 2000:188). Stones or other materials grow and perdure while the artefacts they give rise to are only temporary forms. What follows is the challenge to explore how the tree as individual organism with its own metabolism not only grows in the 'natural' sense but is also made (Hallam and Ingold 2014:17). One of Ingold's answers to this question leads us to consider the variation in the degree to which humans are involved in the generation of their form (2013:21–22). While a house is obviously human-made, the tree can be said to have a life-path that is much more autonomous and independent from human action. However, and decisively for Ingold, the

Figure 12.3 Materials on the move: who used to live here, and how?

holm oak is just as much affected by the activities of other, human and non-human, beings. Apart from obvious interventions in the planting, pruning, and harvesting of its acorns, humans also tend to the tree's surroundings and nurture its growth, thereby "creating the conditions under which the tree, over the centuries, has grown to assume its particular form and proportions" (Ingold 2000:187).

A second and much more intriguing answer to the question why a tree is not only grown but also made is given by Hallam and Ingold by drawing on ethnographic insights of Christopher Tilley (2004, 2009:176) who interprets English gardens – in which plant organisms grow – as artefacts, "especially as they have associated stories, memories and biographical meanings such that persons and the plants they cultivate grow together. Growing here becomes tantamount to making, even though plants are taken to have their own lives" (Hallam and Ingold 2014:17). Though autonomous in their growth, the plants have become vested with meaning by their gardeners and thus made, too. What is remarkable about this second argument in favour of the made-ness of trees is that making is no longer understood to occur only in the context of skilled practices such as artefact production; it has gained a decisively interpretive constituent in the reference to *human* meaning making by way of attaching personal stories to organisms. These interpretations may plausibly be argued to continue beyond the highly situated engagement of the human with the tangible environment, as for example in their representation in oral and written accounts. In the introduction to this chapter, former shepherd Rafael invited me to imagine the dehesa filled with *chozos*, however, memory in this case was only partially environmentally situated: firstly, we were not moving about the dehesa at all, instead sitting in front of a wooden hut; secondly, the shepherd's huts do not exist anymore, which is why Rafael must have drawn on some kind of abstract image. This runs counter to Ingold's assertion that remembering cannot be about "calling up representations" (2011:148). After reviewing Ingold's arguments on the likeness of trees and houses in their equivalent involvement in making and growing, the next question is if the differences between organism and artefact should be considered meaningful at all.

House or tree: a matter of degree?

To Ingold, form-generation in the case of artefact and organism, or house and tree, basically amounts to the same process, since "the form of the tree is no more given, as an immutable fact of nature, than is the form of the house an imposition of the human mind" (2000:187).[9] Rather, houses and trees are "never complete but continually under construction" (Ingold 2000:154), calling for a blurring of the boundaries between the organic and the inorganic (Hallam and Ingold 2014:3). The mutual identification of artefacts and organisms goes so far that Ingold, in reference to Blier (1987), even suggests that houses "are living organisms" because they "have life-histories, which consist in the unfolding of their relations with both human and nonhuman components of their environments" (Ingold 2000:187). Both buildings and trees are mutually involved with human and nonhuman dwellers and therefore, according to Ingold, there can "be no absolute distinction between 'natural' and 'artificial' structures" (2000:154).

In fact, Ingold grants a certain difference between artefacts and organisms, however, it is "relative [...] to the scope of human involvement in the form-generating process" (2000:187). The distinction between trees and houses is therefore just a matter of human perception and not of a categorical kind, because "[w]hether, at a certain point in its life history, a structure looks to us like a building or not will depend on the extent and nature of human involvement in its formation" (Ingold 2000:154), whereas "to the extent that the nonhuman component prevails, it will seem less so" (Ingold 2000:187). Holm oak and shepherd's hut only *appear* to be different; their final blurring occurs as soon as they 'die,' that is, their materials leave the temporary forms which constitute them:

> What is the opposite of making if things cannot be unmade? What is the opposite of growing if things cannot ungrow? The immediate answer to the first question is breaking or dismantling, the answer to the second is decomposition or decay. And whereas the first may call for a remedial response in the form of repair, the second calls for healing. Yet just as it is hard to draw the line between making and growing, so the distinctions between breakage and decomposition, dismantling and decay, and repair and healing, are all problematic in their various ways.
>
> (Hallam and Ingold 2014:8)

Ingold insists that the degree of human involvement in the form-generating process, or production, does not impede his argument that organisms and artefacts are subject to the same dynamics of growth – acquiring and losing temporary forms as a result of mutual involvement with human and nonhuman activities – so that they may as well not be distinguished at all. But is this 'human involvement' really negligible?

Discussion: going with the flow? Things and the passage of time

The substages of the all-encompassing form-generation, namely, making and growing or deterioration and decay, are indeed processes which occur at quite different temporal scales, and for the most part do so gradually. The dehesa's holm oaks and *chozos* have outlasted or been survived by recent human generations. Since the mid-20th century, former farmworkers have been able to afford a house in the village and left the rudimentary shelters in the dehesa, whereas trees are worked with machines[10] and scarcely anybody pays attention to the fact that for many oaks that had been living in the dehesa and used gently as a resource for more than a century, changes in management practices were drastic once agriculture was industrialised. From Ingold's perspective of making-in-growing, there is no meaningful difference between a house and a tree. Neither of them is an instance of either 'artificially built' or, respectively, 'naturally grown' elements of the environment. Rather, both may be described as artefacts or organisms at just the same time. But even if we think of houses and trees as distinct loci on a continuum from human to nonhuman involvement, a distinction remains.

What seems at first sight an appealing dissolution of only seeming differences is in fact a glaring bias towards the all-embracing force of growth – of life on the move – at the expense of the closer inspection of human meaning making which making-in-growing construes as the result of humans' faulty assumptions about their own absolute distinctiveness. Ingold argues that subsuming making under growing is an enhancement of our understanding of what it means if time – and, for that matter, life – goes on, however, it also runs the risk of reducing makers to mere passengers along life-paths without escape. Kindly, Ingold demonstrates the friction in his concept of making-in-growing himself: while making in the case of a house may be said to occur as a skilful improvisation along a flow of materials as making-in-growing suggests, making in the case of a plant organism has obtained a rather fuzzy meaning as it simply refers to the impact of human activities on things as perceived by humans.[11] This friction, however, proves key to my endeavour of enhancing the scope of what it means to make, since we may speculate whether a world without humans would be meaningless, but there is no doubt that perception and meaning making by human beings does bear some distinctive qualities.

Disappearances and the complexities of remembering

Usually, a central role is played by material traces in the remembrance of past events, pleasant or dreadful. Things may function as reminders of and even as 'witnesses' (Filippucci 2017, 2020) to the past so that they authenticate and even star in the stories about it. However, things come and go, and memories about difficult pasts may actually be repressed, making deterioration of material witnesses to unpleasant events an almost welcome process. In the example discussed here, memories of the most difficult aspects of the former life of the rural population in southwestern Spain are only hesitatingly recounted: among them are sparse references to atrocities like the exploitation of whole families including their children and the sexual abuse of girls and women by the superiors on the farms.

From the dwelling perspective, remembering is an embodied and situated practice; but does it follow that everything that is not tangible anymore is bound to be forgotten? Objects, if not even completely preserved in their form, leave material traces such as stone ruins and other kinds of remnants. Things and their traces have the capacity to endure "in a non-discursive way" (Filippucci 2020:392) and thus challenge human perceptions of the past in the present that are all too detached from their physical surroundings. At the same time, however, objects are also incorporated into a memorial space of abstractions and representations (Filippucci 2020). These spaces do not only constitute which kinds of objects are foregrounded in public remembrance, but may also induce forgetfulness about others, as in instances of politically expedient forgetting (Fewster 2007). As is well known, the public relation to the past in Spain has long been guided by the *Pacto del Olvido* which forges forgetfulness about the violent relations between the Spanish in the past, which comprise both the atrocities committed during the civil war (1936–1939) and the ensuing dictatorship of Franco (1939–1975) as well as the abuse which occurred on rural fincas fairly independently of the political regime (Fewster 2007; Muñoz-Encinar 2019). Even if we subscribe to the mutual playoff of an experienced and a 'representational' remembrance of the past (Ingold 1993:152–153, 2000:138, 146–148): when forgetting is politically expedient, how do we deal with ruins with only glimpses of earlier forms that, in Ingold's words, soon continue their relentless flow as materials – and whose perdurance could very well function as a critical counterpoint to obtruded public representations?

My conversation with Rafael and Emilio started with an invitation to *imagine* an inhabited dehesa populated with *chozos* as the centres of shepherds' and families' lives in the past. There were only scarce or no material traces at all left of what Rafael sought to bring home to me. Situated and relational approaches to the environment, present or past, fail to recognise the role of absent things which still inform accounts of the past precisely because they can be 'called up' (Ingold 2000:138). As a child, Rafael witnessed the times when the dehesa hosted more *chozos*, but I too, as his listener, can invite people to imagine this landscape with buildings and human activity. In other words: Although the relentless flow continues to change the landscape, it has been vested with stories and thus *made*. Ultimately, remembering is not only a faculty reducible to a dweller's engagement with their environment; it is also a practice guided by moral and ethical considerations. It is misled to assume that because life continues, it would always do so in sympathetic correspondences of knots that are joined in *with*-ness (Ingold 2015:23–24). What about the blatant *against*-ness exerted and experienced in the dissonances, frictions, and even malevolent violent interruptions of lives, as in the case of mid-20th century rural Spain? And given the combination of hesitation and willingness exhibited by Rafael and Emilio when they shared their stories with me, how do we account for the ambiguities involved in remembering itself?

Conclusion: the relentlessness of growing

In their introduction on making and growing, Hallam and Ingold conclude that "even as lives come and go, life itself is carried on" (2014:9). This phrase captures accurately the relentlessness of the truism that 'life goes on,' at least when it is equated with an all-encompassing growth, an ongoing movement in which human and nonhuman agents are mutually involved in their immediate environment, which is how artefacts and organisms, postulated as temporary forms, are generated. According to Ingold, not only is making, defined as the human involvement in this production process, just a variation of growing; since artefacts and organisms are subject to the same dynamic of making-in-growing, their distinction is insignificant. I am afraid that the subsumption of human activities under the fundamental principle of growth not only turns attention away from the meaning making humans engage in to deal with life's relentlessness; what is worse, Ingold's absolutising of the growth paradigm necessitates the defaming of those anthropological accounts which explicitly deal with meaning making in the form of abstract representations (Ingold 2016). Ingold is right to criticise all too detached engagements with the world we live in; I in turn argue we should insist on keeping sight of the 'abstract representations' which form part and parcel of our everyday lives and shape our meaningful environment; for if not only human but also material witnesses have disappeared from the scene, how are we ever to be reminded of past rights and wrongs?

In anthropology, taking people seriously implies learning *with* them (Ingold 2018:11) but also involves close listening to what matters *to* them. While Rafael and Emilio recalled good and bad moments of their childhood and only hesitantly shared memories of past atrocities, they also expressed worries that their past will be forgotten. Memories are often connected to buildings or other elements of the landscape subject to constant decay, but not restricted to these material traces of the past. It is only from the entanglements of the passage of time and the memory of the past, which in turn encompasses embodied *and* representational forms of remembering, that the complexity emerges which does justice to anthropological research on the Spanish dehesa. This research entails embodied and situational engagement with this landscape, however, it does so *without* falling into the trap of inveighing against anything 'representational,' instead seeking to make both approaches fruitful in "an energising tension" (Harvey and Wilkinson 2019:180). Only by learning from the tangible *and* intangible past is there a chance that we will not tread on the spot ethically.

Notes

1 I am very grateful to the organisers and participants of the masterclass with Professor Tim Ingold which took place at the University of Tübingen in September 2019 and provided a locus for insightful discussions and critical exchange on a wide range of topics. My sincere thanks also go to both reviewers and Tim Ingold for their helpful comments on a first draft of this text. All photos in this chapter are by the author.

2 The names of my informants that appear in the text are pseudonyms.

3 *Chozos* could be built of straw or stones. The latter were of local types of rocks such as slate or granite and layered as dry-stones or joined with mud. Both types of *chozos* were either temporary shelters for shepherds on the move or provided longer-term accommodation of families living in the open countryside and not in the village (in the case of the straw huts, this was mostly a group of a few *chozos*, each dedicated to a different purpose, such as matrimonial bed, sleeping place for children, and cooking zone). While the more frequent makeshift huts of straw disappeared from the landscape without leaving any trace (only in some museums or sheds a few specimens have been maintained), the stone huts have fallen into disrepair, and the ruins of some can still be viewed today.

4 In earlier times, *ganadero* used to refer to the owners of livestock (such as sheep), while shepherd (*pastor*) denotes the labourer who takes care of the flock. Today, many livestock farmers run their own business, which means that they both own and look after their animals themselves. While the *pastor* is considered an extinct profession, today's livestock farmers usually refer to themselves as *ganaderos*.

5 For example, according to Emilio, his mother used to go to the landowner's house "not only to clean"; other interlocutors told me of draconian punishments if the malnourished farm workers, desperate to feed their family, dared to collect even a handful of the acorns provided by the dehesa's numerous holm oaks and destined to fatten the farm's pigs.

6 "Whenever we read that in the making of artefacts, practitioners impose forms internal to the mind upon a material world 'out there', hylomorphism is at work" (Ingold 2013:20–21). Ingold's understanding of hylomorphism as the rendering passive of matter warrants that his approach offers a counter-perspective in which he ascribes materials the same activity during the production process as to the human maker. By positing a matter-flow and production as a form-giving process, he curiously upholds the distinction between matter and form – which is the basic assumption on which concepts of hylomorphism are premised– rather than genuinely challenging it.

7 As one reviewer argued, one may of course question whether the wood of my chair has merely been given a new form after the tree has been felled – that is, killed – and sawn up in order to obtain its materials. To Ingold, however, materials such as wood or hair, although they have been nurtured by a living organism and are then removed from this metabolic cycle, do not lose activity as they continue to change, even though this may simply reduce to the fact that fabricated wood "splits, warps and cracks, eventually settling into a shape quite different from that given to it by the sculptor's initial intervention" (Ingold 2011:27). In their activity, materials "forever threaten [...] the things they comprise with dissolution or even 'dematerialization'" (Ingold 2011:26). I will critically discuss the consequences of Ingold's 'life-flow' perspective in the upcoming sections.

8 One of the oldest holm oaks in Spain is located in the northwest Andalusian natural park Sierra de Aracena y Picos de Aroche. The holm oak was declared a natural monument of the park since its age is estimated to be around half a millennium and is neighboured by a likewise centuries-old cork oak which was included in the natural monument in 2019. The trees are located on the farm of an ecological foundation whose founder recalls that the ancient holm oak was the meeting point where the day labourers received modest payment for their hard work. Both trees are much larger than the average oaks of the dehesa and their metre-long limbs are stabilized by metal poles at their ends. They continue to provide large shades where pasture is often lusher and taller.

9 In order to avoid confusion, it should be noted here that Ingold's discussion of the difference "between those parts of the environment that are, respectively, built and unbuilt" (Ingold 2000:187) is basically identical to his considerations on making and growing. Both pairings refer to the common distinction between 'human-made' artefacts and 'naturally grown' organisms which Ingold seeks to dissolve.

10 With the important exception of the cork harvest that is carried out by the skilled workers as manually as hundreds of years ago: with an axe.

11 At least I infer this specific human component in the concept of making in the context of making-in-growing; it may of course be that Ingold grants the same quality of making to nonhuman agents, as in the example of the beaver that builds its lodge (Ingold 2000:174–175).

References

Blier, S. P. 1987. *The anatomy of architecture*. Cambridge: Cambridge University Press.

Bunn, S. 2014. Making plants and growing baskets. In *Making and growing. Anthropological studies on organisms and artefacts*. E. Hallam and T. Ingold, eds. Pp. 163–181. Surrey: Ashgate.

Deleuze, G. and F. Guattari. 1988. *A thousand plateaus: Capitalism and schizophrenia*. 2nd edition. Minneapolis: University of Minnesota Press.

Fewster, K. 2007. The role of agency and material culture in remembering and forgetting: An ethnoarchaeological case study from central Spain. *Journal of Mediterranean Archaeology* 20(1):89–114.

Filippucci, P. 2017. *Témoins muets*/Mute witnesses: Ethnography and archaeology encounter the objects of the Great War. In *Témoignages et médiations des objets de guerre en musée*. M. Géllereau, ed. Pp. 15–25. Villeneuve d'Ascq: Presses Universitaires du Septentrion.

——— 2020. *Morts pour la France*: Things and memory in the 'destroyed villages' of Verdun, *Journal of Material Culture* 25(4):391–407.

Hallam, E. and T. Ingold. 2014. Making and growing: An introduction. In *Making and growing. Anthropological studies on organisms and artefacts*. E. Hallam and T. Ingold, eds. Pp. 1–24. Surrey: Ashgate.

Haraway, D. 2008. *When species meet*. Minneapolis: University of Minnesota Press.

Harvey, D. and T. J. Wilkinson. 2019. Landscape and heritage: Emerging landscapes of heritage. In *The Routledge companion to landscape studies*. 2nd edition. P. Howard, I. Thompson, E. Waterton, and M. Atha, eds. Pp. 176–191. Abingdon: Routledge.

Ingold, T. 1993. The temporality of the landscape. *World Archaeology* 25(2):152–174.

——— 2000. *The perception of the environment: Essays on livelihood, dwelling and skill*. London: Routledge.

——— 2005. Towards a politics of dwelling, *Conservation and Society* 3(2):501–508.

——— 2011. *Being alive: Essays on movement, knowledge and description*. Abingdon: Routledge.

——— 2013. *Making: Anthropology, archaeology, art and architecture*. Abingdon: Routledge.

——— 2015. *The life of lines*. Abingdon: Routledge.

——— 2016. Rejoinder to Descola's 'Biolatry: A surrender of understanding'. *Anthropological Forum* 26(3):329–332.

——— 2018. *Anthropology: Why it matters*. Cambridge: Polity.
Ingold, T. and G. Palsson, eds. 2013. *Biosocial becomings: Integrating social and biological anthropology*. Cambridge: Cambridge University Press.
Muñoz-Encinar, L. 2019. Unearthing gendered repression: An analysis of the violence suffered by women during the civil war and Franco's dictatorship in southwestern Spain. *World Archaeology* 51(5):759–777.
Tilley, C. 2004. *The materiality of stone: Explorations in landscape phenomenology*. Oxford: Berg.
——— 2009. What gardens mean. In *Material culture and technology in everyday life: Ethnographic approaches*. P. Vannini, ed. Pp. 171–192. New York: Peter Lang.
Tsing, A. L. 2013. More-than-human sociality: A call for critical description. In *Anthropology and nature*. K. Hastrup, ed. Pp. 27–42. Abingdon: Routledge.

13 Living along infrastructural lines

Following electricity in Hunza

Quirin Rieder

Karim waved at me and invited me into his house for *chai*.[1] I met him some minutes earlier on a street in Hunza, northern Pakistan, and we chatted for a while in English before he offered me to have tea. Pleased, I said yes, we took off our shoes and he led me into his living room. Karim hit the light switch, stared at the celling for a split second and smiled as the headlight went on. "There isn't much electricity these days", he said while he also turned on a small TV and started boiling water on a gas stove. With a hint of anger, he looked through the window towards another house some hundred metres away and said: "But he has a special line, and he is doing it openly. He has electricity all day". This neighbour is the son of an influential politician with good connections to the local Water and Power Department. Therefore, Karim explained, this man somehow managed to get a 'special' transmission line carrying electricity 24 hours that were originally designed for health units and government buildings only.

In this chapter, I demonstrate the value of Tim Ingold's work on lines for anthropological studies of 'infrastructure'. If we take infrastructure as a knot in Ingold's sense in which flows of materials and practices mingle, we start seeing the everyday entanglements happening around and with us. In this perspective, infrastructure arises as a form of those flows in which we participate, and along which the lines of life run. As such, it is neither a pre-existing and passive thing ready to use for political purposes, nor does it contain any intrinsic agency. Rather, infrastructure emerges as a fluid shape in the flows of materials and lives.

After a brief discussion of recent anthropological studies of infrastructure, the chapter focuses on Ingold's notions of lines and corresponding materials. Then, based on two short periods of ethnographic fieldwork in the years 2017 and 2018 in Hunza, Pakistan, I will point out how approaching phenomena like electricity with Ingold's writings might widen our understanding of life along infrastructure.

DOI: 10.4324/9781003162773-18

Figure 13.1 Various 'transmission lines' in Karimabad, Hunza. Photograph by Q. Rieder, March 2018.

An anthropology of infrastructure

Currently, infrastructure is 'in vogue' in anthropology, as Luke Heslop rightly observes (2016:54). For some years now, a wave of publications dealing with all kinds of infrastructure has been flooding the discipline. Some even dare to speak of an 'infrastructural turn' (Harvey, Jensen, and Morita 2017:3) while others – less spectacularly – see infrastructure as a timely reconfiguration of researching the political (Venkatesan et al. 2018). Yet, the topic in general is not entirely new. In social and cultural theory, scholars have long been paying attention to infrastructure from Marxist, evolutionary, Modernist, and cultural materialist points of view (Appel, Anand, and Gupta 2018; Larkin 2013), and even some early ethnographic research, too, has taken the importance of infrastructure for social dynamics into account (e.g., Gluckman 1940). Additionally, critical scholarship of development discusses the role of infrastructure in international development aid (Ferguson and Lohmann 1994). The very recent focus on infrastructure might be rooted in seminal works in the fields of science and technology studies (STS) and actor-network-theory, more specifically in their attention towards things and nonhumans. Being confronted with large scale technological systems and practices of scientific communities, authors like Susan Leigh Star or Geoffrey Bowker focused on the networks and material structures that have to be installed in order to secure the smooth exchange of (certain) materials and ideas (Bowker 1995; Star and Ruhleder 1996; Star 1999). For anthropologists, infrastructure developed conceptually from being something like a marker of 'cultural evolution' at the beginning of the twentieth century into a relational structure that enables certain practices.

The general concept of infrastructure as it figures in current anthropological research can be summarised broadly in Brian Larkin's word as: "built networks that facilitate the flow of goods, people, or ideas and allow for their exchange over space" (Larkin 2013:328).[2] One important stream of research investigates the political relations incorporated into such networks. Nikhil Anand, for example, writes about how political subjectivities are recreated in water pipes and conduits for marginalised 'slum' communities in Mumbai, since these infrastructures often "deliver more than water" (Anand 2017:15). Anand analyses infrastructure as a major battleground for negotiating recognition and citizenship because he takes access to infrastructural services to be crucial in stratifying society. Likewise, Antina von Schnitzler (2016) emphasises the processes in which township inhabitants in Soweto and elsewhere in South Africa refuse to pay for infrastructural services and thereby reject the post-apartheid state on a general level. Up to this day, von Schnitzler points out, infrastructural services have been materialising "the biopolitical relationship between state and population" (von Schnitzler 2016:76). Infrastructure is often picked as a field of study in order "to work ethnographically on the state" (Harvey and Knox 2015:186), frequently linked to broader issues of financial capitalism and political economy (e.g., Barry 2013; Bear 2015; Collier 2011; Mitchell 2013). This literature on infrastructure slightly runs risk of theoretically instrumentalising its object of study as primarily "a form of political recognition, materialized and made possible by a material and technical connection" (Cross 2019:79) while leaving out the multiplicity of experiences and relations in and around it. Thus, the perspective tends to overlook the potentiality of infrastructure in re-forming relations between lives and its environment (but see Carse 2012; Simone 2004).

Another influential stream of infrastructural studies focuses on the aesthetic and affective aspects of those material networks. Scholars observe that infrastructures do more than just function technically or govern politically. Here, infrastructures are conceived through terms like 'desire', 'form', or 'poetics' (Larkin 2013:329) for they "also operate aesthetically" (Larkin 2018:175). Their symbolic value is stressed as they are not merely the undetected base of practices and actions but exist on "a range of visibilities that move from unseen to grand spectacles and everything in between" (Larkin 2013:336). This kind of research focusses on expectations and the often impressive futures – or sometimes pasts – that infrastructural projects epitomise (e.g. Khan 2006; Schwenkel 2018), even if those projects might eventually never be realised (Rippa, Murton, and Rest 2020; Weszkalnys 2016).

These political and aesthetic anthropological approaches to infrastructure have produced a body of insightful literature, but only a small part of it takes into account the entanglements of infrastructural materials in our everyday lives, with even fewer studies recognising the potential of Tim Ingold's ideas for doing so. Instead, infrastructure is either instrumentalised as a platform of political recognition or raised as a symbol of a larger cultural issue. Only a handful of authors, predominantly in the fields of STS and political ecology, conceptualise infrastructure as strongly tied to the environment (see Carse 2012, 2019; Hetherington 2019). In one of the few attempts to reconcile studying infrastructure with Ingold's ideas Rest and Rippa write we need to understand infrastructure "as being in life, and not just as distinct, bounded entities" (Rest and Rippa 2019:377). This perspective explicitly avoids giving infrastructure any kind of individual agency, preferring to locate infrastructural 'networks' in the dynamic meshwork which consists of "nothing other than the web of life itself" (Ingold 2012:435).

Ingold and infrastructure

Tim Ingold is no big fan of the nowadays popular concept of infrastructure, neither its idea, nor its realisation. In fact, Ingold brings forth a "charge against infrastructure" (Anusas and Ingold 2015:550) blaming it (*inter alia*) for two things. First, infrastructure creates the appearance of a world consisting of hard surfaces, on which enclosed and separated blocks rest, arranged according to principles laid down in the structure. And second, thanks to this, infrastructure attempts to shield our perception from the omnipresent entanglements of materials and lives all around us (Anusas and Ingold 2015:550; Ingold 2015:45; see also Anusas and Ingold 2013). I want to show how this argument is embedded in Ingold's writings in general.

Broadly speaking, Ingold's work is characterised by an ontological commitment to movement, a strong argument against dichotomies, and a plead for attention to the everlasting correspondence of humans and nonhumans. For Ingold, the world is not built out of separated, fixed entities, but is always in becoming (see Gisinger, this volume). Everything is in movement through materials which "are the active constituents of a world-in-formation" (Ingold 2011:28). Even if there might be differences in terms of their degree of involvement in the constitution of our world, they are more the products of ontogenesis (and differentiation) than of ontology (Ingold 2018). As Ingold recurrently shows, in reference to French philosophers like Gilbert Simondon and more often Henri Bergson and Gilles Deleuze, instead of pre-existing entities, there is merely the "co-responsive movement of occurrent things along their manifold lines of becoming" (Ingold 2012:437).

It is against this backdrop that Ingold comes up with his notion of lines. Taking lines neither as a metaphor, nor as a theory, but as "phenomena in themselves" (Ingold 2016:xv), Ingold proposes to see lines as traces of movement and the relations made by them, whether durable or elusive. As such, they escape the classical anthropological 'human exceptionalism' since movements are by no means limited to human beings. In general terms, Ingold distinguishes two major kinds of lines, the wayfaring line, and the straight line. The first one moves freely, it takes its time and "goes out for a walk", as Ingold puts it, echoing the words of the artist Paul Klee (Ingold 2016:75). The other goes directly from point to point, ideally in no time at all. One is the result of a free, bodily movement without predetermined destination while the other is static, mapped out and produced in advance. Now Ingold doesn't want to argue normatively for a style of living and being more like Klee's line on a walk; instead, he urges us to realise we have never been doing anything else. Only because of 'modern' innovations (like infrastructure), which created the appearance of a world with straight edges and lines, do people frequently "find themselves in environments built as assemblies of connected elements". "Yet", Ingold goes on, "in practice they continue to thread their own ways through these environments, tracing paths as they go" (Ingold 2016:77). Ingold calls this way of being in life, which extends well beyond human boundaries, 'correspondence'. With this term he describes "the process by which beings or things literally answer to one another over time" (Ingold 2017:14). Things thus come into being through the mingling and corresponding of (material) lines. The same is true for humans, who are additionally practising what Ingold explains as one form of correspondence, the "attentionality of going along with things, opening up to them" (Ingold 2017:19). They are bound together by such everlasting, responding, and interlacing movements, creating specific forms as 'knots' (Ingold 2015:13–16; 2016:103f.). Hence, through processes of correspondence – which are not necessarily as gentle as the term might sound but also encompass "contrary forces of tension and friction" (Ingold 2017:10) – things and places emerge. For Ingold, materials and attentive beings engage with each other's lines and go along together, all running in flowing lines of becoming something, not being something. Accordingly, Ingold describes the always evolving world in which we live, encompassing human and nonhuman beings, as a meshwork. Writing against both Modernist perspectives and actor-network-theory, Ingold wants to capture with this term the ubiquity of movements forming "a field not of interconnected points but of interwoven lines; not a network but a meshwork" (2011:70).

When thinking about infrastructure or any built structure, and Ingold's charge against it, we first of all have to erase the idea that things are solid entities independent of their surroundings. Rather, Ingold urges us to see infrastructure as a part of 'the ground' itself. Like a mountain growing high because of tectonic shifts in the earth's crust, infrastructure too, for Ingold, is something that arises in the ground like a fold, but nevertheless always remains part of the ground. The reason lies in the fact that buildings are fashioned out of materials which are not categorially different from the 'resources' they are made of, and that the same forces of wear and tear work on them (Ingold 2015:32–45). Thus, instead of seeing the world in dichotomies, we should rather recognise that the boundary between 'artificial' and 'natural' environment is fluid and relative. Ingold goes even further, acknowledging the process through which built environment, like infrastructure, emerges as neither finished at any point, nor only human made. Indeed, humans and nonhumans live, dwell, and thereby alter their world in 'spheres' that are inseparably culturally and biologically: "To the extent that the influence of the human component prevails, any feature of the environment will seem more like a building; to the extent that the non-human component prevails, it will seem less so" (Ingold 2000:187). Infrastructure, then, forming a "built network" in Larkin's words (Larkin 2013:328), is part of an active environment and as such, it is involved in a process of continual rebuilding and growing. For this reason, it also is webbed into the meshwork. Since infrastructure is not just one single line but rather a bundle of lines, it is what Ingold would call knotted. Yet the knot, in his terms, does not appear as a central "hub" (Ingold 2016:101), for the lines of flowing materials tie themselves together with the lines of the beings that perceive and engage with infrastructure.

A few studies already draw on Ingold for researching infrastructure. A recent piece by Rest and Rippa (2019) stands out, as they bring forth an advanced theoretical discussion of Ingold's theory for studies of infrastructures, or at least for studies of roads. Thinking about infrastructure with Ingold, Rest and Rippa argue, means accepting the manifold relevance it has for everyday life and for human (and nonhuman) worlds in general. Moreover, their approach does not remit any intrinsic agency to separated infrastructural entities (like for instance an actor-network-theory perspective probably would). For the authors, life is not in roads; "roads, however, are in life, enmeshing social worlds, environmental configurations, imaginaries, and temporalities" (Rest and Rippa 2019:372). Following Ingold's concept of meshwork, they do not simply emphasise the relational quality of infrastructure, as against the assumed separation of spheres such as environment and society; they also take infrastructure as "being these very relations", becoming part of the world only through corresponding practices and materials (Rest and Rippa 2019:385). While this approach is clearly helpful for understanding roads, I think Ingold's ideas fit even better when speaking of electricity.

In this field, Vannini and Taggart (2015) have carried out important research on life off-grid in contemporary Canada. For those voluntarily living disconnected from service networks and generating their own energy supply (and who are often self-sufficient in many other ways too), it is very clear that life is "a coming into being together with different materials" (Vannini and Taggart 2015:18). In their making of a liveable home by generating their own electricity or establishing a running water connection, they practice inhabitation and become involved in their environment in a way different from people living on grid. Yet, the involvement they experience is not simply a 'more', since involvement is not a state that is measurable on a quantitative scale. Rather, Vannini and Taggart refer to this involvement as encompassing the "bindings of people and of non-human inhabitants of the life-world through which substances, intelligences, feelings, and intensities are wrought together" (2015:53). Speaking of renewable energy generation on the Orkney Islands in Scotland's Northern Isles, Laura Watts (2018) makes a similar observation. The strong winds that turn the turbines in the 'energetic' island archipelago are extremely tangible to each of its inhabitants, for they constantly tear on people, car doors or umbrellas, and thus impact on everyday behaviour (Watts 2018:41). This millennia-old intimate bond with wind gets transformed with the emergence of renewable energy generation. Since the huge capacity of the Orkney Islands for tidal and wind energy is recognised, new powerful lines of infrastructure correspond with many facets of life. Creating a suitable energy infrastructure tries to knot the flows of wind, tides, and life together harmoniously.

So, as these authors show, to study infrastructure with Tim Ingold makes us keenly attentive to the materials involved and to the bonds created in their correspondence. In the following section, I describe unstable energy generation and its usage in Hunza, in the high mountains of northern Pakistan. In this case too, infrastructure is a changing relation in life, which brings another kind of quotidian involvement, and through this a feeling for materials in flow. The experience of many people in Hunza shows how life runs along infrastructural lines – even if those frequently come to a halt.

Following electricity in Hunza

The Hunza valley is a remotely appearing mountainous region including several villages and one small town, most of them loosely linked by the Karakoram Highway, which traces parts of the old Silk Road and connects Pakistan with the Chinese Border. It is situated in Gilgit-Baltistan, the Pakistani part of the politically sensitive Kashmir region. At the time of my stays in 2017 and 2018, Hunza had no connection to the national energy grid. Most of its decentralised energy is generated through small run-of-river hydro power plants whose electricity then gets distributed to households according to a governmentally fixed schedule in rolling blackouts (load shedding). Depending on the generally scarce amount of melting water from nearby glaciers, the villages in this rather arid region have access to electricity for around two to five hours per day, more in summer, less in winter. Each village has an assigned slot of electricity supply; however, the promised availability of energy is not guaranteed then. The central and regional governments have been promising to increase electricity generation for years, but due to complications like unforeseen landslides at construction sites, faulty design, corruption and political misconduct, and other difficulties, the situation has not changed for decades. The unreliable availability of electricity has led people to develop a variety of ways to cope with blackout periods. Depending on the occasion and on socio-economic means, households are using solar panels, diesel generators, rechargeable lamps, car batteries, gas lamps, or candles in order to run at least some small devices or to have at least a bit of light. I will show how the role of such infrastructural lines for the meshwork of many lives in Hunza can be better understood by drawing on Ingold's work.

Corresponding electricity

Following Anusas and Ingold, studying electricity "has the capacity to reveal the true extent of our energetic entanglements" (2015:551). Every society – and in fact every kind of life – has depended by some means or other on forms of energy, and their respective patterns of usage have influenced their histories (Anusas and Ingold 2015:546; Vannini and Taggart 2015:9; see also Mitchell 2013). But in order to understand how people live their lives, anthropologists have also to focus on infrastructure to observe the ways and flows of movements, materials, and energies. "Electricity", according to Anusas and Ingold, "is first and foremost a property of materials, as in their movement they rub against one another" (Anusas and Ingold 2015:547). Electricity infrastructure, I argue, means not generating but organising and channelling energy. While electricity is never completely absent from Hunza – because of technical back-up solutions and a variety of electric phenomena inherent in the 'natural' world in general (Anusas and Ingold 2015:547f.) – it is infrastructure that makes electricity flow in certain ways, spinning out infrastructural lines alongside which people live.

The production of hydro energy and its unequal distribution in Hunza shows impressively how infrastructure is enmeshed in social and material worlds. Electric power does not simply emerge on the spot from one power plant. The whole environment around the site has to be arranged (and made to stay) in a certain disposition. First of all, there has to be a steady flow of water – the more and the faster, the better. This flow needs to be channelled to a turbine whose rotation is transmitted to a generator. Now, the Hunza region is full of steep valleys which would afford brooks and rivers as well as usable altitude to create falls for water. But the mountains in the area are also prone to landslides and rockfalls, and during winter most water supplies are frozen. Additionally, the weather mingles with power generation in Hunza. According to Ingold, weather is "continually woven in the multiple rhythmic alternations of the environment" (2015:71), and therefore equally woven into the flows of electricity. On a very general level, weather – as well as climate change – impacts on snowmelt and through this on electricity generation. Moreover, since solar electricity depends on sunlight and this technique is used by many as a back-up energy source in Hunza, the connection with weather is quite visible. Likewise, weather shapes the conditions of electricity use. A warm and sunny day calls for different work tasks and activities, involving different devices, compared to a rainy day. Consequently, the season and the time of day play important roles. The infrastructure of electricity generation arises from knotting materials together and at the same time altering their flows, showing the close relation between weather, water, and current.

The relevance of limited flows of water is not new in Hunza; since irrigation systems have been playing an influential role in political and social processes for centuries (Grieser 2018; Sidky 1996). Due to low annual rainfall, most of Gilgit-Baltistan's agriculture depends on irrigation systems fed by meltwater from glaciers (Sökefeld 2014:9). Often these streams power the hydro power plants too. In spring 2018, when I visited the oldest power generation site in Hunza, a senior engineer complained about the freezing temperatures this year and put the interconnection in a nutshell: "Less water, less electricity. No water, no electricity". Electricity, then, is not simply the output of a power station, but runs as a relation alongside materials like water, guided by transmission lines and influences the possibility of everyday practices.

In the case of such small scale powerplants we see why Ingold argues against the idea of finished buildings and infrastructures standing opposed to a growing and moving natural world, or of the human subordination of materials. Hydropower generation is not a 'cultural' exploitation of 'natural resources'. Infrastructure comes into being because it brings together rare flows of water, concrete channels, and turbines made of steel with skilled engineers and contested power lines. Infrastructure, like anything built, is not simply set above a numb earth; it arises as part of it. As Rest and Rippa emphasise, it is "in life" (2019:375), in so far as all the things involved in infrastructure only exist because of "the generative fluxes of the world of materials in which they came into being and continue to subsist" (Ingold 2011:29). It is just a temporary form continuously entangled in the correspondences of "drawing out or bringing forth of potentials immanent in a world of becoming" (Ingold 2012:435). What makes infrastructure slightly special is its way of participating in this "form-giving" (Ingold 2011:210) since it strives to be a powerful knot, attempting to guide lines of water and electricity, and – as I will show below – also the everyday experience of enmeshed human beings. For now, we note how flows of electricity run with what Ingold calls the corresponding movements of materials and their lines, loosely bound together by the knots of infrastructure. In re-forming water and electricity, infrastructure becomes entangled with these mutable currents as with other lines of life.

Living semi-electrified

What distinguishes Hunza's electric infrastructure – much to the chagrin of most of its inhabitants – is its discontinuous availability. Having a scheduled service is not uncommon in many – especially rural – areas of the world, yet it challenges the still prevailing view of infrastructure as something hidden, and visible only when it breaks down (Star 1999:382), as well as the opposite position that stresses the spectacular and symbolic aspect of highly visible infrastructures (Larkin 2013). In most villages in Hunza, an ordinary day comes with less time on grid than off. Harvey's paraphrase of Deleuze and Guattari, stating "that infrastructures work only by breaking down" (Harvey, Jensen, and Morita 2017:13) has a particular resonance when these breakdowns are the rule. Starting from this point of view, the present section is concerned with the entanglements of electricity in its unstable presence. This situation reveals not only the active involvement with electricity but also the strong emotional line running through infrastructure.

Having a scheduled, yet still unreliable electricity connection can have a major impact on the rhythm of everyday life. On a cold day in April 2018, I spoke to Nosheen, a young woman living and working for an NGO in Hunza, and she explained the role electricity plays for her:

> Like for me as a human – It is like water. Like, for humans, to be alive is to have water, right? It gives life, water. Either for humans or for plants – you will just have it and you will be ok, just fresh and like that. Right now, electricity is like that. I just call it a life. It just comes, and we are happy. [...] You know, when there is light, the feeling is enough. I can't express it, we are happy, and the pent-up work, we do all our pent-up work. How can I say – we have the feeling, we are on track, we are on the right way. And when there is no light, sometimes when we have only a small, small light, I think like 'I don't know what to do...'. If there is light, I will think bigger. About ideas, about business, about going somewhere for education.

There are many things to say about the way life is lived alongside electricity. Nosheen emphasises the value of electricity by relating it to the massive importance of water for life in general, and it is even more vital in Hunza since adjusting to rivers and meltwater rhythms is key to achieving irrigation and creating a livelihood in the region. Nosheen describes how electricity circulates into everyday life and out again, like the partly controllable flow of water for cultivating the fields of wheat, potatoes, and fruit trees, carrying certain activities and feelings. As Vannini and Taggart (2015:53) put it, one can be involved in energy generation in different ways, but every involvement consists of several different activities instead of one fixed state, and in Hunza these activities are closely bound to the availability of electricity. During my talk with Nosheen, she mentioned that nowadays, her village in Hunza has up to six hours of service per day. In another village where she lived a few years ago, there were only two hours:

> When I think of that time, you know, it was painful. We had to boil the water, we had to press the dresses, wash the dresses, we had to vacuum the house – so many works. There were just two hours of light! And we had to do the office work too.[3]

Life runs along infrastructural lines and sometimes one needs to hurry to 'catch up'. However, this is not independent of personal circumstances and possibilities in the sense of how many hours of grid supply one can access. For example, Nosheen as well as Karim, the man we met in the introduction, adjust their lives to an unstable supply, whereas Karim's neighbour with his 'special line' has electricity nearly all the time. The way one lives along infrastructure is related to one's socio-economic status. According to Ingold, every being is continuously caught in a process of becoming, and it is "by their lines that they can live, move and hold on to one another" (Ingold 2015:16). In Hunza, it becomes very apparent how these lines are also infrastructural lines. Relaying on their flow, but also the interrelated inequalities bound to them (see Hornborg 2018), one can or cannot do certain activities.

Listening to Nosheen reveals how this living along infrastructure is open to emotional perception. The presence of electricity enables tasks within and beyond the household and although Nosheen previously described the hope and happiness linked to it (see also Pedersen 2017), its brief availability can also be stressful. This again reassembles Ingold, who claims that in being alive humans attentively follow lines and lay out paths. And the "key quality that makes a movement attentional lies in its resonance with the movements of the things to which it attends – in its going along *with* them" (Ingold 2017:19, emphasis in original). In dealing attentionally with electricity, infrastructural lines become emotional too. "It just comes, and we are happy"

Figure 13.2 A broken hydropower plant in Hunza, its lines interrupted by a swelling river. Photograph by Q. Rieder, March 2018.

Nosheen has said. Electricity as described here can be felt, the current can be experienced, as lifelines runs along the lines of electricity.

During time off grid streets in the centres of Hunza's larger villages were regularly filled with the noise and smell of burning fuels. Especially in the evening, shopkeepers run generators to power their lighting and electronic devices to sell dried fruits and souvenirs to domestic and a few international tourists or anthropologists – often to the anger of some neighbours disturbed by the pollution of power generation. Infrastructure in Hunza occurs in the flowing lines of materials, enmeshed with emotionally charged activities along with the unstable electricity supply. When Laura Watts observes how "people see and feel energy" in Orkney (2018:41), the same might be said for people in Hunza, because electricity is something you see at night-time, hear in the sound of the generators, feel in the everyday and get on with. Influenced, yet not determined, by the governmentally scheduled service, life in Hunza is lived along the fluid lines of electricity.

Conclusion

With this short ethnographic note on Hunza, I have sought to show how attention to the flows of materials and lives can help in further developing thinking about infrastructure. Taking Tim Ingold's ideas into account enables the ethnographer to observe the "energetic entanglements" (Anusas and Ingold 2015:551) around infrastructural lines, instead of being preoccupied with single entities containing 'agency', direct materialised political connections, or spectacular symbolic constructions. Ingold's work can be read as an invitation to follow closely the ways in which people and things like electricity and roads go along together – while also investigating the meaning of the enmeshed unequal access to infrastructure. Seeing infrastructure as a loose knot in the lines of continuously flowing materials, sometimes halting energies, everyday practices and feelings might help us to better understand how life is lived.

Notes

1 All names of research interlocutors changed.
2 Although this definition (especially the notion of infrastructure as *built* networks) is by no means undisputed (see Harvey, Jensen, and Morita 2017:5).
3 I do not want to ignore the impact electricity has on the gendered division of housework; however, this is beyond the scope of this work and will be investigated more closely elsewhere (see also Walter and Grieser 2020).

References

Anand, N. 2017. *Hydraulic city: Water and the infrastructures of citizenship in Mumbai*. Durham, NC: Duke University Press.

Anusas, M. and T. Ingold. 2013. Designing environmental relations: From opacity to textility. *Design Issues* 29(4):58–69.
——— 2015. The charge against electricity. *Cultural Anthropology* 30(4):540–554.
Appel, H., N. Anand, and A. Gupta. 2018. Introduction: Temporality, politics, and the promise of infrastructure. In *The promise of infrastructure*. N. Anand, A. Gupta, and H. Appel, eds. Pp. 1–36. Durham, NC: Duke University Press.
Barry, A. 2013. *Material politics: Disputes along the pipeline*. Chichester: Wiley-Blackwell.
Bear, L. 2015. *Navigating austerity: Currents of debt along a South Asian river*. Anthropology of Policy. Stanford, CA: Stanford University Press.
Bowker, G. 1995. Second nature once removed: Time, space, and representations. *Time & Society* 4(1):47–66.
Carse, A. 2012. Nature as infrastructure: Making and managing the Panama Canal Watershed. *Social Studies of Science* 42(4):539–563.
——— 2019. Dirty landscapes: How weediness indexes state disinvestment and global disconnection. In *Infrastructure, environment, and life in the anthropocene*. K. Hetherington, ed. Pp. 97–114. Durham, NC: Duke University Press.
Collier, S. 2011. *Post-Soviet social: Neoliberalism, social modernity, biopolitics*. Princeton, NJ: Princeton University Press.
Cross, J. 2019. No current: Electricity and disconnection in rural India. In *Electrifying anthropology: Exploring electrical practices and infrastructures*. S. Abram, B. R. Winthereik, T. Yarrow, and A. Sarkar, eds. Pp. 65–81. London: Bloomsbury Academic.
Ferguson, J. and L. Lohmann. 1994. The anti-politics machine: "Development" and bureaucratic power in Lesotho. *The Ecologist* 24(5):176–181.
Gluckman, M. 1940. Analysis of a social situation in modern Zululand. *Bantu Studies* 14(1):1–30.
Grieser, A. 2018. *Den Verlauf kontrollieren: eine Ethnographie der Waterscape von Gilgit, Pakistan*. Bielefeld: transcript.
Harvey, P. and H. Knox. 2015. *Roads: An anthropology of infrastructure and expertise*. Ithaca, NY: Cornell University Press.
Harvey, P., C. Bruun Jensen, and A. Morita. 2017. Introduction: Infrastructural complications. In *Infrastructures and social complexity: A companion*. P. Harvey, C. Bruun Jensen, and A. Morita, eds. Pp. 1–22. London: Routledge.
Heslop, L. 2016. Review: "Roads: An anthropology of infrastructure and expertise" by P. Harvey and H. Knox. *LSE Review of Books*. https://blogs.lse.ac.uk/lsereviewofbooks/2016/01/18/book-review-roads-an-anthropology-of-infrastructure-and-expertise-by-penny-harvey-and-hannah-knox/ (accessed 28/08/2020).
Hetherington, K., ed. 2019. *Infrastructure, environment, and life in the Anthropocene*. Durham: Duke University Press.
Hornborg, A. 2018. Relationism as revelation or prescription? Some thoughts on how Ingold's implicit critique of modernity could be harnessed to political ecology. *Interdisciplinary Science Reviews* 43(3–4):253–263.
Ingold, T. 2000. *The perception of the environment: Essays on livelihood, dwelling and skill*. London: Routledge.
——— 2011. *Being alive: Essays on movement, knowledge and description*. London: Routledge.
——— 2012. Toward an ecology of materials. *Annual Review of Anthropology* 41(1):427–442.

——— 2015. *The life of lines*. Abingdon: Routledge.
——— 2016. *Lines: A brief history*. London: Routledge.
——— 2017. On human correspondence. *Journal of the Royal Anthropological Institute* 23(1):9–27.
——— 2018. One world anthropology. *HAU: Journal of Ethnographic Theory* 8(1–2):158–171.
Khan, N. 2006. Flaws in the flow. *Social Text* 24(4):87–113.
Larkin, B. 2013. The politics and poetics of infrastructure. *Annual Review of Anthropology* 42(1):327–343.
——— 2018. Promising forms: The political aesthetics of infrastructure. In *The promise of infrastructure*. N. Anand, A. Gupta, and H. Appel, eds. Pp. 175–202. Durham, NC: Duke University Press.
Mitchell, T. 2013. *Carbon democracy: Political power in the age of oil*. London: Verso.
Pedersen, M. A. 2017. The vanishing power plant: Infrastructure and ignorance in peri-urban Ulaanbaatar. *The Cambridge Journal of Anthropology* 35(2):79–95.
Rest, M. and A. Rippa. 2019. Road animism: Reflections on the life of infrastructures. *HAU: Journal of Ethnographic Theory* 9(2):373–389.
Rippa, A., G. Murton, and M. Rest. 2020. Building Highland Asia in the twenty-first century. *Verge: Studies in Global Asias* 6(2):83–111.
Schwenkel, C. 2018. The current never stops: Intimacies of energy infrastructure in Vietnam. In *The promise of infrastructure*. N. Anand, A. Gupta, and H. Appel, eds. Pp. 102–129. Durham, NC: Duke University Press.
Sidky, H. 1996. *Irrigation and state formation in Hunza: The anthropology of a hydraulic kingdom*. Lanham, MD: University Press of America.
Simone, A. 2004. People as infrastructure: Intersecting fragments in Johannesburg. *Public Culture* 16(3):407–429.
Sökefeld, M. 2014. Anthropology of Gilgit-Baltistan: Introduction. *Ethnoscripts* 16(1):9–30.
Star, S. L. 1999. The ethnography of infrastructure. *American Behavioral Scientist* 43(3):377–391.
Star, S. L. and K. Ruhleder. 1996. Steps toward an ecology of infrastructure: Design and access for large information spaces. *Information Systems Research* 7(1):111–134.
Vannini, P. and J. Taggart. 2015. *Off the grid: Re-assembling domestic life*. New York: Routledge.
Venkatesan, S., L. Bear, P. Harvey, S. Lazar, L. Rival, and A. Simone. 2018. Attention to infrastructure offers a welcome reconfiguration of anthropological approaches to the political. *Critique of Anthropology* 38(1):3–52.
von Schnitzler, A. 2016. *Democracy's infrastructure: Techno-politics and protest after apartheid*. Princeton, NJ: Princeton University Press.
Walter, A.-M. and A. Grieser. 2020. Feminine intrastructures in a men-made city. *Roadsides* 4:52–60.
Watts, L. 2018. *Energy at the end of the world: An Orkney Islands saga*. Cambridge, MA: MIT Press.
Weszkalnys, G. 2016. A doubtful hope: Resource affect in a future oil economy. *Journal of the Royal Anthropological Institute* 22(1):127–146.

Part V

Art beyond the image

14 Introduction

Art beyond the image

Martin Porr and Niels Weidtmann

The creation of art is often regarded as a genuinely human activity. It is regularly presented as the only characteristic that truly distinguishes humans from animals. Accordingly, in the academic search for human origins, the appearance of art objects in the archaeological record is often interpreted as reflections of 'people like us', and the origins of art are equated with the origins of humanity (Lorblanchet and Bahn 2017). Although this view continues to be perpetuated in public discourses, archaeologists and palaeoanthropologists have been questioning it for some time (Conkey et al. 1997; Palacio-Pérez 2013). Apart from the fact that the concept of art and the definition of art objects remain extremely slippery and belong to a narrowly Eurocentric history, recent findings increasingly suggest that so-called artistic practices and expressions are not restricted to our own sub-species. Finds from Neanderthal contexts suggest that these hominins made geometric markings, used pigments, created personal ornaments and ritual underground structures, and, possibly, applied paint to cave walls (Clauset 2019; Hoffmann et al. 2018; Jaubert et al. 2016). The boundary between so-called anatomically or behaviourally modern humans and other hominins is becoming ever more porous and problematic.

Tim Ingold has interrogated many aspects relevant to this discussion of human origins (see e.g., Ingold 1988, 1991, 1994, 2004, 2006). One of the key areas of critique is related to the population thinking that underlies most of recent human evolutionary theory. With their prioritisation of heritable information, evolutionary models suppose that organisms are genotypically prespecified before they engage in processes of growth and development. In the context of the discussion of the origins of art, this thinking translates into the assumption that the ability to make art objects, or objects that have social or symbolic significance, can be related to an innate capacity for the creation of art. Accordingly, this capacity must have originated at some point in the past, in the form of a suite of modifications to the genotype. Ingold (e.g., 2004, 2006) categorically rejects such an essentialist view of human beings (and other organisms) (see also Porr 2014). He finds that the idea of 'anatomically modern humans', who allegedly originated sometime in the past, and

DOI: 10.4324/9781003162773-20

have remained essentially the same until the present, needs to be discarded as well (Ingold 2000:373–391). Human beings continue to create themselves in response to their respective environments, along with other human beings and fellow creatures.

Similarly, art is what humans do, but humans in the past did not set out expressly to create artistic objects or to engage in artistic practices. They engaged with the world around them and created their lives in their own particular ways. The idea, long considered axiomatic in Eurocentric art history, that humans have always distinguished categorically between works of art and other objects, is also one that Ingold has critiqued extensively during his career. It rests on the so-called hylomorphic model, according to which material artefacts are the realisations of representations in the minds of their makers. This understanding has a long tradition in Western thought, going back to the Aristotelian distinction between form (*μορφή/morphḗ*) and matter (*ὕλη/hylē*) (Ingold 2011:210–219, 2013) (see also Gisinger, this volume). But it is incompatible with the understanding of the world as constantly in formation, in which everything is a going-on. Acts of making, from this latter perspective, do not impose ideal concepts onto inert matter. They intervene in flows of materials and forces. Creatures mark their environments, the ground, and other surfaces through their ongoing activities. Together, they form a reticulate meshwork. The creation of what we call 'art' is but one facet of these encompassing processes that reflect the dynamics of life itself.

Ingold has gone on to explore correspondences and convergences between different human practices such as reading, writing, drawing, painting, and walking, in order to develop a non-representational understanding of so-called art objects and activities. Following Heidegger, he prefers the term 'things' in this context, to stress their emergence from confluences of materials, forces, and gestures (see esp. Ingold 2011). To understand expressions of art, researchers should not ask what they represent or signify. To find their real meaning, one has to understand the relationships between drawings, paintings, or markings and their environments and surfaces. The contributions in the following section show how these aspects are particularly relevant in relation to archaeological objects and markings on rock surfaces (see also e.g., Porr 2018, 2021; Porr and Bell 2012). They show the value of Ingold's work across a wide range of geographical and cultural contexts, and beyond established disciplinary boundaries.

References

Clauset, A. 2019. Symbolic behavior in Neanderthals. *Science* 366(6465):583.

Conkey, M. W., O. Soffer, D. Stratmann, and N. G. Jablonski, eds. 1997. *Beyond art: Pleistocene image and symbol*. San Francisco: California Academy of Sciences.

Hoffmann, D. L., C. D. Standish, M. García-Diez, P. B. Pettitt, J. A. Milton, J. Zilhão, J. J. Alcolea-González, P. Cantalejo-Duarte, H. Collado, R. de Balbín, M. Lorblanchet, J. Ramos-Muñoz, G.-Ch. Weniger, and A. W. G. Pike. 2018. U-Th dating of carbonate crusts reveals Neandertal origin of Iberian cave art. *Science* 359(6378):912–915.

Ingold, T. 1988. The animal in the study of humanity. In *What is an animal?* T. Ingold, ed. Pp. 84–99. London: Unwin Hyman.

Ingold, T. 1991. Becoming persons: Consciousness and sociality in human evolution. *Cultural Dynamics* 4:355–378.

Ingold, T. 1994. Humanity and animality. In *Companion encyclopedia of anthropology*. Tim Ingold, ed. Pp. 14–32. London: Routledge.

Ingold, T. 2004. Between biology and culture: The meaning of evolution in a relational world. *Social Anthropology* 12(2):209–221.

Ingold, T. 2006. Against human nature. In *Evolutionary epistemology, language and culture*. N. de Gontier, J. P. van Bendegem, and D. Aerts, eds. Pp. 259–281. Dorbrecht: Springer.

Ingold, T. 2011. *Being alive. Essays on movement, knowledge and description*. London: Routledge.

Ingold, T. 2013. *Making. Anthropology, archaeology, art and architecture*. London: Routledge.

Jaubert, J., S. Verheyden, D. Genty, M. Soulier, H. Cheng, D. Blamart, C. Burlet, H. Camus, S. Delaby, D. Deldicque, R. L. Edwards, C. Ferrier, F. Lacrampe-Cuyaubère, F. Lévêque, F. Maksud, P. Mora, X. Muth, É. Régnier, J.-N. Rouzaud, and F. Santos. 2016. Early Neanderthal constructions deep in Bruniquel Cave in southwestern France. *Nature* 534(7605):111–114.

Lorblanchet, M. and P. Bahn. 2017. *The first artists. In search of the world's oldest art*. London: Thames & Hudson.

Palacio-Pérez, E. 2013. The origins of the concept of 'Palaeolithic art': Theoretical roots of an idea. *Journal of Archaeological Method and Theory* 20:682–714.

Porr, M. 2014. Essential questions: 'Modern humans' and the capacity for modernity. In *Southern Asia, Australia and the search for human origins*. R. Dennell and M. Porr, eds. Pp. 257–264. Cambridge: Cambridge University Press.

Porr, M. 2018. Country and relational ontology in the Kimberley, Northwest Australia: Implications for understanding and representing archaeological evidence. *Cambridge Archaeological Journal* 28(3):395–409.

Porr, M. 2021. Art, representation, and the ontology of images. Some considerations from the *Wanjina Wunggurr* tradition, Kimberley, Northwest Australia. In *Ontologies of rock art: Images, relational approaches, and Indigenous knowledges*. O. Moro Abadía and M. Porr, eds. Pp. 178–199. Abington: Routledge.

Porr, M. and H. R. Bell. 2012. 'Rock-art', 'animism' and two-way thinking: Towards a complementary epistemology in the understanding of material culture and 'rock-art' of hunting and gathering people. *Journal of Archaeological Method and Theory* 19:161–205.

15 'Dwelling' with Siberian rock art

Irina A. Ponomareva

Introduction

Rock art creates and maintains a strong connection between people, their past, and their land. Being able to tell us about the past, it belongs to the present and the future. Rock art is a phenomenon of constant form but changing meaning. It remains where it was placed, but the impression and interpretation of rock art differs between every epoch and every person. Rock art sites can be seen as joints, or knots in human–nature–art relationships. The sites are alive because they are active in these relationships, and "every living being is a line or, better, a bundle of lines" (Ingold 2017:10). The engagement of people with the land and rock art can be understood through the exploration of routes and pathways:

> Our perception of the environment as a whole, in short, is forged not in the ascent from a myopic, local perspective to a panoptic, global one, but in the passage from place to place, and in histories of movement and changing horizons along the way.
>
> (Ingold 2000:227)

This chapter phenomenologically explores the Gorodovoy Cliff rock art site located in South Buryatia, Siberia (Figure 15.1). It expands on Tim Ingold's observation that "the practice of archaeology is itself a form of dwelling [...]. For both the archaeologist and the native dweller, the landscape tells – or rather is – a story, 'a chronicle of life and dwelling'" (Ingold 2000:189). The cave with the art is located at the top of the Khugtey-Khan Mountain overlooking the valley of the Chikoy River (Figure 15.2). The mountain is sacred in the beliefs of the Buryat peoples and is worshipped. The site is not easy to reach and requires several hours of hiking and climbing along the mountain top which is the only possible way to get to the cave, and the cave is a dead end of this pathway. Following this path is as if following the footsteps of those who created this art. However, are my feelings in any way similar to those that the people of the past experienced walking this pathway? How can my experience of 'dwelling' with the art enhance my

DOI: 10.4324/9781003162773-21

Figure 15.1 The location of the Gorodovoy Cliff site. Map by I. Ponomareva (based on www.freeworldmaps.net/russia/siberia/map.html).

Figure 15.2 Khugtey-Khan Mountain: the location of the Gorodovoy Cliff cave and the *suburghan* 'Lkhabab'. Photograph by I. Ponomareva.

understanding of it? This chapter will engage with questions regarding the value of experiences related to the current research process for the purpose of comprehending rock art and its numerous relationships.

The dwelling perspective and rock art research

When I started my research as an undergraduate student, I learned about Siberian rock art from archival documents and books. Rock art data was presented and published in a completely detached way whereby inventories of rock art motifs would be accompanied by tracings arranged on a page to comply with the book format. It was a revelation for me when I went on fieldwork and saw rock art as it was in the landscape. In my chapter, I will be speaking specifically about the rock art of Trans-Baikal, a region in South-East Siberia. This art looks stunningly homogeneous and uniform on book pages – countless figures of the same birds, simple stick anthropomorphic figures and groups of dots. It was assumed to belong to the Bronze Age and to be related to the early nomadic cultures of the region. When reading key books on this rock art (Okladnikov and Zaporozhskaya 1969, 1970), the impression was that there is nothing else to say. All rock art has already been collected, described, classified, analysed, culturally and chronologically attributed, and interpreted with references to ethnographies of the Siberian peoples. What more can be added? However, when doing fieldwork in this region and working with the same sites that were previously studied, it became apparent that the rock art is not homogeneous; there are many styles of various ages, and many sites feature multiple events of rock art production (Ponomareva 2021). Moreover, my impression was that each site was unique in its art and landscape setting. By looking at random photographs of rock art images from my fieldwork, I can definitely say what site out of the 91 visited is this one or that one. Certainly, I cannot complain about my visual memory as, for me, every site has its own personality which leaves its traces on my experiences of every rock art site I have surveyed. But according to the rules of what counts for science as proper research, these experiences are always put to one side as personal, subjective, and therefore unscientific.

The dwelling perspective, which "treats the immersion of the organism-person in an environment or lifeworld as an inescapable condition of existence" (Ingold 2000:153) has positive consequences for understanding human–nature–art relationships when applied to rock art studies. An important point to make here is that the 'art' of non-Western cultures should not be perceived from a Western point of view, as symbolic representations expressing an aesthetic appreciation of various objects in the world. As Ingold (2000:111–112) noted, to interpret depictions is to understand the relationships between people and their environment.

The dwelling perspective may also have consequences for the methods of fieldwork. Rock art sites are alive within lines of connections, and this can be grasped only through active engagement, such as walking and living with rock art. However, the methods of rock art documentation and presentation remain static even though the quality has considerably improved over the years from black-and-white tracings to stunningly detailed 3D models. The recordings are still detached from the environment of the site, from the play of light on rock surfaces, from seasons of the year, and from sounds of birds in the air, leaves in the wind and a river nearby. Notwithstanding how detailed modern recording might be it disconnects rock art from the innumerable relations in which it lives. Many rock art researchers would agree on that disparity between the feelings of fascination and amazement when working with rock art in the field and that sheer boredom experienced when reading someone else's accounts and reports on their rock art research.

In written reports, the way rock art is presented is completely detached from our perception and our experience. A scientific approach attempts to present knowledge distilled from the researcher's subjectivity. However, it appears that this subjectivity might be the key to look behind the wall of cold facts:

> If science is to be a coherent knowledge practice, it must be rebuilt on the foundation of openness rather than closure, engagement rather than detachment. And this means regaining the sense of astonishment that is so conspicuous by its absence from contemporary scientific work.
>
> (Ingold 2011:75)

When we work with rock art, we touch it, sense it, crawl on rocks, catching glimpses of light on rock surfaces. But all this is lost in the processes that follow, of data assemblage, analysis, and interpretation. We describe panels, categorise images, define types, and make inferences about style and the age of the depictions. Then, we attempt to provide an interpretation depending on our preferred theoretical framework. By the end of the study, we produce a totally different entity of knowledge almost completely disconnected from what we experienced when conducting the survey. This essay is an attempt to bring our attention back to rock art.

Walking to the rock art

Spending more than three months doing my PhD fieldwork in Siberia was a period of living with rock art. Every day I walked countless kilometres up and down hills searching for and recording rock art, and most of the time was spent on walking to and from sites. This made me think about the importance of not just sites as crossroads of time and space but also about the importance of the process of approaching these crossroads, of anticipating the encounter, of living through the walking.

> For it is surely through our feet, in contact with the ground (albeit mediated by footwear), that we are most fundamentally and continually 'in touch'

> with our surroundings ... Locomotion, not cognition, must be the starting point for the study of perceptual activity.
>
> (Ingold 2011:45–46)

Some of the rock art sites that I surveyed are difficult to reach and there is a restricted number of ways to them. The Gorodovoy Cliff site is one such site and it provides a unique case because there is only one possible way to get to the cave, and the cave is the dead end of this route. The unique setting of the site may shed light on the understanding of the diversity of Siberian rock art.

Gorodovoy Cliff is located in South Buryatia, Siberia (Figure 15.1). This is a cave rock art site featuring Bronze Age imagery typical for the region. The cave with the art is located on the southern side at the top of the Khugtey-Khan Mountain overlooking the valley of the Chikoy River, 400 m above the river (Figure 15.2). This mountain was also used as an observation post by Cossacks and the cave was used as a shelter to watch Mongols. The mountain is still worshipped by local people. There are two smaller caves on the mountain but there is no rock art in them. Even though there are more than 200 figures recorded, the most outstanding are three large bird figures depicted on the ceiling of the cave. The site is not easy to reach – on the first day, it took 3.5 hours of hiking and climbing.

The route to the site was explained to me by Zhargal Buyantuyev, the head of the Altai village, which is located nearby. He instructed me to ascend to the mountain top and walk along the peak until the cave is reached. Zhargal also mentioned that another way is possible, descending from the top of the mountain, but this route is dangerous. It is difficult to find the spot from which to descend and would require special skills and equipment. Therefore, the first option was chosen since the explanation was clear and seemed easy to perform. Interestingly, that meeting with Zhargal was a sheer coincidence. On the previous day, I was surveying another site not far from a road. Zhargal was driving and stopped by to enquire about my purpose. Learning that I was a researcher conducting a rock art survey and was going to visit the Gorodovoy Cliff site located not far from his village, Zhargal offered help. Without this coincidence on the road, I would not have found the way to the amazing site of Gorodovoy Cliff!

However, it was midday of 23rd of August 2017 when my driver Sergey Krainov and I arrived at the Altai village, the following day after the encounter on the road. Zhargal assured me that it would take just an hour to get to the site. The weather was grey and cloudy; although conditions can change quickly in the steppe, the clouds did not look threatening. I went up the mountain at 1.30 pm and started walking in the indicated direction. There was no beaten track and I had to find the way myself. Walking just below the rocky peak would mean stumbling on accumulations of rocky debris. Walking along the mountain further down would mean trudging through thorny bushes and crossing many little creeks on the way. The medium path

Figure 15.3 View from the Khugtey-Khan Mountain on the valley of the Chikoy River. Photograph by I. Ponomareva.

had to be found. The cave was expected at each turn because that is what Zhargal had told me – follow the peak and the cave will be just around the corner. Eventually I saw a cave, ran towards it with utter delight, and all of a sudden intense hail began to fall. To my disappointment, no rock art was found in this cave. After the hailstorm was over, I kept walking. Ultimately, it took 3.5 hours to get to my destination. Another cave with no rock art was encountered and hail fell one more time. Notwithstanding all these difficulties and impediments, the walk was full of excitement and astonishment with magnificent scenery unfolding around me as I trudged my way through this landscape (Figure 15.3). Below my feet were the bends of the Chikoy River which is the actual border with Mongolia; Mongolian yurts were seen on the other side of the river. Mountain-Steppe landscape lay all around.

Eventually the cave was reached (Figure 15.4), and it was the dead end of this pathway. It was clear that it was impossible to reach the cave from the other side of the mountain except with climbing gear. On the way back, I attempted to explore the possibility of following the watercourse, but it also turned out to be impossible because the mountain slope was precipitous. When walking back, the sun was setting behind me. At this time of year, sunset occurs at around 8 pm. I started my way back at 7 pm, and therefore had little time to get to our camp (which still remained to be set up) before dark. Now I felt anxious about returning through an uneasy terrain without being able to see anything under my feet. I hurried and this time spent 2.5 hours rushing through rocks and thorny bushes. The following day I had to return to the cave because on this day I had been able to spend only 2 hours there, which was not enough to record all of the amazing rock art at the site. When following this path for the third- and fourth times on the next day, just 1.5 hours was spent walking each way. The route was learnt, the landscape

Figure 15.4 General view at the Gorodovoy Cliff cave. Photograph by I. Ponomareva.

around was expected, and my skills of trudging through rocky and harsh obstacles were upgraded.

Pathways, rock art, and experience

It was apparent that the way along the mountain peak was the only possible way to reach the cave without special gear, which means that ancient people almost certainly had to follow the exact same route. They would have seen the exact same scenery around and felt that same astonishment on seeing the whole world on the palm of the hand. However, was my experience the same as other peoples'?

The character of human experience in the past has been the focus of phenomenological archaeology in the 1990s (Thomas 1996; Tilley 1994), especially in British prehistoric studies of landscape (Brück 2005; Johnson 2012) and Scandinavian rock art research (Ljunge 2013; Tilley 2008). A phenomenological approach is inevitably constrained by the researcher's cultural background and worldview. We see things differently. This was emphasised by critics of the application of phenomenology in archaeology (see Brück 2005), as well as by researchers who held the view that all experience is socially constructed (see Snead, Erickson, and Darling 2009).

Important work on the phenomenology of landscape was carried out by Tilley (1994, 2008). In his later work, Tilley studied Neolithic monuments in

Ireland and rock carvings in Scandinavia through the kinaesthetics of bodily movement. He noted that

> different persons, according to knowledge and circumstances, experience these monuments in different ways, and what ultimately is important about this are the experiences and impressions that they take away with them and remember and the narratives and meanings that they are able to construct from these experiences.
>
> (Tilley 2008:116–117)

Exploring the movements of the body in the spaces of Irish Neolithic temples, and of rock art sites of Norway and Sweden Tilley concluded that "rock art images were not just *expressive* of cognitive thought but constituted a major element in the *formation* of those cognitive thoughts – by virtue of their kinaesthetic experience" (Tilley 2008:255; emphasis in original).

However, in many instances Tilly speculates what these monuments meant for the people who created them, drawing on his personal bodily experience. This research approach, however, was criticised as unconvincing by some authors (Brück 2005; Fleming 2005). Ingold (2005) identified six paradoxes in Tilley's work and also noted the speculative nature of claims about past people's beliefs. Other researchers of phenomenological archaeology were more cautious about the temporality of being and problems concerning the cultural and historical background in the context of human experience (e.g., Clack 2009; Ljunge 2010; Thomas 1996). An interesting study focused on auto-phenomenology which helped to identify researcher's biases when studying rock art (Hurd 2011).

Smith and Blundell (2004), in their critical assessment of phenomenological approaches in rock art studies, inferred that relevant ethnography is crucial for such research. While this is available in some regions, it is absent from others. In Australia, studies of Aboriginal cultural traditions provide insights into the relationships between people and their land though the enactment of stories in the landscape (Porr 2018). Specific rock art styles are means through which people construct their identities and revive their belonging to the land (Blundell 2003). In Siberia, no such stories are preserved from as long ago as the Bronze Age. The ethnography of Siberian peoples provides a rich record of various cultural traditions, but the earliest records date to the 16th–17th centuries, and there is no cultural continuity from the Bronze Age to the present day since the history of Siberia has seen many culturally disrupting events such as migrations and invasions, often on a large scale (see History of Siberia 2019).

We do not know how the people of the past perceived this landscape, and each and every experience is unique. What, then, is the value of my experience for understanding this rock art? Without having had this experience, I would not have come to ask questions about the multiple relations of rock art with its surroundings, its creators, and its appreciators. Nor would I have come to think about the importance of pathways, routes, and the movement along them in general and in relation to rock art in particular. None of these questions are raised by illustrations on the pages of books, in which rock art is reduced to cartoonish images. Although I may not find all answers, the questions have set me on this journey which might or might not open new horizons.

Walking a path is not just crossing space but also passing time, thus the metaphoric association of roads and pathways with time are noticeably to be present in many languages and cultures; "by walking on a road, one senses the passage of time physically: what is behind me is in the past, what lies ahead is in the future" (Keller 2009:156). As Tilley (2008:268) put it,

> to walk is to fuse past with present with future. Walking thus gathers known past histories, practices, and traditions; following a path (for the most part), I am walking where others have walked, in the footsteps of previous generations and the ancestors.

In this regard, an interesting study was conducted on Hopi pilgrimage trails to the Grand Canyon and Zuni Salk Lake (Ferguson, Berlin, and Kuwanwisiwma 2009). During the search and survey of archaeological traces of the trails, many archaeological sites including temporary shelters, camps, resting areas and rock art were documented in close association with the studied trails. One of the rock art sites is Tutuventiwngwu along the Hopi Salt Trail where more than 2,000 petroglyphs are believed to have been pecked by Hopi men who participated in the salt pilgrimage to the Grand Canyon. Importantly, "many trails lead to ancestral villages that connect past and present Hopi use of landscape" (Ferguson, Berlin, and Kuwanwisiwma 2009:24). Thus, notwithstanding the scepticism around the possibility of comprehending past experiences of pathways, trails, and movement along them, a researcher's experience is still valuable because it might grasp persistent qualities of landscapes and monuments. The exact tracks are considerably more difficult to retrace in archaeological research but moving around is no less important to unveil the relational settings of artefacts left to researchers. Movement is also temporal, and the monuments are not relics but continue to live on in the present and into the future; thus, their present setting and present experience of them is no less significant. Since to dwell is to move along a way of life (Ingold 2011), we now move to the next bundle of lines of experience which is the cave itself and the rock art present there.

A blend of sky and earth

Around the world, caves were noticed to exhibit a special value for different societies and were places used for habitation, interment, shelter, and the performance of various rituals (see Bergsvik and Skeates 2012; Clack 2009; David 2017; Moyes 2012b). For instance, in the Ancient Maya culture, caves were related to water rituals (Moyes 2007). For Palaeolithic Europe, it has been suggested that caves were places of initiation and shamanic journeys (Lewis-Williams 2002). In Bronze Age Italy, caves were related to initiation, and a restricted access to the religious knowledge was noted (Whitehouse 1992). In California, the symbolics of rock art sites and specifically those associated with caves was shown to contain reversed gender metaphors within shamanic religious system. Rock art sites were female-gendered but were owned by male shamans (Whitley 1988, 2000). Researchers studying different regions and cultures noticed that caves or other settings with restricted light and other conditions may have had a particular impact on human psychological states restricting or altering the senses and, thus, heightening the experience of the sacred (Hodgson 2008; Lewis-Williams 2002; Montello and Moyes 2012; Skeates 2007; Tilley 2008). Rock art found in caves adds more symbolic significance to the setting. Phenomenology also influenced the field of cave studies. Bjerck (2012) explored the sensory qualities of caves with Bronze Age rock art in Norway through his personal embodied experience concluding that the caves were used for rites of passage and were connections to other worlds. Bjerck shares Tilley's views about the resemblance of present bodily experience with that of the prehistoric people. However, while the experiences were colourfully described, the rock art itself was overall neglected in Bjerck's interpretation (Goldhahn 2019:317–318; Ljunge 2013).

'Cave' has many meanings and is usually understood quite broadly. An exhaustive review of this term's definition, its usage and applicability for cultural studies was undertaken by Moyes (2012a). She emphasises the importance of distinguishing between rock shelters and caves where the key difference lies in the quality of the light. While rock shelters feature light and twilight zones which might have been useful for habitation, caves contain dark zones rarely used for this purpose. These dark zones could, however, have strongly impacted on sensory experiences. Following Moyes's analysis that dark zones are an essential characteristic of caves, the Gorodovoy Cliff cave should be described as a shelter. However, it is traditionally referred to as a cave in the literature and by local people, and for this reason, I will retain this designation.

The Gorodovoy Cliff is 9 m wide, 5.1 m deep and 2.5 m high (Tivanenko 1990:41), oriented towards south-south-west, and located 975 m above the sea level, 400 m above the Chikoy River (Figure 15.4). Although it does not contain a dark zone, it features a rather small twilight zone in the north-west corner of the cavity. Its location almost at the top of the mountain and its openness to majestic scenery gives a thrilling feeling of transition between realities. This place does not heighten some senses by restricting others as dark caves do. Instead, the world opens up around you (Figure 15.3), but you still feel safe and grounded as if in a bird's nest. This metaphor is further heightened by the presence of three large depictions of birds of prey on the ceiling of the cave (Figure 15.5).

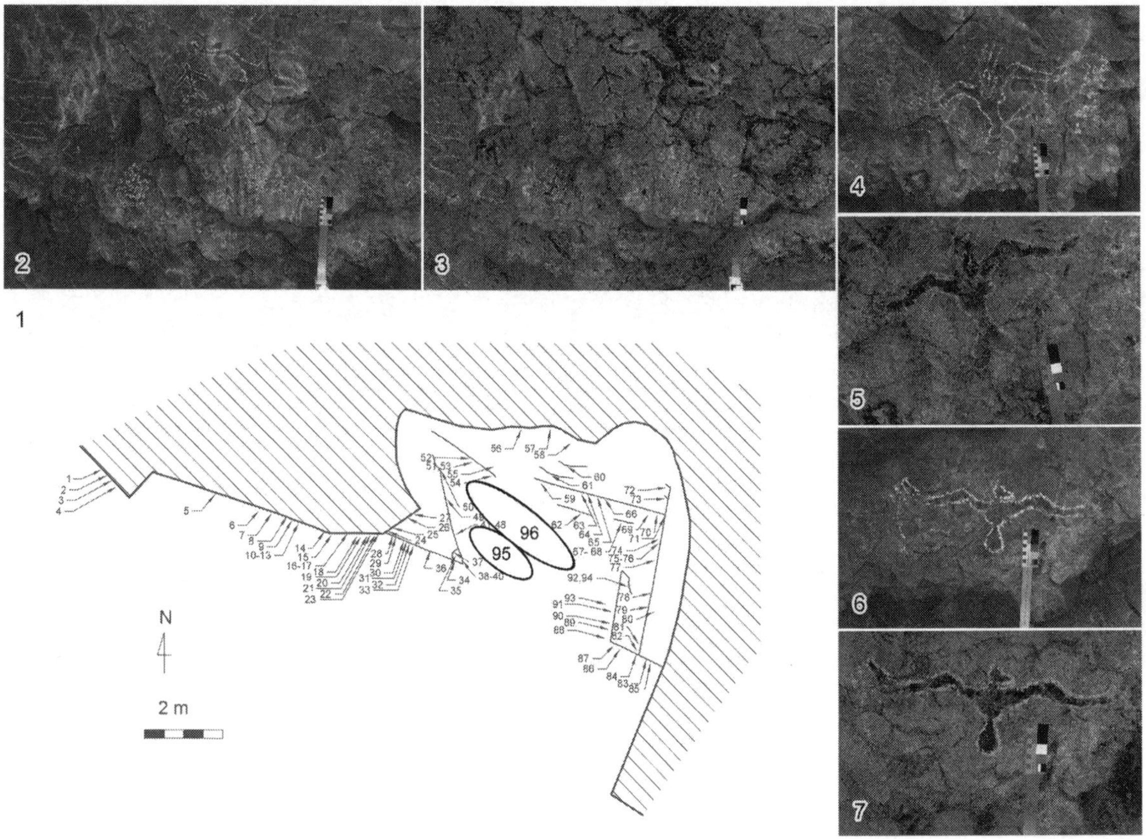

Figure 15.5 Central bird depictions and their location in the cave: 1 – plan of panels; 2, 3, 4, 5 – panel 96; 6, 7 – panel 95; 2, 4, 6 – original photographs; 3, 5, 7 – DStretch-enhanced. Photographs by I. Ponomareva.

Attaining the cave and becoming a bird

Birds of prey are an essential element of the Trans-Baikal Steppe landscape. There are more than 40 species present in the region such as eagles, kites, falcons, hawks, etc. (Dorzhiev 2016). The motif of the bird of prey depicted in flight with the wings spread is one of the predominant features of the Bronze Age rock art tradition. In addition, eagles and falcons are important characters in Siberian mythology and are believed to be the spirit-guardians of shamans (Okladnikov and Zaporozhskaya 1970). From ethnographic sources we know that Mongols and Buryats have had cults of mountains, rocks, and other natural places which they believed were inhabited by guardian spirits. They also had cults of caves. In Mongolia and Buryatia there were special caves related to female fertility cults and these rituals were performed by shamans (Humphrey 1995).

Simple statistics do not reveal the centrality of bird images at the site (Figure 15.5). The total number of designs is 213, and most (122) are non-figurative, consisting of apparently chaotic assemblages and rows of dots. There are also 31 anthropomorphs, 2 enclosures, and 22 undefined designs. These numbers, however, do not tell us the whole story of the site. Three central figures are among the 36 ornithomorphic figures recorded in and around the cave. Interestingly, although rock art depictions are found everywhere inside and outside the cave, various depictions of birds (naturalistic, stylised and schematic) are mostly found in lighter areas – on the walls outside of the cave, on the cornice, on the walls near the entrance inside the cave, and on the ceiling. Only four figures at the back of the cave were identified as ornithomorphic, two of which are ambiguous due to weathering. Thus, the birds remain on the border of light and shade highlighting their metamorphic character as creatures who dwell between the worlds.

It is not surprising that the transformative nature of the birds, their ability to transcend realities has attracted the imagination of the artists who painted here in prehistoric times. The birds of prey are an essential element of this land, and when doing my survey, I often watched as eagles and kites flew above my head high in the sky. Once I even encountered a kite's nest on top of a rock art site in Eastern Trans-Baikal with a fluffy kite nestling in it. The depictions of birds on rocks are not just depictions. They are birds. The three large bird figures of the Gorodovoy Cliff are not depicted on the ceiling of the cave; they dwell there. This is their nest, located high above and overlooking the valley.

Art is about corresponding with the world. It connects the lifelines of people, animals, and the land. Through art we express our soul, open a door for it and touch other souls. Goldhahn expressed a similar feeling about the Solsemhulen cave in Norway, "By entering the cave, the *humanness* of humans faded, while their *animalness* and *birdness* increased" (Goldhahn 2019:333, original emphases). The depictions of birds are often accompanied in the Gorodovoy Cliff by groups of dots which are of the size of a fingertip. Half the motifs in the cave are composed of simple dots in various combinations. These are common in all rock art sites in the region, and in some instances, preservation allows one to distinguish fingerprints. Possibly, these dots are evidence that people who visited this cave wanted to touch the surface and leave their traces on it. They wanted to connect directly and personally with the place and with the birds on the ceiling.

Visiting this rock art site engages all the senses (see also Ouzman 2001; Lahelma 2010; Skoglund, Persson, and Rédei 2020). When walking towards it, you perceive the opening world around you with the whole body. You see, you smell, you stumble upon rocks and strike out through thick thorny bushes. When reaching the cave, you see live birds on the ceiling of the cave, you touch the walls which were touched before many times. The perception of rock art is all-encompassing. This is how it is meant to be, alive and thrilling. Visiting this site opens all your feelings and make you closer to the sky where eagles dwell. You become an eagle because you are here, and you experience what they see and feel.

The lifelines of the Khugtey-Khan sacred mountain

Rock art is often considered as evidence or a reflection of past events, and we attempt to understand it in the context of the time of its creation. However, rock art continues to live into the present day and into the future. It is therefore important to consider rock art as it exists now. Together with the mountain where it is located, the site is not considered a relic of the past by the Indigenous people of the region. In their culture, it is alive. Importantly, the mountain Khugtey-Khan is one of the five sacred mountains in Buryatia according to Buddhist beliefs (Batomunkueva 2012).

In the 17th Century, Tibetan Buddhism spread from Mongolia to Trans-Baikal where until then, shamanism had been practiced. In Buryatia, Buddhism incorporated and assimilated many local traditions and beliefs, and in many cases, shamanic sacred places were converted into Buddhist shrines and included in the Buddhist belief system. In Buryat Buddhism, the cult of five sacred mountains is present and the origins of this cult are related to the concept of five dhyani-buddhas which are emanations of the five qualities of the Adi-Buddha or 'first Buddha'. The mountain Khugtey-Khan, or Gorodovoy Cliff, located in the South of Buryatia is thus considered to be the guardian of the South. In Buryat, 'Khan' means ruler, tsar, monarch, and Khugtey means cheerful, joyful. It is also believed that there is a place near the mountain where *avarga mogoj* (the giant serpent in Mongolian and Buryat mythology) lives. The master of the mountain has the appearance of an elder with a grey beard dressed in a black silk robe (Batomunkueva 2012).

In 2002, on the western side of the mountain, in the village of Tsagan-Chelutai, *suburghan* (stupa in Buryatia) 'Zhanchub' was erected devoted to Damba Darzha Zayayev, the first Buryat Khambo Lama. In 2004, on the eastern side of the mountain, at the foothill, *suburghan* 'Lkhabab' was constructed (Bazarova 2009). These are recent stupas, and their appearance is related to the religious resurgence during the post-Soviet period. Budaeva and Semyenov (2018) also mention the remains of four *oboo* at the foothill and on the top of the mountain. The *oboo* is a sacred stone cairn used as a shrine devoted to the master of a place. On the official website of the Kyakhtinskiy district where the Khugtey-Khan Mountain is located, the Gorodovoy Cliff cave is listed among the most significant places of the district. In addition to its archaeological identification as a rock art site, the cave is described as a "sacred place, several *oboo* are constructed here" (Republic of Buryatia. Kyakhtinskiy district. Sights).

I must admit that I did not know all these details about the importance of the Khugtey-Khan Mountain and other places with rock art in contemporary Buryat beliefs before setting out on this journey. When preparing for the fieldwork, I gathered information from the few existing publications, notably the works are by Okladnikov and Zaporozhskaya (1969, 1970), Tivanenko (1989, 1990), and Mazin (1986, 1994). These are archaeological studies which treat rock art sites as sources to inquire about the human past. They pay no attention to the role of these places in contemporary Indigenous cultures. Okladnikov and Zaporozhskaya (1969, 1970) occasionally mention the *oboos* constructed at a site. However, in Buryatia, *oboos, khadags* (colourful ceremonial scarves in Tibetan Buddhism) attached to trees and other offerings such as coins and cigarettes are commonly found at rock art sites. Tivanenko (1989:5–7) noticed that in 90% of the cases, rock art sites "coincide with tribal and clan shrines" and used this as an indication to search for 'new' rock art sites, which were discoveries for academia but not for local people. Only by coming to Buryatia and visiting those places personally could I grasp their significance. They are not points of interest on a map and data for analysis. They are living places.

Conclusion

Answering the question set at the beginning, about the value of personal experience in the comprehension of rock art and its relations, my experiences provoked me to contemplate on this journey and to learn more about the significance of various things seen and felt. Before setting foot on my trip towards the Gorodovoy Cliff cave, I did not know about its significance or of the mountain's importance for the Buryat. Notwithstanding my ignorance, I grasped its significance through my bodily experience of the place. There are some eternal qualities in landscapes, which are accessible to anyone who is prepared to be sensitive and open.

> Astonishment, I think, is the other side of the coin to the very openness to the world that I have shown to be fundamental to the animic way of being. It is the sense of wonder that comes from riding the crest of the world's continued birth.
>
> (Ingold 2011:74)

People continue venerating the same places through millennia, and this persistence cannot be explained by cultural continuity or transmission alone. Certain places are felt to be endowed with special powers, and people from different cultural backgrounds are able to perceive it. This is where this pathway has brought me so far.

References

Batomunkueva, S. R. 2012. Five Buryat sacred mountains worship cult. *Bulletin of Banzarov Buryat State University. Pedagogy. Philology. Philosophy* 6a:257–261 [in Russian].

Bazarova, E. B. 2009. Istoricheskiye traditsii vozdvizheniya suburganov (buddiiskikh stup) v severnom buddizme [Historical tradition of constructing suburghans (Buddhist stupas) in Northern Buddhism]. *Rossiiskiy ekonomichskiy internet-zhurnal*:1–9 [in Russian].

Bergsvik, K. A. and R. Skeates. 2012. Caves in context: An introduction. In *Caves in context: The cultural significance of caves and rockshelters in Europe*. K. A. Bergsvik and R. Skeates, eds. Pp. 1–9. Oxford and Oakville: Oxbow Books.

Bjerck, H. B. 2012. On the outer fringe of the human world: Phenomenological perspectives on anthropomorphic cave paintings in Norway. In *Caves in context: The cultural significance of caves and rockshelters in Europe*. K. A. Bergsvik and R. Skeates, eds. Pp. 48–64. Oxford and Oakville: Oxbow Books.

Blundell, V. 2003. The art of country: Aesthetics, place, and Aboriginal identity in north-west Australia. In *Disputed territories: Land, culture and identity in settler societies*. D. Trigger and G. Griffiths, eds. Pp. 155–185. Hong Kong: Hong Kong University Press.

Brück, J. 2005. Experiencing the past? The development of a phenomenological archaeology in British prehistory. *Archaeological Dialogues* 12(1):45–72.

Budaeva, A. Z. and Y. Semyenov. 2018. Natural and cultural heritage of the village Ust-Dungui of the Kyakhta District of the Republic of Buryatia: History and modern condition. *Bulletin of East-Siberian State Institute of Culture* 1(5):22–30 [in Russian].

Clack, T. 2009. Sheltering experience in underground places: Thinking through Precolonial Chagga Caves on Mount Kilimanjaro. *World Archaeology* 41(2):321–344.

David, B. 2017. *Cave art*. New York: Thames & Hudson.

Dorzhiev, T. Z. 2016. *Ptitsy Buryatii i organizatsiya ekologicheskogo turizma: uchebno-metodicheskoe posobie* [Birds of Buryatia and the organization of ecological tourism]. Ulan-Ude: Izd-vo Buryatskogo gosuniversiteta [in Russian].

Ferguson, T. J., G. L. Berlin, and L. J. Kuwanwisiwma. 2009. Kukhepya: Searching for Hopi trails. In *Landscapes of movement. Trails, paths, and roads in anthropological perspective*. J. E. Snead, C. L. Erickson, and J. A. Darling, eds. Pp. 20–41. Philadelphia: University of Pennsylvania Museum of Archaeology and Anthropology.

Fleming, A. 2005. Megaliths and post-modernism: The case of Wales. *Antiquity* 79(306):921–932.

Goldhahn, J. 2019. *Birds in the Bronze Age: A North European perspective*. Cambridge: Cambridge University Press.

Hodgson, D. 2008. The visual dynamics of Upper Palaeolithic cave art. *Cambridge Archaeological Journal* 18(3):341–353.

Humphrey, C. 1995. Chiefly and shamanist landscapes in Mongolia. In *The anthropology of landscape. Perspectives on place and space*. E. Hirsch and M. O'Hanlon, eds. Pp. 135–162. Oxford: Oxford University Press.

Hurd, R. 2011. Integral archaeology: Process methodologies for exploring prehistoric rock art on Ometepe Island, Nicaragua. *Anthropology of Consciousness* 22(1):72–94.

Ingold, T. 2000. *The perception of the environment. Essays on livelihood, dwelling and skill*. London and New York: Routledge.

——— 2005. Comment on Christopher Tilley: The materiality of stone: Explorations in landscape phenomenology. *Norwegian Archaeological Review* 38(2):122–129.

——— 2011. *Being alive: Essays on movement, knowledge and description*. London and New York: Routledge.

——— 2017. On human correspondence. *Journal of the Royal Anthropological Institute* 23(1):9–27.

Johnson, M. H. 2012. Phenomenological approaches in landscape archaeology. *Annual Review of Anthropology* 41:269–284.

Keller, A. H. 2009. A road by any other name: Trails, paths, and roads in Maya language and thought. In *Landscapes of movement. Trails, paths, and roads in anthropological perspective*. J. E. Snead, C. L. Erickson, and J. A. Darling, eds. Pp. 133–157. Philadelphia: University of Pennsylvania Museum of Archaeology and Anthropology.

Lahelma, A. 2010. Hearing and touching rock art: Finnish rock paintings and the non-visual. In *Changing pictures: Rock art traditions and visions in Northern Europe*. J. Goldhahn and I. Fuglestvedt, eds. Pp. 48–59. Oxford and Oakville, CT: Oxbow Books.

Lewis-Williams, D. 2002. *The mind in the cave*. London: Thames & Hudson Ltd.

Ljunge, M. 2010. Rock art and the meaning of place: Some phenomenological reflections. In *Changing pictures: Rock art traditions and visions in Northern Europe*. J. Goldhahn and I. Fuglestvedt, eds. Pp. 88–105. Oxford and Oakville, CT: Oxbow Books.

——— 2013. Beyond 'the Phenomenological walk': Perspectives on the experience of images. *Norwegian Archaeological Review* 46(2):139–158.

Mazin, A. I. 1986. *Tayozhnye pisanitsy Priamur'ya* [The Taiga rock art sites of the Amur region]. Novosibirsk: Nauka [in Russian].

——— 1994. *Drevnie svyatilishha Priamur'ya* [Ancient sanctuaries of the Amur region]. Novosibirsk: Nauka [in Russian].

Ministerstvo nauki i vysshego obrazovaniya Rossiiskoy Federacii, Rosssiiskaya akademiya nauk, Sibirskoye otdelenie, Institut arheologii i etnografii, Institut istorii, Rossiiskoye istoricheskoye obshchestvo, eds. 2019. *History of Siberia*. Novosibirsk: IAET SO RAN [in Russian].

Montello, D. R. and H. Moyes. 2012. Why dark zones are sacred. Turning to behavioral and cognitive science for answers. In *Sacred darkness: A global perspective on the ritual use of caves*. H. Moyes, ed. Pp. 564–581. Boulder, CO: University Press of Colorado.

Moyes, H. 2007. The Late Classic drought cult: Ritual activity as a response to environmental stress among the ancient Maya. In *Cult in context*. D. A. Barrowclough and C. Malone, eds. Pp. 217–228. Oxford: Oxbow Books.

——— 2012a. Introduction. In *Sacred darkness: A global perspective on the ritual use of caves*. H. Moyes, ed. Pp. 22–37. Boulder, CO: University Press of Colorado.

Moyes, H., ed. 2012b. *Sacred darkness: A global perspective on the ritual use of caves*. Boulder, CO: University Press of Colorado.

Okladnikov, A. P. and V. D. Zaporozhskaya. 1969. *Petroglify Zabaikal'ya. Chast' I* [Petroglyphs of Trans-Baikal. Part I]. Vol. 1. Leningrad: "Nauka", Leningradskoye otdeleniye [in Russian].

——— 1970. *Petroglify Zabaikal'ya. Chast' II* [Petroglyphs of Trans-Baikal. Part II]. Vol. 2. Leningrad: "Nauka", Leningradskoye otdeleniye [in Russian].

Ouzman, S. 2001. Seeing is deceiving: Rock art and the non-visual. *World Archaeology* 33(2):237–256.

Ponomareva, I. A. 2021. *Change and continuity in the prehistoric rock art of East Siberia. An archaeological and anthropological exploration into ethno-cultural identity, belonging, and symbolism*. London: BAR Publishing.

Porr, M. 2018. Country and relational ontology in the Kimberley, Northwest Australia: Implications for understanding and representing archaeological evidence. *Cambridge Archaeological Journal* 28(3):395–409.

Republic of Buryatia. Kyakhtinskiy district. Sights. https://egov-buryatia.ru/kyakhta/o-munitsipalnom-obrazovanii/dostoprimechatelnosti/index.php (accessed 22 December 2021) [in Russian].

Skeates, R. 2007. Religious experience in the prehistoric Maltese underworld. In *Cult in context*. D. A. Barrowclough and C. Malone, eds. Pp. 90–96. Oxford: Oxbow Books.

Skoglund, P., T. Persson, and A. Cabak Rédei. 2020. A multisensory approach to rock art: Exploring tactile and visual dimensions in the Southern Scandinavian rock art tradition. *Proceedings of the Prehistoric Society* 86:95–110.

Smith, B. W. and G. Blundell. 2004. Dangerous ground: A critique of landscape in rock-art studies. In *The figured landscapes of rock-art. Looking at pictures in place*. C. Chippindale and G. Nash, eds. Pp. 239–262. Cambridge: Cambridge University Press.

Snead, J. E., C. L. Erickson, and J. A. Darling. 2009. Making human space: The archaeology of trails, paths, and roads. In *Landscapes of movement. Trails, paths, and roads in anthropological perspective*. J. E. Snead, C. L. Erickson, and J. A. Darling, eds. Pp. 1–19. Philadelphia: University of Pennsylvania Museum of Archaeology and Anthropology.

Thomas, J. 1996. *Time, culture and identity: An interpretative archaeology*. London: Routledge.

Tilley, C. 1994. *A phenomenology of landscape. Places, paths and monuments*. Oxford and Provenance: Berg.

——— 2008. *Body and image. Explorations in landscape phenomenology 2*. London: Routledge.

Tivanenko, A. V. 1989. *Drevnie svyatilishha Vostochnoy Sibiri v epokhu kamnya i bronzy* [Ancient sanctuaries of Eastern Siberia in the Stone and Bronze Ages]. Novosibirsk: Nauka [in Russian].

——— 1990. *Drevnee naskal'noe iskusstvo Buryatii* [Ancient rock art of Buryatia]. Novosibirsk: Nauka [in Russian].

Whitehouse, R. D. 1992. *Undeground religion. Cult and culture in prehistoric Italy*. London: Accordia Research Centre, University of London.

Whitley, D. S. 1988. Finding rain in the desert: Landscape, gender and far western North American rock-art. In *The archaeology of rock-Art*. C. Chippindale and P. S. C. Taçon, eds. Pp. 11–29. Cambridge: Cambridge University Press.
——— 2000. *The art of the shaman. Rock art of California.* Salt Lake City: The University of Utah Press.

16 Rock art conservation and living heritage

Performance and the transformation of 'paintings' in rock art

Ana Paula Motta

Introduction

During the 1990s and 2000s there was a surge in rock art research that cast doubt on the use of 'rock art' as a suitable word to describe wall markings. It was alleged that the use of the word 'art' was tainted by a Western aesthetic appreciation of the past (see Chippindale 2001; Loubser 2001; Whitley 2001 for a discussion of this topic). Despite this initial interest in the (re)definition of categories used in the study of the past, no explicit understandings of what rock art researchers meant by 'paintings' were offered. In more recent attempts to define images (see Back Danielsson and Jones 2020; Jones and Cochrane 2018), *painting* was described as the practice of applying paint to a rock surface. However, the lack of definition and exploration of the word 'painting' erased other meanings and interpretations associated with this term. This phenomenon seems to be specific to archaeology and rock art research, since other disciplines (e.g., art history and cinematography) have vigorously defined painting/s, its multiple meanings being context-specific and dependent upon the author/artist (see Vacche 1996 for an example of the use of paintings as art in film).

The portrayal of paintings as an object/noun – while simultaneously ignoring painting as performance/verb – not only presents paintings as static phenomena, but has profound consequences for the way we think about the conservation of rock art. In this sense, conservation derived from an object/noun understanding of painting/s creates a discourse in which rock art must remain intact for future studies and generations. According to this definition (conservation as protection), the maintenance and repainting of rock images by living communities remains prohibited as it is perceived as 'destructive' in nature. In doing so, the social aspect of paintings as part of a living world that must be taken care of for the renewal of resources is overlooked.

Overall, Western notions of art and its principles for conservation are instead prioritised in the protection of cultural and natural heritage. This means that cultural and natural sites are isolated from any type of 'unqualified' influence that might jeopardise their conservation (Maynard 1975). A similar argument can be unmasked when considering the conservation of natural

DOI: 10.4324/9781003162773-22

heritage by wildlife protection agencies. Ingold (2000:67) argues that the responsible agencies conceive nature as separated from humanity. In turn, wildlife protection agencies promote the idea that the conservation of nature and its species can only be achieved by isolating them from (all) human populations. This vision poses a problem for non-Western concepts of nature and culture, which, in turn, affects the way Indigenous populations relate to the environment (e.g., Kirksey 2015). Ingold's argument reveals a dialectic between scientists and Indigenous populations. On the one hand, we have Western scientists that envision (Western/qualified) humans as the sole agents in charge of the conservation of nature. On the other hand, we have Indigenous populations with a deep knowledge of environmental conservation (Ingold 2000:68). Ultimately, as science prevails in setting the agenda for conservation, other significant ways of engaging with the environment are neglected or ignored.

The way environmental protection is portrayed by wildlife conservation agencies is analogous to how cultural heritage management is understood in rock art studies. The idea of conservation that is based on a static understanding of rock paintings – promoted by archaeologists and other institutions – is not only detrimental for some sites in which access is restricted to local communities. It also limits the overall interpretation of rock images and our appreciation of paintings among past and contemporary communities.

In this paper, I engage with the polysemy of the word 'painting' and use this to reflect on rock art conservation. Painting has many meanings. As a noun, it signifies the end product or an art object in itself. As a verb, however, it refers to the act of marking a surface. The first concept is passive, whereas the second one is active. Although the term 'rock art' is used to refer specifically to the attributes of painting as a noun, artists and viewers often think of painting as a verb or performance. This is manifested in the meaningful engagements between paintings and artists/viewers through the act of painting and by living in these painted landscapes (e.g., Maynard 1975:57). In other words, as Ingold (2000:72) notes, just as hunters 'get to know their prey' through hunting, artists get to know and reproduce their world through painting/s.

Finally, I will discuss what happens when the idea of conservation, defined as the protection of heritage from unauthorised human interference, enters the policymaking process. This will be illustrated through the analysis of Tsodilo Hills in Botswana. The declaration of this site as World Heritage in 2001 brought a series of unforeseen problems to the Indigenous communities living in the vicinity of the rock art area, brought forward by an eagerness to 'preserve' and maintain the site for tourists, while restricting and destroying some of its natural features. In sum, viewing paintings (n) vs painting (v) has profound repercussions for how we think about the conservation of cultural heritage and brings into play epistemological and ontological differences between the West and the 'rest' regarding the interpretation and subsequent conservation efforts of significant sites. As will be shown, for some Indigenous groups, conservation is about the painting and repainting of rock art, rather than the preservation of original objects.

Painting (n.) vs Painting (v.)

In considering Indigenous 'art', it has been noted that labels originally used for referring to European art objects have been directly applied to Indigenous decorated objects and paintings (Maynard 1975:55). These objects were not meant to be taken out of their original context and be exhibited in museums but were rather designed to be part of daily activities and ceremonies and intended to be destroyed or left behind (Maynard 1975). For example, in the Kimberley, north-western Australia, the regular repainting of Wanjinas was done to reactivate the paintings, to renew resources, and to bring rain (Crawford 1968; Maynard 1975; Mowaljarlai et al. 1988; Stanton 2006). This treatment of 'art' objects by some Indigenous groups is often seen by Western researchers as vandalism (see Motta 2019 for a review of these approaches), rather than considering how art and paintings can be perceived as performance. However, some anthropologists, archaeologists, ethnographers, and art historians have highlighted the different properties of Indigenous rock art. For example, Morphy's (1999) work on Yolngu art emphasises its spiritual power and how it relates to the Ancestral Past and origin stories. In other words, paintings have an aura of aliveness that communicate Ancestral Power (Rose 2008:114). In this sense, Australian Indigenous art is used to learn about mythical events and is primarily referential (Morphy 1999:13). Therefore, the meaning of the art is encoded in landscape features and events that took place during Ancestral times and are revealed by Elders through ceremonies. However, Yolngu art is not only about revealing meaning; it also is a direct 'manifestation of the Ancestral Time' (Morphy 1999:13–14). Along these lines, Rose (2008) draws on Morphy's work to propose that, among the Yarralin Walangeri, "the painting can also be understood to express power in the form of the enduring time and motion of creation" (114). In other words, she conceptualises Ancestral Power as shimmering, as being alive and communicating Dreaming Power, where painting and dancing are viewed as motion and performance.

Another relevant contribution to the study of Indigenous art is the work of Indigenous scholar Leuthold (1998). His work focuses on Indigenous aesthetics applied to the study of Native filmmakers and films among First Nations people in North America. He suggests that Western conceptions of art do not necessarily apply to Indigenous notions of this term (Hart 2000:145). Instead, Leuthold proposes that modern definitions of art should be broadened, while acknowledging the "ties among art, ethics, and spirituality" (Leuthold 1998:9).

By contrast, Western definitions of art are grounded in Classical philosophy, more particularly in Plato's and Aristotle's theorisations about paintings. Both Plato and Aristotle saw art as a form of *mimesis* or imitation

(Halliwell 2002:37–38). The main difference between the two is that for Plato art was inferior as it was a copy of nature, while Aristotle argued that art contained 'cognitive value' through which one would gain a better understanding of reality. Following Aristotle's definitions of art and painting, Bell (1999) locates 'paintings' within two categories: *paintings and painting*. The first category is closely related to Aristotle's views of paintings. According to this definition, paintings are seen as objects or as the agglomeration of markings produced by human action. The second category can be defined as "the concept that unites these objects, one that makes us think of them as demonstrations of a certain 'art', rather than as surfaces that merely happen to have paint on them" (Bell 1999:24–25). In a similar fashion, Sullivan (2008) notes that painting – as a verb – allows us to access another dimension, that of practice. In other words, in this second definition, *painting is* conceived of as a process, where Western and Indigenous conceptions come into close proximity.

What happens, then, when we apply some of these definitions to the study of rock art? While discussing how images (and paintings) have been understood in archaeology, Jones and Cochrane (2018) argue that images can be defined as having four dimensions: the first dimension refers to gesture; this gesture gives origin to two-dimensional representations or paintings. Three-dimensional images include the material representation of two-dimensional objects, such as figurines and statues. They argue that thinking images in two and three dimensions is static and often concentrates on one particular aspect of the art. To overcome this static materiality of art, the authors call for an understanding of images in four dimensions that also incorporates the temporal dimensions of images. Thinking in four dimensions is to consider the materiality of art, to ponder on the events that gave rise to these images and the events that affected their physical permanence. For the authors, "an archaeology of art thus considers the role of materials in image-making, considers how images are brought about by intra-actions between past people and materials, and how such intra-actions are sustained or altered over time" (Jones 2018:184). In other words, this fourth dimension takes into consideration the images' life histories (see Hoskins 1998 for a definition), materials, and temporality. In considering the life histories of paintings, or their fourth dimension, we are able to further expand how we think about rock art images as a process or action. In this sense, I have discussed above how painting practices are not frozen in time; instead, many populations continuously engage with rock paintings and incorporate them into ceremonies or other practices. As such, by taking into account Jones and Cochrane's (2018) proposal of integrating the temporal dimension of images with their interpretation, we are able to understand paintings under a new light, one that incorporates their active role in society, by focusing on their ongoing transformation through performance, rather than deeming them as sacred objects that must remain untouched. Thus, painting – in its active form – is a way of world-making (Jones 2018:186).

It could be noted that Jones and Cochrane's (2018) proposition of images in four dimensions does not explicitly include in their definition the relationships between images and their surrounding physical world. However, in another contribution, Back Danielsson and Jones (2020) address this dimensionality of images and suggest that images are in continuous movement – in an ongoing process of making. They argue that images have been traditionally seen as symbols, which portrays images as static objects. Their proposal, in contrast, recovers the unfolding meanings of images, which do not stop once they have been placed, but rather enter different sets of relationships through viewing and intra-action (Back Danielsson and Jones 2020:4). Their proposal resonates with some of Ingold's ideas about growth, transformation, and drawing. Ingold (2011a) uses the notion of growth to describe how organisms go through a series of transformations through movement or performance. In other words, things are not transformed while being produced, but grown (Ingold 2000:18–19). This last argument is later revisited by Ingold (2011b) and applied to actions such as drawing, making, and writing. In the particular case of drawing, he argues that drawing is better understood in relation to walking (or wayfaring) and not so much as 'the projection of images' (Ingold 2011b:178). Through the comparison of these two modes of action, he draws on the transformational dimension of walking as leaving a trace through the act of breaking vegetation. This way of thinking about drawing and painting as interconnected, as part of a continuum in which images and objects are part of an 'ongoing movement', is closer to the second definition of painting as performance/action/verb.

In summary, we must not only focus on the events that gave rise to images as we know them in the present, but also on the images' relations to the surrounding landscape and beings (plants, animals, bacteria, spirits, humans, etc.) in shared spaces. It is by adding this layer of significance to images that we are able to come closer to Leuthold's (1998) expanded definition of Indigenous art. Altogether, this redefinition of images and paintings that focuses on the active and ever-evolving engagements with paintings holds the potential of bringing together the life processes that images undergo, such as the seasonal repainting and re-activation of paintings and their reincorporation into new compositions, with the various beings that interact with these paintings. As such, four-dimensional images are active (Jones 2018:184) and break ontological barriers between Western and Indigenous perceptions of paintings and art.

Painting as action

Going back to Bell's (1999) dual categorisation of paintings, we could then propose that painting as object and painting as practice correspond to thinking about them as noun and verb, respectively. In its most widely accepted definition, painting is known as a noun. As such, painting is characterised as the final product of the act of painting or as an image. Bell's first category, painting as object/noun, fits this description. In the second definition, painting refers to the *act* of marking a surface or painting as *practice/performance*. In this active form, "distinctions between terms such as painter, object, and viewer melt away [...] the practice of painting can be argued to be a robust form of human engagement that has the potential to reveal new insights and understandings" (Sullivan 2008:241). In sum, in painting as an object/noun, the focus is placed on the ability to act independently from the act of making, whereas painting as a verb is connected to the act of marking a surface, its production, and its consumption. I am interested here in the active/performance understanding of painting/s.

This second classification is more dynamic than previous conceptualisations and sets the stage for the expansion of our understanding of painting, while it allows a simultaneous focus on the relational properties of images, bringing forward their active dimension. In their active form, images are closely related to places, the landscape, and beings that come into contact with them; they become part of the site they have been placed on and provide information about their life histories. As such, they can tell us about the materials that were used for making them, the natural and cultural processes that affected their 'conservation', their reincorporation into new compositions, and their perception and interpretation, among many others.

On traditional knowledge and conservation

What are then the implications of understanding paintings as in constant transformation for their conservation? To properly address this question, let us go back to Ingold's argument about the type of environmental conservation promoted by wildlife protection agencies. According to Ingold (2000:62), the conclusion that humanity could transcend nature was taken by Western wildlife conservation agencies to mean that, in order to protect the environment, it must be isolated from any *unqualified* human action. Indigenous communities and their notion of conservation are absent from this equation, despite some of these groups being recognised as custodians and caretakers. Furthermore, among some Indigenous groups, paintings should be maintained for their conservation (maintenance meaning their recurrent repainting). By ignoring the role Indigenous populations and other local communities played in the conservation of natural and cultural heritage for many millennia (Mazzochi 2006:463), wildlife conservation agencies, as well as cultural heritage professionals, place Western science above ancestral knowledge. This situation continues in the present and leads to protection measures that are purely based on Western values.

Nonetheless, despite conservation efforts conducted by environmental protection agencies and heritage professionals, the relevance of traditional knowledge and its role for the conservation of biological diversity has been recognised by the United Nations as early as the 1990s (United Nations 1992). More recently, a report conducted by the Intergovernmental Science-Policy

Platform on Biodiversity and Ecosystem Services (IPBES) on biodiversity loss found that Indigenous groups and local communities were better at managing natural resources than other human groups (IPBES 2019:35–36). Overall, despite Indigenous and local communities being recognised as assisting in the conservation of their dwelling places, either directly or indirectly, wildlife protection agencies often ignore these conditions.

Cultural and natural conservation

Discussions around archaeological conservation follow a similar trend to nature conservation in that cultural heritage must be isolated from (unqualified) human action in order for it to be preserved. As many have argued, implicit in this statement is a concern for maintaining the authenticity of cultural remains (Walderhaug Saetersdal 2000).

Where does the interest in the conservation of archaeological sites, and particularly rock art, comes from? An early concern for the discovery of past remains can be traced back to the 16th century and the so-called Antiquarians – a loosely defined group of people across Europe – who were interested in the study of the past and the collection of antiquities (Schnapp 2014). This fascination for the collection of ancient artefacts led to the organisation of expeditions across the world that provided the basis for archaeological practice today and had a major influence on how ancient monuments were protected (Schnapp 2014:218). Other concerns for the conservation of monuments and sites emerged in the 1800s and early 1900s across Europe, when an acknowledgement of the non-renewable properties of cultural resources emerged (Loubser 2018:1001). Conservation efforts were often associated with attempts to repair structures and one of the first attempts to apply scientific knowledge in restoration was conducted between 1846 and 1858 (Caldadaro 1987:86). Many decades later, following the International Congress of Restoration and Monuments in 1931 the Charter of Athens was created, which outlined the principles of conservation (Matero 2010). In 1964, the Venice Charter was established, which described the general principles for the restoration of cultural heritage. These principles were expanded after the development of the Amsterdam Declaration (1975), the Burra Charter (ICOMOS 2013 [orig. 1979]), and the Nara Document on Authenticity (ICOMOS 1994) among others. As a result of the United Nations Conference on the Human Environment held in 1972 in Stockholm, Sweden, a convention concerning the protection of the world's cultural and natural heritage was adopted and later ratified by 20 State parties. This convention is composed of 38 articles and promotes the adoption of conservation practices to safeguard cultural and natural sites. In 1978, the World Heritage Committee developed the selection criteria to inscribe sites in the World Heritage List. The protection and conservation of world cultural and natural heritage is grounded on an idea of conservation as "a moral obligation upon all human beings" (ICOMOS 1990), where protecting sites is a way of exercising 'humanity itself' (Haskovec 1991:97).

More recently, a concern for conservation has been pushed forward as a response to an increase in tourism in certain areas (Deacon 2006a). In its basic definition, the objective of conservation is to protect cultural sites from damage (Matero 2010). This includes the protection of sites from any influences that may pose a threat to their integrity, the removal of organic materials, and the management of other environmental factors (see also Renfrew and Bahn 2004:560). As Deacon (2006a:381) points out "conservation, by its very name, is assumed to be 'good' because it reacts against what is perceived to be detrimental impact or *malpractice* at the other end of the scale" (highlight my own).

Rock art conservation and Indigenous worldviews

The general principles established by the United Nations Educational, Scientific and Cultural Organisation (UNESCO) in 1972 (and further advanced by subsequent charters and documents) for the protection and conservation of cultural and natural sites were later expanded through the implementation of the "principles for the preservation and conservation/restoration of wall paintings" by ICOMOS in 2003. This document contains 10 articles outlining the principles for the protection, investigation, documentation, and restoration of wall paintings. Despite the recognition that wall paintings can be composed of rock art murals, and frescoes belonging to different time periods, the principles mostly reference European art and attempt to outline universal principles of wall paintings conservation. In doing so, the document creates a division between Western and non-Western art, thus failing to engage with non-normative ways of knowledge.

It has been highlighted that during the process of conservation, decisions are made with regard to what is going to be preserved and under which standards (Schiffer and Gumerman 1977), recreating in this process a selected image of the past (Lowenthal 1985:278). At the very centre of these efforts is a concern for authenticity where sites are assumed to have remained unchanged through the course of their life span, so that they need to be isolated from any other future impacts. Implicit here is the Western concern for permanency or the attempt to freeze sites in time, based on a fear of the passing of time and decay (Walderhaug Saetersdal 2000:165). According to an object biography framework, objects, as well as people, are subjected to a series of transformations, movements, and changes throughout their lifetime that can be accessed by archaeologists through the study of their physical properties (Appadurai 1996; Hoskins 1998; Kopytoff 1986). There has been an ever-increasing concern with the traces left by the passing of time in cultural remains as comparable to those by humans (Lowenthal 1985).

Furthermore, the existing guidelines, intended to protect rock art sites because of their universal value to humanity, grounded in colonial ideas of conservation as keeping an original state with little to no room for transformation and change, does not take into consideration non-Western and Indigenous perceptions towards their management (Chirikure et al. 2010; Mowaljarlai et al. 1988; Pwiti and Mvenge 1996). As I have explained above, Western protection, conservation, and restoration efforts (encouraged by UNESCO and other organisations) often conflict with Indigenous views on how sites should be preserved. As discussed by Maynard (1975), European artists strive to make their art permanent with any interventions on works of art seen as detrimental and conservation efforts trying to replicate the original work and intention. The author argues that conservation views of European art objects determined how Palaeolithic art was managed. By contrast, some Indigenous decorative objects, such as those in Australia, are not meant to be preserved; they are intended to be used for ceremonies and left to decay once the ceremony is finished (Maynard 1975:56). Another example that differs from European art conservation attitudes is that of Australian rock art. In the Kimberley, Wanjina rock art depictions were seasonally repainted in order to maintain their 'strength and vitality' (Stanton 2006:415) and secure the replenishment of natural resources (Crawford 1968). The reuse and subsequent repainting of rock art as part of renewal practices might not necessarily go hand in hand with scientific ideas of conservation – as maintaining a pristine state (Mowarjarlai et al. 1988). Other groups such as the Dogon in Mali see the weathering of rock art images as a natural process, where the regular repainting of images is also practiced (Kleinitz 2006 in Deacon 2006a:381). In other words, "conservation in the Western perception constitutes the preservation of static images for all time; conservation from an Indigenous perspective means visible and tangible continuity of the spiritual content of the image" (Mowaljarlai et al. 1988:693). In these contexts, it is possible to approach the conservation and painting of rock images in a way that is consistent with Traditional Owners' worldviews as renewal practices, and they have been extensively recorded by anthropologists and were still performed at the time of European colonisation. However, in locations where there are no traditional custodians, the application of conservation principles will differ and might closer align with Western views.

This argument will be further expanded in the following section through the discussion of heritage management practices at the Tsodilo Hills site, Botswana. It will be argued that conflict often arises when Western/scientific and non-Western/traditional ontologies come together during negotiations of conservation strategies at archaeological sites.

The case of Tsodilo Hills

Let me now expand on this last point by considering some of the main challenges stakeholders from Tsodilo Hills, Botswana, faced when this site was included in the World Heritage List in 2001. The site is in the northwest of Botswana, in the Kalahari Desert Region (Figure 16.1). It extends through four hills denominated by local Hambukushu and Ju/'hoansi populations as *mosadi* (female), *monna* (male), and *ngwana* (child and grandchild; Figure 16.1). It is around these hills where more than 4,500 motifs are located across 400 panels, constituting one of the largest concentrations of rock art in the world (Keitumese and Nthoi 2009:145). The paintings from Tsodilo Hills were depicted in a schematic technique (National Museum, Monuments and Art Gallery 2000) using red and white pigments, made between 850 and 1,100 AD (Munjeri 2001). The area has also been used during the Middle and Late Stone Age, as evidenced by stone tools and fish bone remains from about 100,000 BP onwards (Campbell and Robbins 2010:35). These layers were followed by occupations during the Iron Age, where more permanent settlements are recorded for the 7th and 8th centuries AD. At around AD 1,000, cattle and sheep herders settled in the area and were later joined by metal-working farmers coming from the north (Wilmsen and Denbow 2010).

The paintings

The art is predominantly composed of red paintings (3,800 motifs), whereas a smaller number is comprised of white paintings. Other art forms include polychrome paintings, cupules, and grooves. Half of the red paintings show animals (with giraffe, eland, rhino, and zebra being the most frequently represented species), a third are geometric designs, and almost 15% are human figures and handprints (Campbell and Robbins 2010; Rudner 1965). These paintings are also characterised by silhouette and outline figures (two shades of outline and a heavy outline). Outline figures are scarce and only present in one rock shelter, which led researchers to propose that they were the product of a single artist (Rudner 1965:56). The white paintings are not as widely distributed as the red ones and are mostly found at one rock shelter. The remaining white paintings are scattered in caves and shelters or found at open air sites. Motifs are composed of geometric designs (50% of the figures), human stick figures (25%), and animals (25%). Among the depicted animal species are antelopes, cattle, snakes, giraffes, elephants, rhinos, zebras, and goats. The only polychrome paintings described in the area are of two adult rhinos and a baby rhino (Figure 16.2). Finally, there is a large number of cupules (2,000 motifs) and a smaller number of grooves (100 motifs). These were produced by grinding the surface creating spherical or elongated forms.

There are no direct dates for the art, but cattle images have been correlated with dates obtained from cattle remains found in the archaeological record of Toteng and dated to AD 100 (Robbins et al. 2005). Late Stone Age pastoralists working with cattle have been reported to occupy the region around AD 650–700 (Wilmsen and Denbow 2010). Based on this data, it has been estimated that the red paintings were probably made in the first millennium AD (Campbell and Robbins 2010:43). The white paintings contain horse depictions, which were introduced to the area

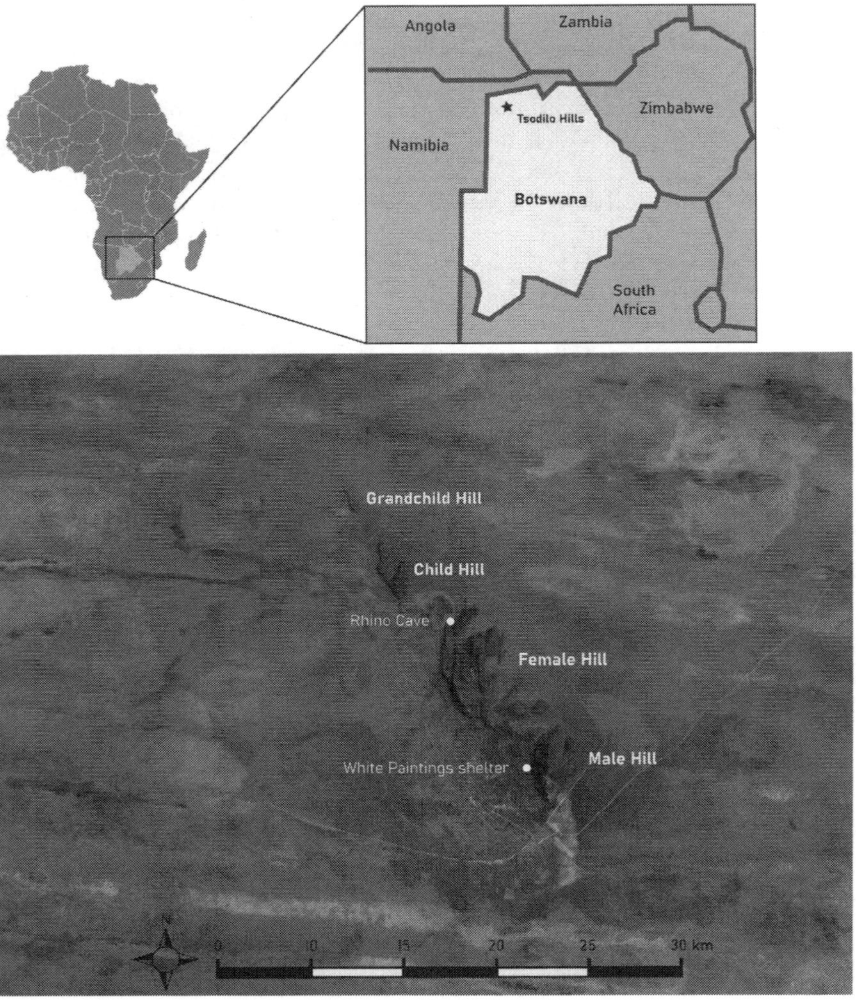

Figure 16.1 Map of Tsodilo Hills (created by the author).

no earlier than 1852. The cupules have been estimated to belong to the Palaeolithic, but no dates are available for this assemblage (Campbell and Robbins 2010:42).

The red paintings have been speculated to relate to fertility, health, and resource abundance. The white paintings are believed to have a similar significance, and their location on top of the red paintings might relate to a purposeful placement to draw power from the underlying red paintings (Campbell and Robbins 2010:44). As reported by a member of

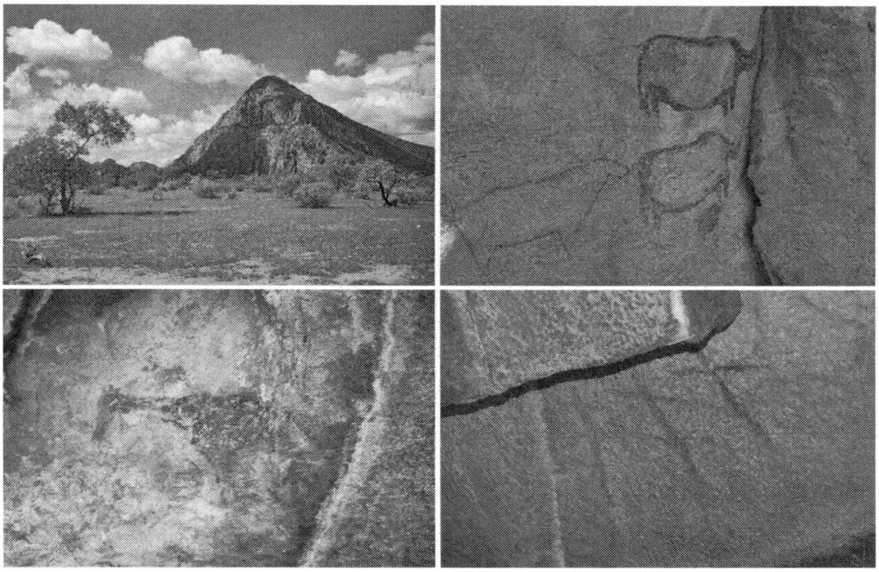

Figure 16.2 Top left, a view of Tsodilo Hills (© Mike Richardson/Creative Commons). Top right, example of art found at Tsodilo Hills (© Robertharding/Creative Commons). Bottom left, photograph of a giraffe (© Oliver Vass/Creative Commons). Bottom right, painting of human figures (© Joachim Huber/Creative Commons).

the Hambukushu community, the site has been used since the 20th century by his ancestors to perform healing ceremonies (Campbell and Robbins 2010:44).

The artists

The two local communities living in the area – Hambukushu and Ju/'hoansi – arrived around 1850 (Campbell and Robbins 2010). The Hambukushu people are sedentary pastoralists and practice farming, while the Ju/'hoansi-San are hunter-gatherers (Segadika 2018). There currently exist conflicting versions about the authorship of the rock art. It has been proposed that Ju/'hoansi ancestors made the red paintings, although some informants also credit God with the creation of these paintings (Campbell 1994). The images also share some similarities with engravings found in Southern Africa that are credited to Khoe herders (Smith and Ouzman 2004). Regarding the white paintings, it has been suggested that Bantu-speaking groups painted them (Rudner 1965:60), although residents deny the link between Bantu-speaking populations and these paintings (Campbell and Robbins 2010:43). The differences in lifestyles by these two groups are also translated into distinct engagements with the art: Ju/'hoansi people practice trance ceremonies in the area, whereas Hambukushu people use the site for rainmaking and cleansing ceremonies (Segadika 2018:32).

Both communities living in this area regard Tsodilo Hills as having a significant 'spiritual, cultural, recreational and religious' relevance (Keitumetse et al. 2007:108). The Hills are a place of worship, where spiritually significant medicinal plants and water sources are found (Campbell and Robbins 2010:44). They are also regarded as a place of creation (Segadika 2018:33). The natural shapes and markings in the outcrops in the form of vulvas and animal traces are linked to places where human beings were created and where animals were brought to Earth (Campbell and Robbins 2010). Finally, if local interpretations of the art are considered, the Hambukushu interpret animal images as the tracks left by animals when the land was wet, while the Ju/'hoansi see some eland depictions as representing rain spirits (Monamo and Keitumetse 2003 in Keitumetse et al. 2007).

World Heritage listing of Tsodilo Hills

> Heritage that belongs to all is not a good point. It is Tsodilo people´s culture. They say it is for all people. But we have not been explained to what exactly that means.
>
> (Informant in Keitumetse et al. 2007:111)

Tsodilo Hills was listed as a World Heritage Site (WHS) in 2001. However, the site has been protected by local laws since the 1920s. The site was declared a National Monument in 1927 and has been protected by the Monuments and Relics Act since 2001. The area is also protected by the Anthropological Research Act of 1967, which regulates the permissions for carrying out anthropological research (Botswana Statute Law: B232). In 1994, the first management plan for Tsodilo Hills was developed, which recommended the construction of a site museum, housing for the staff, a tourist camp, and a fence to control cattle (Campbell 1994). The declaration of Tsodilo Hills as a WHS necessitated that a core and a buffer zone should be created, in order to 'protect' the rock paintings. Consequently, local communities living in what was to become the core zone had to be relocated to a permanent settlement (Ecosurv 2005).

As expected, one of the major challenges faced by the local communities' relocation was the interference with their traditional way of living (Smith 2006). A fence was built around the core area to prevent cattle from entering the site, which meant that local communities could only access the site through a gate (Ecosurv 2005). Although the Integrated Management Plan (IMP 2005) states that the communities have free access to this area, this measure also implies a control over the flow of visitors (Abungu 2006). The two communities were granted hunting and gathering rights in the buffer zone, but these activities were prohibited in the core zone (Campbell 1994).

Further issues with the implemented management plan relate to the lack of acknowledgement of these two communities to the overall conservation of Tsodilo Hills. For example, a Hambukushu member reported destructive incidents at the hands of tourists to the Ngamiland authorities (Monamo 2004 in Keitumetse et al. 2007). Additionally, the community also faced the removal of beehives located in a main rock art panel so they would not pose a threat to tourists, disregarding that these were used by local groups for rainmaking ceremonies.

In sum, the management plan developed for Tsodilo Hills solely focused on the economic benefits achieving a WHS status would bring (e.g., increase in tourism) while disregarding the contemporary value the area has for the two local communities. Analogous to how wildlife protection agencies envision the protection of the natural environment, the view promoted by UNESCO and other agencies has at its core a Western appreciation of heritage, which functions as a tool for colonialism that could transform stakeholders' experiences into 'negative heritage' (*sensu* Meskell 2002). For example, at Domboshava, Zimbabwe, a member of a San community covered a rock art panel with brown paint to avoid its inclusion in the World Heritage List (Smith 2006:327). Archaeologists and heritage professionals must consider that rock art images are sometimes being maintained (repainted) by local communities (Deacon 2006b), which affects their use for future scientific studies. These practices are not perceived by local communities as 'vandalistic acts' (see Motta 2019 for an extensive discussion of this topic), but as ways of cultural continuity (Meskell 2002:567).

Concluding remarks

If we are to propose that paintings also contain a dynamic/performative element, how can heritage management practices incorporate paintings in their noun and verb definitions? As I have shown, Tsodilo Hills' inclusion in the WHS list was done on the grounds of its cultural and natural values. The former includes the rock paintings (Campbell et al. 2010), the archaeological occupations dating back to 100,000 years ago (Campbell and Robbins 2010), the local communities, and the production of traditional crafts by Hambukushu and Ju/Hoansi communities (Keitumetse and Nthoi 2009:146). The natural values refer to geomorphological features, flora, and fauna. Even though rock art was used as one of many attributes for the inclusion of this site in the WHS list, it is paradoxical that contemporary appreciations of the paintings by local communities have overall been disregarded in the listing process. We must then acknowledge how paintings found at Tsodilo Hills relate to other cultural and natural features contained in this area. If we, in turn, solely focus on the contextual features of the rock art, or painting as noun/object, we would only attain a very limited interpretation of the art. However, by including another layer of meaning into this initial explanation, or painting as verb/performance, we can achieve a more dynamic and holistic

Figure 16.3 *Der Zeichner des liegenden Weibes* by Albrecht Dürer showing a draftsman mathematically depicting a female model (Albrecht Dürer/ Public Domain [Wikipedia Commons]).

characterisation of the art, where rock paintings are entangled in a series of active relationships. As such, Tsodilo Hills and its paintings are used for healing practices, accessing power contained in the art, and rainmaking ceremonies (Campbell and Robbins 2010:44). By including this second sphere of meaning, other hidden values associated with the art become more prominent, thus bringing forward the relationship between past and present Indigenous groups inhabiting this area. Due to the unfolding characteristics of rock art images, we are able to break away from a static definition of painting as an object that separates artists/painters from their immediate world. As argued, this dichotomy stems from a Western understanding of what an artist is, in which painters distance themselves from the (real) world to attain an externalised vision of nature (Figure 16.3). I have argued that by regarding painting as performance/verb, both painters and painting/s become active components of the world and, as such, are deeply entangled with their environment and the beings inhabiting it. In other words, they become alive.

Finally, painting as performance/verb means to be present in the act of painting. In this process, the boundaries of what it means to be human are blurred through a process of transformation. During this process, paintings grow, identities are shaped and becomings occur. These processes are part of peoples' perception of rock art, other beings, and the landscape. To conclude, I have proposed that to think of painting as verb highlights the active role images have throughout time. By reframing the role of rock paintings in society, we are able to expand Western conservation principles and values to include other non-normative ontologies.

Acknowledgements

The research conducted for this paper was originally presented at the 'One World Anthropology: A masterclass with Tim Ingold' event organised by

Martin Porr and Niels Weidtmann in September 2019 and hosted at Tübingen University, Germany. I am thankful to the event's organisers, Tim Ingold, and other attendants s for the feedback received during my presentation. I am grateful to the paper's reviewers, Matthew Chrulew, Andrew Jones, and Tim Ingold for their advice and critical comments on an earlier version of this manuscript. This paper has also profited from conversations with Martin Porr and Bruno Vindrola.

References

Abungu, G. O. 2006. Rock art management in Eastern Southern Africa: Whose responsibility? In *Of the past, for the future: Integrating archaeology and conservation*. Proceedings of the Conservation Theme at the 5th World Archaeological Congress, Washington, DC, 22–26 June 2003. Getty Conservation Institute Symposium Proceedings Series. N. Agnew and J. Bridgland, eds. Pp. 331–335. Los Angeles: Getty Conservation Institute.

Appadurai, A. 1996. *The social life of things: Commodities in cultural perspective*. Cambridge: Cambridge University Press.

Back Danielsson, I.-M. and A. M. Jones. 2020. *Images in the making: Art, process, archaeology*. Manchester: Manchester University Press.

Bell, J. 1999. *What is a painting? Representation and modern art*. London: Thames & Hudson.

Caldadaro, N. L. 1987. An outline history of conservation in archaeology and anthropology as presented through its publications. *Journal of the American Institute for Conservation* 26(2):85–104.

Campbell, A. 1994. *Tsodilo management plan scheme of implementation*. Gaborone: Government Printer.

Campbell, A. and L. Robbins. 2009. Tsodilo Hill, Botswana. *Adoranten*. www.rockartscandinavia.com/tsodilo-hill-botswana-by-alec-campbell-and-lawrence-robbins-aa21.php (accessed 07/06/2022).

Campbell, A., L. Robbins, and M. L. Murphy. 2010. Cupules and grooves. In *Tsodilo Hills: Copper bracelet of the Kalahari*. A. Campbell, L. Robbins, and M. Taylor, eds. Pp. 64–71. East Lansing: Michigan State University Press/Gaborone: The Botswana Society.

Chippindale, C. 2001. Studying ancient pictures as pictures. In *Handbook of rock art research*. D. S. Whitley, ed. Pp. 247–272. New York: Altamira Press.

Chirikure, S., M. Manyanga, W. Ndoro, and G. Pwiti. 2010. Unfulfilled promises? Heritage management and community participation at some of Africa's cultural heritage sites. *International Journal of Heritage Studies* 16(1–2):30–44.

Crawford, I. M. 1968. *The art of the Wandjina: Aboriginal cave paintings in Kimberley, Western Australia*. Melbourne: Oxford University Press.

Deacon, J. 2006a. Rock art conservation and tourism. *Journal of Archaeological Method and Theory* 13(4):379–399.

Deacon, J. 2006b. Introduction. In *Of the past, for the future: Integrating archaeology and conservation*. Proceedings of the Conservation Theme at the 5th World Archaeological Congress, Washington, DC, 22–26 June 2003. Getty Conservation Institute Symposium Proceedings Series. N. Agnew and J. Bridgland, eds. Pp. 322–330. Los Angeles: Getty Conservation Institute.

Ecosurv. 2005. *Tsodilo Hills World Heritage site. Integrated management plan.* Gaborone: Ecosurv.

Government of Botswana. 1967. *Statute Law, 1967*. Gaborone: Government Printer.

Government of Botswana. 2001. *Monuments and Relics Act N° 12, 2001*. Gaborone: Government Printer.

Halliwell, S. 2002. Introduction: Mimesis and the history of aesthetics. In *The aesthetics of mimesis: Ancient texts and modern problems*. Pp. 1–34. Princeton: Princeton University Press.

Hart, D. 2000. Indigenous aesthetics: Native art, media, and identity by Steven Leuthold. *Wicazo Sa Review* 15(2):145–147.

Haskovec, I. P. 1991. On some non-technical issues of conservation. In *Rock art and posterity: Conserving, managing, and recording rock art*. Occasional AURA Publication 4. C. Pearson and B. K. Swartz, eds. Pp. 97–99. Melbourne: AURA.

Hoskins, J. 1998. *Biographical objects. How things tell the stories of people's lives.* London: Routledge.

ICOMOS. 1931. *The Athens charter for the restoration of historic monuments*. www.icomos.org/en/167-the-athens-charter-for-the-restoration-of-historic-monuments (accessed 07/06/2022).

ICOMOS. 1964. *International charter for the conservation and restoration of monuments and sites (The Venice Charter)*. www.icomos.org/charters/venice_e.pdf (accessed 07/06/2022).

ICOMOS. 1975. *The declaration of Amsterdam*. www.icomos.org/en/and/169-the-declaration-of-amsterdam (accessed 07/06/2022).

ICOMOS. 1990. *Charter for the protection and management of the archaeological heritage*. www.icomos.org/images/DOCUMENTS/Charters/arch_e.pdf (accessed 07/06/2022).

ICOMOS. 1994. *The Nara document on authenticity*. www.icomos.org/charters/nara-e.pdf (accessed 07/06/2022).

ICOMOS. 2003. *Principles for the preservation and conservation-restoration of wall paintings*. www.icomos.org/images/DOCUMENTS/Charters/wallpaintings_e.pdf (accessed 07/06/2022).

ICOMOS. 2013 [1979]. *The Burra charter: The Australia ICOMOS charter for places of cultural significance*. https://australia.icomos.org/publications/burra-charter-practice-notes/ (accessed 07/06/2022).

IMP. 2005. Integrated management plan for the Tsodilo Hills World Heritage site. https://awhf.net/wp-content/uploads/2015/10/Tsodilo-Core-Area-Management-Plan.pdf (accessed 07/06/2022).

Ingold, T. 2000. *The perception of the environment: Essays on livelihood, dwelling, and skill*. London: Routledge.

Ingold, T. 2011a. Making, growing, learning. Lecture presented at IEAT/FUNDEP, 2-10 October 2011. www.ufmg.br/ieat/2015/06/timothy-ingold-university-of-aberdeen/ (accessed 07/06/2022).

Ingold, T. 2011b. Naming as storytelling. Speaking of animals among the Koyukon of Alaska. In T. Ingold, *Being alive. Essays on movement, knowledge and description*. Pp. 165–175. London: Routledge.

IPBES. 2019. *Global assessment report on biodiversity and ecosystem services of the Intergovernmental Science Policy Platform on Biodiversity and Ecosystem Services*. E. S. Brondizio, J. Settele, S. Díaz, and H. T. Ngo, eds. Bonn: IPBES Secretariat.

Jones, A. M. 2018. Art in the making. In *The archaeology of art: Materials, practices, affects*. A. M. Jones and A. Cochrane, eds. Pp. 183–192. London: Routledge.
Jones, A. M. and A. Cochrane. 2018. *The archaeology of art: Materials, practices, affects*. London: Routledge.
Keitumetse, S. O. and O. Nthoi. 2009. Investigating the impact of world heritage site tourism on the intangible heritage of a community: Tsodilo Hills World Heritage site, Botswana. *International Journal of Intangible Heritage* 4:143–150.
Keitumetse, S. O., G. Matlapeng, and L. Monamo. 2007. Cultural landscapes, communities, and World Heritage: In pursuit of the local in Tsodilo Hills, Botswana. In *Envisioning landscape. Situations and standpoints in archaeology and heritage*. One World Archaeology. D. Hicks, L. McAtackney, and G. Fairclough, eds. Pp. 101–119. Walnut Creek: Left Coast Press.
Kirksey, E. 2015. Species: A praxiographic study. *Journal of the Anthropological Institute* 21(4):758–780.
Kopytoff, I. 1996. The cultural biography of things: Commoditization as process. In *The social life of things: Commodities in cultural perspective*. Arjun Appadurai, ed. Pp. 63–91. Cambridge: Cambridge University Press.
Leuthold, S. 1998. *Indigenous aesthetics: Native art, media, and identity*. Austin: University of Texas Press.
Loubser, J. 2001. Management planning for conservation. In *Handbook of rock art* research. D. S. Whitley, ed. Pp. 80–115. Walnut Creek: Altamira Press.
Loubser, J. 2018. The conservation and management of rock art: An integrated approach. In *The Oxford handbook of the archaeology and anthropology of rock art*. B. David and I. McNiven, eds. Pp. 993–1020. Oxford: Oxford University Press.
Lowenthal, D. 1985. *The past is a foreign country*. Cambridge: Cambridge University Press.
Matero, F. F. 2010. *Heritage, conservation, and archaeology: An introduction*. Boston, MA: Archaeological Institute of America.
Maynard, L. 1975. Restoration of Aboriginal rock art: The moral problem. *Australian Archaeology* 3:54–60.
Mazzocchi, F. 2006. Western science and traditional knowledge. *European Molecular Biology Organization* 7(5):463–466.
Meskell, L. 2002. Negative heritage and past mastering in archaeology. *Anthropological Quarterly* 75(3):557–574.
Morphy, H. 1999. Encoding the Dreaming – a theoretical framework for the analysis of representational processes in Australian Aboriginal art. *Australian Archaeology* 49:13–22.
Motta, A. P. 2019. From top down under: New insights into the social significance of superimpositions in the rock art of Northern Kimberley, Australia. *Cambridge Archaeological Journal* 29(3):479–495.
Mowaljarlai, D., P. Vinnicombe, G. K. Ward, and C. Chippindale. 1988. Repainting of images on rock in Australia and the maintenance of Aboriginal culture. *Antiquity* 62:690–696.
Munjeri, D. 2001. *Tsodilo dossier, 1999*. Gaborone: Botswana National Museum.
National Museum, Monuments and Art Gallery. 2000. *Tsodilo: Mountain of the gods. World Heritage nomination dossier*. Gaborone: National Museum, Monuments and Art Gallery.
Pwiti, G. and G. Mvenge. 1996. Archaeologists, tourists and rainmakers: Problems in the management of rock art sites in Zimbabwe, a case study of Domboshava

national monument. In *Aspects of African archaeology. Papers from the 10th Congress of the PanAfrican association for prehistory and related studies*. G. Piwiti and R. C. Soper, eds. Pp. 817–823. Harare. University of Zimbabwe Publications.

Renfrew, C. and P. Bahn. 2004. *Archaeology: Theories, methods, and practice*. 4th edition. London: Thames & Hudson.

Robbins, L. H., A. C. Campbell, M. L. Murphy, G. A. Brook, P. Srivastava, and S. Badenhorst. 2005. The advent of herding in southern Africa: AMS dates on domestic livestock from the Kalahari Desert, Botswana. *Current Anthropology* 46:671–677.

Rose, D. B. 2008. Dreaming ecology: Beyond the between. *Religion and Literature* 40(1):109–122.

Rudner, I. 1965. Archaeological report on the Tsodillo Hills, Bechuanaland. *The South African Archaeological Bulletin* 20(78):51–70.

Schiffer, M. B. and G. J. Gumerman, eds. 1977. *Conservation archaeology. A guide for cultural resource management studies*. New York: Academic Press.

Schnapp, A. 2014. The birth of the archaeological vision: From antiquaries to archaeologists. *West 86th. A Journal of Decorative Arts, Design History, and Material Culture* 21(2):216–229.

Segadika, P. 2018. Managing intangible heritage at Tsodilo. *Museum International* 58(1–2):31–40.

Smith, B. W. 2006. Rock art tourism in Southern Africa: Problems, possibilities, and poverty relief. In *Of the past, for the future: Integrating archaeology and conservation*. Proceedings of the Conservation Theme at the 5th World Archaeological Congress, Washington, DC, 22–26 June 2003. Getty Conservation Institute Symposium Proceedings Series. N. Agnew and J. Bridgland, eds. pp. 322–330. Los Angeles: Getty Conservation Institute.

Smith, B. W. and S. Ouzman. 2004. Taking stock: Identifying Khoekhoen herder rock art in Southern Africa. *Current Anthropology* 45(4):499–526.

Stanton, J. E. 2006. Wandjina. *Art and Australia* 43(3):414–419.

Sullivan, G. 2012. Painting as research: Create and critique. In *Handbook of the arts in qualitative research: Perspectives, methodologies, examples, and issues*. J. Gary Knowles and Ardra L. Coles, eds. Pp. 240–251. Thousand Oaks: SAGE Publications.

United Nations. 1992. *Convention on biological diversity*. www.un.org/en/observances/biological-diversity-day/convention (accessed 07/06/2022).

Vacche, A. D. 1996. *Cinema and painting: How art is used in film*. Austin: University of Texas Press.

Walderhaug Saetersdal, E. M. 2000. Ethics, politics and practices in rock art conservation. *Public Archaeology* 1(3):163–180.

Whitley, D. S. 2001. Rock art and rock art research in a worldwide perspective: An introduction. In *Handbook of rock art research*. D. S Whitley, ed. Pp. 7–51. Walnut Creek: Altamira Press.

Wilmsen, E. N. and J. R. Denbow. 2010. Early villages at Tsodilo: The introduction of livestock, crops and metalworking. In *Tsodilo Hills: Copper bracelet of the Kalahari*. A. Campbell, L. Robbins, and M. Taylor, eds. Pp. 72–81. East Lansing: Michigan State University Press/Gaborone: The Botswana Society.

17 Many ways to see yams

An ecological analysis of Yam Figures in the Aboriginal rock art of Balanggarra Country, Northeast Kimberley, Western Australia

Emily Grey and Balanggarra Aboriginal Corporation

The well-known importance of yams and other tubers in forager-hunter cultures sits in contrast with the many issues posed by their organic and biodegradable nature, and presents a persistent conundrum when attempting to assess their significance in the archaeological record (for examples, see Atchison and Head 2012). The current archaeological understanding of yam and tuber plants in Australian forager-hunter lifeways is centred on economy and subsistence, and structured by an ecologically fragmented depositional record. This record is exacerbated in northern Australia due to the fluctuating nature of wet-dry tropical weather systems (Dilkes-Hall et al. 2019b; Florin et al. 2020). To explore the significance of yams in past forager-hunter lifeways, an examination of the rock art record of the Kimberley is presented, where yams and other plants are depicted in unusually rich numbers (Veth et al. 2016). The high level of variation in yam depictions across the region's major stylistic periods and the presence of yam and other plant depictions at up to ~15% of rock art sites is evidence of the continual entanglement of people and plants through time in the Kimberley. This chapter explores these entanglements through a case study of human-yam motifs, or Yam Figures, in the rock art of Balanggarra Country, northeast Kimberley, to examine the ways rock art can inform on multispecies dimensions of forager lifeworlds. Drawing on theoretical frameworks developed by Tim Ingold (2000, 2002, 2008) and others (e.g., Bawaka Country et al. 2016; Alberti and Fowles 2018), Yam Figures are here located in an entanglement of yam socioecologies and rock art traditions.

Research context

This chapter draws on archaeological research undertaken in the Balanggarra Native Title Determination area of the Kimberley, Western Australia (see Figure 17.1), and utilises data from the ARC project *Kimberley Visions: Rock*

DOI: 10.4324/9781003162773-23

Art Style Provinces in Northern Australia (LP 150100490). Indigenous occupation of Balanggarra Country extends back to at least ~50,000 BP (Veth et al. 2019), and across northern Australia sites such as Carpenter's Gap 1 (Maloney et al. 2018; Dilkes-Hall et al. 2019b), Riwi (Balme et al. 2018; Dilkes-Hall et al. 2019a), and the Northern Territory site of Madjedbebe (Florin et al. 2020) attest to over ~60,000 years of complex people-plant interactions. These sites provide a viable range of palaeoenvironmental analogues for cross-regional reconstructions, and have produced a complex chronology for forager-plant interactions (Veth et al. 2016; Dilkes-Hall et al. 2019). Importantly, evidence for human-yam interaction in the form of vegetable parenchyma is identified from multiple stratigraphic units dating between ~41,000 BP to 300 BP at Carpenter's Gap 1 (Dilkes-Hall et al. 2019), and from ~50,000 BP onwards at Madjedbebe (Florin et al. 2020).

These fragments were identified as part of a detailed macrobotanical record, which provides evidence for regionalised niche vine thicket refugia during periods of dramatic climate change (Dilkes-Hall et al. 2019; Florin et al. 2020). Evidence of the antiquity of tuber consumption is also identified from Holocene deposits at Riwi (Dilkes-Hall et al. 2019b) and Borologa 1, in Balanggarra Country, where processed ochre and waterlily tuber traces on

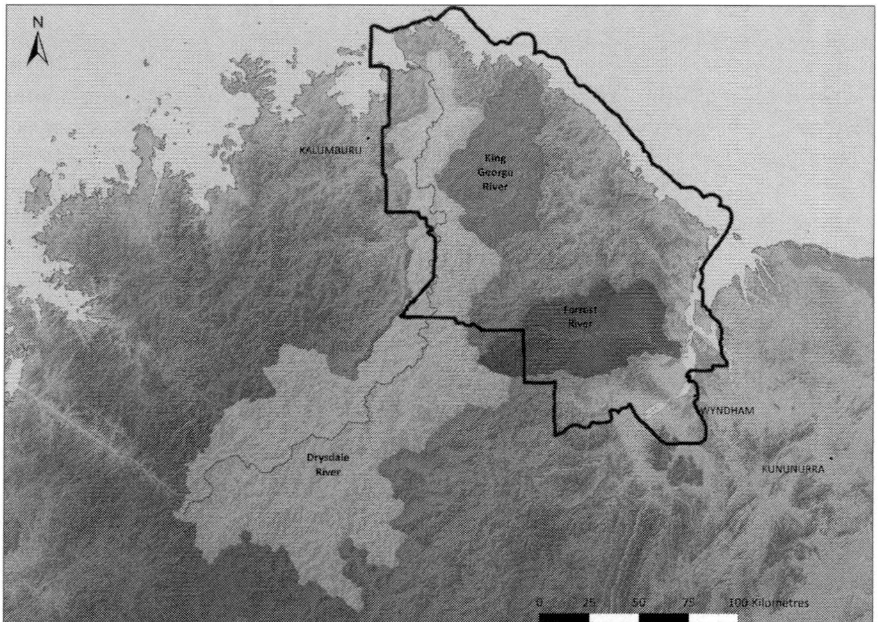

Figure 17.1 A map of the Balanggarra Native Title Determination (black outline). Kimberley Visions and Emily Grey 2018.

grindstones are dated to 630–340 BP (David et al. 2019). More tangible evidence of people-plant interactions is present in the extensive rock art of the Kimberley, where the proliferation of plant-depictive or *planty* imagery exists in contrast to its relative dearth in world forager rock arts (see Taçon et al. 1996; Boyd et al. 1996, 2016; Mguni 2009; Hammond 2019). Formative work by Veth et al. (2016) has identified in the wider Kimberley a unique archaeological record of plant depictions at up to ~15% of rock art sites, "suggesting an accrued memory bank of collecting and even cultivation or 'management' practices" (36).

Early work by Walsh (1994) and Welch (1990, 1993, 2003) identified variable forms of plant depictions across a six-phase chronology of rock art – Cupule Period, Irregular Infill Period, Gwion Period, Static Polychrome period, Painted Hand period, and Wandjina period – shown in Table 17.1. These motifs are described by Welch (2003) as reflections of food resources and creation figures, while Doring and Nyawarra (2014) describe how some plant motifs articulate kinship and initiation systems and exemplify women's ecological practices and trade systems. Recent work by Finch et al. (2020, 2021) has provided date ranges for Irregular Infill rock art (17,500–13,000 BP) and Gwion rock art (16,600–12,400 BP), while Ross et al. (2016) have securely dated Wandjina depictions to the mid-Holocene. Currently, the only absolute dates for plant motifs have been produced by Ross et al. (2016) from the west Kimberley, bracketing yammy motifs at 16,000 BP for a bifurfaced or split yam-like motif and 650 BP for a multi-lobed yam-like motif.

Yam Figures in East Kimberley rock art

Yams and other botanical underground storage organs (USOs) are the most common plant type described in both historical and recent ethnographies from the Kimberley, used primarily for food and connected to multiple cultural narratives surrounding plant distribution, ancestral movements, and ecological niche management (see Elkin 1930; Crawford 1982; Head, Atchison and Fullagar 2002; Welch 2003; Atchison and Head 2012; Cheinmora et al. 2017). Similarly, USOs are by far the most common plant depictions in the rock art record, accounting for 46% of all plant motifs currently recorded (Grey 2018). The two most commonly referenced USO types, both in the ethnographic literature and identified in Kimberley plant-depictive rock art, are the long yam *Dioscorea transversa*, known in Kwini language as *ganmanggu* (Cheinmora et al. 2016), and the round yam *Dioscorea bulbifera,* or *kunu*. These two yam types provide robust morphological profiles, which have been assessed against rock art motifs for identification, where motifs demonstrate a high level of variability in form, size, and botanical characteristics (Veth et al. 2016; Grey 2018). *Kunu*, alongside other round tubers, is depicted with an ovoid or rounded shape, fine, hair-like adventitious roots, and dotted or solid interiors (Welch 2003; Veth et al.

Table 17.1 Synthesis of rock art and palaeoenvironmental studies from the Kimberley and northwest Australia

Art Period	*Rock Art Summary*	*Ecological Context*
Cupule Period ~50KBP – ongoing 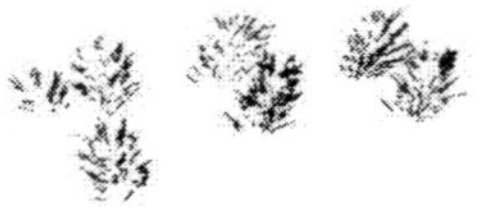	Pecked and abraded cupules and grooves on vertical surfaces, often associated with grinding hollows. Plantforms are present as positive grass stem and head prints, which may be contemporaneous with cupule production. Grass prints are also identified in Irregular Infill and Gwion rock art styles.	Multiple permanent and semi-permanent freshwater sources are dispersed between a mosaic of rainforest, grassland, and open Eucalypt woodland. Presence of rainforest taxa in Carpenter's Gap 1 and Madjedbebe suggest utilisation of a wide range of plants.
Irregular Infill ~18–13KBP 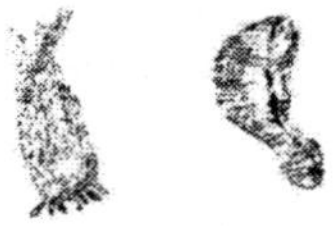	First figurative rock art in the Kimberley; large painted naturalistic depictions of animals, as well as plant and human motifs. Depictions are outlined, have solid external features, and irregular striated infill. Imagery is reflective of emerging territorialities, changing resource mosaics. Plants are present at 25% of sites.	The Last Glacial Maximum (LGM; ~25–16KBP) lowered sea and rain levels, producing an expanded arid zone. Lacustral and rainforest areas retract to isolated refugia, but tuber remains at Carpenter's Gap 1 suggest a preference for those limited resources.
Gwion ~17–12KBP 	Highly decorated anthropomorphs feature multiple types of plant-based material items, such as digging sticks, dilly bags, and hafted weapons. Smaller animals and plants are depicted, as well as human-plant and Yam Figures. Plants are present at 2% of sites.	LGM aridification has left sea levels up to -130m, leaving the plains of the Bonaparte Basin plains exposed. Stylised Gwion figures reflect both local territorialities and long-distance cultural exchange across the Kimberley and Arnhem Land.

Table 17.1 (Continued)

Art Period	*Rock Art Summary*	*Ecological Context*
Static Polychrome ~14–9KBP 	Human figures are polychrome, painted primarily in red and orange with missing or faded sections. Motifs are highly stylised, with diverse headdresses and barbed spears. Plantforms are limited to linear-style botanicals and Yam Figures. Plants are present at 4% of sites.	Re-established monsoon post-LGM results in rising sea levels and the loss of coastal plains. Rainforest and open woodlands expand, and lacustral taxa and tuber parenchyma increase at Carpenter's Gap 1.
Painted Hand 9–5KBP 	Animals and humans are depicted with sectioned bodies. Figures are depicted in social and ritual scenes, and feature sex attributes. Decorated hands are painted with elongated nails and internal patterns. Plant depictions include fruits, yams, and Yam Figures. Plants are present at 18% of sites.	The monsoon system stabilises and expands, and an Early Holocene Wet Phase produces an inferred population increase. This is reflected in increasing rock art territoriality and iconographic shift from previous naturalistic styles to more stylised imagery.
Wandjina ~5KBP-ongoing 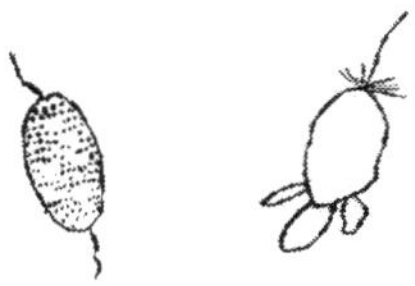	Dominated by depictions of large ancestral figures known as Wandjina, connected to the environment and weather systems. Dingos and other animals are depicted alongside yams, fruits, and Yam Figures. Plants are present at 19% of sites.	Increasing climate variability stems from the onset of the El Niño-Southern Oscillation (ENSO) system, marked by intermittent high aridity. High levels of macrobotanical diversity at Carpenter's Gap 1 and Riwi suggest an increase in site and plant usage.

Illustrations by Emily Grey.

2016; Grey 2018) (see Figure 17.2). Motifs occur in groups of two or more, depicted as individual tubers or a string of yams connected by roots. In comparison, *ganmanggu* demonstrates a higher level of morphological variation with multi-lobed and patterned ovoid forms often depicted with sprouted tendrils and rootlet fringes (see Figure 17.3).

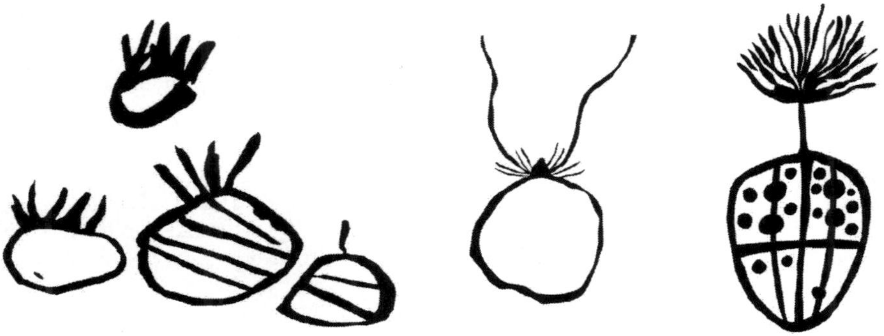

Figure 17.2 Different types of round yam representations in East Kimberley rock art. Illustrations by Emily Grey.

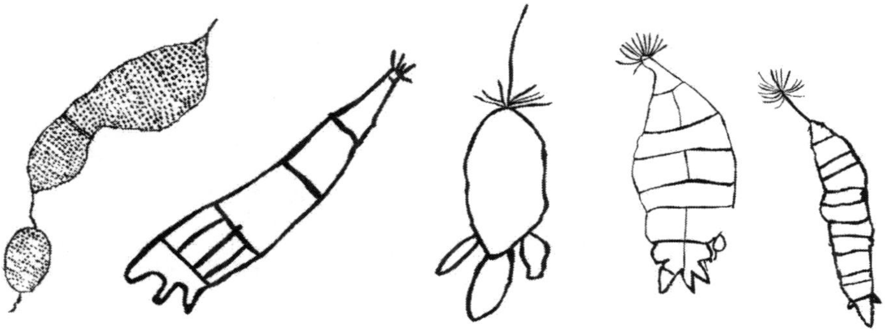

Figure 17.3 Different types of long yam representations in East Kimberley rock art. Illustrations by Emily Grey.

Yam Figure motifs incorporate these variable features into anthropomorphic forms, which have also been identified in Arnhem Land rock art by Chaloupka (1993) and Hammond (2016, 2019). Hammond (2019) details a transition in motif subject matter from early Holocene *Dioscorea bulbifera* depictions to a later emphasis on anthropomorphic *Dioscorea transversa* figures, which has expanded into contemporary paintings and cultural practices. These figures are associated with a period of environmental resource abundance argued by Williams et al. (2015) to have increased low-intensity food production. In the Kimberley, early research by avocationalist Walsh (n.d., in Veth et al. 2016:38) identified two categories of Yam Figures: "a) motifs that are highly stylised and essentially yams with limbs" and "b) schematised stick figure-like anthropomorphs with variations of distinctive yam heads". These preliminary identifications have been critically assessed by both Veth et al. (2016) and Ouzman et al. (2018), and are here expanded on to

Table 17.2 Yam Figure types and motif counts

Type	*Sub type*	*Attributes*	*Sites*	*Motifs*
Yam Head	Type A	Linear figures with large round or obovate tuber heads, infilled with irregular gridding and/or longitudinal lines. Depicted in pairs, triplets, and larger compositions, in direct association with Gwion and Static Polychrome imagery.	28	80
	Type B	Simple stick-figures with linear bodies covered in lobes, dots, and/or short barbs and rootlet fringing. Heads are large, obovate tubers infilled with dots. Depicted in pairs and larger compositions, in direct association with Gwion and Static Polychrome imagery.	4	19
Yam Body	Type A	Round bulbous figures with curvilinear arms and legs ending with rootlet-like fingers and toes. Figures can be dotted, striped, and/or segmented. Depicted in pairs, triplets, and multiples, in association with Painted Hand and Wandjina imagery. Figures are also repeatedly associated with figurative plant imagery, particularly long and round yam and tuber motifs.	13	35
	Type B	Elongated figures with linear limbs, often only represented as short lines and rootlet fringes. Motifs can be dotted, striped, and/or segmented. Depicted as individuals or pairs, in association with all currently defined Kimberley rock art styles.	13	26

Data taken from Grey (2018).

incorporate wider morphological variability in a sample of 84 'Yam Figures'. These motifs were identified in 30 rock art sites out of ~1,251 sites recorded by the *Kimberley Visions: Rock Art Style Provinces of North Australia* project. Yam Figure sites were recorded during remote fieldwork undertaken between 2016 and 2019, through systematic survey, and photographic and written site records. Depictions are differentiated from figurative plant and ornamented anthropomorph motifs through anthropomorphic and botanical morphological markers defined by plant taxonomies and Indigenous traditional ecological knowledge (TEK; see Crawford 1982; Cheinmora et al. 2017). Identifications are also informed by intra-site and intra-panel motif associations, with ~85% of all Yam Figures depicted in site or panel associations with figurative plant motifs. Figures are unsexed, not featuring any primary or secondary sexual characteristics that would make identifying sex or gender possible within the current research framework.

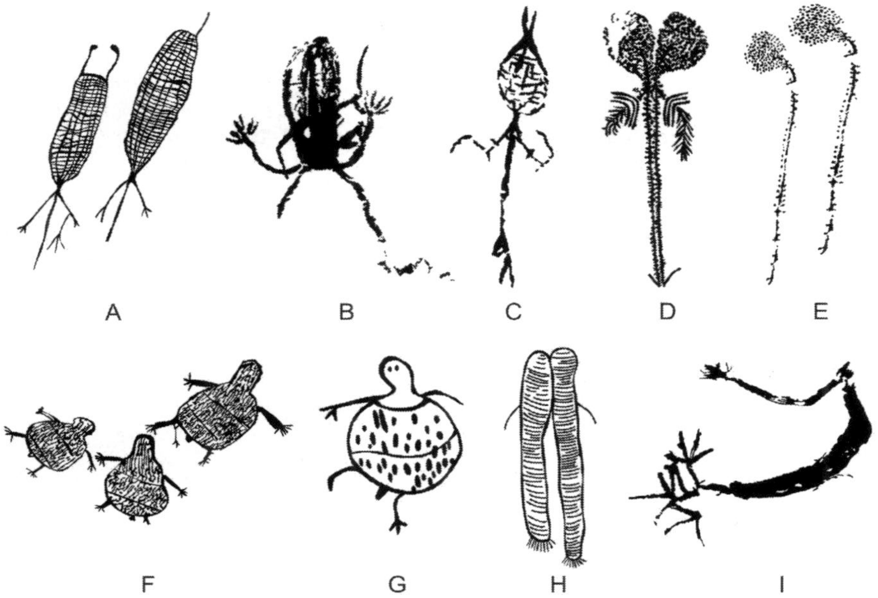

Figure 17.4 Examples of Yam Figure motif types – Yam Head Type A (A–C), Type B (D–E), and Yam Body Type A (F–G) and Type B (H–I). Illustrations by Emily Grey.

A combination of anthropomorphic and botanical markers enable the identification of specific yam attributes in Yam Figure motifs, specifically as part of the head and body of each figure (see Table 17.2). These include ovoid tuberous head and body shapes, bodies infilled with adventitious dotting and longitudinal and irregular ridgelines, and linear rootlet-like limbs. Yam Head Type A figures are morphologically most comparable to *ganmanggu*, with elongated ovoid yam heads infilled with irregular longitudinal lines suggestive of surface root ridging; in comparison, Type B images are more comparable to *kunu*, with ovoid heads infilled with adventitious dotting, tapering to an elongated body and stem line covered with fine fringed rootlets. Yam Body figures are similarly defined, with Type A figures featuring rounded *kunu* bodies with rootlet limbs and bulbous heads, and Type B most comparable to the elongated tuber forms of *ganmanggu* and other long tubers (see Figures 17.4 and 17.5). The identified emphasis on specific morphological attributes such as ovoid shape and rootlets suggests an association of yam attributes and ecologies with anthropomorphic identity markers. This emphasis is reflective of the nature of yams and USOs as keystone food types across northern Australia, where yams and other tubers are also part of many mythological narratives (Akerman 2016; Veth et al. 2016; Ouzman et al. 2018).

Figure 17.5 A Yam Body Type A panel from a site in the King George River catchment. Illustrated by Emily Grey.

Multispecies lifeworlds and planty relationships

Plants have historically been under researched in archaeology. Despite their clear cultural value, the association of plants with women-coded activities has worked against their recognition in a field with a traditional focus on male subsistence practices, especially hunting. Plant remains are further disadvantaged in this respect because of their depositional characteristics (Balme and Bowdler 2006; Atchison and Head 2013; Sterling 2014). In the context of rock art, this disadvantage is further compounded by a perceived absence of botanical imagery in world forager rock arts, particularly in comparison to the wealth of detailed animal depictions (Veth et al. 2016). This perceived absence has created a bias in archaeological inference, where animals are considered part of the "imaginative construction of lifeworlds" (Ingold 2000:9), while plants are part of a separate and profane female economy. Crittenden and Schnorr (2017:86) link these assumptions to "an observational bias of only attending to men's activities", while Atchison and Head (2012, 2013) note a similar dichotomous approach when investigating the importance of yams in the East Kimberley. Emphasis is placed on the nutritious components of yams and their economic exploitation by forager-hunter communities over their socioecological significance (see Keeley 1995; Bird and O'Connell 2006).

This emphasis and associated biases sit in contrast to Indigenous engagements with plant resources, which are recognised both for their valuable materials and resources, and their ancestral connection with humans: "everything come up out of ground – language, people, emu, kangaroo, grass. That's Law" (Danyari in Rose 1992:57 and Hall 2011:101). A Western emphasis on economic function and gendered biases demonstrates the inadequacy of the scientific epistemology in conceptualising and connecting with such non-Cartesian lifeworlds (Ingold 2000, 2002, 2008; Zedeño 2013). In addressing such inadequacies, researchers increasingly take into consideration other-than-human ecologies and the entanglement of human and other-than-human lifeways. Work by Atchison and Head (2013) embodies this understanding of forager lifeways "with the materiality of the plants themselves, and… what kinds of relations this material makes possible" (168). This kind of engagement is conducive to a multispecies approach, a theoretical framework which considers the biocultural modalities of forager-plant relations (Hussain and Floss 2015; Alberti and Fowles 2018).

Multispecies archaeologies engage with evidence of human interactions with other-than-humans in the archaeological record to understand non-Western lifeworlds, which are neither solely 'nature' or 'culture' (Aisher and Damodaran 2016; Alberti and Fowles 2018). Plants, animals, people, and wider ecologies such as seasons and landscapes, are connected in manifold forms, and lifeworlds include the experiences, activities, and phenomena shared between these inhabitants. Drawing on concepts of ecological entanglement (Bawaka Country et al. 2016; Alberti and Fowles 2018) and the 'life of lines' (Ingold 2015), multispecies ecology argues that relationships between humans and other-than-humans are co-constructed through shared experiences, encounters, and perceptions. These experiences are shaped by what Ingold (2000:27) refers to as the "ground[ing of] human intention and action within the context of an ongoing and mutually constitutive engagement between people and their environments". Humans and other-than-humans do not exist as separate entities, but as bundles of relations, which interact with, intersect, and influence each other. An example of this can be seen in Ingold's (2008:1808) concept of the riverbank, where the tangling of vegetation extends into multiple lifeways:

> in the tangled bank, lines of growth issuing from multiple sources become comprehensively bound up with one another, just as do the vines and creepers of a dense patch of tropical forest, or the tangled root systems that you cut through with your spade every time you dig your garden. What we have been accustomed to calling 'the environment' might, then, be better envisaged as a zone of entanglement.

Ingold's riverbank description enmeshes plantlife with soil, insect life, and other animals; it is shaped by wind, rain fall, and sunshine, through the continuance of seasons, the movement of people through the landscape searching for food and sourcing plants, all of which further entangles each aspect together into a meshwork, which extends far beyond plants lining a riverbank. This concept is similarly embodied in traditional Indigenous concepts of landscape animacy, where plants and animals can communciate and call out in their own languages to signal change and transition (Crawford 1982; Head, Atchison and Fullagar 2002; Atchison and Head 2012; Cheinmora et al. 2017). In the Forrest River region of the east Kimberley, female elders emphasise the importance of the smell of ripening fruit and flowers: "smellem from long way"; and the humming of bees as indicators of valuable plantlife: "listen all the sugarbag singing out" (Head, Atchison, and Fullagar 2018:185).

The '*following*' of plants in these ways means that people encounter not just one plant, but many plants, animals, and landforms simultaneously, and constantly engage in a complex sensory communication with the wider environment (Rose 2005, 2013). The immersion of forager lifeways in agentive environments, which can communicate and act, can be understood as the building of relations *between* nodes of intentionality and agency, or relations *along* lines of multispecies lifeways (Ingold 2008:1808). These lines of relations include the ways both people and yams co-occupy the landscape, the ways yams grow up through stones and trees, how people move through shared environments, and the tangible impacts of plants and art at rock art places (Bawaka Country et al. 2016; Alberti and Fowles 2018). These types of planty actions entangle rock art and rock art places with the experiencing and conceptualising of plants themselves. The extension of figurative plant depictions to human-plant conflation motifs is, according to Ouzman et al. (2018:475), part of an iterative process serving to articulate and mobilise complex worldviews in which people and plants are entangled and co-identified. These processes are part of wider environmental management traditions, termed *ecoscaping*, which involve "collective plant gathering, processing, and social activity" (Ouzman et al. 2019:476).

Ecoscapes and yamscapes

As one of a host of other-than-agriculture Indigenous environmental practices (see Denham 2008), ecoscaping is a meshwork of recursive human-plant relationships; it involves knowledge and practice surrounding the location and usage of waterways, landscape formations, and floral and faunal communities (Lidicker 2008; Ouzman et al. 2019). The assemblage of known locations of plant resources is referred to as an *ecoscape*, and in reference to yams, *yamscape* (Atchison and Head 2012). The act of cultivating, gathering, foraging, and harvesting these resources is referred to as *wild harvesting*, a process which is undertaken at specific times according to the cyclical calendar of the Australian Monsoonal Tropics (AMT). Six seasons are recognised by Kwini people, and their onset and duration are marked by changes in plants, animals, and weather; an example of this is seen during the onset of the early dry season *Bandemanya/Kolorûrru*, when above-ground tuber vines dry and desiccate to send energy into fattening below-ground tubers (Cheinmora et al. 2017, after Crawford 1982). Both *kunu* and *ganmanggu* can be found and harvested from a range of environments, categorised in Kwini tradition according to soil and vegetation communities: *bura/bera,* leached sand plains with gravel admixture; *wungkaylia/wunggaila,* outcrops of basalt with clay-rich deposits which support a host of rainforest species; *kololor/gololor*, the water-washed sand and scrub, which lines the banks of beaches and freshwater rivers; and *wumangarr*, sandstone outcrops whose crevasses are filled with a rich humus supporting fruits, yams, and other tubers (Crawford 1982:23; Cheinmora et al. 2017:18). While their locations are shared, the long and round yam require different processes for consumption; *ganmanggu* requires little processing, and can be eaten roasted or raw, while *kunu* requires processing to remove irritating raphide bundles composed of calcium oxalate crystals in the skin (Padhan and Panda 2020). As members of the *Dioscoreaceae* family, these yams are monocotyledonous vines, which feature cordate leaves with pronounced acuminate apices, undulating margins, and palmate venation.

Kunu's dark green leaves alternate along clockwise-twining stems, which sprout small aerial bulbils, while *ganmanggu's* leaves sit opposite one another on anti-clockwise-twining stems free of growths (Western Herbarium 1994). Vines extend through neighbouring vegetation and stone, and tubers can grow up to two metres below ground. While the round tuber is ovoid, bulbous, covered with nodules from which adventitious rootlets extend, the long yam is elongated, multi-lobed, and covered with rootlets. A preference for long and round yams growing in stony soils over sand stems from the quality of yams from stony substrates, which grow long and thin through soil punctuated by stony material, which once excavated is used for stone tool production (Atchison and Head 2009, 2012); this preference also stems from the fact that yams in sandy soils are regularly dug up and consumed by kangaroos, while those from stony outcrops are harder to excavate and rarely targeted. The excavation of highly valued stony yams, a practice traditionally undertaken by women, leaves a noticeable footprint in the landscape, with "mounds of piled up stones and holes… evidence of [women's] gathering activities" (Atchison and Head 2013:169). These piles produce depressions, which fill with worked soil and leaf litter, creating deep stone-free soils in which yam tops are transplanted to grow longer and stronger. The replanting of yams ensures the same tuber re-grows and re-develops each season, meaning "women are not just digging yams from the same place… they are often re-digging and collecting the same genetic plants" (Atchison and Head 2013:171). This creates a complex mosaic of yamscapes embodying intergenerational knowledge and social prestige, evidence of the importance of these ecoscapes and wild harvesting practices, and the complex interplay between social and ecological contexts shared between people and yams. Such interplay is embodied in the variable depictions of Yam Figures, which articulate a dialogue between plants and people, and, in particular, women foragers.

Conclusion: people, plants, and painting

Research concerning the intersection or entanglement of forager lifeways, environments, and rock art, is still in its developing stages. Veth et al. (2016)

and Ouzman et al. (2018) have built on early avocational plant art studies in the Kimberley (i.e., Welch 2003) to better understand the significant role of plants in past forager lifeways, both economically and spiritually. Yam Figures are one unique form in which these forager-plant relationships were expressed through rock art. The identification of these motifs involves the use of morphological botanical features of keystone yam species referenced in Kimberley ethnographic and archaeobotanical research. An understanding of these motifs requires a more detailed study of the socioecology of these plant types, their environments, and their relationships with forager lifeways. Emphasis on the merging of anthropomorphic identity markers such as the head and body with yam morphologies is suggestive of a close co-identification of foragers with keystone plant species, particularly by women. While Yam Figures do not feature any physical primary or secondary sexual characteristics, their incorporation of plant features with the human form may also indicate potentially female-coded identity constructs. A repeated reference to the replanting of yam tops in the literature (see Crawford 1982; Atchison and Head 2012, 2013) may also be connected to this emphasis, tying together the women-led replanting of yam tops with Yam Head Figures in particular. This co-identification is referred to as a "recursive scaping of human and plant identities" by Ouzman et al. (2018:475), and has been connected to wider archaeobotanical and palaeoecological research across northern Australia (Atchison and Head 2013; Bawaka Country et al. 2016; Barton and Denham 2018; Florin and Carah 2018). These relationships are entangled with the ways that yams live and move through the landscape, growing in attachment to surrounding trees, twining between boulders, and rooting into stony substrates, much in the way Ingold (2008:1808) describes the entangling of vegetation on the banks of a river. The repeated presence of both figurative and anthropomorphised yams in northeast Kimberley rock art suggests the continued importance of these plants in similar social, economic, and symbolic lifeways. As such, the visual salience of yams becomes intimately connected with their landscapes and is embodied in their depictions.

References

Aisher, A. and V. Damodaran 2016. Introduction: Human-nature interactions through a multispecies lens. *Conservation and Society* 14(4):293–304.

Akerman, K. 2016. *Wanjina: Notes on some iconic ancestral beings of the Northern Kimberley*. Carlisle: Hesperian Press.

Alberti, B. and S. Fowles. 2018. Ecologies of rock and art in northern New Mexico. In *Multispecies archaeology*. S. Pilaar Birch, ed. Pp. 133–153. New York: Routledge.

Atchison, J. and L. Head. 2009. Cultural ecology: Emerging human-plant geographies. *Progress in Human Geography* 33(2):236–245.

Atchison, J. and L. Head. 2012. Yam landscapes: The biogeography and social life of Australian *Dioscorea*. *The Artefact* 35:59–74.

Atchison, J. and L. Head. 2013. Exploring human-plant entanglements: The case of Australian *Dioscorea* yams. In *Archaeology in environment and technology:*

Intersections and transformations. D. Frankel, S. Lawrence, J. Webb, W. S. F. Pickering, and G. Walford, eds. Pp. 167–180. London: Taylor & Francis Group.

Balme, J. and S. Bowdler. 2006. Spear and digging stick: The origins of gender and its implications for the colonisation of new continents. *Journal of Social Archaeology* 6(3):379–401.

Balme, J., S. O'Connor, T. Malony, D. Vannieuwenhuyse, K. Aplin, and I. E. Dilkes-Hall. 2018. Long-term occupation on the edge of the desert: Riwi Cave in the southern Kimberley, Western Australia. *Archaeology in Oceania* 54(1):35–52.

Barton, H. and T. Denham. 2018. Vegecultures and the social-biocultural transformations of plants and people. *Quaternary International* 489:17–25.

Bawaka Country, S. Wright, S. Suchet-Pearson, K. Lloyd, J. Sweeney, L. Burarrwanga, R. Ganambarr, M. Ganambarr-Stubbs, B. Ganambarr, and D. Maymuru. 2016. Co-becoming Bawaka: Towards a relational understanding of place/space. *Progress in Human Geography* 40(4):455–475.

Bird, D. W. and J. F. O'Connell. 2006. Behavioural ecology and archaeology. *Journal of Archaeological Research* 14(2):143–188.

Boyd, C. E. and K. Cox. 2016. *The White Shaman mural: An enduring creation narrative in the rock art of the Lower Pecos*. Austin: University of Texas Press.

Boyd, C. E. and J. P. Dering. 1996. Medicinal and hallucinogenic plants identified in the sediments and pictographs of the Lower Pecos, Texas Archaic. *Antiquity* 70(268):256–275.

Chaloupka, G. 1993. *Journey in time: The world's longest continuing art tradition*. Chatswood: Reed.

Cheinmora, D., A. Charles, T. Karadada, B. Waina, F. Nyalerin, L. Waina, M. Punchi, A. Chalarimeri, D. Unghango, T. Saunders, M. Sefton, T. Vigilante, and G. Wightman. 2017. *Belaa plants and animals: Biocultural knowledge of the Kwini people of the far north Kimberley, Australia*. Darwin: Batchelor Press.

Chippindale, C., B. Smith, and P. S. C. Taçon. 2000. Visions of dynamic power: Archaic rock-paintings, altered states of consciousness and 'Clever Men' in Western Arnhem Land (NT), Australia. *Cambridge Archaeological Journal* 10(1):63–101.

Clarkson, C., M. Smith, B. Marwick, R. Fullagar, L. A. Wallis, P. Faulkner, T. Manne, E. Hayes, R. G. Roberts, Z. Jacobs, Z. Carah, K. M. Lowe, J. Matthews, and S. A. Florin 2015. The archaeology, chronology, and stratigraphy of Madjedbebe (Malakunanja II): A site in northern Australia with early occupation. *Journal of Human Evolution* 83(2015):46–64.

Crawford, I. M. 1982. *Traditional Aboriginal plant resources in the Kalumburu area: Aspects in ethno-economics*. Records of the Western Australian Museum Supplements, Supplement No.15. Western Australian Museum, Perth, WA.

Crittenden, A. N. and S. L. Schnorr. 2017. Current views on hunter-gatherer nutrition and the evolution of the human diet. *American Journal of Physical Anthropology* 162:84–109.

David, B., J. J. Delannoy, F. Petchey, J. Huntley, R. Gunn, P. Veth, K. Genuite, R. J. Skelley, J. Mialanes, S. Harper, S. Ouzman, Balanggarra Aboriginal Corporation, P. Heaney, and V. Wong. 2019. Dating painting events through by-products of ochre processing: Borologa 1 Rockselter, Kimberley, Australia. *Australian Archaeology* 85(1):57–94.

Denham, T. 2008. Traditional forms of plant exploitation in Australia and New Guinea: The search for common ground. *Vegetation History and Archaeobotany* 17(2):245–248.

Dilkes-Hall, I. E., S. O'Connor, and J. Balme. 2019b. People-plant interaction and economic botany over 47,000 years of occupation at Carpenter's Gap 1, south central Kimberley. *Australian Archaeology* 85(1):30–47.

Dilkes-Hall, I. E., J. Balme, S. O'Connor, and E. Dotte-Sarout. 2019a. Archaeobotany of Aboriginal plant foods during the Holocene at Riwi, south central Kimberley, Western Australia. *Vegetation History and Archaeobotany* 29(3):309–325.

Doring, J. and P. Nyawarra 2014. Gwion artists and Wunan Law: The origins of society in Australia. *Rock Art Research* 31(1):3–13.

Elkin, A. P. 1930. Rock-painting of north-west Australia. *Oceania* 1(3):257–279.

Finch, D., A. Gleadow, J. Hergt, V. A. Levchenko, P. Heaney, P. Veth. S. Harper, S. Ouzman, C. Myers, and H. Green. 2020. 12,000-year-old Aboriginal rock art from the Kimberley region, Western Australia. *Science Advances* 6(6):1–9.

Florin, S. A. and X. Carah. 2018. Moving past the 'Neolithic Problem': The development and interaction of subsistence systems across northern Sahul. *Quaternary International* 489:46–62.

Florin, S. A., A. S. Fairbairn, M. Nango, D. Djandjomerr, B. Marwick, R. Fullagar, M. Smith, L.A. Wallis, and C. Clarkson. 2020. The first Australian plant foods at Madjedbebe, 65,000-53,000 years ago. *Nature Communications* 11(924):1–8.

Grey, E. 2018. *Plant, person, or both? An archaeological attribute analysis of human-plant 'florianthrope' conflations in east Kimberley rock art*. Unpublished BA(Hons) thesis, School of Social Sciences, Archaeology, University of Western Australia, Crawley.

Hall, M. 2011. *Plants as persons: A philosophical botany*. New York: State University of New York Press.

Hammond, J. W. 2019 The spatial distribution of unique motifs featuring *Dioscorea bulbifera*, the round yam, in western Arnhem Land rock art. *Australian Archaeology* 85(2):215–219.

Head, L., J. Atchison, and R. Fullagar. 2002. Country and garden: Ethnobotany, archaeobotany and Aboriginal landscapes near the Keep River, northwestern Australia. *Journal of Social Archaeology* 2(2):173–196.

Head, L., J. Atchison, and R. Fullagar. 2018. Country and garden: Ethnobotany, archaeobotany and Aboriginal landscapes near the Keep River, northwestern Australia. *Journal of Social Archaeology* 2(2):173–196.

Hussain, S. T. and H. Floss 2015. Sharing the world with mammoths, cave lions and other beings: Linking animal-human interactions and the Aurignacian "belief world". *Quartär* 62(2015):85–120.

Ingold, T. 2000. *The perception of the environment: Essays on livelihood, dwelling and skill*. London: Routledge.

Ingold, T. 2002. Between evolution and history: Biology, culture, and the myth of human origins. In *The evolution of cultural entities*. M. Wheeler, ed. Pp. 43–66. London: Oxford Publishing.

Ingold, T. 2008. Binding against boundaries: Entanglements of life in an open world. *Environment and Planning* 40(8):1796–1810.

Ingold, T. 2015. *The life of lines*. New York: Routledge.

Kaberry, P. M. 1939. *Aboriginal woman: Sacred and profane*. London: Routledge and Kegan Paul Limited.

Keeley, L. H. 1995. Protoagricultural practices among hunter gatherers: A cross-cultural survey. In *Last hunters, first farmers: New perspectives on the prehistoric transition to agriculture*. T. D. Price and A. B. Gebauer, eds. Pp. 243–272. Santa Fe: School of American Research Press.

Lidicker, W. Z. Jr. 2008. Levels of organization in biology: On the nature and nomenclature of ecology's fourth level. *Biological Reviews* 83(1):71–78.

Maloney, T., S. O'Connor, R. Wood, K. Aplin, and J. Balme. 2018. Carpenter's Gap 1: A 47,000 year old record of Indigenous adaptation and innovation. *Quaternary International* 191:204–228.

Mguni, S. 2009. Natural and supernatural convergences. Trees in Southern African rock art. *Current Anthropology* 50(1):139–148.

Mowaljarlai, D. 1992. Ngarinyin perspective of repainting: Mowaljarlai's statement. In *Retouch: Maintenance and conservation of Aboriginal rock imagery*. Occasional AURA Publication 5, Archaeological Publications. G. K. Ward, ed. Pp. 8–9. Melbourne: AURA.

Ouzman, S., P. Veth, C. Myers, P. Heaney, and K. Kenneally. 2018. Plants before animals? Aboriginal rock art as evidence of ecoscaping in Australia's Kimberley. In *The Oxford handbook of the archaeology and anthropology of rock art*. B. David and I. J. McNiven, eds. Pp. 439–479. Oxford: Oxford Publishing.

Padhan, B. and D. Panda 2020. Potential of neglected and underutilised yams (*Dioscorea spp.*) for improving nutritional security and health benefits. *Frontiers in Pharmacology* 11(1):496.

Pilaar Birch, S. E., ed. 2018. *Multispecies archaeology*. Oxford: Routledge.

Porr, M. 2018. Country and relational ontology in the Kimberley, Northwest Australia: Implications for understanding and representing archaeological evidence. *Cambridge Archaeological Journal* 28(3):395–409.

Porr, M. and H. R. Bell. 2012. 'Rock-art', 'animism', and two-way thinking: Towards a complementary epistemology in the understanding of material culture and 'rock-art' of hunting and gathering people. *Journal of Archaeological Method and Theory* 19:161–205.

Rose, D. B. 1992. *Dingo makes us human: Life and land in an Aboriginal Australian culture*. Melbourne: Cambridge University Press.

Rose, D. B. 2005. An Indigenous philosophical ecology: Situating the human. *Australian Journal of Anthropology* 16:294–305.

Rose, D. B. 2013. Val Plumwood's philosophical animism: Attentive inter-actions in the sentient world. *Environmental Humanities* 3(1):93–109.

Ross, J., K. Westaway, M. Travers, M. J. Morwood, and J. Hayward. 2016. Into the past: A step towards a robust Kimberley rock art chronology. *PLoS ONE* 11(8):1–33.

Sterling, K. 2014. Man the hunter, woman the gatherer? The impact of gender studies on hunter-gatherer research (a retrospective). In *The Oxford handbook of the archaeology and anthropology of Hunter-Gatherers*. V. Cummings, P. Jordan, and M Zvelebil, eds. Pp. 151–176. Oxford: Oxford University Press.

Taçon, P. S. C., M. Wilson, and C. Chippindale. 1996. Birth of the Rainbow Serpent in Arnhem Land rock art and oral history. *Archaeology in Oceania* 31(3):103–124.

Veth, P., C. Myers, P. Heaney, and S. Ouzman 2016. Plants before farming: The deep history of plant-use and representation in the rock art of Australia's Kimberley region. *Quaternary International* 489:26–45.

Veth, P., K. Ditchfield, M. Bateman, S. Ouzman, M. Benoit, A. P. Motta, D. Lewis, S. Harper, and Balanggarra Aboriginal Corporation. 2019. Minjiwarra:

Archaeological evidence of human occupation of Australia's northern Kimberley by 50,000 BP. *Australian Archaeology* 85(2):115–125.

Wallis, L. A. 2001. Environmental history of northwest Australia based on phytolith analysis at Carpenter's Gap 1. *Quaternary International* 83(85):103–117.

Walsh, G. n.d. Unpublished notes. Copy held by M. Myers. North Carlton.

Walsh, G. 1994. *Bradshaws: Ancient rock paintings of North-West Australia*. Geneva: Edition Limiteé.

Welch, D. 1993. Stylistic change in the Kimberley rock art, Australia. In *Rock art studies: The post-stylistic era or where do we go from here?* Oxbow Monograph 35. M. Lorblanchet and P. G. Bahn, eds. Pp. 93–113. Oxford: Oxford Publishing.

Welch, D. 2003. Plant motifs in Kimberley rock-art, Australia. *Before Farming* 4:1–13.

Western Australian Herbarium. 1994 *Dioscorea bulbifera* L. Ganmanggu. Western Australian Flora Department of Biodiversity, Conservation and Attractions. Retrieved 10 June from https://florabase.dpaw.wa.gov.au/browse/profile/1508

Wightman, G. M. and M. R. Andrews. 1989. *Plants of Northern Territory monsoon vine forests*. Darwin: Conservation Commission of the Northern Territory.

Williams, A. N., S. Ulm, C. S. M. Turney, D. Rohde, and G. White. 2015. Holocene demographic changes and the emergence of complex societies in prehistoric Australia. *PLoS ONE* 10(6):1–17.

Zedeño, M. N. 2013. Methodological and analytical challenges in relational archaeologies: A view from the hunting grounds. In *Relational archaeologies: Humans, animals, things*. C. Watts, ed. Pp. 117–134. New York: Routledge.

18 Ontological reversals, correspondences, and archaeological 'arts of noticing'

Benjamin Alberti

The idea of a thing grows alongside the thing itself.

(Ingold 2020)

Introduction

I have been worrying about the relationship between the form of made things and what they mean for a long time. Standing in a museum in St. John's, Newfoundland, in 2016, staring at several small, Inuit ivory carvings, I had a sudden intuition: meaning and form emerge together out of a long, intimate history of stories and materials. There never is a separation. Tim Ingold has been saying this for a long time, of course. In this chapter, I explore the uniquely archaeological problem of how to understand the meaning of ancient things to which we have no historical connection. The idea that meaning and thing are separate entities is an Enlightenment legacy. Ingold (2013:20–21) characterises one symptom of this way of thinking as 'hylomorphism', the idea that form is imprinted by thought onto matter. Standard methodologies for object analysis in archaeology obey this logic, the distancing enacted performing a separation between meaning and thing. Useful quantitative and comparative data are accrued using such methodologies but are often considered the only form of valid knowledge. Archaeological artworks, in this scheme, are understood as the outcome of technical processes that are given meaning *a posteriori*. It is taken as given that we have the physical object, but the original meaning is gone.

Ingold provides tools to think about both how things become meaningful and how archaeologists might get meaning out of things. Since the 1990s, Ingold has proposed a series of reversals in ontological priority: from made thing to making, from form to growth, from building to dwelling, and from image to image making. In a typical paper, an ontological truth is presented as such, until a pivotal moment in the argument when the ontology is flipped, and a key insight revealed. It is always intellectually gratifying to read an Ingold article for this reason. His work has grown, I would argue, from one central reversal: that doing is prior to thought. There are two aspects

DOI: 10.4324/9781003162773-24

of Ingold's thought I draw on in this chapter: that the idea of a thing and the thing itself grow together, encapsulated in his theory of correspondence (Ingold 2016, 2017, 2021); and his insistence that we "follow the materials" (Ingold 2007). There is a puzzle, nonetheless, that Ingold's work does not fully resolve: how does meaning emerge from making in the particular case of an art-like object?[1]

'Correspondence' is Ingold's substitute for thinking about specific meanings, one that provides the resources to do so by enabling us to see that the making of artworks and their study are ontologically equivalent. Archaeologists act in the same way as the ancient artist did. Following cues from Ingold's work, I explore craft, art practices, and the nature of the art object, ultimately arguing for a reappraisal of an 'archaeological sensibility' (Shanks 2020). Experiences such as the sense of alterity in the ruins of a castle (Alberti 2016), or the excitement of touching 1,000-year-old ceramics from the Yungas of Argentina, can be dismissed as the almost inevitable feeling that develops when one is brought up in a world and trained in a discipline infused with the romantic tradition of ruins and old things. I argue that such attunement to past things is an analytical advantage, not the noise of context to be dispensed with. It is an error to think that the sensibilities we bring to the study of archaeological things suffocate all other meanings. Moreover, the fact that we can engage with things deeply means that we can be impacted by them beyond taking their scientific measure. In what follows, I present ideas for observational practices designed to capture the lingering residue of the conceptual worlds – the meaning – that grew alongside archaeological artworks in their original contexts, providing examples from a body of anthropomorphic ceramic vessels from first millennium AD northwest Argentina. The goal of these 'arts of noticing' (Tsing 2015) is not to resuscitate ancient meanings wholesale but rather to reveal the material consequences of concepts that show up precisely because they are not ours.

Compulsive creativity

> It takes concrete histories to make any concept come to life.
>
> Anna Tsing (2015:66)

The difficulties introduced by the Cartesian substance ontology's separation of all entities into material things and things of thought has been long recognised in archaeology (e.g., Thomas 1996). In line with Ingold's thinking, it is generally recognised by archaeologists influenced by Latour, new materialism, or the 'ontological turn', that the distinction between meaning and thing is artificial: material culture is meaningfully constituted, as Hodder (1986) claimed. Symmetrical archaeologists go further, arguing that things are meaningful beyond any contact with humans (see Olsen 2010). The co-constitution of what we study and our way of studying it has been stressed, developing insights by new materialist authors such as Barad (e.g., Marshall and Alberti 2014; Fowler and Harris 2015).

Even so, a majority of archaeologists continues to treat the thing and its meaning as ultimately distinct, even if objects are considered to be more than blank slates onto which we project culturally specific meanings. The concept of 'social construction', for example, continues to undergird work on landscape and materiality. Moreover, there is little work that addresses the question of how specific meanings and practices emerge together in the making of an object, nor how to leverage that insight in our methodologies. If the separation of meaning from things is an artefact of modern thought (Henare et al. 2007:3), we need a better way to understand the processes whereby things take on specific meanings. That is the wrong question to ask of Ingold; the two are never separate in his work. However, Ingold's world tends to be surface-focused, concerned with immanent, visible relations. How can we explain the production of art-like things such as the La Candelaria pots that seem to carry a meaning beyond the interactions that led to their growth?

For Ingold, any meaning is always present. The often-overlooked end point of his hugely influential 1993 essay *The temporality of the landscape* is that meaning awaits animating stories in the features of the world. In a classic reversal, meaning is not applied to landscapes by sentient humans, but rather "is there to be *discovered* in the landscape, if only we know how to attend to it" (Ingold 1993:172; emphasis in original). Similarly, forms are not the product of minds but are the consequence of perception and the natural template of bodies. The form of the Acheulean handaxe, for example, which remained virtually unchanged for hundreds of thousands of years, is an outcome of the morphology of the body, the gestures associated with flake removal, and the fracture properties of materials (Ingold 2013:33–45). The bifacial form is thus almost inevitable. Though Acheulian handaxes are not art-like in the way I have described, similar arguments can be made for things that are. Jones (2020) shows that the regularity in form and design of the carved stone balls of Neolithic Britain emerged out of the act of subdividing a sphere. The material guides intention. Forms that appear to exceed the form-producing properties of materials and bodies present more of a challenge. Nonetheless, Ingold (2015) has written a compelling analysis of the La Candelaria ceramics, arguing that their form is related to the potter's gestures in working clay as they would also have experienced the caressing and forming of human infants. The pot and infant are both "made-in-growth" (Ingold 2015:122), such that "form and our awareness of it" emerge together (Ingold 2017:118).

Ingold's (2016:14) ideas have coalesced into his theory of 'correspondence':

> Limbs move, stones settle, timbers bind, voices harmonize, and family members get along through the balance of friction and tension in their affects. They are not 'and ... and ... and' but 'with ... with ... with' [...] In answering – or responding – to one another, they correspond.

Within this framework, 'paying attention to' materials characterises the act of making rather than 'imposing' intention on them. Even so, acts of human making are never mechanical or unconscious, however often repeated. Concentration is required as each action strives to keep itself attuned to the prior action of which it is the continuation: sawing a kerf in wood responds with each pull of the saw to the ever-changing depth and texture of the cut (Ingold 2011:51–53). Ingold (2021:171) describes the builder's chalk line as "a kind of pivot in the balance between conceptual and material worlds". The mark it leaves *is* the concept of straight line. Concepts owe their existence to "the ground of experience" (Ingold 2021:14).

Meaning is not ignored but is tied to a non-intellectual space of natural goings on. My question is, how do these forms, latent in materials and practices, accrue *specific* meanings? That hands experienced in childbirth and the properties of clay grow both children and pots is an argument that could be made about any anthropomorphic ceramics. Craftwork reveals a tighter connection between Ingold's general theory, specific activities, and specific meanings, which remain very concrete. Wheelwright George Sturt (1974 [1923]; Alberti 2018), writing of his experiences, shows how specific concepts grow from generations of skilled wheelwrights and sawyers working with materials. He can distinguish between "ash that is 'tough as whipcord,' and ash that is 'frow as carrot,' or 'doughty,' or 'biscuity' " (Sturt (1974 [1923]:24). Recalling Ingold's discussion of landscape, Dryfus and Kelly (2011:209; emphasis in original) write of Sturt that the craftsman "does not *decide* to treat the ash as if it were 'frow as a carrot' ", as the "task of the craftsman is not to *generate* the meaning, but rather to *cultivate* in himself the skill for *discerning* the meanings that are *already* there". In her discussion of the Middle Magdalenian *contours découpés* – engraved images of horses' heads, executed on horse hyoid bones – Conneller (2011:36) notes that the shape of the bone recalls that of an animal's head. Magdalenian peoples were expert horse hunters, which provided the necessary, concrete experiences to suggest the resemblance. In this case, a different body provides materials for the form. As Conneller (2011:36) argues, even when the idea of form is suggested by material, knowledge of that particular form is only there "for those who know how to see it".

Archaeology played a role in the separation of historical thing from past meaning through the isolation of artefacts in museums and archives (Olsen et al. 2012). The eighteenth century's separation of craft from fine art, in which the latter became an autonomous, meaningful realm of aesthetic contemplation free from everyday life (Shiner 2002) has its counterpart in the practice of archaeology.[2] Art-like archaeological objects such as the La Candelaria ceramics are the outcome of craft-like practices, practices which the fine arts consider to be mechanical rather than meaningful. Yet, as I have argued, through the processes of craft we can understand how meaning in the form of concepts might inhere in them. Their art-like nature provides a clue as to how meaning sticks (see Alberti 2018). Ingold cites Paul Klee

(1961 [1920]:76), who famously wrote, "art does not reproduce the visible but makes visible". In line with Klee, Grosz (2011:60) asks "what affect is produced" by art? "And how does this affect wrench from its materiality what has not been sensed or perceived before?" Affect and sensation, Grosz argues, find homes in the materials – paint, canvas, concrete, steel, marble, words, sounds – as a direct consequence of how those materials are put together. The materials themselves become expressive, are transformed into sensation, making visible 'invisible forces'. Grosz (2011:84–85) takes from Gilles Deleuze the example of the work of Francis Bacon. What Bacon's 'screaming popes' makes visible as 'meat-sensation' are forces such as isolation, deformation, and gravitational pull that act through bodies.

Archaeological artworks, in contrast, are taken to work by referencing something beyond their immediate physical presence, such as past peoples' beliefs. Taking a cue from Grosz's idea of artworks as compounds of sensations that endure, archaeological objects can be usefully thought of as compounds of concepts created through craft-like practices that reside in the materials. Some objects take on a quasi-autonomous state as concept-holders. Holbraad and Pedersen (2017:236) have made the case that "certain materials may be said to 'emit concepts'". Mongolian shamanic costume, for example, constitutes "an explanatory context in and of itself"; its material properties "set in train conceptual trajectories in their own right" (Holbraad and Pedersen 2017:235). Archaeological artworks, we could argue, intensify what is latent in daily experience. The iterative nature of concepts, melded through practice, compels the compulsive making of concept-holders such as the La Candelaria ceramics. The La Candelaria pots can be thought of as both conceptually unsettling and stabilising: repeated acts that renew or demonstrate the indeterminacy of the world (Strathern 2018). These are residues, concretisations of the concepts their makers lived through.

The art of noticing

The question remains of how to develop techniques to capture something of the motivation, experience, and concept-ridden reality of the makers of archaeological art objects. Following Tsing (2015:1), I adopt the idea of 'the arts of noticing' to describe an attitude of anticipation, openness, and curiosity that does not require a pre-established theory of how the world is. There is a "virtue in seeing the world for the first time" (Ingold 2017:105). If you know the scientific name of something, Ingold suggests, you may have too much knowledge. Strathern (1999:6–11) writes of the 'dazzle' of certain, mesmerising ethnographic moments, those that offer a revelatory promise; the "startle of surprise [that] interrupts common sense" (Tsing 2015:293). Being open to such moments is to be open to the 'epistemic mood' of wonder (Ballestero 2015; see also Alberti 2016; Stengers 2011). With this attitude in mind, I recommend three principles to work by. First, we must recognise an equivalence in how we model the taking on of meaning and how we plan our own analysis. What the ancient artist was doing was as experimental, unpredictable, and unstable as our own practices; she, too, was trying to induce an effect in her world. In this regard, I agree with Ingold (2013:6) when he stresses that research should be craft-like, allowing "knowledge to grow from the crucible of our practical and observational engagements with the beings and things around us". Research mirrors practices common to all artful or craft-like activity. Consequently, to conduct analysis of archaeological artworks is to work with two sets of proximities: between everyday actions and artworks; and between artistic production and the archaeological work of analysis.

Second, we can learn from how artists work. Ingold (2013:7) advises us that most practitioners of research as correspondence are to be found among practicing artists, not anthropologists. "Could certain practices of art", he asks, "suggest new ways of *doing* anthropology?" (Ingold 2013:8). Both study 'with' the world; the artwork, therefore, is a result of something like an anthropological study rather than its object. What I propose is that archaeological inquiry can also follow artistic practices to make visible, or sensate, past difference. There is an important body of work that addresses the relationships between art practice and archaeology (see, for example, the "art/archaeology" project curated by Doug Bailey; Jones and Cochrane 2018; Alberti 2018 for an overview). Here, I am concerned with what it is about artists working with materials that produces an effect and the nature of that effect. Artworks capture sensations. But Bacon's paintings are not simply the expression in paint of the 'meat-sensation' of the natural force of gravity; they are also the expression of an ontological commitment to a world of gravity. The concept and artwork resonate with our experience. Similarly, one can understand the intense, physical struggle with plaster that the sculptor Antonio Giacometti frequently underwent, "often subjecting it to so much pressure that it finally crumbled away" (Feigel 2017), as illustrative of muscular artistic practices that wrestle reality into being in a given way.

Creating artworks is to struggle with materials, but it is also a form of materials analysis. On the cover of the edited volume *The way of the shovel* (Roelstraete 2013), that accompanied the eponymous exhibition, is an artwork by Jean-Luc Moulène, entitled *Orant*. *Orant* is a photograph of a broken ancient Mesopotamian figure hung on a wall, one of 24 objects drawn from the Louvre's collections, photographed, and exhibited in both newsprint (*Le Monde*) and in the museum. Berrebi (2013) notes that Moulène is performing a reframing and critique of media and the museum context. I would argue, however, that it is also a concrete reperforming of itself *by* the figure. The arms are broken off at the shoulders, no lower extremities remain, the nose is smashed, and it has one remaining, black-rimmed ivory eye staring intensely, as if in a state of shock or utter helplessness.[3] The third principle, then, is that things provide the means for their own analysis. Things guide our attention in particular ways. Ingold's now famous call to "follow the materials" (Ingold 2007) focused attention on the constituent materials out of which things are made and their inherent vitality. He has since described the entire research process in similar terms:

> [T]here comes a point [...] when, in our observations, the things we study begin to tell us how to observe ... [I]n attending to them, we find that they are also guiding our attention. Our eyes and ears, hands, and minds, absorb into their ways of working a perceptual acuity attuned to their particular ways of moving, of feeling and of being.
>
> (Ingold 2018)

Importantly, such observations are not impressionistic; they are based on the properties of materials as they present themselves through histories of practice and attentiveness. Archaeologists recognise the affect artworks can have but limit their comments to the impact such affect was intended to have on the original viewers, not on us (Hamilakis 2013; Jones and Cochrane 2018). 'Correspondence' implies we should be as interested in the affective impact on the researcher of archaeological things, as clues provided by the things themselves that can guide analysis.

If art can capture our commitment to and experience of force or history, then it can also – as technique – encourage that original sensation to come out. We are not all Bacons, but many archaeologists have a strong intuition for the ancient and otherworldly. We suffer from a kind of 'hypersensitivity' when confronted with things of the past; or as Shanks (2020:47) calls it, we have an "archaeological sensibility", an "affective attunement to the dynamic interplay of the presence of the past in remains". An archaeological sensibility includes an attuned sense of the difference that signifies the pastness of a place or thing. This may sound like mysticism or at the least highly subjective. Subjectivity is not a deficit, however, as it fosters our engagement with the past. Rather than some wooly notion of affinity with old things, an archaeological sensibility is an asset that can be honed by developing a particular 'art of noticing' and a set of descriptive practices capable of receiving the greatest possible influence from the things themselves. Artists analyse, whether self-consciously or not, their world's ontological commitments when they make their works. The ancient La Candelaria artists analysed their worlds when they made their ceramics. Archaeologists, I suggest, can respond to the ceramicist's response to their world using similar processes as artists, both ancient and modern.

Drawing something into being

> [E]very work is an experiment [...] in the sense of prising an opening and following where it leads [...].
>
> (Ingold 2013:6–7)

In this section, I sketch suggestions for analytical techniques, or 'tools to wonder' (Ballestero 2019), framed by the premises of correspondence. Ingold (2013:7) defines research as a form of correspondence: "To practice this method is not to describe the world or to represent it, but to open up our perception to what is going on there so that we, in turn, can respond to it". Analysis of this kind brings together bodies, theories, and passions that "coalesce around the desire [...] to draw something into being" (Winthereik and Ballestero 2021:8). Even so, Ingold's 'corresponding with' tends to occur in a neutral space of encounter, free of contradiction, strong emotion, or strangeness. Archaeologists have noted the analytical possibilities, however, of the feeling of uncanniness the past can stimulate (often inspired by Walter Benjamin, see Dawdy 2016; Pétursdóttir 2013). The moment of initial encounter with archaeological artworks tends to be when our sense of the alterity of the past is most heightened and we are affected by the concrete thing we have in front of us, in an instant of "pre-discursive or prehistoric wonder" (Pétursdóttir 2013:46). There is something of the past that makes itself known at this moment but becomes diluted through overfamiliarity.

This original encounter presents a fissure, a propitious moment to explore difference, though it is not easy to record our response given the nature of fieldwork. Even so, the experience and habits of fieldwork are crucial to the construction of archaeological knowledge from the first moment of encounter (see Edgeworth 2012) and train the sense to the uncanny and unexpected (Pétursdóttir 2013). It is not easy to break the hold of a given set of practices that condition our ways of noticing when confronting an object in the laboratory. Descriptive practices designed to keep the fissure open through acute, studious attention to what is in front of us, are required to prolong our captivation. Preparation for analysis can include reading and slowing things down, avoiding the rush to familiarise and know the thing. I would argue that the impact of our reading on what we 'see' is undertheorised, given that everything we bring with us to the analysis has a bearing. We can read for inspiration with an eye to difference. Concept priming, the intellectual engagement with new concepts prior to working with the materials, more specifically increases receptivity.

Slowing things down includes 'slow looking'; being slower and more creative in our object observation and descriptions (Mol 2021). If we pause, then the art-like nature of the objects might become more available to us. Moreover, our relationship to things will change as the analysis carries on. Mol (2021) and her students have experimented with ways to study an object (a pot) that matches theory with practice, bringing to life insights from recent theory on alterity.[4] Mol organised their activity into 'rounds' of descriptive techniques, experiments with different kinds of 'vantage points, embodiment, and empathy'. This circular organisation highlights the fact that this is not a checklist. Each round changed the meaning of the object for the group. Ultimately, Mol (2021:95) notes, "for those involved, it became almost impossible to turn the pot back into an object". Mol (2021:94) notes that in this process the object "becomes a centre to which one can attach every new thing one learns, every new perspective". That is, the thing itself creates the context for its continued analysis and understanding.

Words

We should not underestimate the power of banal, descriptive writing (see also Olsen et al. 2012). Straightforward, intense observation can reveal hidden patterns within a body of material. Writing or dictating detailed descriptions, listing unique features of each thing, following unusual contours or features, and tracing shapes can avoid normative description based on pre-established elements. This practice could take the form of serial redescription, in which a thing is described in detail by members of a group in turn. Colleagues and I are currently in the experimental process of 'serial re-describing' a (different) set of anthropomorphic pots from northwest Argentina. Our descriptions incorporate old descriptions and any associated element (materials, colours, dimensions, metaphors, etc.) that were not initially included. More creative writing, or oral dictation, can be done on the basis of prompts suggested by the material. An anthropomorphic pot may suggest 'body'; but it may also suggest 'stunted', 'incomplete', or fierce'. The materials may suggest hard, cold, rough, or smooth. We could describe this as using a bait concept to snare something of the original concept. In the La Candelaria material, obvious candidates for bait concept would include 'body' or 'pot'. Others might be 'vessel', 'anthropomorph', 'zoomorph', 'human', 'orniform', and so on. It is used as a lens through which to see what about the thing does not fit, to attract difference. For example, a cursory look at the La Candelaria ceramics shows basic volumes that do and do not align with our idea of a body: ambiguous limbs where legs or arms should be and a common bulge shape as a basic form that repeats itself (Alberti 2020). What kind of 'body' is this? Creative writing can also take the form of describing how the thing moves you. Pétursdóttir (2016:384) pushes us to name our feelings boldly, "name their colour, smell, texture, sounds and movements – and [...] name the sensations, memories, fears, and dreams that their sheer presence may provoke [...] no matter how banal these declarations may appear".

Images

Archaeologists have always used images – photography, drawings, digital renderings – as translations. Each produces a quite distinct sense of an artefact. Photography, for example, is usually a conventional tool, though it has been experimented with (Bailey 2017; McFadyen and Hicks 2019). Pétursdóttir and Olsen (2014:51) in their study of ruins show photography is "capable of bringing forth memories, meanings and pasts that tend to filter out" in standard usage. Bender et al. (2007:288) equipped crew members on the Leskernick Hill archaeological landscape project with cameras and asked them to photograph something evocative or meaningful around the Hill. Their claim was that photography "has the capacity to deal with the banal and the emotion of everyday experience", revealing "participants' ontologies [...] within the single 'snapshot'" (Bender et al. 2007:288). My project is not reflexive in that same sense, the objective being to grasp something of the maker's 'ontology' rather than participants' meanings. Non-conventional photographs of the La Candelaria pieces can draw our attention to details through intense close-ups and impact through techniques such as portraiture (Figure 18.1), much like Moulène's *Orant*. Juxtaposing portraits with intentionally isolated elements of the 'body' may serve to both disaggregate what our mind wants to group together and jolt us into intuitive understanding (Bergson 1999). Masking the surrounding context, close-ups isolate marks in clay, changing the emphasis of the image and establishing relationships on the basis of the gestures that produced the marks rather than images retrojected onto the complete piece.

Archaeologists draw a great deal – from initial sketches in field notebooks to highly detailed penned drawings for publication. Standard archaeological drawing is an intense exercise in focused observation. Archaeological drawings, however, tend to be guided by conventions that enable comparison, creating a universal language without borders (Wickstead 2013). Such standardisation, however, flattens differences, reducing the chances of working outside received categories (Ballestero and Wintheriek 2021). Moreover, there is a tendency to allow one's overall interpretive framework to overdetermine what is drawn. In contrast, the act of drawing as a form of correspondence stresses the activity itself, in which the subject and your relationship to it change. Leveraging archaeologists' drafting skills can serve in at least two ways. First, drawing can turn up details that would otherwise go unnoticed, focusing the gaze and forcing you to pay attention. Second, the act of drawing is a potent vehicle for engaging with what is in front of you, obeying the "desire to get closer and closer, to enter the self of what is being drawn" (Berger 2011:156). Drawings do not need to remain simple representations, but can establish a very specific, physical relationship to the subject through the body of the drawer. As Mol (2021:89) stresses, "[d]rawing or sketching is a different way of kinesthetic and multimodal observation that will generate knowledge through performance". It is the performative aspect of drawing that is stressed by Ingold (2013:128); drawings are "the trace of a gesture". Drawings as gesture are intimately connected to the thing drawn: "[Y]ou become what you draw: not in shape but in affect [...] You know it from the inside, and in your gesture, you relive its movement" (Ingold 2013:129). Drawing is thus a process of correspondence and transformation. Berger (2011:8) writes of the moment when things change during the act of drawing:

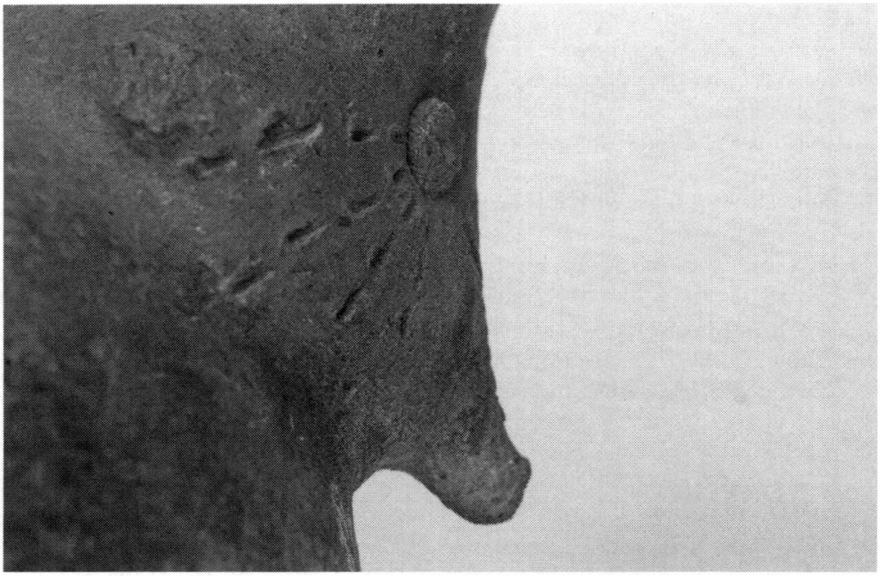

Figure 18.1 Portrait of a Candelaria anthropomorphic ceramic vessel (photo by the author).

> At first you question the model [...] to discover lines, shapes, tones that you can trace on the paper. The drawing accumulates the answers. [...] At a certain moment [...] the accumulations become an image – that's to say it stops being a heap of signs and becomes a presence. [...] This is when your looking changes. You start questioning the presence as much as the model.

Something 'true' has to be in the drawing by that point. A drawing snags on some aspect of the thing drawn; tension emerges in the movement from thing to drawing. The drawing takes on or makes visible forces or resistance. In his struggle to draw the dancer Maria Muñoz, for example, Berger (2011:14) describes how the strength and tension in the pose she is holding are translated through repeated gestures into dark lines outlining her shape on the page. But more than an image emerges; it is the 'resilience' of Muñoz' body that Berger experiences and transmits into the forceful impressions on the paper (Alberti 2018). Drawing is a visceral encounter.

Drawing does not finish (Ingold 2011:218). In practice, our materials should be drawn and re-drawn rather than relying on one, definitive version. Many archaeologists sketch objects during the course of thinking about them. These sketches should be recognised as an active part of the process of analysis. Something forceful about the subject can emerge out of the exercise of drawing.

Haptic relationships established between bodies and materials leave their mark on the La Candelaria ceramics. The lines that are impressed into the pre-fired clay are often rough, tearing the clay, and a kind of careless superposition of marks is frequent. Resolving one incised line into a tear (see Figure 18.1), and another into female genitalia (Figure 18.2), masks the line itself as a definite trace, a mark that is identical in both instances. A short, quickly executed mark versus a longer mark, for example, are both incised marks in ceramic made with specific tools and specific gestures that differ therefore on that basis. Moreover, the action of marking may be more significant than the finished mark. Plastic decorative elements of the La Candelaria pots are linked through form but also through similar gestures. For example, the same technique, fold, shape, and pressure is used to make the eyebrows and nose of the humanoid faces and the front legs and nose of small frog-like appliques. The flattened clay piece and point/nose are, morphologically, identical (Figure 18.3). The lines transcribed require the same gesture, whether tracing with graphite or pushing thumbs over clay.

Ideally, archaeologists would be able to hold, examine, and interact fully with artefacts. Handling La Candelaria ceramics for the first time was an experience that enthralled and surprised me; they were so cold, hard, small, and vulnerable (Alberti 2013). If I let one slip, it would shatter against the stone tiles of the museum floor. The shape of the 'head' of one, almost cartoonish piece drew me to it. Before I was aware, my mouth was moving

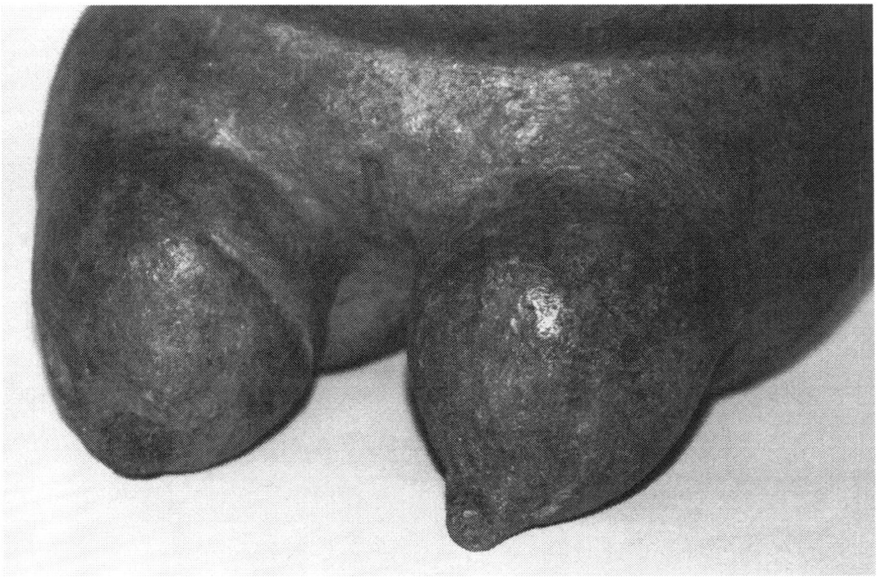

Figure 18.2 Incised line on a Candelaria anthropomorphic ceramic vessel (photo by the author).

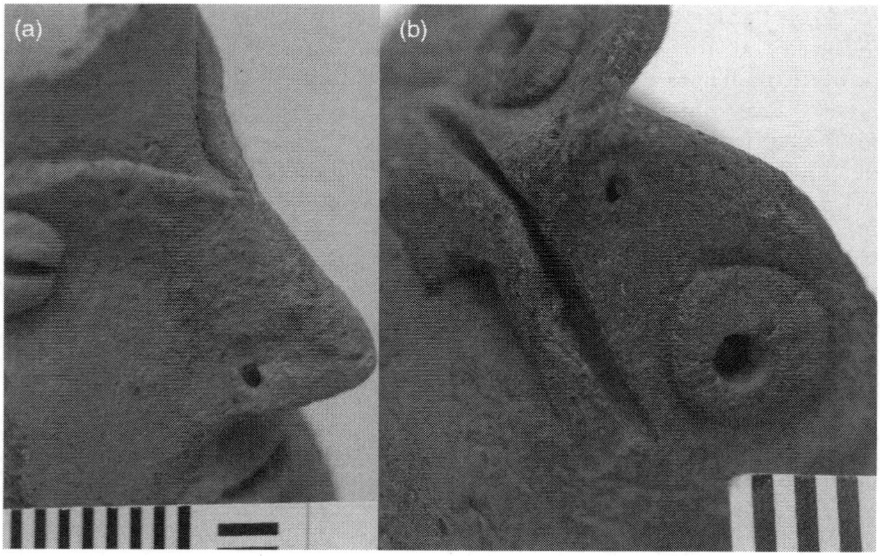

Figure 18.3 The nose-snout and eyebrow-legs of (a) a humanoid face and (b) an applied frog figure on Candelaria ceramic vessels. (c) Sketch of the formal relationship (photos and drawing by the author).

towards it, drawn to the shape that seemed perfect for nestling my bottom lip. I stopped before I made contact. I subsequently discovered the piece is a whistle; one could argue that the shape of the thing compelled its own blowing.

Conclusion

Ingold (2017:121) has characterised correspondence, after Henri Bergson, as an intuitive mode that is ontologically prior to intellect. The procedural equivalence (Alberti 2016) I am suggesting recognises that researcher and ancient artist 'follow' materials in identical ways. Hands formed the ceramics. Working with our hands, copying movements and gestures, we can induce intuitive connections – "the places in things and events where differences most directly emerge" (Grosz 2011:85). The total phenomenon influences the outcome of our encounter with these concept-things, including the knowledge and sensibility promoted by excavation and the initial context of encounter with the objects, archives, and images. 'Arts of noticing' promote the emergence of those differences, which can then serve to ignite our own compulsive conceptual creativity. The pots can be thought of as ontological emissaries, bringing something of the alterity or difference of the past forward to us. In this paper, I have focused on cumulative practices that

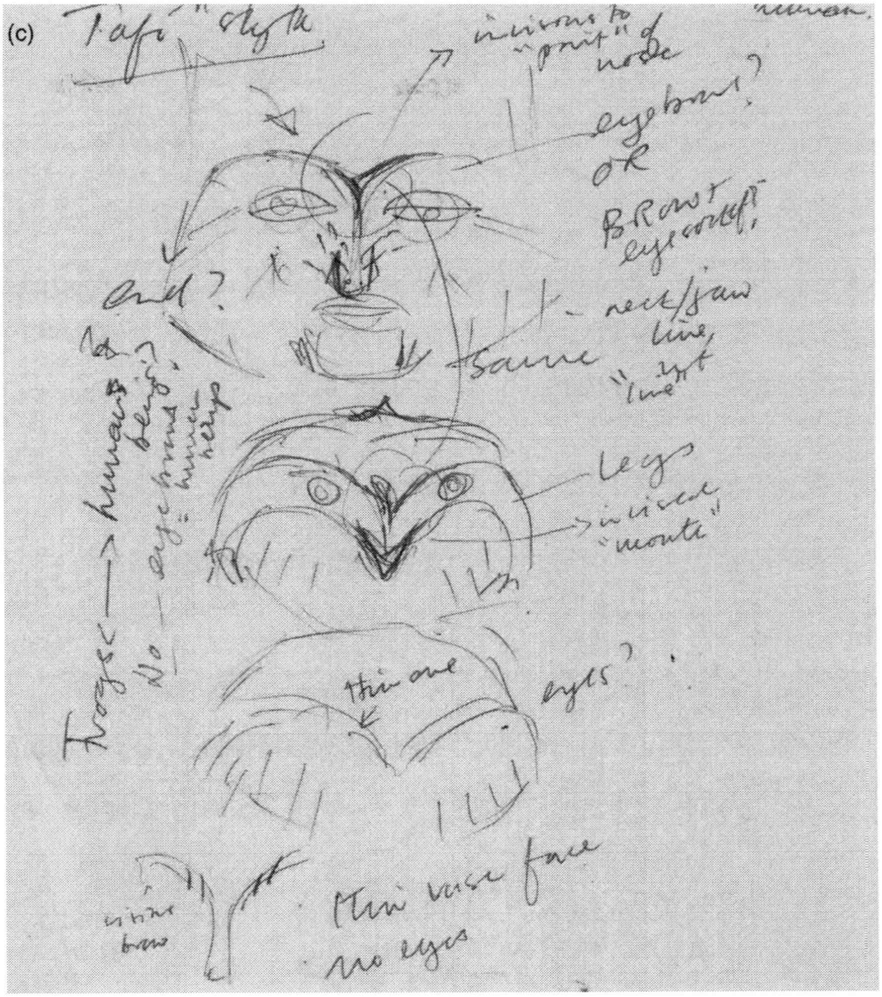

Figure 18.3 Cont.

can be used or directed at art-like archaeological materials. Such practices include the full range of scholarly interpretive practices, including accounting for context, history, material analysis, theoretical exploration, but not in a way that over-determines the continued exploration of the piece-in-itself as the outcome of past practices.

I have emphasised the affective side of the encounter, not in the belief that the objects contain in themselves an essence that only they can reveal to us. Singling out the extraordinary is a deliberate strategy: we are primed to be affected by such things, not because they are in essence extraordinary – or were to their creators – but because we are archaeologists. Privileging that response is a methodological decision, not an aesthetic evaluation. It is a step towards the craft-like practices that gave rise to these art-like things, the effects of which linger in them. When we work on those materials in craft-like ways we may enable that residue of the past to affect us. What we finally get out of the encounter is neither 'theirs' – belonging to the La Candelaria – nor 'ours' – belonging exclusively to the modern world of archaeology. While rooted in both worlds, what we 'draw into being' will be something ontologically quite new.

Acknowledgements

This paper has benefitted enormously from conversations with Eva Mol, who I thank for sharing with me an advance copy of her *Slow looking* paper. All errors remain my own. Many thanks also to Martin Porr and Niels Weidtmann for the invitation to contribute to this volume. I am grateful to the Instituto de Arqueología y Museo, Tucumán, and Museo Arqueológico El Cadillal, Tucumán, for access to their collections.

Notes

1 It is a struggle to find a way to describe the things I am interested in, especially in the face of the critique of the notion of a non-Western art which accompanies the claim that art is an exclusively Western category. I settled on 'art-like' with the hope that it points towards the phenomenon I am interested in (excessive things, decorated things, embellished things?) while remaining sufficiently vague to avoid getting hung up on definition. I distinguish between Acheulean handaxes and anthropomorphic ceramics to highlight an analytically useful distinction between craft and art, though that distinction itself is the product of eighteenth-century practices (Shiner 2002).
2 I am grateful to an anonymous reviewer for this observation.
3 An orant is a type of supplicant, usually with outstretched arms; this orant has lost its arms.
4 Mol's (2021) paper contains a wealth of exercises that can be tried in relation to alternative descriptions of objects, especially within a classroom or group situation.

References

Alberti, B. 2013. Archaeology and ontologies of scale: The case of miniaturization in first millennium northwest Argentina. In *Archaeology after interpretation*. B. Alberti, A. Jones, and J. Pollard, eds. Pp. 43–58. Walnut Creek: Left Coast Press.

——— 2016. Archaeologies of risk and wonder. *Archaeological Dialogues* 23(2):133–137.

——— 2018. Art, craft, and the ontology of archaeological things. *Interdisciplinary Science Review* 43(3–4):280–294.
——— 2020. An archaeology of anthropomorphism: Upping the ontological ante of Alfred Gell's anthropology of art through a focus on making. In *Images in the making: Art, process, archaeology*. I.-M. Back Danielsson and A. Jones, eds. Pp. 34–50. Manchester: Manchester University Press.
Bailey, D. W. 2017. Art/archaeology: What value artistic-archaeological collaboration? *Journal of Contemporary Archaeology* 4(2):246–256.
Ballestero, A. 2015. Theory as parallax and provocation. In *Theory can be much more than it used to be: Learning anthropology's method in a time of transition*. D. Boyer, J. D. Faubion, and G. E. Marcus, eds. Pp. 171–180. Ithaca: Cornell University Press.
——— 2019. *A future history of water*. Durham: Duke University Press.
Ballestero, A. and B. R. Winthereik 2021. Introduction. In *Analysis as experimental practice in experimenting with ethnography: A companion to analysis*. A. Ballestero and B. R. Winthereik, eds. Pp. 1–14. Durham: Duke University Press Books.
Bender, B., Hamilton, S., and C. Tilley. 2007. *Stone worlds: Narrative and reflexivity in landscape archaeology*. Walnut Creek: Left Coast Press.
Berger, J. 2011. *Bento's sketchbook: How does the impulse to draw something begin?* New York: Pantheon Books.
Bergson, H. 1999 [1912]. *An introduction to metaphysics*. Indianapolis: Hackett Publishing Company.
Berrebi, S. 2013. Not-so-transparent things. In *The way of the shovel: On the archaeological imaginary in art*. D. Roelstraete, ed. Pp. 266–276. Chicago: The University of Chicago Press.
Conneller, C. 2011. *An archaeology of materials: Substantial transformations in early prehistoric Europe*. London: Routledge.
Dawdy, S. L. 2016. *Patina: A profane archaeology*. Chicago: University of Chicago Press.
Dryfus, H. and S. Kelly. 2011. *All things shining: Reading the western classics to find meaning in a secular age*. New York: Free Press.
Edgeworth, M. 2012. Follow the cut, follow the rhythm, follow the material. *Norwegian Archaeological Review* 45(1):76–92.
Feigel, L. 2017. On the edge of madness: The terrors and genius of Alberto Giacometti. *The Guardian*. www.theguardian.com/artanddesign/2017/apr/21/the-terrors-genius-of-alberto-giacometti-artist-sculptor-tate-modern (accessed 6 April 2021).
Fowler, C. and O. J. T. Harris. 2015. Enduring relations: Exploring a paradox of new materialism. *Journal of Material Culture* 20(2):127–148.
Grosz, E. 2011. *Chaos, territory, art: Deleuze and the framing of the earth*. New York: Columbia University Press.
Hamilakis, Y. 2013. *Archaeology and the senses: Human experience, memory, and affect*. Cambridge: Cambridge University Press.
Hodder, I. 1986. *Reading the past: Current approaches to interpretation in archaeology*. Cambridge: Cambridge University Press.
Holbraad, M. and M. Pedersen. 2017. *The ontological turn: An anthropological exposition*. Cambridge: Cambridge University Press.
Ingold, T. 1993. The temporality of the landscape. *World Archaeology* 25(2):152–174.
——— 2007. Materials against materiality. *Archaeological Dialogues* 14(1):1–16.

——— 2011. *Being alive: Essays on movement, knowledge and description*. London: Routledge.
——— 2013. *Making: Anthropology, archaeology, art and architecture*. London: Routledge.
——— 2015. *The life of lines*. London: Routledge.
——— 2016. On human correspondence. *Journal of the Royal Anthropological Institute (N.S.)* 23:9-27.
——— 2017. *Correspondences*. Aberdeen: University of Aberdeen.
——— 2018. Anthropology between art and science: An essay on the meaning of research. *Field: A Journal of Socially Engaged Art Criticism* 11. http://field-journal.com/category/issue-11 (accessed 06/06/2022).
——— 2020. Making growing thinking. *Architecture Foundation*. www.youtube.com/watch?v=FptmjWzj6Vw (accessed 12 April 2021).
——— 2021. *Correspondences*. Cambridge and Medford: Polity.
Jones, A. 2020. An archaeology of affect: Art, ontology, and the carved stone balls of Neolithic Britain. *Journal of Archaeological Method and Theory* 27:545–560.
Jones, A. and A. Cochrane. 2018. *The archaeology of art: Materials, practices, affect*. London and New York: Routledge.
Klee, P. 1961. *Notebooks. Volume 1*. J. Spiller, ed. London: Percy Lund, Humphries & Co., Ltd.
McFadyen, L. and D. Hicks 2019. Introduction: From archaeography to photology. In *Archaeology and photography: Time, objectivity, and archive*. L. McFadyen and D. Hicks, eds. Pp. 1–20. London: Bloomsbury.
Mol, E. 2021. Trying to hear with the eyes: The art of slow looking in archaeological object analysis. *Norwegian Archaeological Review* 54(1–2):80–99.
Olsen, B. 2010. *In defense of things: Archaeology and the ontology of objects*. Lanham: Rowan and Littlefield Publishers.
Pétursdóttir, Þ. 2013. Concrete matters: Ruins of modernity and the things called heritage. *Journal of Social Archaeology* 13(1):31–53.
Pétursdóttir, Þ. 2016. For love of ruins. In *Elements of architecture: Assembling archaeology, atmosphere, and the performance of building spaces*. M. Bille and T. F. Sørensen, eds. Pp. 365–386. London: Routledge.
Pétursdóttir, Þ. and B. Olsen 2014. Imaging modern decay: The aesthetics of ruin photography. *Journal of Contemporary Archaeology* 1(1):7–56.
Roelstraete, D., ed. 2013. *The way of the shovel: On the archaeological imaginary in art*. Chicago: The University of Chicago Press.
Shanks, M. 2020. The archaeological imagination. In *The Cambridge handbook of the imagination*. A. Abraham, ed. Pp. 47–63. Athens: University of Georgia Press.
Shiner, L. 2002. *The invention of art: A cultural history*. Chicago: University of Chicago Press.
Stengers, I. 2011. Wondering about materialism. In *The speculative turn: Continental materialism and realism*. L. Bryant, N. Srnicek, and G. Harman, eds. Pp. 368–380. Melbourne: re.press.
Strathern, M. 1999. *Property, substance, and effect: Anthropological essays on persons and things*. London: Athlone Press.
Strathern, M. 2020. Opening up relations. In *A world of many worlds*. M. de la Cadena and M. Blaser, eds. Pp. 23–52. Durham and London: Duke University Press.

Sturt, G. 1974 [1923]. *The wheelwright's shop*. Cambridge: Cambridge University Press.

Thomas, J. 1996. *Time, culture, and identity: An interpretative archaeology*. London: Routledge.

Tsing, A. 2015. *The mushroom at the end of the world. On the possibility of life in capitalist ruins*. Princeton: Princeton University Press.

Wickstead, H. 2013. Between the lines: Drawing archaeology. In *Oxford handbook of the archaeology of the contemporary world*. P. Graves-Brown, R. Harrison, and A. Piccini, eds. Pp. 549–564. Oxford: Oxford University Press.

Part VI

Conclusion

19 Let the world teach!

Some closing reflections

Tim Ingold

I

What does it take to make oneself invisible, inaudible, insensible? Pondering the question of skill, I have usually veered to the other extreme. I have imagined the practitioner – be they a carpenter, a painter or a scribe – in the midst of things, surrounded by all the materials and tackle of their trade. There is noise, bustle, movement. Words and gestures mingle with all the other sights and sounds that make the workshop, the studio or even the scriptorium a hive of activity. This is a far cry, I have argued, from the scenario promulgated by so many social theorists, of skilled practitioners absorbed into the unconscious depths of their own bodies, going about their business in wordless silence, with a zombie-like automatism, punctuated only by moments of lucid reflection that interrupt the flow. Only the theorist – a stranger to practical work – could possibly imagine that the knowhow of the practitioner is *tacit*, or that it is literally *embodied*. In truth, it is both animate and full of feeling, as it is continually produced and performed in a visceral engagement with tools, materials and surroundings.

There is one field of practice, however, that I had not thought about. It is not one I have tried myself, nor am I familiar with any who have. Yet it is arguably a field in which skill reaches its highest peak of perfection. I mean the art of burglary, demonstrated in its most spectacular form in the theft of priceless masterpieces from a heavily defended art gallery. The light-fingered robber, who can pick any lock, circumvent any tripwire and evade every roving spotlight, all the while making no sound and leaving no trace, is surely a master of the art! His skill, indeed, bears comparison with that of the magician, who likewise contrives to make things disappear, only to reappear in quite another place. Is this not the very opposite of the workshop? In a way it is. But in other ways, the ability to glide frictionlessly through the narrowest of slits in the structure of security calls upon the same dexterity, the same precision of response to ever-unfolding conditions, the same concentration of awareness, that we find in the practice of any craft.

The robber, like the magician, turns invisibility, inaudibility and insensibility into a form of presence. He haunts the space of the gallery precisely by hiding

DOI: 10.4324/9781003162773-26

in the cracks. But he is not the only one hiding there. In fact, what led me to think of art-theft was my reading of Laura Harris's account, in this volume, of the work of gallery technicians. It struck me that technicians are like robbers in reverse. Where the latter spirit artworks out of the space, the former spirit them into it. Their job is to lift works intended for display across the threshold, and to set them in place in their intended positions, without leaving the slightest trace of their activity. So far as the visiting public is concerned, the works have appeared as if by magic. Yet as Harris shows, the task of installation calls for a great deal of judgement and dexterity, to ensure not only that the works are displayed correctly, in accordance with the wishes of the artist and the curator, but also that their own role in this is comprehensively occluded.

Gallery technicians, however, are not alone in this kind of endeavour. Research scientists are complicit in a similar game. They creep up upon the scene of their inquiry intent upon stealing nature's secrets, ideally without her noticing, and moving them across the threshold to the laboratory, for conversion into objects of scientific knowledge. Again, researchers put as much effort into the task of making themselves inconspicuous as they do in harvesting what they call 'the data'. For should they slip up, revealing their presence for all to see and hear, the objectivity of their results would be fatally compromised. The ideal is covert surveillance, such as by means of a concealed camera, which sees all while itself remaining unseen. In the translation of this ideal from the natural to the social sciences, the invisible observer would be compared to a fly on the wall, present in the room, taking everything in, while unnoticed by any of the assembled company. The researcher-technician became a spy. Anna Bloom-Christen, in this volume, notes how in eighteenth century France, observing others came to mean spying on them. Observation equalled surveillance.

II

Many theorists have insisted on the opposition between observation and participation. One can participate from the inside, they say, or observe from the outside, but you cannot do both at once. For them the very idea of 'participant observation', the mantra of ethnographic fieldwork, is an oxymoron. Yet literally, as Bloom-Christen notes, to observe is to *follow the way things are going*, and to respond accordingly. Far from remaining on the sidelines, this means entering into the grain of things. The craftsman does this, with his materials, but so also do the robber and the spy, to the different ends of concealment. The robber is no more outside the gallery than the technician. On the contrary, he is hiding inside. Hiding is a form of participation that actively produces invisibility. Perhaps we could call it 'counter-participation'. The opposite of participation, then, would be counter-participation, not observation. The spy, likewise, is a counter-participant, and so is the fly-on-the-wall social researcher. The claim to 'objectivity' amounts to no more than an admission that he has got away with it, and not been caught in the act.

There is more to be said, however, about inside and outside. Paradoxically, as Melanie Greiner observes in her contribution to this volume, the more scholars position themselves on the outside, vis-à-vis their objects of study, the more they tend to lock themselves indoors, preferring to deal with the data of experience only *after* it has been extracted from its living habitat. And locked up with them, more often than not, are their students. There they are, huddled together inside the classroom; beyond them the great outdoors, otherwise known as the 'field'. What difference would it make if this outdoors itself became a place of study? What if the room, enclosed by walls, floor and ceiling, with only a window to let the light in, were to give way to the open world of earth and sky, extending to the horizon and beyond? Suppose, for argument's sake, that the students on the outdoor education programme in which Greiner participated, instead of trekking in the Australian landscape, have been magically whisked to Siberia, to join archaeologist Irina Ponomareva on her mountainside hike to a remote rock shelter. What would they find?

Ponomareva is in search of prehistoric paintings. Eventually, as she recounts in her contribution, after an arduous scramble over difficult terrain, she reaches the shelter. Looking up, she is rewarded by the sight of huge birds of prey, wings outstretched in flight, painted into the rock above her head. Such birds are a common sight in the mountains. Soaring in the sky at one moment, plunging to earth the next, they are above all denizens of the open. What, then, are they doing tucked away in the folds of the rock? Perhaps it is precisely because it places them on the threshold, whence they can be launched from their stony eyrie into the world of earth and sky. And people, as they painted these birds into being, into existence, could have taken flight with them, albeit in their dreams. In our imaginary scenario, Ponomareva invites the students who have accompanied her on the trek to become birds themselves, to imagine themselves growing wings and to feel their bodies buoyed up by thermal air-currents. This is not something, she says, that could ever be experienced indoors.

For even while deep inside the shelter, neither she nor the students doubt that they are nevertheless outdoors. The folds of the rock, in their experience, give out into the open in a way that the interior space of the classroom could never do. This cannot simply be due to the presence or absence of a door. Many a hidden shelter is accessed via a doorway, yet still remains of the open. The difference, I think, is that the shelter, like a nest, is a place-holder for life, whereas the classroom is imagined as a space in which data, extracted from the settings of 'real life', are reassembled into a simulacrum of the world beyond its walls. Where the door to the shelter, if there is one, marks the threshold between earth and sky; that of the classroom stands between the earth-sky world, *in toto*, and its interior reconstruction. Could we, then, envisage an education in which inside and outside are not so much opposed as mutually enfolded? Could the classroom be a creative nest, an incubator for life, as the rock shelter was for the bird-people who once frequented it?

III

The answer, as Dylan Gaffney and Leor Zmigrod suggest in their contribution, turns on the meaning of creativity. Ever since psychologists, in the mid-twentieth century, appropriated the concept to denote a faculty of intellect, characterised by the virtuosic capacity of great minds to reassemble information into unique and unprecedented combinations, it has been conventional to equate creativity with innovation. Missing from this equation, however, is growth, becoming, the actual forming or making of persons and things, or in a word, *ontogenesis*. In this latter sense, as Gaffney and Zmigrod show, creation is fundamentally a process – or better, a bundle of processes – of material-organic generation. And the place to look for it is not inside individual heads, but in an ecosystem comprised of neural pathways that spread their mesh throughout the entire living world. In this mesh, organisms and persons show up as knots of concentration. This doesn't mean that we have to sever brain from mind, leaving the former inside the head while the latter trails beyond it into the environment. It means, rather, reconfiguring the brain itself as an immense neural tangle, untrammelled by the architectures of anatomy.

The question, then, is how to conceive of this ecosystem as a whole, without falling for what some critics call 'conflationism'. If everything runs into everything else, they say, are we not left with a picture of the world as one big mess? There is a connection in this volume, perhaps unexpected, between Quirin Rieder's account of the tangled lines and knots of electrical power transmission in Pakistani Kashmir, and what Emily Grey, with the Balanggarra Aboriginal Corporation, has to say about the 'yamscapes' of the Northeast Kimberley region, in Western Australia. For Rieder, the messy reality of the electrical infrastructure is a tangle of lines, knotted here and there into points of concentration. For the Aboriginal people of the Kimberley, their 'infrastructure' is an ever-extending, rhizomatic mesh of roots and runners, while the knots are the wild yams that have fed countless generations of their ancestors. There is something mobile and fluid about both infrastructures, as there is about the equally protean mesh of neural connections. They remind us of Charles Darwin's famous comparison of the living world to an entangled bank, clothed with plants and bushes.

For mainstream science, this flux and tangle has always been a problem. Its metaphors of choice have rather been the solid foundation and the building block. Reality may indeed be messy, say scientists, but assertions to this effect are of little help if our aim is to understand it. To advance our knowledge, it is necessary to simplify. Usually, this means imagining the world as an articulated or joined-up structure, assembled from more fundamental units – and the still more fundamental units of which they may be composed – and to get to know it better from experimental attempts first to isolate the units, and then to piece them together again. But as Ralf Gisinger suggests in this volume, there is another way, which is to join *with* things, entering into the processes of their ongoing differentiation. If we imagine these processes as bundled together, then – as Gaffney and Zmigrod also imply – it is to their bundling, or gathering, that we should attend, rather than to the assembly of forms to which they give rise. Once again, this is to prioritise the becoming over the being of things, their ontogenesis.

Of course, this shift from assembly to gathering, and from ontology to ontogenesis, is not without political implications. Power tends to work through top-down, vertically integrated assemblies, in which everything is joined up, while life flourishes in the cracks, spreading its tentacles through every nook and cranny it can find. In putting becoming before being, or creative growth before structural articulation, we risk downplaying the forces of oppression that, throughout history, have blighted the lives of the relatively powerless. This is the burden of Maike Melles's powerful critique, in this volume, of a paradigm of making-in-growing which sees no essential difference between purpose-built human constructions and things like trees that, once planted, grow of their own accord. Even today, the ruined remains of artificial structures dotted around in the landscape call up memories of the cruelty and exploitation that humans have wreaked not upon nature but upon their own kind. These structures, Melles argues, did not grow. They were made, in order to work *against*, not *with*, the forces of life and growth they sought to control. No other creature does this. Are humans, then, exceptional after all?

IV

It would not be fair, perhaps, to tarnish all humans with the same brush. This, as Gisinger notes, is the objection commonly levelled against the idea of the Anthropocene. Human beings, *en masse*, have not ravaged the planet. What *has* caused world-wide devastation is a colonial project driven by the insatiable thirst of capital for raw materials and markets. All capitalists are human, but not all humans are capitalists! Those who are not, crushed historically under the weight of the colonial juggernaut, have suffered centuries of enslavement, abuse and exclusion, often under the mantra of 'race'. Antony Pattathu, in his contribution, shows how thoroughly the exclusionary logic of colonisation has wormed its way into the canons, curricula and classrooms of present-day academia. Even research is charged with epistemicide – with turning other people's ways of knowing into objects of scientific analysis. Is the very word 'research', then, irredeemably tainted by extractivism? Should we get rid of it, in the name of decolonisation? Or might it better be redefined in a way that accords more closely with its original meaning: *to search and search again*?

Perhaps Ana Motta's discussion, in this volume, of the rock art of the Tsodilo Hills, in Botswana, suggests an answer. Now conserved as a World Heritage site, any tampering with the art is considered by the conservation authorities as tantamount to vandalism. Yet for the Indigenous communities of the region, both hunter-gatherers and pastoralist-farmers, the site is a place of spiritual renewal, achieved through the very performance of painting and repainting. In this performance, every repainting both remembers the contribution of generations past in creating the conditions of present life, and reaffirms the creative potential of the place to bring forth generations to come. What if we were to think of research in the same way, as the epistemic analogue of repainting? Its aim, then, would not be to extract the data, or to come up with final results. It would be a practice not of innovation but of renewal. Research, in this sense, is the guarantor that life can move on, in continuity with the values of the past. And for this reason, research for the scholar, like repainting for Indigenous people, is a primary responsibility of the living.

Decolonisation surely begins here, in practices of renewal. Yet how, Pattathu asks, can students who have suffered systematic exclusion be expected to correspond in their studies with teachers like me, from privileged backgrounds, who have never experienced it for themselves? The middle-aged, middle-class, white male professor that I am is not best placed to lead the crusade for decolonisation! Is that why, in my own work, I scarcely mention it? Well, yes and no. For no reader familiar with the literature in postcolonial studies can also fail to notice that it is predominantly couched in a language so abstruse as to make sense only to a coterie of like-minded theorists. This literature creates and perpetuates its own exclusions. To my mind, the emancipatory potential of scholarship lies as much in *how* one writes as in what one writes *about*. I believe we should write in a way that respects the intelligence of our readers, whatever their background and experience, and draws them into the conversation in a spirit of inclusion. To preach decolonisation amounts to little more than posturing, unless it is borne out thus, in scholarly practice.

Thanks to the generosity of its editors, Martin Porr and Niels Weidtmann, this volume is a testament to inclusivity. As Stephanie Bunn so nicely puts it, in her opening contribution, here I am among friends. The thing about friendship is that it welcomes all-comers keen to join the conversation, whatever their differences. You don't have to talk the talk of any particular tendency to gain admission. And thanks to the gift of writing, the circle of friendship is not limited to our contemporaries. We can read the works of predecessors as if we were conversing with them, greeting their well-thumbed books like old friends as we retrieve them from the shelf. And we can hope, in turn, that through our writings, scholars of generations to come will befriend us. That's what Benjamin Alberti is getting at, in his closing contribution, with his gesture towards the 'art of noticing'. To practice such an art is to let the world in on our deliberations. It is to study *with* things. Could science and scholarship, then, instead of teaching us about the world, be the world's way of teaching us?

Index

Note: **Bold** numbers indicate use of the indexed term within tables while numbers in *italics* indicate use in figures. Use of indexed terms in notes is indicated by an 'n' plus the note number after its page reference, e.g., 48n2.

Made in the USA
Las Vegas, NV
31 October 2024

1dee88da-2ec3-4c63-93cb-02e351cccdd4R01